DILEMMAS OF FREE EXPRESSION

Edited by Emmett Macfarlane

Free expression is under threat. Social media and "fake news," misinformation, and disinformation have prompted governments to propose new forms of regulation that are deeply challenging to free expression. Hate speech, far-right populism, campus speech debates, and censorship consistently make headlines in Canada and abroad.

Dilemmas of Free Expression evaluates the ways to confront challenging moral issues, policy problems, and controversies that pay heed to the fundamental right to free expression. The essays in this volume offer timely analyses of legal, policy, and philosophical challenges, as well as social repercussions to our understanding of expressive freedom in relation to government obligations and public discourse.

Free expression and its limits are multifaceted, deeply complex, inherently values-based, and central to the ability of a society to function. *Dilemmas of Free Expression* addresses the challenges of limiting free expression across a host of issues through analyses by leading and emerging voices in a number of disciplines, including political science, law, philosophy, and Indigenous studies.

EMMETT MACFARLANE is an associate professor in the Department of Political Science at the University of Waterloo.

DILEMMAS OF FREE EXPRESSION

EDITED BY

EMMETT MACFARLANE

UNIVERSITY OF TORONTO PRESS
Toronto Buffalo London

© University of Toronto Press 2022
Toronto Buffalo London
utorontopress.com
Printed in the U.S.A.

ISBN 978-1-4875-2929-1 (cloth)   ISBN 978-1-4875-2932-1 (EPUB)
ISBN 978-1-4875-2930-7 (paper)   ISBN 978-1-4875-2931-4 (PDF)

Library and Archives Canada Cataloguing in Publication

Title: Dilemmas of free expression / edited by Emmett Macfarlane.
Names: Macfarlane, Emmett, editor.
Description: Includes bibliographical references and index.
Identifiers: Canadiana (ebook) 20210313250 | Canadiana (print) 20210313145 |
    ISBN 9781487529321 (EPUB) | ISBN 9781487529314 (PDF) | ISBN 9781487529307
    (paper) | ISBN 9781487529291 (cloth)
Subjects: LCSH: Freedom of expression – Canada.
Classification: LCC KE4418.D55 2022 | LCC KF4483.C524 D55 2022 kfmod |
    DDC 342.7108/53–dc23

This book has been published with the help of a grant from the Federation for the
Humanities and Social Sciences, through the Awards to Scholarly Publications
Program, using funds provided by the Social Sciences and Humanities Research
Council of Canada.

University of Toronto Press acknowledges the financial assistance to its publishing
program of the Canada Council for the Arts and the Ontario Arts Council, an agency
of the Government of Ontario.

Canada Council   Conseil des Arts
for the Arts   du Canada

ONTARIO ARTS COUNCIL
CONSEIL DES ARTS DE L'ONTARIO
an Ontario government agency
un organisme du gouvernement de l'Ontario

Funded by the   Financé par le
Government   gouvernement
of Canada   du Canada   Canada

Contents

Acknowledgments

The contributions in this book were first presented at a conference I organized co-sponsored by the Courts & Politics Research Group (CPRG), the Department of Political Science at the University of Waterloo, and the research cluster for Indigenous Peoples, Decolonization, and the Globe at the Balsillie School of International Affairs. The conference took place in October 2019 at the Balsillie School in Waterloo, Ontario. The CPRG was established in recognition of the regional concentration of political scientists studying law and politics in southern Ontario, and currently includes over twenty faculty members at ten universities. This book is the second such collaborative effort under the CPRG banner.

I would like to thank the contributors to this volume for their excellent work and for their commitment to bringing a substantial volume together quickly. My thanks to the Department of Political Science at the University of Waterloo and to the Indigenous Peoples research cluster for providing funding to support the conference. I am also grateful to the Balsillie School for providing facility support and to Joanne Weston, the school's events and administrative coordinator, for her assistance.

I am grateful to Dan Quinlan and the editorial team at University of Toronto Press for ushering the book through the editorial process. Dan once again joined us at the conference to see the work presented first-hand. This is my third edited book conducted under Dan's skillful guidance, and it is always a tremendous pleasure to work with him. My thanks to Ryan Perks for copy-editing.

As always, this book would not have been possible without the support of my colleagues at Waterloo. A special thanks to Jasmin Habib for suggestions and guidance she provided when I was organizing the conference, as well as our many discussions on all manner of topics connected to this book.

Finally, thanks to my family – my parents, Don and Eileen, and my sister, Aingeal – for their continued support. My amazing wife Anna, and our daughter Thea (who exercises her own expressive freedom with aplomb), are key to my success.

DILEMMAS OF FREE EXPRESSION

Introduction: The Challenge and Controversy of Free Expression

EMMETT MACFARLANE

Among the panoply of traditional civil rights, freedom of expression stands as the alpha and omega. Rights like the right to protest, freedom of association, freedom of religion, and freedom of the press quickly disintegrate into charred vessels absent the foundation provided by free expression. Other rights, like the right to vote, similarly hinge on our ability to freely communicate, argue, debate, and advance ideas. And where would equality rights or other values related to the cultivation of a just society be without free expression? As the Supreme Court of Canada enunciated in one of its earliest judgments under the *Charter of Rights and Freedoms*, "the freedom to express oneself openly and fully is of crucial importance in a free and democratic society," and as such it is "an essential value of Canadian parliamentary democracy."[1] The protection of free expression is integral, the Court outlines in another judgment, for seeking and attaining the truth, for participation in social and political decision making, and for "diversity in forms of individual self-fulfillment and human flourishing."[2]

What, then, to make of a contemporary context in which free expression is seemingly under threat on a variety of fronts and in which public discourse around free speech itself appears increasingly polarized along ideological lines? A gamut of political and social issues related to free expression demonstrate quite clearly that the limits of the right are no more easily identifiable now than they ever were. Some of this is the direct result of new challenges and technologies. The federal government's intentions to ensure that social media companies expunge hate speech and other forms of illegal material from their sites arguably reflects the application of existing laws to new contexts, albeit ones that raise new and complex threats to expression (see Mathen, this volume). Social media also presents *new* challenges, including nefarious efforts to spread "fake news," misinformation, and disinformation – some of it even organized by hostile foreign states – and these have prompted governments to propose new forms of regulation that represent deep challenges to free expression principles (see Crandall and Lawlor, this volume). The growth of informational deception and the unreliability of increasingly disparate and disaggregated sources of news online incites one of Canada's foremost experts on free expression to question its future vitality (see Moon, this volume).

The law itself is unlikely to provide clear solutions to these challenges. Indeed, even on traditional matters of protecting free expression against state intrusion, the *Charter*, or at least its interpretation by the courts, has hardly proven a reliable defence. The Supreme Court has upheld a wide range of laws infringing on the right, including relatively severe limits on third-party advertising during election campaigns, criminal and statutory hate speech laws, a (now repealed) law prohibiting the dissemination of election results from one part of the country to another when polls are still open, and laws prohibiting advertising directed at children. Some of these laws may be justifiable, either as designed or in a modified form, to better protect expressive rights. Instead, the core problem has been that, in many of these cases, the Court has not required a particularly robust justification from the government for upholding these infringements as reasonable limits under section 1 of the *Charter*. The Court has failed to require much evidence to demonstrate that the purported harms at stake exist or that the laws meaningfully address them (see Macfarlane, this volume). This is particularly dangerous in a context where the state has often demonstrated an incapacity for restraint, as well as poor judgment when it is permitted to intrude on expressive activity,[3] or where appropriate decision-making processes for placing limits on the right are lacking (see Cameron, this volume).

Yet free expression extends beyond its status as a constitutionally entrenched right. It is equally fundamental as a societal value. The ongoing presence of far-right populism in Western politics and heightened sensitivities to "free speech controversies," particularly the "deplatforming" of controversial speakers on university campuses (see D'Orazio, this volume), have contributed to a broader sense that free expression is either under attack or, conversely, that it is used as a cudgel of oppression to defend odious views. Broader discourses about immigration, diversity and multiculturalism, racism, equality, language rights (see Chouinard and Richez, this volume), and academic freedom all end up ensnared in this debate. Serious policy issues relating to the threat of fake news, the regulation of social media, the integrity of elections, compelled speech (see Sirota, this volume), and the potential dangers of messaging from anti-vaxxers or climate deniers (see Bennett, this volume) all have consequences for how society navigates the waters of free discourse and whether the principle of free expression is protected or eroded.

Aside from the plethora of substantive legal and policy issues at stake, one of the animating features of this collection is recognition that the quality of public debate around free expression has generally been poor, and that in the news and social media terrains it has felt very much like a pitched ideological battle. On the far right, provocateurs seek to win a perverse form of free speech martyrdom when politicians, organizations, or university administrators overreact and censure or investigate controversial or discriminatory messages. Notorious public figures like Jordan Peterson, a University of Toronto professor who garnered media coverage after questioning whether human rights law would require him to use the preferred pronouns of trans people, and Ezra Levant, who was subject to complaints for publishing anti-Muslim cartoons, have developed a degree of fame for having been on the wrong end of attempts at censorship, be it by universities or human rights tribunals. They have developed a fan base that treats them as champions of free speech, although caution is warranted when it comes to viewing their broader advocacy as genuine. It is not uncommon to see people of their ilk lash out at mere social criticism for their speech, or in some cases even call for, or engage in, attempts at censorship themselves.[4]

There are, it sometimes seems, few principled commentators who speak out against censorship regardless of whether the content of the expression aligns with their ideological world views. I was one of those who spoke out when administrators and faculty at Wilfrid Laurier University famously hauled Lindsay Shepherd, a teaching assistant, before them for questioning after she showed a tutorial group a clip (featuring Jordan Peterson) of TVO's current affairs program *The Agenda* discussing the use of non-binary pronouns.[5] Yet it is also important to acknowledge how disingenuous and hateful some of the expression at the centre of these controversies can be. For example, the debates prompted by the Peterson and Shepherd incidents over the use of preferred pronouns of trans people call into question people's very identities, and arguably their human dignity. In some ways, understanding what prompted this debate is perplexing, because it evinces an unwillingness to treat people with basic respect (one honestly wonders when or how someone could be *forced* to use a particular pronoun to refer to someone rather than simply using their name – the controversy itself has an incredibly manufactured feel to it). It is also a discourse filled with, to put it diplomatically, misleading statements about the law. Peterson, for example, mischaracterized a federal law (claiming the human rights legislation could send him to prison) that did not even apply to his situation as a university employee, where relevant provincial law, not federal, would apply.[6]

Yet far-right discourse is not the only culprit degrading the quality of debates on free expression. Some self-styled progressives have contributed to the illiberal sentiment that the promotion of free speech is *itself* a nefarious thing. There are even efforts among some to equate speech with violence (something the Supreme Court has appropriately rejected). Fundamental to this view is the idea that permitting the free expression of offensive or hateful views is antithetical to equality. Yet there seems to be little recognition that allowing for limits on offensive speech empowers some authority – be it the state, university administrators, or some other person in power – to draw lines of acceptability in a context where there will be widespread disagreement about what counts as hateful. More fundamentally, the deleterious effects of weakening speech protections are just as likely to be turned against equity-seeking and historically oppressed groups than they are to work in their favour. It results in the sort of culture that spurred Dalhousie University to launch a disciplinary investigation against a student for the crime of speaking out against "white fragility" because other students found it offensive.[7]

By setting free expression in opposition to equality, certain progressives forget that the fight for the latter is contingent on the former: free expression is what enables the calling out of white supremacy and racist policies, and it is of course core to the right to protest. In short, free expression is perhaps the most important tool in the arsenal for those who would fight on equality's behalf. Instead, from some progressive circles there is a knee-jerk desire to censor and sanction controversial, hateful, or otherwise offensive opinions and forms of speech. Beyond eroding a principle that equality seekers themselves depend on, this has also directly contributed to the martyrdom and rising profiles of people like Levant, and in so doing creates a broader political culture in which free speech is increasingly seen to be associated with the right wing of the ideological spectrum. The tactic continuously backfires because its most common impact is to bring more media attention to the speaker and the offensive views that those trying to censor or deplatform wanted to quash in the first instance. More importantly, the belief that expression should be regulated on the basis of content implies that there are decision makers who can be trusted with the authority to decide what views are acceptable.

This is not a problem limited to speech deemed unlawful; it applies as much, if not more often, firmly within the boundaries of lawful speech. In 2017, Andrew Potter, then the director of the McGill Institute for the Study of Canada, penned an op-ed after a traffic jam on a Montreal highway left hundreds of people stranded in their cars overnight. In his essay, Potter decried a "mass breakdown in the social order" and wrote that "Quebec is an almost pathologically alienated and low-trust society."[8] Political elites in Quebec, including

Premier Philippe Couillard, condemned the op-ed. Potter soon "resigned." If the Quebec establishment can exert enough pressure on McGill University that the institution would fire[9] an established academic and writer like Potter over an allegedly offensive op-ed, why would we think individuals facing systemic forms of oppression would not be even more vulnerable to such tactics?[10] Indeed, we see across North America that it is not just far-right forms of expression resulting in firings and censorship on university campuses (see Sachs, this volume).

The public debate over free speech too often seems to boil down to the charge of "you can't say that" or the defence of "my free speech." There is no sense on one side that social criticism in the face of unpopular speech *is* free speech. There is no sense on the other side that in a free and democratic society one must learn to live with the right of others to express themselves, not only in saying things you disagree with but also in saying things that might make you angry or sad. This is not an argument for free speech absolutism. Indeed, there is *no such thing* as a free speech absolutist. Any number of legal restrictions or impositions on expression are maintained with little controversy: perjury laws, defamation law (see Sheldrick, this volume), or requirements to disclose information (the mandatory census form, income tax returns, etc.). Beyond the law, we are also routinely constrained in our speech by any number of common social norms and institutionalized processes. For all the controversy over campus speakers, for example, few would argue that a student should be able to monopolize a classroom conversation, let alone on issues irrelevant to a particular course (see Dea, this volume).

Instead, any assessment of the legitimacy of particular restrictions on free expression depend on the purpose, context, and nature of the limit. In a free and democratic society, limits on speech should come with a high justificatory burden. When limits are established, and especially when those limits are not content-neutral, empowering state officials or similar actors to draw lines within the bounds of the law on the permissibility of certain forms of expression is an exercise fraught with difficulty.

This is true even when the purported aim of regulation is to enhance free expression. For example, the Province of Ontario recently mandated, under threat of funding cuts, that every publicly funded university and college develop a "free speech policy" based on the University of Chicago Statement on Principles of Free Expression.[11] The move is designed to ensure that post-secondary institutions remain places for open discussion and free enquiry, that ideas and opinions not be censored based on their offensiveness, and that members of the community not be permitted to obstruct or interfere with the freedom of others to express their views. On the surface, the free speech policy enacts basic rules any sensible university administration would already have in practice in order to protect free expression as a value concomitant with the university's wider mission. Yet the policy has come under criticism for threatening free expression, particularly as it relates to an implicit desire to quash protests against controversial speakers (see Zwibel, this volume). Since peaceful protest itself is a protected form of expression, balancing the interests at stake is exceedingly difficult. When does a protest become so disruptive as to prevent the free expression of ideas by members or invitees of the university community? And why do we think university administrators – or the provincial government, for that matter – are capable of identifying that line?

What is needed are forward-looking appraisals of ways to confront challenging moral issues, policy problems, and controversies that pay heed to the fundamental right to free expression. The contributions in this volume are replete with analyses of the law, policy challenges, and social repercussions that characterize the contemporary environment as it relates to free expression. Some of these contributions also help us to reconceptualize or nuance our understanding of expressive freedom as it relates to government obligations (see Oliphant, this volume) or different ways of approaching public or academic discourse (see Newhouse, this volume).

Free expression and its limits are multifaceted, deeply complex, inherently values-based, and central to a society's ability to function. This fact belies the simple two-sided ideological battle we are so often presented with when free speech controversies arise. *Dilemmas of Free Expression* presents nuanced and trenchant analysis from both leading and emerging scholars with interdisciplinary backgrounds, including those from political science, law, business, philosophy, and Indigenous studies. The contributors either move beyond, or add important context to, the "free speech debates" I have briefly outlined here.

Outline of the Book

This volume is not divided into distinct parts, although, as will become clear, many of the chapters are appropriately grouped according to their content and theme. In chapter 1, Richard Moon warns that the internet age has generated a troubling context for free expression. The increasingly fragmented communication environment, particularly on social media, has rendered society particular vulnerable and receptive to fake news and conspiracy theories. Moon's chapter examines the crisis in which public discourse currently finds itself, and he concludes that traditional protections for free speech may even threaten to exacerbate the crisis.

Chapter 2 explores harms associated with hate speech. I investigate the interdisciplinary research identifying these harms and examine the ways the courts have upheld hate speech laws on the basis of harm (or at least the risk of harm) despite a surprising lack of causal evidence in the context of the very diffuse nature of hate speech. There is also little evidence that hate speech laws are particularly effective in mitigating the harms identified by advocates. In part this stems from the fact that much of the harm associated with hate speech applies just as strongly, if not more so, to lawful speech. I conclude that other policy instruments must be brought to bear to combat hate speech and to enhance the free expression of its targets.

Jamie Cameron examines how a lack of procedural safeguards in the regulatory process of restricting expression can fly in the face of basic *Charter* principles in chapter 3. Analysing a case study of executive power under the *Canada Post Corporation Act* aimed at banning individuals from using the postal service, Cameron illustrates the dangers of exercising prior restraint on expressive acts in a context insensitive to obvious rights implications. The decision-making processes her case study explores also reveals more fundamental problems with existing jurisprudence on free expression.

In chapter 4, Erin Crandall and Andrea Lawlor examine the free expression implications of regulation designed to address disinformation and misinformation in election campaigns. The threat of fake news to Canadian democracy is a real one, and the authors investigate recent efforts by the federal government to address it. Through an analysis of existing case law, Crandall and Lawlor explore an ongoing legal challenge to a new provision of the *Canada Elections Act*, offering an important case study of the difficulties of regulation as it relates to the *Charter*'s free expression guarantees.

Carissima Mathen examines the regulation of expression on social media in chapter 5. She explores a host of technological and interpretative challenges associated with regulating speech on social media platforms, which carry a very real risk of unintended consequences. Mathen also analyses the potential for such regulation to shift responsibility from the state to private entities, something she argues is most likely to result in "a chokehold on expression by means of prior restraint systems employed in an inherently risk-averse business mindset."

Chapter 6 probes the interaction between speech and counter-protest and the implications for expressive freedom. Cara Zwibel provides an assessment of the *Charter* jurisprudence surrounding the right to protest, including recent developments relating to the police power to arrest for an apprehended breach of the peace. She concludes with an examination of cases involving conflict between protesters and counter-protesters, with specific attention to a recent case from the Alberta Court of Appeal. Zwibel argues that the state has an obligation to facilitate free expression even in competitive contexts.

In chapter 7, Benjamin Oliphant examines a number of situations in which some form of positive obligation on the part of the state to ensure free expression may be necessary. While the positive versus negative rights distinction (a distinction between governments needing to take some action to ensure rights are protected and a traditional conception of rights as requiring non-interference) is famously blurred in many contexts, Oliphant traces the complexity present in certain contexts in relation to a right that is most commonly conceived of in the traditional negative sense. In an analysis that avoids positing bright line tests or watertight categories, Oliphant introduces a number of important nuances and difficulties to the way free expression is most often conceived.

Compelled speech is the subject of chapter 8. Léonid Sirota examines the spectrum of legally required speech, from requirements for nutritional information to deeply moral and political violations of conscience, noting that the dividing line between legitimate and illegitimate speech compulsions is difficult to draw. He is especially concerned about state requirements that people subscribe to particular doctrines, a clear violation of respect for individual conscience and integrity. Sirota develops a framework to analyse compelled speech in an attempt to help guide future courts dealing with difficult cases.

Byron Sheldrick explores Ontario's Anti-SLAPP legislation in chapter 9. The new law restricts and regulates lawsuits that threaten free expression or limit debate on issues of public importance. Sheldrick analyses the effectiveness of this law and its interpretation and application by the courts. In both cases he finds that an appropriate balance has thus far been struck between permitting litigation to proceed in private disputes and preventing the use of litigation in the context of attempts to silence critics or limit democratic and political expression.

In chapter 10, Christopher Bennett tackles the complex issue of the truth value of online speech, with specific reference to climate change denial. Bennett writes from the perspective of moral philosophy rather than a legalistic or rights-oriented frame. His chapter thus examines the value of climate change denial or anti-vaccination perspectives, the impulse of some critics to seek to deplatform these views, and the place of social media companies in democratic societies.

Stéphanie Chouinard and Emmanuelle Richez analyse the tension between free expression and language rights in chapter 11. While Quebec language policies implicating *Charter* rights have been the focus of academic scrutiny, an explicit focus on the tensions between free expression and a host of policy areas relating to language remain understudied. Chouinard and Richez explore such issues as commercial signage and advertising, the language of work, municipal powers, and language choice in judicial proceedings. The consequences of the courts' approach to the tensions between language and expressive rights are then investigated.

The remaining chapters examine free expression in the context of academia and campus free speech issues. In chapter 12, David Newhouse provides an analysis of Indigenization efforts at Canadian universities, exploring and reconceptualizing key concepts like academic freedom and the contours of knowledge dissemination, discourse, and free expression. Bringing Indigenous approaches to, and forms of, knowledge and scholarship into universities as institutions that carry a history of colonization and assimilation is not an easy or straightforward task. Written in narrative form, Newhouse's contribution to this volume offers an illuminating perspective and draws on a process he refers to as "extending the rafters," which, in addition to its metaphorical power in describing Indigenization, also brings with it a discussion of ethics and the university as a speech community with an "ever-evolving set of rules regulating what can be said and who can speak with what authority."

In chapter 13, Jeffrey Sachs analyses faculty free speech and provides systematic evidence for the nature and frequency of formal punishment in Canada involving protected speech. Although Sachs finds that such formal disciplinary measures are rare, and that in many cases such punishment happens in the context of criticism of university leadership or corporate and governmental partners, there are cases of punishment for politically incorrect speech. He concludes with an exploration of the nature of administrative responses to controversial faculty speech and a discussion of what has helped – generally – to protect faculty free speech.

Shannon Dea examines student refrainment from speech in chapter 14. One of the key impetuses for analysing this phenomenon are surveys and media reports that post-secondary students engage in self-censorship, a claim that sometimes comes with the implication that certain issues or ideological perspectives are not welcome in the academic setting. Dea writes that the term "self-censorship" itself has negative connotations and effectively creates a typology of refrainment based on the reasons for and consequences of doing so. In short, not all instances of student refrainment are bad; indeed, some may be virtuous and beneficial. Dea's chapter adds important nuance to a phenomenon widely and simplistically reported as part of the "crisis" of campus speech.

Finally, Dax D'Orazio explores deplatforming as a tactic at Canadian universities in chapter 15. Through an analysis of the case of noted right-wing commentator Ann Coulter's aborted appearance at the University of Ottawa, D'Orazio investigates the effectiveness of deplatforming. He concludes that the tactic can lead to unintended consequences and that those who seek to deplatform should consider carefully the outcomes such actions can produce.

NOTES

1 *R v Keegstra*, [1990] 3 SCR 697.

2 *Irvin Toy Ltd. v Quebec (Attorney General)*, [1989] 1 SCR 927 at 976.

3 See, for example, the power of border officials to block "obscene" material under the *Customs Act*. Bruce Ryder, "The *Little Sisters* Case, Administrative Censorship, and Obscenity Law," *Osgoode Hall Law Journal* 39, no. 1 (2001): 207–27; Brenda Cossman, "Disciplining the Unruly: Sexual Outlaws, *Little Sisters* and the Legacy of *Butler*," *University of British Columbia Law Review* 36, no. 1 (2003): 77–99.

4 Richard Warnica, "Inside Rebel Media," *National Post*, 17 August 2017, https://nationalpost.com/features/inside-ezra-levants-rebel-media; Colleen Flaherty, "Truth Teller, Guru, Hypocrite?" *Inside Higher Ed*, 24 September 2018, https://www.insidehighered.com/news/2018/09/24/jordan-peterson-dishes-out-what-he-sees-harsh-truths-can-he-take-them-return.

5 Emmett Macfarlane, "Laurier's Apology to Lindsay Shepherd Was Hardly a Win for Free Speech," *CBC News*, 22 November 2017, https://www.cbc.ca/news/opinion/laurier-free-speech-1.4414696.

6 Lisa Cumming, "Are Jordan Peterson's Claims About Bill C-16 Correct?," *Torontoist*, 19 December 2016, https://torontoist.com/2016/12/are-jordan-petersons-claims-about-bill-c-16-correct/.

7 Anjuli Patil, "Dalhousie Withdraws Disciplinary Action against Masuma Khan over 'White Fragility' Facebook Post," *CBC News*, 25 October 2017, https://www.cbc.ca/news/canada/nova-scotia/dalhousie-withdraws-complaint-against-masuma-khan-1.4371332.

8 Jonathan Montpetit, "Quebec Premier Lashes Out at Maclean's for Suggesting Province Is in State of Serious Dysfunction," *CBC News*, 21 March 2017, https://www.cbc.ca/news/canada/montreal/quebec-premier-lashes-out-at-maclean-s-for-suggesting-province-is-in-state-of-serious-dysfunction-1.4034456.

9 Officially, Potter is said to have "resigned" from his position as director of the McGill Institute for the Study of Canada, although McGill's administration never provided a satisfactory answer to questions about whether the resignation was purely voluntary. Benjamin Shingler, "Andrew Potter Resigns from McGill Post after Maclean's Essay on Quebec," *CBC News*, 23 March 2017, https://www.cbc.ca/news/canada/montreal/andrew-potter-mcgill-institute-for-the-study-of-canada-resignation-macleans-1.4037618.

   Some within McGill allege that there was political pressure on the institution to fire Potter or compel a resignation. See Graeme Hamilton, "Board Member Resigns, Alleges Andrew Potter Was Forced out of McGill Institute Role," *National Post*, 18 May 2017, https://nationalpost.com/news/canada/board-member-resigns-alleging-andrew-potter-was-forced-out-from-mcgill-director-role.

10 Amanda Bittner, Elizabeth Goodyear-Grant, and Erin Tolley, "Threats to Academic Freedom Aren't Just a White-Guy Problem," *Maclean's*, 28 March 2017, https:// www.macleans.ca/news/canada/threats-to-academic-freedom-arent-just-a -white-guy-problem/.

11 Government of Ontario, Office of the Premier, "Upholding Free Speech on Ontario's University and College Campuses," 30 August 2018, https://news.ontario .ca/opo/en/2018/08/upholding-free-speech-on-ontarios-university-and-college -campuses.html.

1 Does Freedom of Expression Have a Future?

RICHARD MOON*

A commitment to free speech (or expression) means protecting speech regardless of its truth or falsity and allowing its audience to make their own judgment about its merits. This commitment, though, depends on certain assumptions or conditions – most notably, that individuals are capable of making reasoned and independent judgments and have access to different opinions and reliable factual information. These conditions, of course, never hold perfectly, but it seems that they are now being eroded at a rapid pace.

The character of public speech has changed in the internet era. How we speak to one another and how we receive that speech is different. Audiences have become more fragmented. Disinformation and conspiracy theories seem to spread easily and widely, so that distortion and deceit rather than direct censorship may now be the most significant threat to public discourse. There is little common ground in the community on factual matters or the reliability of different sources of information, which has made it difficult, even impossible, to discuss issues and to agree or compromise on public policy. Those who hold competing positions seem rarely to engage with one another, and, when they do, their engagement is often combative. A growing number of people feel they should not be expected to hear speech that is critical of, or contrary to, their views. The spaces or platforms in which public speech occurs have become increasingly privatized and therefore outside the scope of the constitutional right to freedom of expression.

What future does the right to free expression have in this changing communication environment?

The Freedom's Foundations

The Freedom's Justification

Freedom of expression does not simply protect individual liberty from state interference. It protects the individual's freedom to communicate with others.

The right of the individual is to engage in an activity that is social or relational in character and that involves socially created languages and the use of collective resources.

There are many arguments for protecting freedom of expression, but all seem to focus on one or a combination of three values: truth, democracy, and individual autonomy/self-realization.[1] Freedom of expression must be protected because it contributes to the public's recognition of truth or the growth of public knowledge, or because it is necessary to the operation of a democratic form of government, or because it is important to individual self-realization or autonomy. But whether the emphasis is on truth, democracy, or autonomy, each of the established accounts of the freedom's value rests on a recognition that the realization of human agency is a deeply social process. While the social character of human agency is seldom mentioned in the different accounts of the freedom's value, it is the unstated premise of each. Each account represents a particular perspective on, or dimension of, the constitution of human agency in community life.

We become individuals capable of thought and judgment, we flourish as rational and feeling persons, when we join in conversation with others and participate in collective life. It is through communicative interaction that an individual develops and emerges as an autonomous agent in the positive sense of being able to direct her/his life and to participate in the direction of her/his community. Through communication, an individual creates different kinds of relationships with others and participates in different collective activities, such as self-government and the pursuit of knowledge.

Communication is valuable because individual agency and identity develop in the joint activity of creating meaning. An individual's ideas and feelings take shape in the social process of expression.[2] When we speak, we bring to "explicit awareness" – to consciousness – ideas or feelings of which before we had only an "implicit sense."[3] The individual reflects upon her/his ideas and feelings by giving them symbolic form and putting them before her/himself and others as part of an ongoing discourse. She/he understands her/his articulated ideas and feelings in light of the reactions of others. At the same time, the views of the listener are reshaped in the process of understanding and reacting to the speaker's words. Understanding is an active, creative process in which the listener locates and evaluates the speaker's words (or other symbolic form) within the framework of his/her own knowledge and memory.[4] Listeners use these symbolic forms "as a vehicle for reflection and self-reflection, as a basis for thinking about themselves, about others and about the world to which they belong."[5] In this way, our knowledge of self and the world emerges in the public articulation/interpretation of experience.[6]

Recognition that individual agency and identity emerge in communicative interaction is crucial to understanding not only the value of expression but also its potential for harm. Our dependence on expression means that words can sometimes harass, intimidate, deceive, manipulate, or denigrate the individual. Expression is valuable because individual agency and identity are shaped by what we say and by what others say to us and about us; but expression can also contribute to a distorted public image of the individual (or group) or undermine his/her standing or sense of security in the community, particularly when conditions of unequal communicative power prevent her/him from playing a meaningful role in the definition of his/her public identity. Similarly, while expression is important as a source of knowledge and insight, it can also serve to mislead or manipulate its audience. While speech is not simply a "cause" of audience thought and action, nor is it ever entirely rational and transparent in its meaning or influence.

At issue in many of the debates about free speech protection is whether a particular form of expression engages the audience and encourages independent judgment or whether instead it intimidates, harasses, or manipulates the audience. The judgment that expression is valuable and worthy of protection, or is instead harmful and appropriately subject to restriction (that it is manipulative rather than informative, or that it is harassing or intimidating rather than simply uncivil), is a relative one that will depend on a number of factors, including the form of the expression and the context in which it occurs. When speech seems intended to harass, deceive, or intimidate its audience, it may no longer be viewed as communicative engagement – as part of a discourse that is entitled to constitutional protection.

In cases involving manipulation, incitement, or intimidation, the courts' task is not to strike the fair or just balance between competing interests (between, for example, the value of expression and the importance of public safety); instead, it is to determine whether the expression engages an audience in a way that deserves protection – that advances the values that are said to underlie the commitment to freedom of expression. This may also be true in cases involving state restrictions on advertising directed at children, tobacco advertising, hate promotion, election spending, and degrading sexual imagery – which are to some extent also based on concerns about manipulation or deception.[7] In these cases, the state may be justified in restricting the *expressive* activity not simply because of the harm it *causes* (such as the spread of hatred, or increased tobacco use) but also, and more importantly, because of how it causes that harm – the way the expression influences or impacts the audience.

The Premises of Freedom of Expression

A commitment to freedom of expression means that an individual must be free to speak to others, and to hear what others may say, without interference from the state. It is said that the answer to bad or erroneous speech is not censorship but more and better speech.[8] Importantly, the listener, and not the speaker, is seen as responsible (as an independent agent) for her/his actions, including harmful actions, whether these actions occur because he/she agrees or disagrees with the speaker's message. In other words, respect for the autonomy of the individual, as either speaker or listener, means that speech is not ordinarily regarded as a *cause* of harmful action. A speaker does not cause harm simply because he/she persuades the audience of a particular view and the audience then acts on that view in a harmful way.

Underlying the commitment to freedom of expression (and the refusal to treat speech as a cause) is a belief that humans are substantially rational beings capable of evaluating factual and other claims and an assumption that public discourse is open to a wide range of competing views that may be assessed by the audience. The claim that "bad" speech should not be censored but instead answered by "better" speech depends on both of these assumptions – the reasonableness of human judgment and the availability of competing perspectives. A third, but less obvious, assumption underpinning the protection of freedom of expression is that the state has the effective power to either prevent or punish harmful action by the audience. Individuals will sometimes make poor judgments. The community's willingness to bear the risk of such errors in judgment may depend on the state's ability to prevent the harmful actions of audience members or at least to hold audience members to account for their actions.

Incitement and Manipulation

Expression cannot be restricted by the state simply because it might persuade its audience to act in a harmful way or because it might negatively affect an individual's or group's self-understanding or self-esteem. The courts, though, recognize that the assumptions about the audience's agency or judgment, which underlie the protection of speech, may not always hold (and indeed never hold perfectly). Prohibitions on false or misleading product claims have been supported because advertisers have overwhelming power in the "marketplace of ideas" and information (so that others have limited opportunities or lack incentives to correct misleading ads) and because so much commercial advertising is non-rational or visceral in its appeal. Similarly, the restriction of defamatory speech rests on a recognition that false claims made about an individual are not easily corrected through "more speech." The harm of defamatory speech may persist, because the audience is not always in a position to assess the false and damaging claims and because (people being as they are) the correcting speech may not spread as effectively as the original defamation.

Freedom of expression doctrine has always permitted the restriction of expression that occurs in a form and/or context that discourages independent judgment by the audience or that impedes the audience's ability to assess the claims made. When speech "incites" or "manipulates" the audience into taking harmful action, the speaker may be seen as responsible for, and perhaps even as a participant in, any violence that follows. For example, in *On Liberty* John Stuart Mill thought that the authorities would be justified in punishing a fiery speech given in front of the home of a corn merchant to a crowd of farmers angry about crop prices. A heated speech delivered to such a group (a "mob") appeals to passion and prejudice and might lead to impulsive and harmful actions.[9] Speech is described as incitement when the time and (reflective) space between the speech and the (called for) action is so limited that the speaker may be viewed as leading the audience into action rather than simply trying to persuade them to take action.

In American free speech jurisprudence, the classic example of a failure in the conditions of ordinary discourse comes from a judgment of Justice Holmes, who said that "The most stringent protection of free speech would not protect a man in falsely shouting fire in a theatre and causing a panic."[10] The theatre audience in such a case would not have time to stop and think before acting on the communicated message. The panic that would follow the speaker's words in these circumstances would almost certainly result in injury.

The examples given by Mill and Holmes involve circumstances that limit the audience's ability to carefully or dispassionately assess the communicated message. The assumption is that, ordinarily, when an individual communicates with others, she/he appeals to their independent and reasoned judgment. In exceptional circumstances, however, an individual's words may appeal to passions and fears and may encourage unreflective action. In these circumstances the state may be justified in restricting or punishing the expression. Speech may be treated as a "cause" of audience action when the time and space for independent judgment are compressed or when emotions are running so high that audience members are unable or unlikely to stop and reflect on the claims being made. While the line between rational appeal or conscious argument, on the one hand, and on the other, manipulation or incitement, may not be easy to draw (and indeed is a relative matter), it is at least possible to identify some of the circumstances or conditions in which reasoned judgment is significantly constrained.

But what happens when the basic assumptions underlying the commitment to freedom of expression – about the reasonableness or rationality of discourse and the scope of communicative engagement – are eroded or undermined, not simply in limited situations of the sort described by Mill and Holmes, but instead by more systemic changes in the character of public discourse?

The Behavioural Approach of the Canadian Courts

The response of the Canadian courts to concerns about the manipulative character of speech or the potential of speech to "cause" harm has been to defer to the legislature's judgment about the need for limits on (harmful) speech or to rely on the "common sense" that such speech is harmful. The courts have been willing to uphold limits on freedom of expression without explaining why we should not trust audience members to make their own judgments about the merits of the expression. Instead, in these cases, the courts have adopted a behavioural approach – asking simply whether the expression "causes" harm without trying to identify or isolate factors that distinguish this particular form of speech as manipulative or as likely to cause harm.

When defining the scope of freedom of expression, the courts regard the individual as free and rational, as an autonomous agent capable of giving direction to his or her life. In expressing him- or herself, an individual gives voice to his or her thoughts and feelings and provides ideas and information for other individuals to consider and to adopt or reject. However, when the courts move from defining the scope of the freedom under section 2(b) of the *Charter* to assessing the freedom's limits under section 1, they appear to shift to a behavioural or causal discourse. In their limitations analysis, the courts rely on a different image of the individual. The individual is seen as irrational, manipulable, directed by unchosen preferences, urges, and desires. Expression is seen as a form of action that impacts the individual, sometimes causing him/her harm or leading him/her to engage in harmful behaviour. When confronted with issues of manipulation, intimidation, and communicative power, the Canadian courts' faith in the freedom and rationality of the individual collapses.

This shift to a behavioural discourse at the limitations stage of the courts' analysis occurs without any reconsideration of the assumptions that underlie their initial account of the value and scope of freedom of expression. When expression takes place in a context in which individual judgment seems distorted or constrained, the courts have found it easier to label and treat the expression as a form of action that impacts the individual, rather than to identify the exceptional character or circumstances of the expression.[11] In addition, because it is difficult to prove the impact of speech on its audience, the courts have either relied on "common sense" or deferred to legislative judgment to complete the causal link between expression and harm.[12]

However, if the courts support the restriction of potentially harmful expression without explaining why the judgment of the audience is not to be trusted (in the particular circumstance), and without acknowledging the costs of removing certain matters from the scope of public discourse, the right to free expression will have ceased to play any meaningful role in their decision making. Freedom of expression has little substance if our trust in the autonomous judgment of the individual is the exception (a condition that must be established); it has no substance if it is protected only when we agree with its message or consider its message to be harmless.[13] The problem with this approach to free speech protection – an approach that formally acknowledges the premises of free speech but supports limits on speech that carries a harmful message – is that it puts the whole free expression edifice at risk.

The Demise of Freedom of Expression?

Systemic Changes in the Last Half of the Twentieth Century

In the last part of the twentieth century, two developments in the structure and character of public discourse raised significant challenges for freedom of expression doctrine. The first was the rise of lifestyle/commercial advertising, a form of speech that was designed to influence its audience non-cognitively, by associating a product with a value or lifestyle. Lifestyle ads make no explicit claims and are generally presented in a context that limits the viewer's ability to reflect upon their images or associations. As John Berger observed, "The publicity image belongs to the moment. We see it as we turn a page, as we turn the corner as a vehicle passes. Or we see it on a television screen whilst waiting for the commercial break to end."[14] The images of advertising stream past us at a speed and in a volume that "defies rational reflection."[15] Indeed, an advertisement is designed to be looked at quickly in passing, and not as something that requires careful reflection.

The second development was the domination of public discourse by a small group of speakers and a limited range of perspectives – resulting from the concentration of media ownership and the high cost of access to the media. In the nineteenth-century, newspapers were numerous and partisan. However, in the century that followed, technological developments, along with the push to increase advertising revenue, led to dramatic growth in the scale of newspapers and the creation of media monopolies in particular geographic areas.[16] Entry costs became so high that control over (and communicative access to) daily newspapers belonged to a remarkably small group of individuals and corporations. These newspapers presented themselves as common carriers of information, providing not only neutral and objective news reporting on a wide range of matters but also a forum for the expression of different perspectives. The shift from partisan proponent to objective reporter and common carrier broadened the appeal of particular newspapers and supported their growth in scale.[17] However genuine the aspiration to objectivity, ownership concentration meant that the values of a small group of corporations played a significant role in shaping public debate. A newspaper had to decide what to include and what to exclude, what to treat with emphasis or in depth and what to treat superficially on the back pages.[18] This selection was bound to reflect the values, concerns, and interests of those who make the decisions and those who employ the decision makers. As well, because newspapers obtained most of their revenue from advertising, the selection of newspaper content was also significantly influenced by the priorities of advertisers.[19]

Manipulation and Inequality

While manipulation and inequality of access are often described and responded to as separate problems, they are linked and might even be viewed as two aspects or dimensions of a more general problem in public discourse – that of the domination of commercial speech.

Commercial advertisements have a manipulative impact only because they so completely dominate public discourse. The overwhelming number of commercial messages that we are confronted with each day reduces the space for critical viewing of individual ads. There are so many ads that it is impossible for the audience to reflect on the claims or associations of each. These ads simply wash over us. The domination of public discourse by advertising also means that the unnatural images or absurd associations of a particular ad seem unexceptional.

Commercial advertising has come to dominate public discourse, not just in the sense that so much of that discourse is comprised of ads (we see ads everywhere), but also in the way in which these ads have become the general model for public expression, for how political and other public actors convey their views and seek to persuade others. Political speech in the commercial model seeks an emotional or visceral response, avoids complexity and nuance, and devalues factual accuracy. The dominance of the advertising model has made it increasingly difficult for us to envision political speech that seeks to persuade citizens of the wisdom of a particular policy rather than simply spin or manipulate the concerns and feelings of political consumers.[20]

Concern that certain messages may dominate discourse and overwhelm or displace other views is more explicit in the debate about limits on spending in election campaigns.[21] Inequality in election spending, though, is only a problem because of the advertising form of most campaign expression, which is composed of images and slogans with little evaluative content. Limitations on election spending, which do not restrict the message or form of expression but only the amount of money that can be spent in support of a particular message, are justified on the ground that unlimited spending will allow the messages of some candidates to "drown out" those of other candidates. How is it, though, that the message of the better-financed candidate "drowns out" the message of his or her competitors? The competitors' messages can still be heard, even if less often. And, of course, a limitation on the speech of one candidate does not increase the other candidates' opportunities to speak. If greater volume has an impact (if repetition of messages makes a difference), it is because so much contemporary political discourse has adopted the form of commercial advertising in an attempt to influence the audience emotionally or non-cognitively.[22]

Restrictions aimed at either the manipulative impact of expression or the dominance of particular messages are partial, or symptom, responses to a systemic problem. Inequality in election spending is a problem because of the advertising form of most campaign expression. Commercial advertisements have a manipulative impact only because they so completely dominate public discourse. Yet the courts in Canada, as elsewhere, have described manipulation and inequality as separate problems, each representing a distinct and limited failure in the ordinary operation of public discourse. A commitment to freedom of expression, at least as a judicially protected constitutional right, rests on a belief that, in the absence of special circumstances, individuals should be permitted to express themselves and to assess the expression of others. Manipulation, then, must be viewed as an identifiable deviation from the ordinary conditions of free and rational public discussion and inequality must be viewed as a particular unfairness in electoral competition that can be addressed by setting basic ground rules that level the "playing field."[23]

The Internet and Democratic Speech

The emergence of the internet as a significant conduit for personal conversation and public discussion seemed to lessen concerns about media concentration and unequal access to communicative resources. The web opened the conversation to more voices. It became possible for individuals to bypass existing media structures and to communicate to others without filters.

It was, and still is, the case that large sections of the community rely on central sources for information and opinion, such as online versions of established newspapers and other traditional media, and so concerns about control and filtering are not entirely gone.[24] However, the more significant issue raised by our reliance on the internet is the fragmentation of audiences – an issue that, even if it predates the internet, has nonetheless been exacerbated by it. Despite their failings, newspapers and broadcast stations often provided a common space (were part of the public sphere) where a large and sometimes diverse group of readers or viewers went to discover different opinions and to acquire reliable information. While the internet provides access to a remarkably wide range of views and information, internet users tend to expose themselves to a relatively narrow range of opinions that reinforce the views they already hold. Selective access occurs by choice but also by design. The habit of going to sources that confirm one's existing views (resulting in what is referred to as "confirmation bias") is reinforced by the algorithms used by search engines such as Google and platforms such as YouTube and Facebook, which direct individuals to sites that are similar to those they have visited in the past.[25] This may not count as censorship, at least as that term is commonly used, but it has the same effect – determining or selecting the information and opinions to which individual

users are exposed, in effect "editing" their experiences.[26] The result of this selection is what is sometimes referred to as an "echo chamber" or "filter bub-
ble" – spaces in which individuals hear their existing views fed back to them or
become immersed in more and more extreme versions of these views.[27]

Most online engagement now occurs on social media platforms such as Facebook and YouTube.[28] These platforms generate revenue though advertising that
is directed at users. Advertisers have always targeted particular audiences by
placing their ads in certain publications or broadcast time slots. However, the
accumulation of personal data by platforms such as Facebook has made possible
micro-targeting – individualized targeting of commercial and political messages
that are designed to play to the individual's particular concerns and prejudices.
These messages are both personal (directed at individual users) and private (visible only to the targeted individual) and so are insulated from outside scrutiny.
While these platforms have enabled individuals with common interests to connect across the community and around the world, they have also enabled powerful commercial and political actors to direct specific, and often deceptive or false,
messages at particular individuals out of sight, away from public examination.

On platforms such as Facebook, individuals share stories with close friends, social acquaintances, and political allies – a broad group of "friends" who are generally
like-minded. A consequence of this "scrambling" of the personal and the political
is that adherence to a particular political outlook often becomes a matter of group
identity and loyalty.[29] Even if social media users are not entirely insulated from opposing views, they may be unwilling or unable to engage with those views in a serious way. When competing positions are formed around particular social groups
(often linked to ethnicity, religion, class, location), debate between these groups
ceases to be about persuading others or understanding their views and becomes
instead a clash with opponents and a declaration of group identity or allegiance.
These exchanges seem only to deepen the divide and intensify partisan loyalties.

This divide is often reinforced by interested corporate and political actors.
The online news/opinion sites that many rely on (particularly on the political right) often provide users with "partisan confirming" (dis)information and
opinion, while also encouraging them to dismiss other sources as "false news."[30]
And so, as Yochai Benkler observes, even when partisans are exposed to the
positions and claims of "the other side," they often discount those positions:

> When the propagandist's efforts are exposed to external criticism and fact checking,
> the mechanisms that developed for reducing the cost of disconfirmation – lower
> attention and lower trust to external media – kick in to insulate the propagandists'
> efforts from this external criticism.[31]

A growing number of individuals reject traditional authorities and distrust
anyone with a different outlook, and as a consequence they have become

vulnerable to conspiracy theories and the deceptive claims of populist politicians and corporate interests.

The visceral or emotional character of so much of our online communication, along with the undermining of competing sources, makes any real engagement with other positions difficult or impossible. John Stuart Mill argued that the "collision" of truth with error would give us a "clearer perception and livelier impression of truth."[32] In his view, any acceptance by the individual of the truth (what happens to be true) that is not the outcome of reasoned judgment (and open to challenge) will be weak and easily reversed when the winds of opinion shift. Yet the opposite seems to be the case. Opinions that are adopted without judgment often become entrenched (a matter of group identity) and vigorously defended, not through argument but through assertion and attack.

The breakdown of consensus about sources of information or expertise is a reminder that traditional accounts of free speech often focus on the individual's direct/personal judgments about ideas and information, while ignoring his/her judgments about sources and expertise – about whom or what to trust or rely on. In the absence of any agreement about which sources to trust, public discussion of pressing issues, such as global warming or vaccine safety, becomes impossible.

The principal threat to public discourse is no longer censorship – and state censorship in particular – but rather the spread of disinformation (within a fragmented public sphere) that undermines agreement on factual matters and trust in different sources of information or knowledge.[33] Zeynep Tufekci describes the problem in this way: "In the networked public sphere, there is too much information, and people lack effective means to quickly and efficiently verify it, which means that information can be effectively suppressed by creating an ever-bigger glut of mashed-up truth and falsehood to foment confusion and distraction."[34] In a piece I wrote a little over a decade ago about the attack on human rights commissions by right-wing bloggers and columnists, I noted that the merits of the cases for or against the commissions had become "lost in a sea of exaggerations and fabrications," with the result that the audience had been left to make a choice based on their ideological predispositions rather than reasoned judgment:

> [Spin or disinformation] will not advance democratic engagement or meaningful discussion of public policy, and it cannot bring about consensus or compromise or even respectful disagreement based on an awareness of the costs and benefits of the different responses. Spin encourages the fragmentation of the civic audience into insular ideological communities that are unable to engage with each other. The costs of spin are even more fundamental than this though. Spin degrades public discourse, so that we no longer expect to be told the truth and are no longer able to evaluate positions based on the accuracy of their claims or assumptions.[35]

The Case of Hate Speech

The use of the internet as a vehicle for the expression of hate speech has strengthened the case for its restriction; it has also made such a restriction more difficult to define and enforce. The internet enables individuals and groups with common interests to connect with one another at low cost and little personal risk. These characteristics have made the internet the preferred medium for hate promoters. The internet's complex public/private character makes it a potent vehicle for the promotion and reinforcement of hateful views.[36] While most websites are public in the sense that they are generally accessible, the audience for a particular site is self-selecting and often quite small.

Hate speech generally occurs at the margins of public discourse, where the opportunity for response or engagement is limited. It often circulates among the members of a relatively insular racist subculture, who are uninterested in exposing themselves to other views. When targeted at such an audience, extreme speech may reinforce and extend bigoted views without being subjected to critical scrutiny. Smaller hate sites (or those that are less easily accessed, such as chat rooms) that link like-minded individuals can encourage a sense of intimacy and shared identity among their members and are able to operate below the radar. These sites may be an effective means for individuals and groups who hold hateful views to encourage others to adopt more extreme views or to take radical action. Speaking in a "safe place" free from challenge may also encourage the speaker to express more extreme views and even perhaps to believe more strongly in the views she/he is expressing.

Hate speech laws, though, may be ineffective, and perhaps even counterproductive, in suppressing less extreme bigoted views, such as stereotypes, that circulate more widely in mainstream discourse.[37] Such views cannot simply be expunged from public discourse through censorship. Any attempt to exclude all expressions of prejudice from the public sphere would require extraordinary intervention on the part of the state. Hate speech law, then, cannot effectively address bigoted views that are part of mainstream discourse, even though such views may contribute significantly to the marginalization of particular groups. The scope of the ban on hate speech must be narrowly drawn so that it extends only to extreme speech – speech that either explicitly or implicitly advocates or justifies oppressive action against the members of a particular group.[38] The primary concern of contemporary hate speech law must be to prevent speech that encourages "isolated" acts of violence against members of an identifiable group, acts such as "gay-bashing." Hate crimes are most often committed not by organized groups but by individuals who have immersed themselves in extremist subcultures that operate at the margins of public discourse, and principally on the internet. However, the hateful views that are fostered in the hidden corners of the web have, recently, found expression in popular right-wing radio, newspaper, and television outlets and have begun to circulate more widely on social media platforms. Once hate speech enters the mainstream, the legal ban on hate may no longer be workable (see Macfarlane, this volume).

Privately Owned Public Forums

The constitutional right to free speech is focused on state censorship – on limiting the state's power to restrict or regulate speech.[39] Yet the most significant public forums – the places where individuals communicate with others – have been, and continue to be, privately owned. Publicly owned spaces, such as parks and streets, have increasingly been displaced by privately owned shopping malls and office building concourses as the locations in which individuals interact or congregate. Because these spaces are privately owned, the decisions of their owners to exclude certain speakers or to curtail certain forms of speech fall outside the scope of the *Charter's* protection of freedom of expression.

The web is open and accessible and permits individuals to engage on a wide range of matters. However, most online activity occurs on privately owned social media platforms such as Facebook, Twitter, YouTube, and Instagram. These platforms may claim or aim to be neutral towards content and open to a wide range of users and views, but they have the power, if they choose, to exclude any speakers or viewpoints. And, as earlier noted, these platforms employ algorithms that direct individuals to particular topics, perspectives, and sources. Even if these algorithms are intended simply to retain users' attention – to keep users on the platform so that they will continue to view ads – their effect is to inhibit access to other sources and viewpoints.

Most of the criticism of social media platforms has centred on their accumulation of users' personal data and their failure to filter out (or their facilitation of) false news and hate speech.[40] While we should be concerned about the use of these platforms by hate-mongers and political manipulators (who are able to direct misleading messages at very specific audiences), we should, perhaps, also be concerned about the platforms' authority, as private providers, to exclude certain speakers or messages, without any need for justification. A particular risk is that these platforms, in responding to popular or legal demands to remove speech that is hateful or harassing, will be over-inclusive in their enforcement of such a ban and exclude speech that is lawful. Given the volume of material that is posted on Twitter and Facebook, these platforms must make quick and simple judgments, and must often rely on automated means to do so, that cannot take adequate account of context and nuance (see Mathen, this volume).[41]

Public Spaces and Private Purposes

Street speech, including public demonstrations and street-corner leaflet-ting, was once viewed as an important alternative to communication in the mainstream/established media. At an earlier time, the concentration of media ownership, and the reliance on advertising as the primary source of revenue for newspapers and broadcasters, meant that critical perspectives were often excluded from these forums. The streets were sometimes the only platform available to those who lacked either the resources or connections to access the mainstream media. However, the communication landscape has changed dra-matically since the courts first championed the individual's access to the "poor man's printing press."[42] The emergence of the internet as a significant conduit for the expression of ideas and information seemed to lessen concerns about media concentration and unequal access to communicative resources. Yet de-spite the rise of new media, street speech continues to occur with the same and perhaps even greater frequency. As several commentators have noted, online communication and street demonstrations are not simply alternative modes of protest but are instead complementary components of all contemporary protest movements.[43]

The continuing appeal of street speech may reflect, first, a desire to recreate a common space in which public engagement – politics – is possible. The frag-mentation of public discourse, quickened by the rise of new media, has led to the loss of a shared public conversation and a common body of information upon which to engage in discussion and decide on collective action. Because street speech occurs in a publicly accessible and visibly open space, its message can (appear to) reach a general (non-self-selecting) audience. Second, while the internet overcomes geographic distance, a demonstration in public space bridges physical and emotional distance, by bringing individuals together and giving them a sense of presence and connection with others that is lacking in mediated forms of communication.[44] In contrast to the disembodied, deper-sonalized, and passive character of internet communication, street speech is experienced as performative and physically engaging.

Street demonstrations are often intended as a challenge, rather than simply a contribution, to the dominant political discourse. They are a reaction to a perceived failure of the prevailing political conversation to take any or adequate account of important public issues or positions. Demonstrations, then, are in-tended, and can be viewed, as democratic participation but also as an opting out of mainstream public discourse or a rejection of ordinary politics. They seek to create a more truly democratic conversation that challenges established institutions and the forms of discourse that legitimate those institutions. They make visible the extent and depth of opposition to a government or its policies. They confront the authorities or the larger community with demands for public recognition or action. This was most clearly so in the case of street protests in places such as Iran and Egypt, where the protestors sought to reopen a public space that the state had shut down, but it is also true of demonstrations in democratic societies such as Canada, where protestors seek to highlight issues that are given little attention in mainstream discourse.[45]

The courts, and other state actors, may describe demonstrations as valuable political speech, but they are often quick to see them (and other forms of street speech) as disruptive or harassing. In a society in which communication (other than with family and friends) is generally mediated (through broadcast, print, and internet platforms) listening is generally a choice. The individual is free to tune in or out. Because most speech is mediated, face-to-face communication with strangers in public spaces such as the streets is often experienced as a nuisance and sometimes even as intimidating.[46] Many believe they should not have to listen to views with which they disagree. And any requirement that they do so is regarded as an interference with their autonomy. This assumption (that everyone has a right to speak but no one has a right to be heard) impedes meaningful engagement in the community across political differences.

As well, when most public communication is about consumption (the promotion of goods and services), face-to-face speech that challenges or disrupts this message and calls on individuals to take political action (e.g., public demonstrations) or to assist others (e.g., panhandling) is often viewed as invasive or disruptive of ordinary life. Because public spaces such as the streets and the parks often serve personal (private) purposes, such as shopping and transportation, speech that impedes the individual's pursuit of these purposes is sometimes viewed as an unjustified interference with her/his liberty of movement. Once again, even though the courts stress the importance of street speech, the value of this speech is often depreciated in an assessment or balancing of competing/conflicting uses of public property.[47]

Commercial advertising often escapes these complaints of nuisance and disruption, not just because it is ordinarily mediated, but, ironically, because it is ubiquitous. Indeed, the effectiveness of commercial advertising depends on it being everywhere, on its normalcy, so that it is viewed without serious, careful reflection. It makes no argument and does not ask anything directly of us, but simply presents a product that we may or may not choose to purchase. In contrast, political speech asks something of us. It takes a position and argues for agreement or action. Even though we attach formal value to political speech, we may experience it as more intrusive than commercial speech.

What Is to Be Done?

Recent changes in the character and structure of public discourse raise significant questions about the future of free speech. A reliance on "more speech" as the answer to bad speech – to false or deceptive claims – seems inadequate in a communication environment that is increasingly fragmented and in which a significant element of the population is not only receptive to "false news" and conspiracy theories but is also (reflexively) hostile to competing opinions and evidence that contradicts their views. The constitutional right to freedom of expression protects individuals from state censorship. Yet because the most important public forums – the places where public discourse occurs – are now privately owned, private censorship is the greater concern. These private platforms can take down speech or block speakers without any need for justification. However, the main threat to public discourse is no longer censorship (state or private), at least as it is understood in the traditional free speech model, but is instead the barrage of (targeted) disinformation that is undermining our ability to make judgments about what is true and right and our willingness to engage with those who hold different views. Social media platforms have made possible the micro-targeting of audience members with messages that play to their fears and resentments. The volume of unfiltered speech with which we are daily confronted makes it impossible for us to sift through it all and to distinguish the true or trustworthy from the untrue and dissembling.

Ignoring these changes in the form and forums of public discourse may have considerable costs. We cannot carry on as if we live in a world of rational or reasonable engagement. Holding to a laissez-faire approach to free speech (as the US courts seem inclined to do) will only further erode the common ground necessary for a democratic public discourse – which requires some level of agreement about facts or authorities. Public discourse is in crisis, but the remedy is no longer simply "free speech" – the breaking down of state censorship. Indeed, a robust protection of free expression may actually contribute to the crisis. The courts do not have the capacity to repair our deteriorating discourse – although they do have the power to make it worse by holding to the view that state censorship is the principal threat to democratic discourse and blocking legislative responses to the crisis. The problem lies with the structure and character of public discourse and cannot be fixed by court decisions that decide that a state restriction on expression should be either upheld or struck down.

There are some imaginable legislative responses to this crisis, but it is difficult to be optimistic about their effectiveness or even the likelihood that they could be implemented politically or practically. There should be limits on the ability of platforms such as Facebook to gather personal data and to engage in direct individualized marketing. Legislatures should require these platforms to remove hate speech – although the drawbacks of such a requirement are obvious and include the likelihood that platforms will be over-inclusive in their enforcement so as to avoid any risk of violating such a ban. Legislatures should also discourage platforms from routinely directing users to sources or content that reinforce their existing views or offer more extreme versions of those views. It may be that we also need to consider legal restrictions on speech that is intentionally deceptive, even though proving intention in such cases may not always be easy.[48] Online speech that is harassing or threatening should be regulated, so that its targets are not simply driven off public platforms such as Twitter. Because these platforms are public forums, we cannot simply leave it to their private owners to decide what counts as hate speech or harassment or false news, without any public oversight of their decisions. Each of these responses carries risks and costs.

NOTES

*   This paper draws on my previous writings, including *The Constitutional Protection of Freedom of Expression* (Toronto: University of Toronto Press, 2000), *Putting Faith in Hate: When Religion Is the Source or Target of Hate Speech* (New York: Columbia University Press, 2018), and R. Moon, "What happens when the assumptions underlying our commitment to free speech no longer hold?" in Marie-Claude Najm Kobeh (ed.), *La liberté d'expression et ses juges* (Beirut: Centre d'études des droits du monde arabe, 2018).

1   McLachlin J. in *R. v Keegstra*, [1990] 3 SCR 697 at 806.

2   "We become individuals," Clifford Geertz observes, "under the guidance of cultural patterns, historically created systems of meaning in terms of which we give form, order, point, and direction to our lives." Clifford Geertz, *The Interpretation of Cultures: Selected Essays* (New York: Basic Books, 1973), 52.

3   Charles Taylor, *Human Agency and Language* (Cambridge: Cambridge University Press, 1985), 256. When we communicate our ideas and feelings – when we give them linguistic form – we "bring them to fuller and clearer consciousness" (257).

4   John B. Thompson, *The Media and Modernity: A Social Theory of the Media* (Stanford, CA: Stanford University Press, 1995) at 39

5   Thompson, *The Media and Modernity*, note 4 at 42.

6   At the same time, individuals adapt the symbolic forms of language to their needs in particular communicative contexts and in so doing recreate, extend, alter, and reshape the language. See Taylor, *Human Agency and Language*, 97. As Mikhail Bakhtin observes, the individual's thought is "born and shaped in the process of articulation and the process of interaction and struggle with others' thought": Mikhail M. Bakhtin, *Speech Genres and Other Late Essays*, Trans. V. McGee (Austin: University of Texas Press, 1986), 92.

7   *Irwin Toy v AG (Quebec)*, [1989] 1 SCR 927; *R. v Keegstra*, [1990] 3 SCR 697; *Canada (AG) v JTI-Macdonald*, 2007 SCC 30; *Harper v Canada (AG)*, 2004 SCC 33; *R. v Butler*, [1992] 1 SCR 452.

8   Brandeis J. in *Whitney v California*, 247 US 357 (1927) at 37: "the remedy to be applied is more speech."

9   John Stuart Mill, *On Liberty* (Harmondsworth, UK: Penguin, 1982), 119.

10 *Schenck v United States*, 249 US 47 (1919) at 52. But note that in that case Holmes J. thought that the distribution of literature encouraging draft resistance during the First World War was the equivalent of the "yell of fire" and so could be restricted.

11 See, for example, *RWDSU v Dolphin Delivery*, [1986] 2 SCR 573; *R. v Keegstra*, [1990] 3 SCR 697; *R. v Butler*, [1992] 1 SCR 452.

12 See, for example, *Harper v Canada (AG)*, 2004 SCC 33.

13 See, for, example the judgment of McLachlin J. in *RJR Macdonald v Canada*, [1995] 3 SCR 199.

14 John Berger, *Ways of Seeing* (London: British Broadcasting Corporation; New York: Penguin, 1977), 129.

15 Anne Marie Seward Barry, *Visual Intelligence: Perception, Image, and Manipulation in Visual Communication* (Albany: State University of New York Press, 1997), 171.

16 Kent Commission, *Report of the Royal Commission on Newspapers* (Ottawa: Minister of Supply and Services, 1981), 72.

17 At the same time, this shift in image was an important defence against attempts to regulate newspapers that operate as a monopoly in a particular geographic area. See Ithiel de Sola Pool, *Technologies of Freedom: On Free Speech in an Electronic Age* (Cambridge, MA: Belknap Press of Harvard University Press, 1983), 238.

18 Ben Bagdikian, *The Media Monopoly* (Boston: Beacon Press, 1992), 16.

19 Sometimes advertisers wanted newspapers to suppress stories contrary to their interests; for example, the cigarette manufacturers who worked very hard to ensure that newspaper content was censored to obscure the link between tobacco and death; see Bagdikian, *The Media Monopoly*, 173. More often, advertisers simply wanted the news content of the paper to complement their message. If a newspaper is to be an effective vehicle for commercial messages, it must not be too critical and opinionated.

20 Richard Moon, "The Attack on Human Rights Commissions and the Decline of Public Discourse," *Saskatchewan Law Review* 73 (2011): 123.

21 *Harper v Canada (AG)*, 2004 SCC 33.

22 This is why the particular criticism of negative election adverting seems misguided. Negative ads are just the flip side of positive image-based advertising – and are a concern for the same reason.

23 Even if there is some acknowledgment that the problem is also with the form or character of campaign speech, the focus of regulation remains on the election period. Yet we now recognize both that politicians are always running for office and that political speech more generally takes the form of commercial advertising.

24 See Matthew Hindman, *The Internet Trap: How the Digital Economy Builds Monopolies and Undermines Democracy* (Princeton, NJ: Princeton University Press, 2018), 13: "Many had hoped that the web would make news and political debate less centralized, expand and diversify the number of journalists and news outlets, and make capital less important in gathering an audience. The number of outlets may have expanded, but the public sphere remains highly concentrated."

25 A number of writers, including Cass Sunstein, have discussed the way in which "confirmation bias" has contributed to the echo-chamber effect and the polarization of public opinion. See Sunstein, *#Republic: Divided Democracy in the Age of Social Media* (Princeton, NJ: Princeton University Press, 2017).

26 Siva Vaidhyanathan, *Antiscocial Media: How Facebook Disconnects Us and Undermines Democracy* (Oxford: Oxford University Press, 2018), 34.

27 Yochai Benkler, Robert Faris, and Hal Roberts, *Network Propaganda: Manipulation, Disinformation, and Radicalization in American Politics* (New York: Oxford University Press, 2018), 73, makes a strong case that the echo chamber is predominantly an issue in the right-wing media sphere: "The right wing of the media ecosphere behaves precisely as the echo-chamber models predict – exhibiting high insularity, susceptibility to information cascades, rumor and conspiracy theory, and drift towards more extreme versions of itself. The rest of the media ecosystem, however, operates as an interconnected network anchored by organizations, both profit and non-profit, that adhere to professional journalistic norms."

28 Zeynep Tufekci, *Twitter and Tear Gas: The Power and Fragility of Networked Protest* (New Haven, CT: Yale University Press, 2017), 135: "The dominance of a few platforms online is not a historical coincidence; rather, it is the product of two important structural dynamics: network effect and the dominance of ad-financing model for online platforms."

29 Vaidhyanathan, *Antiscocial Media*, 50: "We perform our tribal membership with what we post and share on Facebook."

30 Benkler, Faris, and Roberts, *Network Propaganda*, 78.

31 Benkler, Faris, and Roberts, 80. The authors also argue that "members of the public now have media outlets and elites confirming their prior beliefs, contrary to what they hear on other media, and are also told by these outlets and elites that other media that contradict what they say are themselves biased and hence untrustworthy" (78).

32 Mill, *On Liberty*, at 76.

33 Richard Moon, "What Happens When the Assumptions Underlying Our Commitment to Free Speech No Longer Hold?," in *La liberté d'expression et ses juges*, ed. Marie-Claude Najm Kobeh, 110–37 (Beirut: Centre d'études des droits du monde arabe, 2018). See also Tim Wu, "Is the First Amendment Obsolete?," in *The Free Speech Century*, ed. Lee C. Bollinger and Geoffrey R. Stone (New York: Oxford University Press, 2019), 272.

34 Tufekci, *Twitter and Tear Gas*, 230.

35 Moon, "The Attack on Human Rights Commissions and the Decline of Public Discourse," 123.

36 Richard Moon, *Report to the Canadian Human Rights Commission Concerning Section 13 of the Canadian Human Rights Act and the Regulation of Hate Speech on the Internet* (Ottawa: Canadian Human Rights Commission, 2008).

37 Richard Moon, *Putting Faith in Hate: When Religion Is the Source or Target of Hate Speech* (Cambridge: Cambridge University Press, 2018), 53.

38 In *Saskatchewan (Human Rights Commission) v Whatcott*, 2013 SCC 11 at para.
    57, the Court made clear that the provincial hate speech ban caught only a narrow
    category of extreme speech that vilifies the members of a group.

39 The focus on state action/censorship rests on the long-standing assumption that
    the state represents the principal threat to freedom of expression but also on a
    recognition that such a limit may be necessary to contain the scope, and protect
    the legitimacy, of judicial review under the *Charter of Rights*.

40 See, for example, the German law known as the *Network Enforcement Act* (or
    Netz DG, in the German abbreviation), which requires social media platforms to
    remove hate speech and other unlawful forms of speech within a short period of
    time – twenty-four hours if manifestly unlawful, or even days.

41 Benkler, Faris, and Roberts, *Network Propaganda*, 363.

42 The term "the poor man's printing press" was coined by Harry Kalvin Jr., *The Negro
    and the First Amendment* (Chicago: University of Chicago Press, 1966).

43 Tufekci, *Twitter and Tear Gas*, x.

44 Manuel Castells, *Networks of Outrage and Hope: Social Movements in the Internet
    Age* (Malden, MA: Polity, 2015), 10: "Occupied spaces … create community, and
    community is based on togetherness. Togetherness is a fundamental psychological
    mechanism to overcome fear."

45 Most demonstrations aim to bring an issue to the attention of a broader audience by
    attracting media coverage or through social media dissemination. The traditional
    media, though, often has little interest in covering demonstrations or reporting outsider
    political events, except insofar as they can be understood as a public nuisance or a
    potential source of violence. In other words, the media will cover the event as spectacle
    rather than speech. When media attention is paid, it is often to the negative dimensions
    of the protest, such as nuisance or property damage, with its original message being
    either ignored or tainted. And of course, the media's interest in confrontation or
    violence creates an incentive for some protestors to threaten or engage in violence.

46 This feeling may be strengthened by the experience of speech on Twitter and other
    open platforms, where strangers sometimes engage in personal attacks and other
    forms of harassment.

47 This may have been playing a role in the willingness of the courts to issue
    injunctions against the Occupy Movement encampments. See, for example, *Batty v
    City of Toronto*, 2011 ONSC 6862.

48 McLachlin J., in her dissent in *R. v Zundel*, [1992] 2 SCR 731 at 754, made the troubling
    argument that lies sometimes have value and so should fall within the protection of
    section 2(b) of the *Charter*: "Exaggeration – even clear falsification – may arguably
    serve useful social purposes linked to the values underlying freedom of expression …
    A doctor, in order to persuade people to be inoculated against a burgeoning epidemic,
    may exaggerate the number or geographic location of persons potentially infected with
    the virus." This position, and the example given to support it, have not aged well.

2 Hate Speech, Harm, and Rights

EMMETT MACFARLANE

The bottom line is this. While remaining sensitive to the social and political context of the impugned law and allowing for difficulties of proof inherent in that context, the courts must nevertheless insist that before the state can override constitutional rights, there be a reasoned demonstration of the good which the law may achieve in relation to the seriousness of the infringement.[1]

The above caution that the Supreme Court ought to demand evidence from the state when it seeks to impose limits on free expression comes from a landmark 1995 decision. The case at hand did not involve restrictions on political expression or the censorship of literature or art, but laws targeting the advertising of tobacco. In fact, a majority of the Court was unconvinced that there was sufficient evidence of a connection between advertising and the increased prevalence of smoking to justify a broad prohibition. Although the justices on both the majority and dissenting sides acknowledged that the burden of proof on the state does not rise to the level of scientific proof – it is sufficient to make a finding of a causal connection "on the basis of reason or logic"[2] – the Court nonetheless still found in favour of the tobacco companies.

It is noteworthy, then, that the Court has routinely upheld laws restricting freedom of expression in the context of hate speech when the evidence of harm is much less certain, and much more diffuse and subjective, than the evidence that tobacco advertising might contribute to the substantial, and well-established, harms of smoking.

This chapter explores the harms of hate speech and how harms are invoked to justify restrictions on freedom of expression. After examining arguments about harm by the leading proponents of hate speech laws, the chapter analyses the interdisciplinary literature empirically studying harm. The particular focus here is not on hate speech that explicitly advocates violence or threaten illegal acts (incitement), nor do I propose to examine hateful speech that likely violates other laws, such as speech that constitutes harassment via the sustained targeting of an individual. The chapter focuses, rather, on forms of expression that reflect or are designed to foster hatred towards minority or vulnerable groups on the basis of racial, sexual, or analogous characteristics. The harms most often identified with such speech include those from two broad categories: the first is the notion that it contributes to or influences physical and behavioural harms, ranging from violence towards members of targeted groups to inculcating prejudicial attitudes that subsequently increase acts of discrimination in society; the second concerns the belief that such speech is inherently harmful because it imposes psychological and emotional harm on the members of targeted communities, even damaging their equal status and inherent dignity.

Much of this harm is diffuse in nature. That is, in the vast majority of cases falling under the definition of hate speech I adopt here, the speaker or writer does not have an individual target in mind but is maligning an entire category of people. The harm is not a linear or direct harm in the sense that we can realistically trace a specific utterance or written statement to a specific injury of a specific person. Instead, the hate speech considered here is broadly dispersed. It enters the social ether and the harm is effectively conceptualized as a contaminant in the broader system of societal discourse, a poison or form of pollution that negatively affects both its targets and the larger society.

The diffuse nature of the harms of hate speech has many consequences, two of which are the focus of this chapter. First, from a social scientific standpoint, diffusion makes identifying a causal link between hate speech and its purported harms extremely difficult. Second, from the perspective of law, rights, and state regulation of free expression, the justificatory burdens of prohibiting hate speech are grimly challenging in a context where attributing direct legal or even moral responsibility for harms to specific instances of hate speech is virtually impossible. Instead, hate speech laws are largely justified and upheld because hate speech is seen as increasing the *risk* of some *conceivable* but not necessarily identifiable harm. Add to this the fact that, because of this justificatory burden, courts in Canada have set a high threshold before hateful speech becomes unlawful hate speech, such that the law only captures the most extreme forms of hateful expression. The result is that most purportedly harmful speech goes unregulated, increasing the apparent arbitrariness of the line-drawing exercise the state engages in when it seeks to regulate expression in this context.

The lack of a strong social scientific basis for the harms of hate speech – not to mention the *effectiveness* of hate speech laws – does not belie the significant risks that the harms are nonetheless real, especially the subjective harms to the emotional and psychological wellness of the targets of hate speech. The policy response to this quandary, however, needs to reflect the fact that hate speech laws as currently implemented are unlikely to bring any salutary benefits. Our focus should be on dealing with the systemic forms of discrimination and op-pression that reinforce real harms, including hate itself.

The Harms of Hate Speech: Arguments and Evidence

One of the leading contemporary arguments for the regulation of hate speech comes from Jeremy Waldron's book *The Harm in Hate Speech*.[3] Waldron pre-sents a typically nuanced conceptual account of harm that departs from a fo-cus on harmful consequences of speech for society at large (violence, acts of discrimination) for a focus on harm to those targeted by hateful speech. As he explains,

> The harm that expressions of racial hatred do is harm in the first instance to the groups who are denounced or bestialized in the racist pamphlets and billboards. It is not our harm – if I can put it bluntly – to the white liberals who find the racist invective distasteful ... The question is about the direct targets of the abuse. Can their lives be led, can their children be brought up, can their hopes be main-tained and their worst fears dispelled, in a social environment polluted by these materials?[4]

Laws prohibiting or regulating hate speech, then, "are set up to vindicate pub-lic order, not just by pre-empting violence, but by upholding against attack a shared sense of the basic elements of each person's status, dignity, and reputa-tion as a citizen or member of society in good standing."[5] Waldron is not inter-ested in policing thought, nor is he concerned with merely "offensive" speech; his concern, rather, is with damage to people's *dignity*, acknowledging that "[s]hock, distress, or wounded feelings may or may not be symptomatic of indig-nity, depending on the kind of social phenomenon that causes these feelings or that is associated with their causation."[6] For Waldron, a relevant analogy is contempt of court: we do not seek to protect a judge's feelings but to prevent the esteem of the judge and the court from being lowered.[7]

Waldron's arguments warrant serious examination, because the harms he de-scribes, particularly the "dispelling of assurance" that people be afforded equal worth in a society without "fear of being denigrated and excluded as subhuman or second-class citizens,"[8] go to the core of rights and equality in a democratic society. Nonetheless there are serious problems with Waldron's analysis, not least of which is the fact that, despite the title of his book, nowhere does he in-troduce any actual evidence of the harms he describes.[9] As L.W. Sumner writes, "it is clear that hate speakers cannot impair or undermine the dignity of those they hate *on their own*," so what is the causal mechanism at work? In Sumner's view, Waldron "vastly understates the extent to which most hate speakers are ranting away somewhere out there on the lunatic fringes of cyberspace, rather than in the public square. For the most part, their audience is one another ... they might be powerless to dislodge a social consensus of inclusiveness, once it has been achieved."[10]

Sumner might be overconfident on this point. In the Canadian context, for example, there are reasons to be concerned about the fragility of public support for diversity and pluralism.[11] Nonetheless, it is certainly an open question whether the risk of changes to public opinion of that nature constitute a harm that in and of itself justifies restrictions on expression. Any expression might have effects on public opinion that we might view as normatively undesirable, including expression that falls well short of hate speech. Stephen Newman contends that Waldron's argument is in fact a reconceptualization made necessary by the lack of evidence linking hate speech to violence, discrimination, or social upheaval.[12] Indeed, the "merely offensive" speech Waldron insists he does not wish to subject to state sanction may be even more environmentally hazardous in the ways he describes than the extreme messages that are the focus of his concerns.[13]

Despite the general nuance of his thesis, Waldron does occasionally lapse into caricaturizing the positions adopted by critics of hate speech laws. In a passage acknowledging that hate speech laws might reduce transparency and drive malicious speech underground, he cautions that "the notion that what we most need for expression and publication of this kind is a great debate in which Nazis and liberals can engage one another honestly and with respect for each other's points of view is a curious one."[14] Waldron thus erects a bit of a straw man, no doubt premised on the notion of a "marketplace of ideas" or that "good speech will win out against bad," arguments that are frequently heard in debates about free speech. But it is farcical to suggest that a literal public debate between Nazis and liberals is what defenders of free speech imagine. As Newman points out, "[w]hen we engage the hatemonger as private citizens, we do not give credence to his views or seek to convert him to ours. Rather, as historian Pierre Vidal-Naquet argues in regard to the Holocaust denier, 'we do not "debate" him; we demonstrate the mechanisms of his lies and falsifications' as lessons to our fellow citizens."[15]

While Waldron does not provide empirical evidence to demonstrate the harms he describes, he does invoke analogies to further conceptualize them. In fact, he is critical of demands for causal, scientific proof, suggesting the evidentiary bar is drawn so high that all evidence is dismissed by critics "unless it is established beyond a scintilla of doubt."[16] Instead, he argues, it is important to recognize the complex ways in which harms manifest rather than presume simplistic, observable causation. As a result, Waldron asks what would happen if such arguments were made about environmental harms. "Suppose we said," Waldron explains, "that unless someone can show that *my automobile* causes lead poisoning with direct detriment and imminent harm to the health of assignable individuals, I shouldn't be required to fit an emission-control device to my car's exhaust pipe."[17] The environmental analogy proves unfortunate for Waldron's argument. First, we know that lead is physically damaging to those who ingest it; drivers whose cars are spewing lead are thus creating a very real risk of harm. This is distinct from the subjective, emotional harms associated with hate speech, as examined below. Moreover, even at the systemic level, scientific modelling explicitly demonstrates that any amount of environmental emissions – like carbon dioxide, for example – *contributes* to systemic harm, to the point where there exists scientific consensus that *measurable* thresholds of danger exist that ought to be avoided to prevent *measurable* amounts of damage. The same simply cannot be said of hate speech; the analogy is confined to the imagined or conceptual rather than the empirical and verifiable.

Arguably a better analogy is to the purported harms of pornography. Waldron effectively endorses the views advanced by Catharine MacKinnon that pornography is demeaning and both constitutes and contributes directly to sexual violence and discrimination.[18] But feminist scholars are famously divided over such conclusions, with critics of MacKinnon pointing to methodological issues in her work, accusing her of cherry-picking plausible effects from the most extreme and degrading forms of pornography, and providing a sex-positive feminist rebuttal to her core claims and assumptions.[19]

It is worth noting that Waldron has also been criticized by others for not adopting a sufficiently broad conception of harm. Tariq Modood argues that Waldron's account needs to better consider "the feelings of the victim," which are too often "made secondary and contingent, whereas they are part of what hate is about."[20] I discuss feelings and emotions in more detail below.

Karen Zivi similarly criticizes Waldron's account for failing to recognize hate speech as "symbolic and normative violence."[21] Zivi argues that the "forces and sources of harm are far greater and far less individualized than he suggests."[22] As examples, she cites exclusionary education curricula and religious teaching. Yet the setting of education curricula might be better described as discrimination in practice, and Zivi provides no evidentiary link between hate speech and those types of policy decisions. Zivi is hardly alone in attempting to recast expression as "violence," and one could write an entire paper analysing and critiquing this tendency. Referring to speech as violence seems to me a rhetorical device designed to merely assert or analogize harm rather than convincingly demonstrate it. Moreover, as noted below, the Supreme Court has dismissed this analogy in its own analysis of free expression.

Waldron's, Modood's, and Zivi's arguments are part of a much larger literature in which scholars assert rather than demonstrate or provide evidence for the purported harms of hate speech.[23] Some bypass the focus on hate speech as harm for other reasons – for example, to assert that hate speech is itself an act of discrimination[24] (thereby mirroring the claim that such speech constitutes violence), while others bypass questions of evidence in order to flip the argument on its head and contend that hate speech results in silencing that in fact undermines free speech principles.[25] I address this important and intuitive consideration in the conclusion to this chapter, but first I turn to the empirical literature on harm.

Empirically Identifying Harm

The empirical search for the harms of hate speech crosses the disciplinary borders of psychology, sociology, law, political science, communication studies, critical legal and critical race studies, and philosophy. As noted above, this interdisciplinary scholarly literature tends to focus on two broad categories of harm: those harms, usually acts of discrimination or violence, that are incited or influenced by hate speech (consequentialist harms), and the direct harms manifested by the hate speech itself (constitutive harms), which are usually framed as psychic or emotional harms that risk impairing the human dignity of the targets of hate speech.

In the psychology literature, methodological limitations, restrictions imposed by research ethics, and the largely correlative or self-reported nature of data are all recognized problems scholars face when attempting to identify causal connections between exposure to hate speech and harm.[26] As Timothy Jay notes, assertions "that speech alone harms people oversimplifies the role of complex contextual variables underlying harassment, hate speech, and verbal abuse. The final determination of offensiveness generally is not straightforward but rests almost entirely on complex contextual variables such as the location of the conversation, the relationship between the speaker and the listener, and the language used."[27]

Evidence about consequentialist harms leading those exposed to hate speech to engage in harmful conduct are often asserted rather than demonstrated, but include very intuitive ideas that such speech may prompt others to engage in violence or discrimination, that it shapes beliefs about stereotypes, and that it can normalize further hatred and discriminatory acts, thereby causing imitation.[28] Studies attempting to test these hypotheses seem surprisingly rare.

One such attempt, the first of its kind, attempted to correlate online hate speech with racially and religiously aggravated offences in London, England.[29] The authors find a correlation, including temporal evidence that online hate speech preceded offline hate crimes, while incorporating geographical data on specific neighbourhoods. Notably, the study was not limited to instances of criminal hate speech but looked for hateful speech generally that incorporated racial and religious characteristics.[30] However, the authors conclude that "it is unlikely that online hate speech is directly causal of offline hate crimes in isolation. It is more likely the case that social media is only part of the formula, and that local level factors, such as the demographic make-up of neighbourhoods (e.g., Black and minority ethnic population proportion, unemployment) and other ecological factors play key roles, as they always have in estimating hate crime."[31]

Another paper, consisting of three studies based on survey and experimental design, found evidence of desensitization that results from exposure to hate speech and greater resultant prejudice. However, the results were heavily conditional. For example, the first survey-based study actually found a correlational result that exposure to hate speech led to *less* prejudice. The experimental design, which involved thirty-nine people in an experimental group and thirty-six people in a control group, found greater prejudice, mediated by lower sensitivity to hate messages based on exposure, but was unable to control for "unobservable" variables like personality or ideology.[32]

Attempts to correlate hate speech with hate crimes are notoriously difficult, in large part due to the unreliability of statistics on the latter, which are assumed to suffer from serious under-reporting and which vary on a year-to-year basis.[33] There is correlational evidence that people possessing certain norms and ideas are more likely to perpetuate harm. For example, Tanya D'Souza and colleagues cite evidence that men with traditional beliefs about gender roles are more likely to accept violence against women.[34] Yet this is quite distinct from the idea that such ideas *cause* violence.

Studies on constitutive harms appear more common, but their findings require close inspection. Almost all relevant studies cite Mari Matsuda and colleagues' 1993 edited collection *Words That Wound*, which examines through the lens of critical race theory the direct harms of hate speech[35] and details the "physiological symptoms and emotional distress ranging from fear in the gut to rapid pulse rate and difficulty in breathing, nightmares, post-traumatic stress disorder, hypertension, psychosis, and suicide," as well as a range of behaviours that result from exposure to such speech.[36] This emotional and physical harm, as described, clearly transcends the mere taking of offence or the fleeting feelings of sadness or anger. Yet because of its nature, the empirical study of constitutive harm generally relies on self-reporting that ultimately amounts to a tabulation of the different emotions, however extreme, that are felt in response to hate speech.

There are serious methodological and reporting issues within recent studies. One study, based on 101 interviews with members of targeted minority communities, finds that a majority "reported having been personally targeted or knowing others in the community who had been targeted for hate speech."[37] The authors do not cite specific statistics nor do they separate first-hand from the second-hand accounts because interviewees "spoke strongly to the view that this was not an important differentiation to them."[38] The authors also acknowledge that not all incident reports would satisfy a legal definition of hate speech.

Nonetheless, the study reveals self-reporting of a range of emotions consistent with those described above, including different reactions to hate speech, including a silencing effect. Even these reactions are open to interpretation. For example, the authors describe interviewees who "consciously articulated silence and withdrawal as tactics community members could take to avoid hate speech," but the quoted passages arguably evince a lack of any harm.[39] Other harms, such as a feeling of disempowerment, seem to stem from a lack of belief that hateful speakers would be punished or that reporting the speech would result in any changes.[40] This may speak to a potential feeling of disempowerment, but the idea that this alone is a harm risks inviting a sort of circular reasoning: if speech is not punished, that in itself is a harm stemming from the speech, which in turn justifies its punishment.

Another study of the psychological effects of hateful speech focuses on online college communities, but it captures "hateful speech" that does not always target groups or minorities. More significantly, the study's evidence of harmful psychological stress amounts to online written reactions in college subreddits, and comments labelled "high stress" include statements like "That sounds challenging for me. I am a CS major." "College can be very tough at times like this." "Got denied, but I had to act, I'm very disappointed."[41] These do not seem to be particularly compelling examples of psychological harm, let alone lasting harm.

Other studies are somewhat more persuasive. An experimental study of hateful Twitter posts found that tweets from multiple sources, compared to identical messages from a single source, lead to greater emotional distress among members of the targeted group, as well as a greater likelihood of attributing ambiguous social situations to racial prejudice.[42]

A well-cited 2002 study by Laura Leets examines 120 students' self-reported emotional responses to antisemitic and antigay speech. It concludes that the short- and long-term consequences appear to mirror other traumatic experiences. Yet the details are complex. While 69 per cent of respondents had a short-term emotional reaction, fully 25 per cent reported having "none." Asked about the long term, "no reaction" was the plurality outcome among respondents (at 45 per cent) followed by "attitudinal responses" (at 43 per cent), such as a self-reported belief that hate speech has a lasting effect on self-esteem, and "behavioural responses" (at 12 per cent), such as a "heightened awareness" or less willingness to disclose one's identity to others.[43] Leets concludes that "no long-term outcome was frequently reported, which is not surprising, as an encounter with hate speech is reasonably less traumatizing than many other potential crises."[44] Leets's study also has important findings for how we interpret the potential impact of "silencing" on targets of hate speech. In the view of 83 per cent of the study's respondents, a passive response to hate speech was viewed as the higher moral ground, arguably indicating that a refusal to engage or act does not reflect harm or weakness, but rather a position of strength.[45]

So what are we to make of this body of evidence? On consequential harms, the lack of causal evidence is likely more a reflection of problems with data and methodological limitations than a clear suggestion that no link exists between hate and violence or discrimination. It would be difficult, if not absurd, to argue that misogynistic attitudes and systemic behaviour like violence against women (for example) are not somehow related. Yet incidents of hate speech are subsumed in a broader culture of discrimination, entrenched attitudes like stereotypes, and systemic forms of oppression towards minority or disadvantaged groups, such that the *causal* effect of hate speech is usually impossible to know. It is certainly plausible that hate speech increases or entrenches these aspects of our society, but it is just as likely, if not more so, that much of the hate speech generated is a product of those deeper systemic forces. Thus the search for the harms of hate speech may too often assume a causal arrow pointed in only one direction: someone says a hateful thing, and it leads to acts of harm or attitudinal changes and the entrenchment of poisonous ideas.

There are advocates for regulating hate speech who refuse to treat the phenomenon this simplistically when discussing the moral or legal justifications for their position, but even the more sophisticated accounts fail to rebut arguments about the swamping effect fundamental social forces might play. As Robert Mark Simpson writes,

> there is room for doubt about whether speech is making *any* distinctive and significant causal contribution to social hierarchy. After all, it may be that when people say racists things, for instance, this is largely an epiphenomenal symptom of a deeper racist social order whose etiology lies in other material and institutional forces. And in response to this it isn't enough to simply assert that speech *is* doing the work. Our account becomes speculative past the point of credibility if it suggests that words can create social realities *ex nihilo*.[46]

Simpson does not deny the existence of *any* causal relationship, but he is among those who find the existing evidence wanting. He proposes a conceptual account of harm that might enable us to identify moral culpability for certain kinds of harm, such as instances of hateful speech that involve adults influencing the views of children, particularly where they are in a position of authority (such as teachers). Even this does not get us very far in a debate about under what conditions the state can hold citizens legally culpable for the purported harms they contribute to when exercising a right like freedom of expression. The question is not whether teachers spouting hate in the classroom should lose their jobs (for they do not have a "right" to their job, per se) but whether they should be subject to state sanction for the expressive content itself.

Another problem arises in the context of what to do about the constitutive harms identified in the literature. Opponents of state regulation of hate speech do not tend to find emotional responses a sufficiently serious harm – if they count such reactions as harm at all – to justify restrictions on rights.

The self-reported emotional pain and psychological trauma of the members of targeted communities need to be taken seriously. Yet it is not clear that hate speech laws are either an appropriate or effective measure to address these harms. As Dworkin argues in his response to Waldron's arguments, the intrusion into individual autonomy by the state when it sanctions speech traverses a boundary of illegitimacy:

> Government may not adopt any ethical conviction – any opinion about the true basis of human dignity – and enforce that view against dissenting citizens. It must recognize a right of ethical independence. But recognizing that right means that no individual citizen may be forced to accept any official ethical conviction or be prevented from expressing one's own dissenting convictions … Living in a just society – a society whose government respects human dignity – means that I must accept the right of others to hold me in contempt.[47]

Dworkin's argument is the inverse of the argument, noted above, that hate speech laws may be necessary to *protect* free expression; his concern that in pursing the objective of protecting human dignity governments may end up impairing it is an important one. But is his concern overstated? Certainly governments adopt policies reflecting values like equality all the time. Dworkin's body of work does not seem to imply that any and all laws that express or are informed by values are illegitimate in this sense. Instead, like other scholars,[48] his is a specific concern that state limitations on free expression themselves risk creating harm, harm that may outweigh the emotional harms at stake in the absence of such limitations. Further, there are arguably contexts in which the harms of regulating speech will disproportionately fall on historically disadvantaged groups, an example being prohibitions designed to prevent the defamation of religion.[49]

Another set of problems presented by justifying restrictions on expression on the basis of constitutive harms is their nebulous and subjective nature. It is clear that a range of emotional harms are evinced by studies relying on survey and experimental research, but they all ultimately rely on self-reporting or the interpretation of expressions of emotion. This creates a number of specific empirical issues that are virtually impossible to disentangle. First, any incident of hate speech will affect different members of targeted groups in asymmetrical and varying ways. How, then, to assess a particular hateful utterance or message? Does it cross the threshold into illegal hate speech if it is likely to negatively impact the most psychologically vulnerable individual exposed to it, or only the mythical "reasonable person"?

Second, many messages could cause the sorts of emotional harms associated with hate speech and yet fall far below the threshold maintained by most existing hate speech legislation. If harm is the justification for state limitations, and constitutive harms the most likely form of harm produced, then extant hate speech laws do not capture the vast majority of utterances that match the characteristics of their intended target.

A final problem operates as a moral hazard of regulating emotional harm, in that "given the difficulty of actually discovering whether and how much pain has been caused, you motivate people to pretend to have been pained to discourage speech that they happen not to like."[50] This concern, however cynical, cannot be dismissed out of hand.

If self-reported, unobservable harms provide much of the basis for justifying restrictions on hate speech, then the legal basis for permitting such limitations becomes a minefield. I turn now to an analysis of how the Supreme Court has adjudicated these issues under the *Charter of Rights and Freedoms*.

Hate Speech and the *Charter of Rights and Freedoms*

The Supreme Court has assessed the constitutionality of Canada's hate speech laws under the *Criminal Code*, as well as under statutory human rights legislation, and it has routinely upheld the legislation as constitutional. In the 1990 *Keegstra* case, the Court deals with a former high school teacher charged with unlawfully promoting hatred under the criminal law after making antisemitic statements to his students.[51] The Court gives freedom of expression a broad and liberal interpretation, such that it is protected "if the [expressive] activity conveys or attempts to convey a meaning, it has expressive content and *prima facie* falls within the scope of the guarantee."[52] This approach means that almost anything communicative short of physical violence[53] is protected, and thus the bulk of any analysis of freedom of expression will ultimately rest with the reasonable limits analysis under section 1 of the *Charter*. Notably, Chief Justice Brian Dickson's majority decision rejects the idea that hate speech should be considered violence or analogous to it (something to which the dissenting justices agreed, thus the Court is unanimous on this point). Moreover, even threats of violence enjoy section 2(b) protection and can only be limited by law under section 1.

In his section 1 analysis, Dickson heavily endorses the view that hate speech causes very real harm, not only the emotional and dignity-effacing harm suffered by members of the targeted group, but also the notion that hate speech can influence society at large. In support of the latter, Dickson cites the 1966 report of the Special Committee on Hate Propaganda in Canada, which noted that "individuals can be persuaded to believe 'almost anything' if information or ideas are communicated using the right technique and in the proper circumstances."[54] Further, Dickson writes that it "is thus not inconceivable that the active dissemination of hate propaganda can attract individuals to its cause, and in the process create serious discord between various cultural groups in society."[55] Dickson cites no evidence for this. In fact, the only evidence he cites about harm at all is the work on emotional harm by Matsuda, explored above.

To the extent that Dickson considers whether the harms he attributes to hate speech are sufficient to limit the free expression principle, he ultimately concludes that hate speech "is of limited importance when measured against free expression values ... The state should not be the sole arbiter of truth, but neither should we overplay the view that rationality will overcome all falsehoods in the unregulated marketplace of ideas."[56] Of course free expression is not just about the truth, but about public participation in society and especially in the context of political debate. On this point Dickson simply asserts that hate propaganda subverts the democratic process because it denies respect and dignity to other members of the community: "Indeed, one may quite plausibly contend that it is through rejecting hate propaganda that the state can best encourage the protection of values central to freedom of expression."[57]

In upholding the law against the wilful promotion of hatred, Dickson also considers whether the failure of the offence to require proof of actual hatred resulting from communication weighs against its constitutionality. Dickson responds that this argument gives "insufficient attention to the severe psychological trauma suffered by members" of targeted communities. More significantly, he states that "it is clearly difficult to prove a causative link between a specific statement and hatred of an identifiable group. In fact, to require direct proof of hatred in listeners would severely debilitate the effectiveness of s. 319(2) in achieving Parliament's aim."[58] The objective is to prevent the *risk* of harm, and demands for evidence almost belie the point. When addressing the question of minimal impairment, however, Dickson again points to the harms caused by hate speech to justify not requiring Parliament to consider other policy alternatives. In sum, Dickson's reliance on harm – not just the risks of harm – guide his reasonable limits analysis in a manner that is in tension with the lack of evidence.

In dissent, McLachlin acknowledges the constitutive harms of hate speech, noting it "inflicts pain and indignity upon individuals" who belong to targeted groups, and that it "may threaten social stability" in a consequentialist manner too.[59] In fact, she writes that the "process of 'proving' that listeners were moved to hatred has a fictitious air about it."[60] Her primary concern is that there is a lack of evidence that state criminalization of hate speech will lead to its suppression. The term "hatred" is notoriously broad, relying as it does on subjective and vague understandings. Further, the harms imposed by this breadth in the law is that it "has provoked many questionable actions on the part of the authorities ... the record amply demonstrates that intemperate statements about identifiable groups, particularly if they represent an unpopular viewpoint, may attract state involvement or calls for police action."[61] McLachlin points to instances where copies of Salmon Rushdie's *The Satanic Verses* were stopped by border authorities on the basis the book violated the criminal provision, and arrests were made when pamphlets were distributed containing the words "Yankee Go Home."[62] This speaks to the chilling effect of the law. For McLachlin, the "questionable benefit of the legislation is outweighed by the significant infringement on the constitutional guarantee of free expression."[63]

Taylor, a companion case to *Keegstra*, involved section 13(1) of the *Canadian Human Right Act* (*CHRA*) restricting telephone communication that "is likely to expose a person or persons to hatred or contempt by reason of the fact that the person or persons are identifiable on the basis of a prohibited ground of discrimination."[64] The majority decision by Dickson mirrors much of the logic at stake in his *Keegstra* judgment, although it is worth noting that in the context of the *CHRA* provision, Dickson determines that the *Charter* does not mandate an exception for truthful statements (a defence explicitly included in the criminal provision at stake in *Keegstra*). This is a remarkable determination that seems to subvert any analogies between hate speech laws as protecting against "group defamation" (if we consider truth as a defence in defamation law an important principle). In her dissent, McLachlin notes that the human rights procedures for enforcement under the *CHRA* "may considerably lessen the danger of a counter-productive effect."[65] Nonetheless, as with her *Keegstra* dissent, McLachlin finds that hatred (and contempt) is overly broad and vague and risks capturing a host of otherwise protected expression. Moreover, unlike the criminal law, the *CHRA* provision does not rely on any intent on the part of the speaker to expose people to hatred or contempt.

The Court had the opportunity to revisit hate speech restrictions in the context of statutory rights legislation in the 2013 *Whatcott* case.[66] The *Saskatchewan Human Rights Code* prohibits the publication or display of any representation "that exposes or tends to expose to hatred, ridicules, belittles or otherwise affronts the dignity of any person or class of persons on the basis of a prohibited ground." The case involved an individual found to have violated that provision by distributing flyers with virulently homophobic messages. A unanimous judgment authored by Justice Marshall Rothstein upheld the law, albeit with some modification to the Court's majority approach in *Keegstra* and *Taylor*. Rothstein holds that the harmful effects of hate speech must rise to the level of "detestation" and "vilification" of the targeted groups, slightly narrowing the approach adopted by Dickson in *Taylor*.[67] Further, Rothstein cautions that expression must be assessed by an objective, reasonable person standard, and that the reference in *Taylor* to "unusually strong and deep-felt emotions" should not be interpreted as inviting a subjective test or one dealing merely with the intensity of the perceived expression.[68] As such, the decision reads down the provision to exclude references to "ridicules," "belittles," or "affronts the dignity of," and limits the object of the prohibition to "hatred."[69]

In defending the law as a reasonable limit, Rothstein cites no evidence beyond that introduced in *Keegstra* and *Taylor* twenty-three years earlier. Notably, however, Rothstein dismisses emotional reactions from members of the targeted group as sufficient justification for an infringement on free expression:

> While the emotional damage from hate speech is indeed troubling, protecting the emotions of an individual group member is not rationally connected to the overall purpose of reducing discrimination. While it would certainly be expected that hate speech would prompt emotional reactions from members of the targeted group, in the context of hate speech legislation, these reactions are only relevant as a derivative effect of the attack on the group. As a derivative effect, these are not sufficient to justify an infringement of s. 2 (*b*). Instead, the focus must be on the likely effect of the hate speech on how individuals external to the group might reconsider the social standing of the group. Ultimately, it is the need to protect the societal standing of vulnerable groups that is the objective of legislation restricting hate speech.[70]

This is a significant departure from Dickson's general approach in the 1990 cases, which included those emotional harms as part of the basis for upholding the law. It is also the category of harm for which there is much more considerable evidence. By limiting the justification for the law to how individuals external to the group might be influenced, the evidentiary basis for the harms nearly evaporates.

The Canadian jurisprudence on hate speech has been subject to significant critical commentary, particularly for its relatively weak position on whether the state ought to face an evidentiary burden to justify limits on expression.[71] Jamie Cameron accuses the *Keegstra* majority of fundamentally relaxing its standard of justification under section 1. In her view, this included

> altering the requirements of proportionality, including the government's burden to demonstrate that its prohibition is rationally connected to the prevention or punishment of a demonstrable harm. In doing so, the majority effectively assumed that expressive activity that is valueless must also be harmful. Although hate propaganda unquestionably strays from democratic values, value and harm are not synonymous. In the absence of a demonstrable harm, relaxing the standard of constitutionality to validate criminal sanctions against offensive expression unquestionably violates [the] principle of freedom.[72]

Richard Moon is incisive when he points out that Dickson's *Keegstra* approach also evinced "a general skepticism about the exercise of human reason in a racist culture," something that, in his view, "raises questions about the protection of any (negative) claim about race and not just the extreme claim of people like

Keegstra."[73] More recently, Moon notes that Rothstein's unanimous decision in *Whatcott* and its "reliance on a reasonable person standard allowed him to avoid or obscure the two main challenges confronting any form of hate speech regulation: (i) the difficulty in establishing a causal link between hate speech and the spread of hatred in the community (and the occurrence of harmful action) and (ii) the difficulty in distinguishing extreme speech, which is subject to restriction, from other, less extreme forms of speech."[74] In Moon's view, the purpose of the bans in *Taylor* and *Whatcott* cannot be reconciled with the high threshold drawn by the Court before expression is considered hateful.

Add to these criticisms the general and legitimate concern about the ability of the state to effectively and coherently engage in a line-drawing exercise between speech that vilifies and speech that "merely" offends, and you have a recipe for precisely the sort of implementation problems that McLachlin identifies in her *Keegstra* dissent. (And it is interesting that McLachlin effectively reverses her view by signing on to the unanimous judgment in *Whatcott*, an aspect of judicial behaviour beyond the scope of this chapter but worthy of study.[75])

Advocates of hate speech laws like Waldron are relatively sanguine about the dangers of line drawing, acknowledging the complexity involved but ultimately concluding that if "we pay attention to the hurtfulness of this kind of speech – in order to convey how much it matters to those on the sharp end of it – we can indicate certain kinds of suffering and apprehension that are likely to be involved, whatever other emotions are also occasioned."[76] In the context of the Canadian jurisprudence, this seems to belie the Court's 2013 caution that attention to the emotional state of targets of hate speech does not provide a justificatory basis for hate speech laws in the first place.

Nonetheless, perhaps it is an approach that may help guide us in identifying the most extreme forms of speech. Unfortunately, much like the Canadian Court, Waldron seems unconcerned that much more rote, day-to-day microaggressions, coded language, dog whistles, and other forms of rhetoric are also much more pervasive and almost certainly contribute in a much more systemic way to the various harms identified by the advocates of hate speech laws. This is a difficulty other advocates recognize and acknowledge as posing significant problems for justifying laws.[77] The harm-based standard – as exemplified by the Court's approach to it – is ultimately an unsatisfying one if we retain a substantive commitment to the principles of free expression.

Implications and Conclusion

This chapter may seem dismissive of the harms associated with hate speech. If that is the reader's key takeaway, I will not have provided enough nuance to the core argument. From a normative perspective, I view hate speech as nefarious, ugly, and without value. I believe it has the capacity to hurt people and the potential to feed greater forces of inequality and discrimination and to disrupt society. Yet as it relates to the justification of laws restricting hate speech, the diffuse nature of these harms makes it difficult if not impossible to reconcile a number of problems and harms that state restriction on speech itself creates (most specifically, the punitive harms that come from state sanctions in the criminal or civil context).

First, a law that is too broad risks capturing "merely offensive" speech that may not present any realistic risk of harm. Even when laws are defined with a high threshold, as in the Canadian case, there is a broader category of hateful speech that, for different people, may or may not cross the threshold of what is permissible in a free and democratic society. A high threshold also only targets speech that is least likely to influence others; its extremity means people are more likely to recoil than succumb to it. Meanwhile, we are left with the much more penetrating and systemic but less extreme forms of hateful expression in a society that suffers from deeper forces of oppression.

Second, the tendency to inflate the boundaries of what counts as hate speech has proven time and again too tempting for state authorities, as the examples cited by McLachlin in her *Keegstra* dissent confirm (more recent Canadian examples include *Maclean's*, a national affairs magazine, being hauled before a human rights tribunal for publishing Islamophobic material that did not rise to the level of unlawful hate speech[78]). Granting the state or other entities (like university administrators) the power to regulate speech because it is perceived as hateful can even have the absurd consequence of punishing those speaking out in favour of equality and human dignity, as the recent example of Dalhousie University launching an investigation into a racialized student's Facebook post about "white fragility" attests.[79]

Third, and more fundamentally, there is little evidence that hate speech laws prevent harm. One of the few studies of the effects of such laws comes from Australia, and it finds no evidence of a drop in hate speech generally, a perceived burden on the targets of hate speech to initiate complaints and follow up, and mixed evidence that hate speech laws have an educative purpose (with some evidence that hate speech litigation can appropriate the educative purpose in a way at odds with legislative intent).[80] None of those interviewed for the study thought hate speech laws "had a profoundly positive influence on the quality of public discourse."[81] The only direct and nominally positive outcome was that targets of hate speech had a potential remedy for imposing sanction, but hate speech laws, in Canada at least, are not premised on that narrow objective. This may ultimately be a symbolic value, but that, too, is an intangible benefit.[82] Given the harms of imposing restrictions on expression, the lack of evidence that hate speech laws are an effective tool for combating the phenomenon more generally weakens the case for them.

Despite this critique, we should not end on an argument that leaves the targets of hate speech to simply absorb its negative effects. Other responses to hate speech are likely much more effective and should be pursued with vigour. Advocates of hate speech laws tend to be incredibly cynical when it comes to the power of social censure. But discourse around the n-word in North America exemplifies the impact that *social denunciation* can have on people's willingness to invoke hateful and odious language, even in the context of privileged and powerful people for whom being "politically incorrect" is a brand.[83]

The most important alternative remedies would be efforts to address actual acts of discrimination, and to remove barriers that subsist via entrenched prejudice and systemic racism, sexism, and other forms of discrimination. In the context of free expression itself, a specific concern about hate speech is that it can limit freedom of expression for its targets. The state would have a much more legitimate role to play if it focused on ensuring there were venues and opportunities to "lift up" individuals from historically disadvantaged groups to prevent the potential silencing effects.

A culture that protects, rather than constrains, free expression, the right to protest, freedom of the press, and associated rights is needed for this to happen. University campuses, for example, could ensure there are venues for people opposing "controversial speakers" so that they can express their own views. This prescription is consistent with Nadine Strossen's argument that "students' overriding reaction to the widely reported recent incidents of 'hate speech' and bias crimes has not been depression and withdrawal, but active engagement."[84] The state can do much to ensure there are platforms for that activity and that there is greater equity in civil society for political discourse more broadly.

There is no perfect or easy solution to dealing with systemic hatred in modern society. A focus on hate speech laws risks a degree of complacency in dealing with the root causes of hatred itself. When coupled with the relatively weak evidentiary case for justifying limits on freedom of expression, it would be valuable to move beyond this aspect of the debate and start the search for more substantive solutions.

NOTES

1   *RJR MacDonald Inc. v Canada (Attorney General)*, [1995] 3 SCR 199 at para. 129.
2   Ibid., at para. 153.
3   Jeremy Waldron, *The Harm in Hate Speech* (Cambridge, MA: Harvard University Press, 2012).
4   Ibid., 33.
5   Ibid., 47.
6   Ibid., 108.
7   Ibid.
8   Ibid., 160.

9   For this and other critiques, see Stephen L. Newman, "Finding the Harm in Hate Speech: An Argument against Censorship," *Canadian Journal of Political Science* 50, no. 3 (2017): 679–97; L.W. Sumner, Review of *The Harm in Hate Speech*, by Jeremy Waldron, *Law and Philosophy* 32 (2013): 377–83.

10 Sumner, Review, 383.

11 Randy Besco and Erin Tolley, "Does Everyone Cheer? The Politics of Immigration and Multiculturalism in Canada," in *Federalism and the Welfare State in a Multicultural World*, ed. Elizabeth Goodyear-Grant, Richard Johnston, Will Kymlicka, and John Myles (Montreal: McGill-Queen's University Press, 2018).

12 Newman, "Finding the Harm in Hate Speech," 682.

13 Ibid., 691.

14 Waldron, *Hate Speech*, 95.

15 Newman, "Finding the Harm in Hate Speech," 687, citing Pierre Vidal-Naquet, *Assassins of Memory: Essays on the Denial of the Holocaust* (New York: Columbia University Press, 1992).

16 Waldron, *Hate Speech*, 148.

17 Ibid., 97.

18 Ibid., 89–92, citing Catharine MacKinnon, *Only Words* (Cambridge, MA: Harvard University Press, 1993).

19 Carole S. Vance, *Pleasure and Danger: Exploring Female Sexuality* (London: Pandora Press, 1992); Wendy McElroy, *Sexual Correctness: The Gender-Feminist Attack on Women* (Jefferson, NC: McFarland Publishing, 1996); Nadine Strossen, *Defending Pornography: Free Speech, Sex, and the Fight for Women's Rights* (New York: New York University Press, 2000).

20 Tariq Modood, "Hate Speech: The feelings and Beliefs of the Hated," *Contemporary Political Theory* 13, no. 1 (2014): 106.

21 Karen Zivi, "Doing Things with Hate Speech," *Contemporary Political Theory* 13, no. 1 (2014): 96.

22 Ibid., 98.

23 Erik Bleich, *The Freedom to Be Racist? How the United States and Europe Struggle to Preserve Freedom and Combat Racism* (Oxford: Oxford University Press, 2011), 148–9; Abigail Levin, *The Cost of Free Speech: Pornography, Hate Speech, and their Challenge to Liberalism* (Houndmills, UK: Palgrave Macmillan, 2010).

24 Mary Kate McGowan, "On 'Whites Only' Signs and Racist Hate Speech: Verbal Acts of Discrimination," in *Speech & Harm: Controversies Over Free Speech*, ed. Ishani Maitra and Mary Kate McGowan (Oxford: Oxford University Press, 2012).

25 Caroline West, "Words That Silence? Freedom of Expression and Racist Hate Speech," in *Speech & Harm: Controversies Over Free Speech*, ed. Ishani Maitra and Mary Kate McGowan (Oxford: Oxford University Press, 2012).

26 Timothy Jay, "Do Offensive Words Harm People?" *Psychology, Public Policy, and Law* 15, no. 2 (2009): 96.

27 Ibid., 97.

28 Katharine Gelber and Luke McNamara, "Evidencing the Harms of Hate Speech," *Journal for the Study of Race, Nation and Culture* 22, no. 3 (2016): 325.

29 Matthew L. Williams, Pete Burnap, Amir Javed, Han Liu, and Sefa Ozalp, "Hate in the Machine: Anti-Black and Anti-Muslim Social Media Posts as Predictors of Offline Racially and Religiously Aggravated Crime," *British Journal of Criminology* 60, no. 1 (2019): 93–117.

30 Ibid., 102–3.

31 Ibid., 113.

32 Wiktor Soral, Michat Bilewicz, and Mikotaj Winiewski, "Exposure to Hate Speech Increases Prejudice through Desensitization," *Aggressive Behavior* 44 (2017): 136–46.

33 See, for example, "Hate Crimes Drop in Canada for First Time in Years," *BBC News*, 23 July 2019, https://www.bbc.com/news/world-us-canada-49078558.

34 Tanya D'Souza, Laura Griffin, Nicole Shackleton, and Danielle Walt, "Harming Women with Words: The Failure of Australian Law to Prohibit Gendered Hate Speech," *UNSW Law Journal* 41, no. 3 (2018): 965.

35 Mari J. Matsuda, Charles R. Lawrence III, Richard Delgado, and Kimberle Williams Crenshaw, eds. *Words That Wound: Critical Race Theory, Assaultive Speech, and the First Amendment* (Boulder, CO: Westview Press, 1993).

36 Mari J. Matsuda, "Public Response to Racist Speech: Considering the Victim's Story," in *Words That Wound: Critical Race Theory, Assaultive Speech, and the First Amendment*, ed. Mari J. Matsuda, Charles R. Lawrence III, Richard Delgado, and Kimberle Williams Crenshaw (Boulder, CO: Westview Press, 1993), 24–5.

37 Gelber and McNamara, "Evidencing the Harms of Hate Speech," 327.

38 Ibid.

39 Two interviewees whose reactions were recorded as "silencing" were quoted as saying: (1) "They give you a hate speech, okay, just who cares. Just run way," and (2) "It is better to ignore them and not waste our time." Ibid., 334.

40 Ibid., 333–4.

41 Koustuv Saha, Eshwa Chandrasekharan, and Munmun De Choudhury, "Prevalence and Psychological Effects of Hateful Speech in Online College Communities," 11th ACM Conference on Web Science (WebSci '19), 30 June–3 July 2019), Boston, MA.

42 Roselyn J. Lee-Won, Tiffany N. White, Hyunjin Song, Ji Young Lee, and Mikhail R. Smith, "Source Magnification of Cyberhate: Affective and Cognitive Effects of Multiple-Source Hate Messages on Target Group Members," *Media Psychology* 23, no. 5 (2019): 1–22.

43 Laura Leets, "Experiencing Hate Speech: Perceptions and Responses to Anti-Semitism and Antigay Speech," *Journal of Social Issues* 58, no. 2 (2002): 350–2.

44 Ibid., 354.

45 Ibid., 356.

46 Robert Mark Simpson, "'Won't Somebody Please Think of the Children?' Hate Speech, Harm, and Childhood," *Law and Philosophy* 38 (2019): 81.

47 Ronald Dworkin, "Reply to Jeremy Waldron," in *The Content and Context of Hate Speech: Rethinking Regulation and Responses*, ed. Michael Herz and Peter Molnar (Cambridge: Cambridge University Press, 2012), 342.

48 Michael Ilg, "Economy of Pain: When to Regulate Offensive Expression," *International Journal of Constitutional Law* 16, no. 3 (2018): 808; Frederick Schauer, *Free Speech: A Philosophical Inquiry* (Cambridge: Cambridge University Press, 1982), 193.

49 Kwame Anthony Appiah, "What's Wrong with Defamation of Religion?" in *The Content and Context of Hate Speech: Rethinking Regulation and Responses*, ed. Michael Herz and Peter Molnar (Cambridge: Cambridge University Press, 2012), 181–2.

50 Ibid., 176.

51 *R. v Keegstra*, [1990] 3 SCR 697.

52 Ibid., citing *Irwin Toy Ltd. v Quebec (Attorney General)*, [1989] 1 SCR 927 at 969.

53 The Court has clarified or expanded the exception of physical violence from 2(b)'s ambit to include threats of violence over time. See *Greater Vancouver Transportation Authority v Canadian Federation of Students – British Columbia Component*, 2009 SCC 31, [2009] 2 SCR 295; *R. v Khawaja*, 2012 SCC 69, [2012] 3 SCR 555.

54 Ibid., citing Canada, Special Committee on Hate Propaganda in Canada, *Report of the Special Committee on Hate Propaganda in Canada* (Ottawa: Queen's Printer, 1966), 30.

55 Ibid.

56 Ibid.

57 Ibid.

58 Ibid.

59 Ibid.

60 Ibid.

61 Ibid.

62 Ibid.

63 Ibid.

64 *Canada (Human Rights Commission) v Taylor*, [1990] 3 SCR 892.

65 Ibid.

66 *Saskatchewan (Human Rights Commission) v Whatcott*, 2013 SCC 11, [2013] 1 SCR 467.

67 Ibid., at para. 41.

68 Ibid., at para. 56.

69 Ibid., at para. 85.

70 Ibid., at para. 82.

71 L.W. Sumner, *The Hateful and the Obscene: Studies in the Limits of Free Expression* (Toronto: University of Toronto Press, 2004), 158–62; Richard Moon, *The Constitutional Protection of Freedom of Expression* (Toronto: University of Toronto Press, 2000).

72 Jamie Cameron, "The Past, Present, and Future of Expressive Freedom under the Charter," *Osgoode Hall Law Journal* 35, no. 1 (1997): 19.

73 Moon, *The Constitutional Protection of Freedom of Expression*, 139.

74 Richard Moon, *Putting Faith in Hate: When Religion Is the Source or Target of Hate Speech* (Cambridge: Cambridge University Press, 2018), 46–7.

75 See Emmett Macfarlane, *Governing from the Bench: The Supreme Court of Canada and the Judicial Role* (Vancouver: UBC Press, 2013).

76 Waldron, *Hate Speech*, 113–14.

77 Clay Calvert, "Hate Speech and Its Harms: A Communication Theory Perspective," *Journal of Communication* 47, no. 1 (1997): 16; Simpson, "Hate Speech, Harm, and Childhood," 82.

78 Ilg, "Economy of Pain," 817–18.

79 Emmett Macfarlane, "Laurier's Apology to Lindsay Shepherd Was Hardly a Win for Free Speech," *CBC News*, 22 November 2017, https://www.cbc.ca/news/opinion/laurier-free-speech-1.4414696.

80 Katharine Gelber and Luke McNamara, "The Effects of Civil Hate Speech Laws: Lessons from Australia," *Law & Society Review* 49, no. 3 (2015): 631–64.

81 Ibid., 653.

82 Ilg, "Economy of Pain," 816.

83 HBO late-night host Bill Maher apologized for using the racial slur on his show after public criticism. See Dave Itzkoff, "Bill Maher Apologizes for Use of Racial Slur on 'Real Time,'" *New York Times*, 3 June 2017, https://www.nytimes.com/2017/06/03/arts/television/bill-maher-n-word.html.

84 Nadine Strossen, *Hate: Why We Should Resist It with Free Speech, Not Censorship* (Oxford: Oxford University Press, 2018), 125.

3 Process Matters: Postal Censorship, *Your Ward News*, and Section 2(b) of the *Charter*

JAMIE CAMERON*

Expression is dynamic, a power that is temporal, creating potential at its moment of voice. Whether effervescing to obscurity or enduring in some way as text, memory, impression, that moment is the essence and vitality of freedom. When lost, the presence and value of freedom in that moment – whether short or long – are altered by the lapse of time.

Prior restraint is pre-emptive, stopping expression in advance and without knowing whether the exercise of freedom will be harmful, valuable, neither, or both.[1] Restraint works most often by decree and without challenge, because its purpose is to ban content with little or no process. By its very definition, prior restraint represents a disproportionate response to perceptions that expression is harmful. Accordingly, it must be considered constitutionally suspect in every case.

Restraints on expression, including forms of prior approval, demand oversight. When content is censored, a high threshold of justification must apply under the *Charter* to prevent the targeting and exclusion of unwelcome speakers and points of view.[2] Procedural safeguards are equally critical to ensure that the constitutionality of any restraint, injunction, or prohibitory order can be tested through a transparent process and in a timely manner. Absent oversight, freedom of expression is all but defenceless against the power of the censor.

Once a venerable art, the censorship of bygone eras – featuring urgent debate about the degenerative influence of literary and movie titles, for example – may now seem remote, even quaint. At least in Canada, government-staffed film boards no longer protect the moral character of a too-impressionable public, deciding what the community is and is not allowed to view. With one stark exception, mail censorship, which was once a powerful tool to prevent dangerous material from spreading, has come to an end.[3]

Perhaps less an artefact than hoped, censorship is wily, demonstrating the tenacity and versatility to adapt to shifts in social and political culture. At present, access to public library space is ripe for censorial oversight through demands for content-based prior approval schemes. While public libraries in Vancouver and Toronto resisted intense pressure to deny space to a controversial speaker, a less sturdy public library in Ottawa foreclosed controversy by cancelling a rental agreement.[4] Meanwhile, though the *Charter*'s role on campus is unsettled, similar dynamics describe the status of expressive freedom at colleges and universities.[5]

On another front, technology's capacity to facilitate the posting, sharing, and circulation of largely unfiltered, highly polarizing, and frequently disturbing images and commentary has awakened censorial urges.[6] Despite the challenges it presents, would-be internet regulators, both public and private, are developing ways to censor online content.[7] There is no mistaking the upward pressure to extend the censor's net from extreme content that borders on incitement to content that is deemed offensive and unacceptable.

Whatever the context, the censor's invariable goal is preventing the communication of content that is perceived to be harmful. A chilling instance involving Canada Post exposes this danger, and in doing builds a bridge between the historical and present-day realities of censorship. On 26 May 2016, the federal minister of public services issued an order under the *Canada Post Corporation Act* (*CPCA*) banning two individuals, Sears and Ste. Germaine, the publishers of *Your Ward News* (*YWN*), from Canada's national mail service.[8] The minister's interim prohibitory order (IPO) was in place for almost thirty months before being replaced by a final prohibitory order (FPO).[9]

From start to finish, the minister's ban and ensuing process of review was a travesty of fairness.[10] The IPO was legally and constitutionally unsound. The *CPCA* provisions on prohibitory orders are unresponsive to the rights at stake, sketching no more than a bare outline of the process and offering scant safeguards for those subject to an order. Neither discretionary nor dispensable – and far from ancillary – such safeguards are fundamental to the protection of expressive freedom. Throughout a prolonged and irregular process, the review board failed to recognize or accept that prior restraint is a pre-emptive strike with immediate and enduring impacts on expressive freedom. The IPO was a case in point, imposing a complete and timeless ban that prohibited Sears and Ste. Germaine not only from distributing *YWN*, but also from sending a greeting card, contacting their MP, or mailing in a charitable donation. Ultimately, the review board's report failed to address the constitutional issues at stake in any meaningful way and, in the absence of any right of appeal, the process came to an end with the minister's FPO.[11]

The censorship of Sears and Ste. Germaine was exceptional and must be met with analytical force. Whenever content is prohibited, section 2(b)'s promise of content neutrality is challenged and the *Charter*'s concept of harm put to the test. The overlay of prior restraint and lack of a meaningful process escalates the stakes by shifting, compounding, and aggravating the violation of rights. It is that confluence of dynamics that calls for response. The broader concern is that a seemingly isolated case of postal censorship cannot be dismissed as singular. Rather, it exposes and reflects a lack of threshold insight into what distinguishes prior restraint, as a threat to expressive freedom, and demonstrates why safeguards are imperative. Problems that were systemic in the *CPCA* process reflect deeper gaps in the section 2(b) jurisprudence. With that in mind, closing those gaps is the purpose and imperative of this chapter.

Restraining *Your Ward News*

To many, *YWN* is an overbearing and despicable publication. Self-styled as "the world's largest anti-Marxist publication," *YWN*'s overt goal is to satirize, indignify, and offend as many individuals, groups, and organizations as possible. Its pages glorify Hitler, pillory equality and diversity values, insult countless communities, trade in distasteful sexual content, and vilify all manner of public figures by name. In this, *YWN* is headed up by its boastful and self-aggrandizing editor in chief, James Sears.[12]

Prior to the minister's IPO of 26 May 2016, *YWN* was reportedly delivered to approximately 350,000 residential addresses in Toronto under a bulk contract with Canada Post. Homeowners and postal carriers instantly complained of *YWN*'s intrusion into their physical and psychological space, and while Toronto police were urged to conduct a criminal investigation, human rights litigant Richard Warman appealed directly to Canada Post.[13] In March 2016, Canada Post's general counsel advised Warman that "it is not open to Canada Post to censor the mail."[14]

The Section 43 Prohibitory Order

About three months later, the minister issued an IPO banning Sears and Ste. Germaine from sending mail by Canada Post. Grounded in section 43(1) of the *CPCA*, the order declared there were reasonable grounds to believe the mail was being used to send "items" proscribed by the *Criminal Code* – namely, hate propaganda and defamatory libel.[15] In issuing the notice, the minister failed to provide "the reasons therefor" in support of the order, as required by section 43(2).

Under the *CPCA*, an IPO remains in place until revoked, varied, or replaced by an FPO, automatically becoming final ten days later, by statutory presumption.[16] Though there is no right to appeal a prohibitory order, whether interim or final, section 44 provides for a "review," so long as it is requested within ten days.[17] The minister is required to appoint a three-member board to "review the matter" and give "the person affected," and others with "an interest in the matter," a reasonable opportunity to appear, make representations, and present evidence.[18] After the board submits its report and any recommendations, the minister's decision to revoke the IPO or convert it to an FPO is the last step in the process.[19]

The *CPCA* provisions on prohibitory orders have not been amended since the *Charter*'s enactment in 1982, and they are inadequate to address the entitlements at stake. A critical example is timing, which, under the *CPCA*, is entirely one-sided. Whereas the minister can act pre-emptively to remove mail from the system, at her sole discretion and with a presumption of finality under section 46, those named in an IPO can only avoid an FPO by responding within days. Meanwhile, the *CPCA* places no obligation on the minister to name a review board within a specified period, or in any time frame at all. Nor does the *CPCA* require the minister to give notice of a board's appointment or provide recourse where a minister fails to appoint one.

On 6 June and again on 9 June 2016, Sears and Ste. Germaine formally requested a review of the IPO. The minister did not name a board until 9 December 2016 and did not notify the "affected persons" or announce the board's existence until 6 January 2017.[20] The minister never explained why it took seven months to appoint a board, as required by statute.

Likewise, the *CPCA* sets no parameters on the review, placing no duty on the board to report in a timely way, or on the minister to make a decision within a prescribed period. As noted, the statute's sole timeline makes review of an IPO contingent on compliance with a ten-day deadline. In this, the *CPCA* demonstrates statutory ignorance of the rights at stake and the need for safeguards to protect those entitlements. The absence of a statutory process compounded the *CPCA*'s deficits, creating challenges for the board and aggravating the violation of constitutional rights.

The board held its first hearing on 25 April 2017, about five months after being appointed and eleven months after the IPO was issued, and a second hearing led to a preliminary ruling dated 2 November 2017.[21] The board heard submissions from the parties in January and February 2018 but did not submit its report to the minister until 29 August 2018. The minister released the report and issued the FPO on 15 November 2018.[22]

For thirty months, the IPO banned Sears and Ste. Germaine from using Canada Post, thereby prohibiting their distribution of a publication with a substantial circulation and any unrelated correspondence relating to business, personal, and sundry other matters. The scope and severity of that prohibition demanded a fair process in compliance with the *Charter* but was met instead with a protracted and ill-defined review. While the report declared that nothing in the statute prevented a fair process, the *CPCA* failed to impose duties or otherwise address the question of what fairness required.[23] In this instance, the statute's deficiencies were compounded by the minister's failure to provide reasons or particulars and the board's conception of the process.

The Section 44 Review Process

In halting communication, a *CPCA* prohibitory order triggers section 2(b)'s guarantee of expressive freedom. Whether temporary or permanent, a *CPCA* order is a prior restraint because it pre-empts communication proactively, stopping a sender's entire correspondence when it is suspected or deemed that some correspondence might potentially be unlawful. The severity of the violation depends on what is restrained, for how long, and in what venue. Both historically and up to the present, the mail service has been and continues to be an important conduit and icon of communication, operating as a monopoly under the "sole and exclusive privilege" of Canada Post.[24] As Justice Oliver Wendell Holmes Jr. once declared, "the United States may give up the post office when it sees fit, but, while it carries it on, the issue of the mails is almost as much a part of free speech as the right to use our tongues."[25] Under the US Constitution, it is First Amendment dogma that "grave constitutional concerns are immediately raised once it is said that the use of the mails is a privilege which may be extended or withheld on any grounds whatsoever."[26]

Even in an age of digital technology, Canada Post is a vital government service and, as the *CPCA* proceedings demonstrated, Canadians are "emotionally attached" to the mail.[27] Accordingly, the board's November ruling described the IPO and withdrawal of access to the postal system as a "serious matter."[28] Subsequently, its report acknowledged that "losing the right to send and/or receive mail *ever again* through the Canada Post, *a monopolized public service*, is a serious restriction on the use of the postal service."[29]

Despite that recognition, the board's decisions undermined the rights and interests of Sears and Ste. Germaine at almost every step of the process. Initially, the board granted standing to more than 40 parties, comprising 15 potential or alleged victims of defamatory libel, 16 others with an interest in the proceedings, and 11 community and public interest organizations.[30] This reflected the board's view that any person with an interest in the outcome could present evidence and submissions.[31] That conception of the process transformed a statutory review designed to provide recourse for those subject to an IPO into a forum for members of the public to express their views about *YWN*.

Reviewing the minister's grounds for an IPO is the express purpose of review under section 44. At no point in this process did the minister provide reasons or particular details to substantiate the allegations of criminality that grounded the IPO, which meant that there was no basis in the record to review the grounds for the order.[32] Troubled by this, the board's November ruling was harsh on the minister for not providing sufficient detail "to enable the Affected Persons to appreciate why the IPO was issued and the case they have to address."[33] Recognizing that section 44 review was their only recourse, the board stated that "*both* the CPCA *and* the common law requirements of procedural fairness *require* that [the Affected Persons] be given more" than the names and numbers of *Criminal Code* provisions.[34] The board complained that "it is not up to the Affected Persons nor to this Board to attempt to read the mind of the Minister to glean the basis for her decision," and it acknowledged that "for the review process to be *meaningful*, the Affected Persons should be informed of the particulars and the details" that informed the minister's IPO.[35]

In light of those deficiencies, the board could have ended the review and submitted a report recommending revocation of the IPO.[36] Despite criticizing the minister and outlining what was required for a meaningful process, the board never gave that option serious consideration.[37] Determined to proceed, the board promised to address the minister's "failure" to provide reasons in its report, adding with a hint of resignation that in any case the minister might or might not agree with the board's recommendations on the failure to provide reasons.[38]

Having granted standing to so many, the board was unwilling to deny participants "a voice on topics about which they may feel passionately," especially those who considered themselves victims or targets of *YWN*.[39] That objective could only be met by proceeding without the reasons and particulars needed to assess the minister's order. Doing so changed the nature of the hearing. Though the onus necessarily arises from the exercise of authority to order an IPO, the minister was not required to respond to, much less justify, a serious violation of constitutional rights.[40] In essence, that task was outsourced to third-party participants who supplied the missing reasons and particulars, *ex post facto*. Not surprisingly, submissions that took the place of the minister's materials were determinative, and the board's finding of reasonable grounds for the IPO quoted extensively from and placed heavy reliance on those submissions.[41] In this way, a process aimed at reviewing prohibitory orders against those banned from using Canada Post became a venue for third parties to make informal and unchallenged allegations of criminality.

Throughout, the board was diligent but misguided. The decision to proceed, eighteen months after the ban took effect and in awareness that the IPO was irregular, aggravated the unfairness and deepened the violation of Sears's and Ste. Germaine's constitutional rights. In combination, the substantive and procedural deficiencies were a rich mix of the statute's failure to prescribe timelines or a process, the minister's abdication of her responsibilities, and the board's conception of its mandate. The dynamics of procedural irregularity were deepened by the board's constitutional analysis, which was compromised by unsound and ineffective reasoning.

The Section 45 Report to the Minister

Except on the most unavoidable points, the board resisted conclusions that the order, statute, or process were unfair to the affected persons or violated their constitutional rights. On the core issue about the IPO, the report failed to follow up on the minister's lack of reasons and substantial delay. Moreover, and apart from figuring in its recommendations for reform of the *CPCA*, the statute's lack of timelines and guidelines had little or no bearing on the board's findings.[42] Finally, in principle and as a matter of logic, the board's constitutional analysis was confounding and hard to follow.

By the time of the report, the board's earlier critique of the minister had attenuated and played no role in its findings. In the interim, third parties addressed the minister's case, supplying submissions and arguments to support the IPO. The report described the minister's failure to provide reasons as "regrettable" and a violation of section 43(2), but glossed those problems by stating that it was not a basis for recommending revocation of the IPO.[43] Essentially, the board had signalled that the lack of reasons – and any related breach of fairness – was irrelevant because those concerns "should be addressed in any final disposition of this matter."[44] By accepting that the deficits could be fixed by the FPO, the board skipped over the core question of the IPO's legal soundness.[45] Doing so effectively disappeared a prolonged violation of rights, relegating it to insignificance.

The board also dismissed concerns that delays in the process were undue or raised questions of procedural fairness. After noting without comment that the minister never explained her delay in appointing a board, the panel maintained that it "attempted to proceed in an efficient manner" and went to "lengths" to ensure an adequate process, in part by seeking input from the parties.[46] In this, the board seemed unaware of any connection between its decision on standing and the length of the review process. Nor did the board give credence to the requirements of process where prior restraint is at stake, instead concluding that "it does not appear ... that the delay has been egregious or that it has brought the administration of justice into disrepute."[47]

In a larger frame, the board's lack of insight on matters of process was a function and reflection of its fundamental inability or unwillingness to confront the violation. Having found that it had jurisdiction to address it, the report considered the facial validity of the *CPCA* and constitutionality of the minister's IPO. While reluctant to fully acknowledge the violation of rights, the board had less difficulty concluding that the *CPCA* and IPO did not offend the *Charter*. To avoid finding fault with the statute and IPO, the report turned to inconsistent findings and contradictions.

The board was unwilling, in the first instance, to accept that the IPO violated section 2(b), agreeing instead with the attorney general's view that any infringement arose from the *Criminal Code*, not the order.[48] The board was also uncomfortable concluding that the IPO amounted to a prior restraint, reasoning that other channels of communication, such as the internet, were available to Sears and Ste. Germaine. On this, the board missed the essential point that the *Charter* protects individuals from *state* interference in their rights, even when other avenues are open. On settled doctrine, it is beyond doubt that a governmental ban on expressive activity is a prior restraint that *prima facie* engages section 2(b).[49]

As for the *CPCA*, the board stated that the standard for an IPO is not "particularly high," declared that the minister must "still apply known facts," and proclaimed that the reasonable grounds requirement would guard against IPOs being issued "capriciously."[50] In addition, the report discounted the consequences for expressive freedom, reasoning that any FPO will "generally follow a full review of the matter by a board of review."[51] Though inaccurate, this assertion served to ameliorate the facial deficiencies of the statute. With repeated emphasis – also to assuage the absolute ban – the report maintained that interim orders are no more than a "preliminary step" in a "more rigorous regime" that "provides for a full review."[52] In pronouncing that orders "are meant to be temporary and subject to a comprehensive review," the board either overlooked or was unaware that under section 46, an interim order is final within ten days.[53] Recall, as well, that the *CPCA* places the onus on a person named in an IPO to avoid finality by engaging the review process within ten days.

It became evident in the course of the hearing that the minister's total ban on all Canada Post correspondence was overbroad and indefensible for that reason. That led to discussion of whether section 43 permitted the minister to customize an IPO or required an absolute ban. Either way, the IPO was unconstitutional: if an absolute ban was mandatory, the statutory provision was overbroad and unconstitutional; and, if section 43 permitted a narrower order, the minister issued an overbroad IPO of dramatic and unnecessary scope. Declining to resolve the issue, the board simply declared that it was "not prepared to recommend" revoking the IPO because the *CPCA* was unconstitutional.[54]

Beyond the *CPCA*'s facial validity, the minister's order was vulnerable for failing to engage in constitutional balancing, as required by *Doré*.[55] On this, the board was notably uncritical of the minister, observing only that the absence of reasons made it "impossible to determine" whether she "turned her mind" to the constitutional questions at stake.[56] To be clear, the record was unequivocal: there was no evidence the *Charter* was ever considered, and nor did the minister claim that it was.

Once again the board turned to section 43, stating that *Doré* would only apply if the minister had discretion to impose a partial ban.[57] As a matter of constitutional law, a *Doré* analysis was required either way, because the *Charter* applies to the minister's prohibitory order, whether it partially or totally banned expressive activity. Once again, the board discounted the violation, repeating its assertion that an IPO is "an interim measure" and is not subject to a standard of perfection.[58] Rather than hold the minister accountable for an overbroad order, the board went on to suggest that it was open to Sears and Ste. Germaine, the targets of the ban, to approach the minister and request an exemption for non-*YWN* mail.[59]

Ultimately, the board's analysis was trapped in contradiction. After concluding that an interim order imposing an absolute ban was not overbroad, the board maintained that a final order in identical terms – "an absolute ban on the sending of all mail" – would be overbroad.[60] In similar fashion, the board stated that constitutional balancing was not required for the IPO and then declared that "a full balancing exercise should be conducted before any final order is made."[61] On their face, these findings are baffling. Any conclusion that an overtly overbroad order of more than two years' duration did not violate section 2(b) or require constitutional consideration flew in the face of both the evidence and established *Charter* doctrine. Moreover, the report belied the claim that an interim order would be subject to correction through a comprehensive review: the board had no power to make decisions or invalidate the minister's order, and the statute provided no avenue of appeal.

Conclusion

Prior restraint violates expressive freedom by halting or thwarting communication, and it is axiomatic that there is no remedy when expression is banned without process. As the *CPCA* review demonstrates, the process must be fair and meaningful; it must include elements such as mandatory timelines and access to decision making by subject-matter experts. In this instance, the scope and length of the violation underscored the importance of process, as well as the impact of its deficiencies.

There is no question the panel faced obstacles in conducting this review. The *CPCA* withheld decision-making authority, leaving it unclear how far the board could go to make findings on legal and constitutional issues. There was no framework for section 44 review and little assistance to a non-expert panel.[62] For these and other reasons, a hearing that raised contentious issues placed the board in an unenviable, even an unfair, position. In hindsight, these difficulties should have counselled the board to frame the process narrowly, focusing attention on the minister and whether the IPO met statutory requirements. Had the board followed through on its initial conclusion that the order violated section 43, the process could have achieved its purpose, returning the issue to the minister for decision on whether to reissue an IPO with reasons, as required by the provision.

Little in this process withstands scrutiny and, in the end, the burden of a deficient process is two-fold. First, Sears and Ste. Germaine were placed at a disadvantage throughout. The minister responsible for banning them from Canada Post was never required to explain or justify the order to them or the board. Moreover, in a process putatively aimed at protecting individuals from a censorial official, the roles were reversed: Sears and Ste. Germaine were given the task of defending themselves from, and answering to, third-party prosecutors.

These dynamics present a second and deeper concern. The ease with which a ban was imposed, and an inadequate process conducted, exposed a profound gap under section 2(b). Striking in the *CPCA* process was how little it mattered that an unjustifiable and overbroad ban remained in place for two and a half years; how little it mattered that the minister could ban anyone from Canada Post with impunity; and how little it mattered that, in the absence of safeguards, Sears and Ste. Germaine could not effectively challenge or abate the violation of their rights.

Those who despise *YWN* and its publishers will not worry. In that, it bears noting that the power to ban at will can be exercised against any publication, without restraint; equally, this power can be exercised against any individual on any grounds whatsoever, including by random means such as a lottery.[63] Nothing in the *CPCA* prevents the arbitrary exercise of a power to order a prior restraint that is functionally unreviewable under the statute.

Prior Restraint and Procedural Safeguards

Process is a rich and vital fixture in the *Charter* jurisprudence. While self-evident in the setting of the *Charter*'s legal rights, which provide substantive and procedural protections in the justice system, process grounds other entitlements, such as section 35's duty to consult and section 3's concept of meaningful democratic participation.[64] The process of collective bargaining is protected by section 2(d)'s guarantee of associational freedom, and particular considerations apply, under statute and the common law, when the state seeks access to news-gathering materials or confidential journalistic sources.[65] In principle, procedural safeguards should likewise be required whenever a state actor imposes a prior restraint on expressive activity.

As suggested above, the temporal quality of expression – the drama and potency of an expressive moment – is at the root of the freedom principle. Pre-empting that moment without recourse or procedural safeguards distinguishes and escalates the danger of prior restraint. The *Charter* jurisprudence has responded to that danger in settings that include film censorship, the open court principle, and interim injunctions against constitutionally protected expression.[66] In addition, absolute bans on expression are prone to overbreadth and are more difficult to justify as a minimal impairment of rights.[67]

The Supreme Court's decision in *Little Sisters* was of great interest in the *CPCA* process, and the report relied on it in finding the statute was not unconstitutional.[68] Though there was no absolute or timeless ban at stake, *Little Sisters* considered what procedural safeguards were necessary when expressive material was detained by customs at the border. The Court found that Canada Customs committed serious violations of a gay bookstore's section 2(b) rights, in large part because of systemic border delays. In addressing the facial validity of the legislation, Binnie J. maintained that constitutional deficits "were *not* inherent in the statutory scheme."[69] Rather, "very real" obstacles in its implementation had rendered Little Sisters "supplicants to the government."[70] Accordingly, the Court found that invalidating the statutory provision was not the appropriate remedy, because "a failure at the implementation level ... can be addressed at the implementation level."[71]

Justice Iacobucci's dissenting opinion found instead that the flaws in the regime "flow *from the very nature of prior restraint*"; in his view, that was precisely why the *Charter* required procedural safeguards expressly aimed at minimizing the dangers of prior restraint.[72] In *Little Sisters*, the infringement of constitutional rights stemmed from the legislation's failure to fetter the powers of administrators and prevent them from targeting the bookstore and indefinitely detaining its goods. By making "no reasonable effort to ensure that it will be applied constitutionally to expressive materials," the customs legislation "*practically invite[d]*" violations of section 2(b), which could only be remedied by "*an adequate process* to ensure that *Charter* rights are respected ... at the administrative level."[73] Justice Iacobucci's conception of an "open, expeditious process" demanded supplements to the safeguards already in place.[74] Several years later, *Doré* proposed a substantive methodology to determine whether administrative discretion has been exercised in compliance with the *Charter*. In doing so, the *Doré* methodology formalized the principle, in the dissent, that the protection of constitutional rights cannot be left "solely to the good faith discretion of delegated power."[75]

Far from supporting it, *Little Sisters* does more to condemn than validate the *CPCA* process. While dividing on the question of remedies, all members of the Court in *Little Sisters* agreed that Canada Customs violated the bookstore's rights in serious, systemic, and profound ways.[76] It was precisely Justice Binnie's point that operational problems could be addressed at the administrative level. *Little Sisters* was of limited application to postal censorship because the customs legislation contained safeguards that are not found in the *CPCA*.

Specifically, the customs regime prescribed deadlines at every stage of determination and created access to judicial decision making through a statutory right of appeal. The delays in *Little Sisters* did not arise from the absence of statutory timelines, but from non-compliance by staff. Binnie J. made a point of describing those timelines as "an important protection" for importers whose goods were under review.[77] Noting Parliament's intention to "hurry the process along," he declared it essential that the Court give content to the statutory direction that steps in the process be taken with "*all due dispatch*."[78] Moreover, materials detained at customs are subject to a double-step internal review procedure, with a layered series of redetermination and appeal mechanisms. Importers could invoke at least three levels of decision making under the statute, including an appeal to the courts.[79]

Any comparison of the two regulatory regimes reveals how modest and unsophisticated the CPCA's protection is when an IPO is under review. Notably, explicit timelines and appeal mechanisms that are essential features in customs regulation are absent from the CPCA. That said, *Little Sisters* is analogous in one important way, and that is how it addressed the unconstitutional exercise of administrative authority. There, the Court acknowledged that the bookstore was targeted by customs, in violation of the bookstore's rights, and found that Little Sisters suffered "excessive and unnecessary prejudice" as a result.[80] Binnie J. identified seven customs practices that caused prejudice and delay but found a stronger remedy unnecessary, in part because the Court's reasons so fully addressed the unconstitutional violation of rights.[81] Despite the board's reliance on the decision, there is little basis to the claim that *Little Sisters* applied to or excused the procedural and substantive deficiencies of the CPCA. In comparison, *Little Sisters* treated the prior restraint at customs with suspicion and did not hesitate to acknowledge the magnitude and gravity of the section 2(b) violation.

On another front, the board refused to consider First Amendment doctrine because it had not been expressly adopted under section 2(b).[82] In the United States, a cluster of landmark decisions on book, mail, and film censorship established procedural safeguards to protect rights under schemes for the prior approval or restraint of expression.[83] These landmarks of the 1960s and '70s represent settled principle that forms part of the First Amendment bedrock.[84] Safeguards ensuring that prior restraint is subject to the demands of process are consistent with, and should be incorporated into, section 2(b)'s conception of expressive freedom.

Freedman v Maryland, which concerned a prior approval scheme for films, established procedural requirements to address the risks of censorship inherent in prior restraint.[85] Primary among them is delay and the probability that, in the absence of appropriate safeguards, "the censor's determination may, in practice, be final."[86] *Freedman* acknowledged and concluded that prior approval or restraint only avoids "constitutional infirmity" with procedural safeguards in place that are designed to "obviate the dangers of a censorship system."[87] Specifically, the government or state actor must have the burden to prove that material is not protected by the Constitution.[88] In addition, the constitutional status of detained material must be resolved within a time period that is specified either by statutory prescription or authoritative judicial construction.[89] Moreover, any process of prior approval or restraint must include and assure access to a prompt and final judicial decision.[90] Finally, any interim order must minimize the interference with expressive freedom.

None of *Freedman*'s safeguards was present in the *CPCA* process. First, no reasons for the IPO were given and the process never placed an onus on the minister to explain, justify, or substantiate the ban. In this, it should also be noted that *Little Sisters* invalidated the reverse onus provision, because an individual has no onus to establish a right to engage in expressive freedom.[91] As indicated above, an IPO becomes final under the *CPCA* unless the person(s) affected comes forward within ten days to engage the review process. Second, neither the *CPCA* nor the board set or observed any time prescriptions for the review process. In effect, the ill-defined *CPCA* process made delay inherent, if not inevitable; it practically or inevitably invited disrespect for constitutional rights. Moreover, the scope of the ban was a matter of ministerial fiat, not reviewable limits. The review board lacked decision-making authority and this, along with the absence of any framework for the review, compromised its ability to align the process with standards of administrative fairness and constitutionality. Finally, though the system cannot lend "an effect of finality to the censor's determination," that is exactly what the *CPCA* does.[92] Not only does the statutory presumption deem interim bans final, the *CPCA* makes no provision for judicial determination or appeal of any kind.

Three points are especially salient for section 2(b). The first is that prior restraint poses particular dangers when the censorship of expression is not subject to an effective process of oversight and review. Second, to meet constitutional standards, a process of review must be robust and must include access or appeal to a form of judicial determination. Third, timelines must be prescribed, because any process that fails proactively to require compliance with deadlines will lapse into delay and constitutional insufficiency. To summarize, it is constitutionally impermissible for the state to impose a restraint on speech without providing an accessible and timely procedure to determine its constitutional status.

The section 2(b) jurisprudence on prior restraint has not prescribed safeguards as precisely as *Freedman* and other First Amendment decisions. But that does not mean *Little Sisters* can or should be read as a decision that failed to protect expressive freedom from regulatory schemes that enable administrative censorship.[93] To the contrary, the Court found that customs committed extensive and disturbing violations of the bookstore's rights. Though *Little Sisters* is often cited for the proposition that a statutory provision is not facially invalid when it is maladministered, it must be remembered, when considering the *CPCA*, that the customs scheme incorporated a number of procedural safeguards that were not followed. When properly interpreted and applied, *Little Sisters* suggests both that the *CPCA* did not comply with the *Charter* and that the minister's IPO was legally defective and constitutionally unsound.

Systemic Failure and Section 2(b)

The systemic problems of the *CPCA* process are the systemic problems of section 2(b). True enough, the power to ban individuals from the postal service is rarely invoked. Accepted, as well, is the need to prevent Canada Post's misuse for illegal purposes, such as contraband and smuggling, that are not per se constitutionally protected.[94] It is a different matter, however, when the power to ban access to the post is mobilized after a minister is pressured and lobbied to target an offensive publication. Though core *Charter* entitlements were at stake, the process – from the minister's order to the *CPCA* provisions to the section 44 process – demonstrated systemic disregard for the rights of Sears and Ste. Germaine.

The aftermath of these deficits confirms and further compromises the process. In undertaking the review, the panel proceeded without statutory authority or guidance, a procedural framework, or expertise and resources. The board was diligent but powerless and unable, in the circumstances, to manage the procedural and constitutional challenges in an effective way. To the board's credit, proposing a reform of the *CPCA* was one of the report's core recommendations.[95] Five years after the minister's IPO and almost three years after the board's report, there is no indication of any follow-up or action on this recommendation. In the circumstances, the minister's disregard of the board's call for review and revision of the *CPCA*'s provisions is difficult to excuse.[96] In the circumstances, it was incumbent on the minister to respond, both to address the board's experience and to consider what procedural safeguards are necessary to protect the rights at stake. That lack of response cements the point made in this chapter – that the systemic issues at work here and under section 2(b) are deeply entrenched and must be confronted.

The engagement of a power to censor content from Canada Post was isolated and not isolated, singular and yet not singular. At the least it is clear that, without statutory reform, there is little to prevent a recurrence of postal censorship. Beyond the particulars of *YWN*, the broader concern is that the ban on *YWN* is a reflection in microcosm of any number of campaigns to pre-empt and halt the voices of those with difficult and unacceptable views. Once again, the question of content discrimination is one issue, and the need for procedural safeguards another. Vital to any concept of freedom under section 2(b) is principled recognition that the process around schemes for prior approval or restraint is a key variable in their constitutionality. The *Charter* jurisprudence has gestured at this in some decisions without yet institutionalizing it in clear and concrete doctrinal standards.[97] The groundwork is in place, and it is essential at this point to concretize the safeguards that are necessary, under section 2(b), when expression is restrained by an administrative decision maker. Only when that step is taken can the systemic problems of the *CPCA*, and of other forms of restraint – on access to library space, campus free speech, and the regulation of online expression – be avoided.

NOTES

*   I thank Emmett Macfarlane for assembling the workshop and publication, and including me in the project. I also thank Mr. Ryan Ng (JD 2021) for his valuable assistance as my RA. I am grateful to Jim Turk for his comments on a draft of the paper, as well as to the anonymous peer reviewers of the manuscript. Finally, I note my role as counsel in the *CPCA* review, with the Centre for Free Expression. This article expresses my views, not those of CFE.

1   See T. Emerson, "The Doctrine of Prior Restraint," *Law and Contemporary Problems* 20 (1955): 645.

2   Section 2(b), 1, *Canadian Charter of Rights and Freedoms*, Part I of the *Constitution Act 1982*, Schedule B of the *Canada Act 1982* (UK), 1982, c 11. See also *Irwin Toy v Quebec (AG)*, 1989 1 SCR 927 at 989 (protecting all content of expression equally under section 2(b)).

3   But see also *Re Samsidat Publishers Ltd.* (banning Ernst Zundel from the mail on 13 November 1981, completing the hearing by March 1982, and reporting on 18 October 1982). See generally E. de Grazia, "Obscenity and the Mail: A Study of Administrative Restraint," *Law and Contemporary Problems*, no. 20 (1955): 608, 611 (noting the degree of disruption that can occur, for addressees and recipients as well as senders, when the postal service halts distribution of a newspaper or publication); A. Desai, "The Transformation of Statutes into Constitutional Law: How Early Post Office Police Shaped Modern First Amendment Doctrine," *Hastings Law Journal*, no . 58 (2006–7): 671.

4   See, for example, the petition at Change.org, "Toronto Public Library Collaborators Condemn TPL's Decision on Meaghan Murphy Talk," accessed 27 April 2021, https://www.change.org/p/toronto-public-library-toronto-public-library -collaborators-condemn-tpl-s-decision-on-meghan-murphy-talk; R. Christiansen, "The Wrong Kind of Feminism: Meaghan Murphy Speaks in Vancouver," *Post Millennial*, 18 January 2019, https://thepostmillennial.com/the-wrong-kind-of -feminism-meghan-murphy-speaks-in-vancouver. See also *Weld v Ottawa Public Library*, 2019 ONSC 5358 (challenging the termination of Ms. Weld's contract for the rental of library space).

5   See *Alberta Pro-Life v Governors of the University of Alberta*, 2020 ABCA 1 (applying the *Charter* to expressive activities on university campus). Note also that mandatory governmental free speech policies at colleges and universities in Ontario and Alberta now engage section 2(b) of the *Charter* on campus in those provinces.

6 See generally D. Nunziato, "The Beginning of the End of Internet Freedom," *Georgetown Journal of International Law*, no. 45 (2014): 383; D. Nunziato, "How (Not) to Censor: Procedural First Amendment Values and Internet Censorship Worldwide," *Georgetown Journal of International Law*, no. 42 (2011): 1123; S. Kreimer, "Censorship by Proxy: The First Amendment, Intermediaries, and the Problem of the Weakest Link," *University of Pennsylvania Law Review*, no. 155 (2006): 11.

7 These include protocols for taking down content or terminating user access, as well as systems of content review, whether logarithmic or not. See, for example, "Taking Action to End Online Hate: Report of the Standing Committee on Justice and Human Rights," 42nd Parliament, June 2019, https://www.ourcommons.ca/Content /Committee/421/JUST/Reports/RP10581008/justrp29/justrp29-e.pdf.

8 *Canada Post Corporation Act*, RSC 1985, c C-10, s 43(1).

9 The Minister's FPO is dated 15 November 2018. Documents relating to this process are on file with the author.

10 See J. Cameron, "A Travesty of Fairness: *Your Ward News*, Canada Post, and the *CPCA* Review Board," Centre for Free Expression blog, 1 March 2019, https://cfe .ryerson.ca/blog/2019/03/travesty-fairness-your-ward-news-canada-post-and -cpca-review-board.

11 "Report and Recommendations of Board of Review" (henceforth "Report"), 29 August 2018, https://www.tpsgc-pwgsc.gc.ca/apropos-about/cde-bor/2018-rapport -report-eng.html. The FPO replaced the IPO with a narrower order prohibiting Sears and Ste. Germaine from using Canada Post to distribute *YWN* or other forms of hate literature.

12 Copies of *YWN* are on file with the author. *YWN* is no longer online: http:// yourwardnews.com/.

13 On 15 November 2017, Sears and Ste. Germaine were charged under section 319(2) and on 24 January 2019 they were convicted on two counts for material targeting Jews and women.

14 Quoted in J. Cameron, "A True Canadian Value," Centre for Free Expression blog, 5 October 2016, https://cfe.ryerson.ca/blog/2016/10/true-canadian-value.

15 A copy is on file with the author.

16 *Canada Post Corporation Act*, *supra* note 8, s 46.

17 Ibid., s 43(2)(b) (stipulating for "such longer period as the Minister may allow").

18 Ibid., s 44, 45. One member must be a lawyer, and the *CPCA* sets no criteria for the other panel members.

19 Ibid., s 45(3) (along with the materials and evidence gathered in the process).

20 On 16 December 2016, Sears and Ste. Germaine contacted the minister to inquire on the status of their request for a review.

21 Ruling on Preliminary Issues, 25 April 2017 (henceforth "April Ruling)"; Ruling on Preliminary Issues, 2 November 2017 (henceforth "November Report") (copies are on file with the author).

22 Report, *supra* note 11.
23 Despite stating that nothing prevents it from meeting standards of fairness
    and constitutionality, the board concluded that the statute's lack of procedural
    guidelines led to "considerable" delay in appointing a board and establishing a
    "proper mandate and procedures." Ibid. at 13, 48.
24 *Canada Post Corporation Act, supra* note 8, s 14(1).
25 *Milwaukee Pub. Co. v Burleson*, 255 US 407, 421 (1921) (*per* Holmes J., dissenting).
26 *Hannegan v Esquire, Inc.*, 381 US 301, 306 (1965).
27 Task Force for the Canada Post Corporation Review, Executive Summary, "Canada
    Post in the Digital Age: A Discussion Paper," September 2016, https://www.tpsgc
    -pwgsc.gc.ca/examendepostescanada-canadapostreview/rapport-report/consult
    -eng.html.
28 November Ruling, *supra* note 21, at 6.
29 Report, *supra* note 11, at 41 (emphasis added).
30 April Ruling, *supra* note 21.
31 The board advised six parties that they did not meet the criteria and would not be
    granted standing. Ibid.
32 On 31 March 2017, the attorney general provided a list – but not reasons – of
    those who might have been libelled, and all were granted standing. Otherwise,
    the minister provided no reasons or particulars of the grounds concerning hate
    propaganda; on 3 January 2018, the attorney general advised the board that the
    alleged hate propaganda in *YWN* was directed at Jews.
33 November Ruling, *supra* note 21, at 5.
34 Ibid. (emphasis added).
35 Ibid. (emphasis added).
36 The minister could abandon the IPO or reissue an order in compliance with legal
    and constitutional standards. Despite providing submissions on the constitutional
    issues, this was my position as counsel for the Centre for Free Expression.
37 Counsel for Sears and Ste. Germaine supported a continuation of the process for
    the specific purpose of addressing the constitutional issues at stake. The affected
    persons, CFE, and CCLA consistently opposed the board's proposal to hear
    submissions and evidence from third parties on the underlying grounds for the
    IPO. Copies of correspondence and submissions to the board are on file with the
    author.
38 November Ruling, *supra* note 21, at 7.
39 Report, *supra* note 11, at 17, 18.
40 Although the attorney general appeared to address the constitutional issues, the
    minister did not engage with or participate in the process in any way.
41 Report, *supra* note 11, at 15–19 and 20–2 (citing and relying on the submissions
    of third parties to establish reasonable grounds for the minister's IPO). Only two
    alleged victims of defamatory libel participated in the proceedings, and the report
    only addressed allegations concerning two individuals. Ibid. at 20.

42 See *infra*, notes 77–9 and accompanying text (providing a comparison to customs legislation).

43 Ibid. at 11.

44 Ibid.

45 Ibid. at 38, 42.

46 Ibid. at 13. The board maintained that it acted in accordance with submissions of counsel for the affected persons. The correspondence confirms that counsel asked the board to address the constitutional issues but consistently opposed a process that enabled third parties to proffer evidence and make submissions on the minister's behalf. Copies are on file with the author.

47 Ibid.

48 Ibid. at 27. It was the minister's order banning access to Canada Post under section 43(1), not *Code* provisions, that engage the *Charter*.

49 Ibid. at 30. Not only that, the board's contempt for – or focus on – the publication led it to minimize and even overlook the long-time ban on all non-*YWN* correspondence.

50 Ibid. at 33.

51 Ibid. The *CPCA* incorporates a presumption of finality for FPOs, with no necessity or expectation of any process, subject to a request for review within ten days.

52 Ibid. at 35.

53 Ibid. at 38.

54 Ibid. at 36.

55 *Doré v Barreau du Québec*, [2012] 1 SCR 395. See discussion *infra*.

56 Report, *supra* note 11, at 37.

57 Ibid. at 36. To correct the record, the CFE took no position on the question whether section 43 required a total ban or permitted a partial ban.

58 Ibid. at 38.

59 Ibid. It was inappropriate for the board to suggest that Sears and Ste. Germaine should take steps to mitigate the violation. Those whose rights are violated are not required to mitigate the breach.

60 Report, *supra* note 11, at 38, 42.

61 Ibid.

62 Section 44 did not require a panel with adjudicative or subject-matter expertise. Nor did the board have the benefit of counsel in negotiating the procedural and substantive challenges of the review.

63 See *Esquire, Inc.*, *supra* note 26.

64 See, for example, *Haida Nation v British Columbia (Minister of Forests)*, [2004] 3 SCR 511 (Aboriginal context); *Figueroa v Canada (AG)*, [2003] 1 SCR 912 (citizenship rights under section 3 of the *Charter*).

65 See, for example, *Health Services and Support – Facilities Subsector Bargaining Assn v British Columbia*, [2007] 2 SCR 391 (constitutionalizing the right of public-sector labour unions to a process of collective bargaining); *R. v Vice Media Inc.*,

[2018] 3 SCR 374 (prescribing a process to determine when members of the press can be searched or required to produce materials), and *Denis v Côté*, 2019 SCC 44 (outlining the process and rules for disclosure of confidential source material, under the *Journalistic Sources Protection Act*).

66 On film, see *R. v Glad Day Bookshop* (2004), 70 OR (3d) 691; *Re: Ontario Film and Video Appreciation Society and Ontario Board of Censors*, (1984), 45 OR (2d) 80. The leading decision on open court, which is well developed in the jurisprudence, is *Dagenais v CBC*, [1994] 3 SCR 835; on injunctions, see *Canada (Human Rights Commission v Canadian Liberty Net*, [1998] 1 SCR 626 at paras. 46–50 (concluding that the standard for interim injunctions inadequately protects expressive freedom, including defamatory and hate speech).

67 See, e.g., *Ford v Quebec*, [1988] 2 SCR 712; *Rocket v College of Dental Surgeons*, [1990] 2 SCR 232; *RJR-Macdonald v Canada (AG)*, [1995] 3 SCR 199 (invalidating absolute bans on expressive activity).

68 *Little Sisters Book and Art Emporium v Canada*, [2000] 2 SCR 1120. See also Report, *supra* note 11, at 12.

69 *Little Sisters*, ibid. at para 44 (emphasis in original).

70 Ibid. at para 37.

71 Ibid. at para 82.

72 Ibid. at para 237 (emphasis added).

73 Ibid. at paras 211, 234 (emphasis added).

74 Ibid. at para 275 (identifying the right to be informed of any detention, to examine detained materials, to make effective representation, and to receive determinations that are made in a "prompt fashion" and with brief reasons when materials are found obscene).

75 Ibid.

76 Ibid. at para 40, 144 (per Binnie J., describing the conduct of customs officials as "oppressive and dismissive" and stating that free expression is "central to our identity as individual and to our collective well-being as a society"), and para 274 (per Iacobucci J., describing the bookstore's treatment as a "grave injustice"). Justice Binnie's majority opinion did not comment on or oppose the dissent's position on prior restraint or the legislative standards proposed.

77 Ibid. at para 88.

78 Ibid. at paras 92, 93, 94 (emphasis added).

79 Ibid. at paras 88, 93.

80 Ibid. at para 154.

81 Ibid. at para 158.

82 Not only has First Amendment case law been cited, this jurisprudence was clearly on point with the issues raised in this review.

83 See, for example, *Hannegan v Esquire, Inc.*, *supra* note 26; *Freedman v Maryland*, 380 US 51 (1965); *Lamont v Postmaster General*, 381 US 301 (1965); *Blount v Rizzi*, 400 US 410 (1971); and *United States v Thirty-Seven Photographs*, 402 US 363 (1971).

84 M. Meyerson, "Rewriting *Near v. Minnesota*: Creating a Complete Definition of Prior Restraint," *Mercer Law Review*, no. 52 (2001): 1087 (stating that "beginning in 1965, the [US Supreme] Court has announced a rigid set of guidelines to ensure adequate judicial review" of restraints on free expression that apply not only to censorship boards but also to systems of informal censorship).

85 See *Blount v. Rizzi*, *supra* note 83 (confirming *Freedman*'s requirements in the context of mail censorship). There, the Court found a scheme unconstitutional because judicial review was only available after "lengthy administrative proceedings" and then only at the initiative of the addressee. During the interim, the prolonged threat of adverse administrative decisions either to detain or not deliver mail placed a severe restriction on First Amendment rights.

86 *Freedman*, *supra* note 83, at 58.

87 Ibid.

88 Ibid.

89 Ibid. at 59.

90 Ibid.

91 *Little Sisters*, *supra* note 68, at para 101.

92 *Freedman*, *supra* note 85, at 59.

93 For comment, see B. Ryder, "The *Little Sisters* Case, Administrative Censorship, and Obscenity Law," *Osgoode Hall Law Journal*, no. 39 (2001): 207.

94 See "A True Canadian Value," *supra* note 14 (detailing the use of the post for sending a rocket launcher and venomous snakes, as well as guns and drugs).

95 Report, *supra* note 11, at 48, 49 (outlining the need for legislative changes and recommending that that the *CPCA* be amended or regulations enacted to clarify procedure, including time limits for the appointment of boards, standards of proof, and the remedial powers of the minister). The minister complied with two recommendations: namely, to issue an FPO of limited scope and to "*do so in a timely fashion setting out her reasons and demonstrating a balancing of* Charter *considerations.*" Ibid. (my emphasis).

96 The minister complied with two recommendations: namely, to issue an FPO of limited scope and to "*do so in a timely fashion setting out her reasons and demonstrating a balancing of* Charter *considerations.*" Ibid. (my emphasis).

97 See *Christian Heritage Party of Canada v City of Hamilton*, 2018 ONSC 3690, para 47 (concluding that the Christian Heritage Party was denied natural justice when political advertisements that were protected by section 2(b) of the *Charter* were removed from bus shelters without a "sufficiently robust procedure"). See also the Honourable Thomas A. Cromwell C.C., *York University Independent Review* (30 April 2020), https://president.yorku.ca/files/2020/06/Justice-Cromwell%E2%80%99s -Independent-External-Review.pdf (flagging concerns about prior restraint and recommending that York University address procedural deficiencies in its free speech policies, to provide a robust and transparent framework for the regulation of expressive freedom on campus).

4 Freedom of Expression in an Age of Disinformation: *Charter* Considerations for Regulating Political Speech in Canadian Elections

ERIN CRANDALL AND ANDREA LAWLOR

"Fake news" is no longer simply a theoretical threat to Canadian democracy. During the 2019 Canadian federal election, an unsubstantiated rumour spread across the internet that Prime Minister Justin Trudeau left a former teaching position due to a sex scandal. One website known for circulating fake news posted a story on the rumour that was read by an estimated twenty-five million people.[1] At the provincial level, the 2019 Alberta election campaign saw domestic actors, mostly supporters of the United Conservative Party, use coordinated tactics to manipulate online conversations, including those calling for Alberta's secession.[2] While the impact of such false and misleading information on election results is unclear and difficult to measure, these examples do illustrate the real challenges of maintaining the integrity of Canadian elections.

While no one should want false information to be a common feature of election campaigning, the question of how – or whether – disinformation (the deliberate creation and sharing of information known to be false) and misinformation (the inadvertent sharing of false information) should be regulated is not a straightforward one. One complicating factor in the Canadian context concerns the question of how to approach the regulation of disinformation and misinformation without unduly restricting freedom of expression as protected under section 2(b) of the *Canadian Charter of Rights and Freedoms*.

This chapter focuses on one recent effort by the federal government to navigate these murky regulatory waters of disinformation, misinformation, and the right to political expression. Bill C-76, the *Elections Modernization Act*, introduced significant updates to the *Canada Elections Act* (*CEA*), Canada's key piece of legislation for regulating federal elections (see Mathen, this volume). The bill, which received royal assent in December 2018, garnered considerable attention and scrutiny as it wound its way through the legislative review process; however, changes to section 91, which deal directly with disinformation and misinformation, remained largely off the public's radar.[3] Despite a comparative lack of attention to section 91 during the bill's review, it now has the distinction of being the first component of Bill C-76 to be constitutionally challenged.[4] In September 2019, in the heat of the 2019 federal election, the Canadian Constitution Foundation (CCF), an advocacy group focused on constitutional rights and freedoms, served documents to the attorney general of Canada challenging the constitutionality of section 91 of the *CEA*. The CCF argued that the section was inconsistent with section 2(b) of the *Charter*, violating "the right of Canadians to express their political views freely, particularly during an election period, without fear of reprisal."[5] In February 2021, the Ontario Superior Court of Justice ruled in favour of the CCF and struck down section 91(1) for violating section 2(b) of the *Charter*.[6] Soon after, the federal government announced that it would not appeal the decision and would be "actively examining how best to address the decision to ensure deliberate false statements are captured under the elections law, and to protect our democratic system and institutions."[7] This constitutional challenge thus offers a useful case study for considering the difficulty of balancing the need to address the threat of disinformation and misinformation during Canadian elections with the right to political expression.

This chapter begins with a review of different policy approaches for addressing digital disinformation, including recent initiatives by the Canadian federal government. This includes a description of the 2018 revisions to section 91 of the *CEA*. It then moves to a brief overview of the relevant Canadian jurisprudence on disinformation and election regulation, followed by an analysis considering the constitutionality of section 91 of the *CEA*. Given the broad scope of section 91, particularly the fact that it regulates both disinformation and misinformation, our analysis suggests that the government's task of defending the constitutionality of section 91 against a section 2(b) claim is not an easy one, a conclusion that was confirmed by the Ontario Superior Court of Justice's decision. Even so, the more fundamental question is arguably whether using an approach like that of section 91 is desirable for addressing the harms of disinformation and misinformation during elections. We conclude that the approach embedded in section 91 places Canada out of step with other democracies as well as recommended best practices.

Government Responses to Disinformation and Misinformation

While high-profile cases like Russian interference in the 2016 United States presidential election mean that the phenomenon of digital disinformation is now widely known, the public nonetheless struggles to identify it. For example, a 2019 survey commissioned by the Canadian Internet Registration Authority found that 87 per cent of respondents agreed that the spread of fake news on social media is a problem and that 70 per cent were concerned that fake news could impact the outcome of the 2019 Canadian federal election.[8] Worryingly, over half (57 per cent) admitted to having been taken in by a fake news item. Another poll conducted in 2019 found that 90 per cent of Canadians had fallen for fake news online.[9] Given the increasing prevalence of coordinated disinformation campaigns during elections, both in Canada and internationally,[10] what options do governments have for addressing the threats of disinformation to democratic institutions?

According to the European Commission's Independent High Level Group on Fake News and Online Disinformation, disinformation is best addressed by taking a multidimensional approach that offers mutually reinforcing responses.[11] These responses include enhancing the transparency of online news, promoting media and information literacy, developing tools for empowering users and journalists to tackle disinformation, safeguarding the diversity and sustainability of the news media ecosystem, and promoting continued research on the impact of disinformation.[12] A number of recent initiatives launched by the Government of Canada appear to align with these recommended responses.[13] These include the Canada Declaration on Electoral Integrity Online, which asks (but does not require) social media and other online platforms to commit to greater transparency,[14] $600 million in public funding to support news media over a five-year period,[15] and program funding for more than twenty projects aimed at improving citizens' internet literacy (for examples of other international initiatives, see Mathen, this volume).[16] Also noteworthy, however, is the fact that the European Commission's report stresses against "any form of censorship either public or private,"[17] and notes that "legal approaches amounting to well-intentioned censorship are neither justified nor efficient for disinformation."[18] This type of "well-intentioned censorship" arguably describes the 2018 reforms to section 91 of the *CEA*.

So, what does section 91 say and try to do? With the changes brought in with the *Elections Modernization Act*, section 91 of the *CEA* reads as follows:

91 (1) No person or entity shall, with the intention of affecting the results of an election, make or publish, during the election period,

(a) a false statement that a candidate, a prospective candidate, the leader of a political party or a public figure associated with a political party has committed an offence under an Act of Parliament or a regulation made under such an Act – or under an Act of the legislature of a province or a regulation made under such an Act – or has been charged with or is under investigation for such an offence; or

(b) a false statement about the citizenship, place of birth, education, professional qualifications or membership in a group or association of a candidate, a prospective candidate, the leader of a political party or a public figure associated with a political party.

(2) Subsection (1) applies regardless of the place where the election is held or the place where the false statement is made or published.[19]

In sum, section 91 aims to prohibit people and entities in Canada and abroad from making false statements about political actors during a federal election campaign. While a laudable objective, an overview of some of the key changes brought in with the *Elections Modernization Act* helps to highlight a number of the constitutional challenges that section 91 faced. Though these modifications may at first glance appear relatively minor, they are significant, particularly in terms of their potential impact on political expression.

Previously, section 91 barred people from making "any false statement of fact in relation to the personal character or conduct of a candidate or prospective candidate," knowingly and with the intention of affecting the results of an election. The modified version removed "knowingly" from the provision, creating a much lower threshold for charging someone under the act. This change is primarily a response to the fact that the previous higher standard caused enforcement difficulties, such that no one was ever charged under the provision. Whether or not drafters were aware of the full consequences of removing "knowingly," the change broadened significantly the group of people who are potentially impacted by section 91, from those who have participated in disinformation (the deliberate creation and sharing of information known to be false) to those who have participated in either disinformation *or* misinformation (the inadvertent sharing of false information). The survey data noted earlier in this chapter regarding the high percentage of Canadians who have been taken in by fake news offers a glimpse into the potential reach that this provision would have.

The revised language of section 91 also expanded the class of person protected by such false statements to include leaders of political parties and public figures associated with a political party, in addition to candidates and prospective candidates. Depending on how "associated with" is interpreted, this again constitutes a notable broadening of the provisions of section 91. Arguably, the revised language is less broad in terms of the subject matter of statements that are restricted, given that a set of categories, like citizenship and professional qualifications, are now provided.[20] However, even here the ill-defined nature of some of these categories make their scope unclear. The professional qualifications category is a good example. During the 2019 federal election campaign, controversy arose as to whether Conservative Party leader Andrew Scheer had misrepresented his past work as an insurance broker. In particular, it was unclear whether he had ever received the accreditation necessary to practise in the profession.[21] It is not hard to imagine how this type of sincere confusion around Scheer's professional qualifications could lead to a person sharing a news story that later turned out to be false, an action that would seemingly violate this provision of section 91. Altogether, the changes made to section 91 can be understood as an effort to strengthen the *CEA*'s regulation of disinformation and misinformation by making the provision broader and more likely to be engaged.

These changes to section 91 are what prompted the CCF to launch a constitutional challenge. In its notice of application, it describes the detrimental effects of section 91 in stark terms:

> Section 91 of the CEA will not promote the integrity of Canada's federal elections. Rather, by chilling legitimate political expression, it stands to compromise the robust debate on which our democracy depends. It empowers the state to punish individuals for exercising their freedom to express and share information, opinions, and beliefs during federal election campaigns. In doing so, it offends the Constitution and the democratic commitments that it reflects.[22]

Concern over any limitation on political speech is rightly placed. Political speech, especially during election periods, is part of the core of freedom of expression guarantees. That said, there are nonetheless constitutionally recognized limitations placed on political speech during Canadian elections. For example, federal election laws around spending follow an egalitarian model[23] and place limits on the amount of money parties, candidates, and third parties can spend during an election. The egalitarian model is rooted in the idea that all citizens should have relatively equal opportunities to participate in the democratic process. Because the opportunity to speak (advertise) has traditionally cost money, the egalitarian approach calls for spending limits on election advertising so that the voices of the wealthy do not have the chance to overwhelm the voices of the majority.[24] While spending limits on political advertising have faced constitutional challenge, in *Harper v Canada (Attorney General)*, the Supreme Court upheld such limits on political speech for third parties as a reasonable encroachment on section 2(b) of the *Charter*, and the limits remain in place today. That said, while regulations limiting spending on election advertising and restrictions on election-related disinformation are both limitations on political speech, they present different types of challenges in terms of their regulation. Challenges to political advertising in the vein of *Harper* have focused on the dollar value of third-party ads and have assessed whether legislated limits on spending in campaigns are appropriate and constitute a reasonable limit to *Charter* rights. Adjudicating ads according to their monetary value has the advantage of using an indicator (money) that is both quantitatively comparable and (largely) content neutral. The challenge posed by the restrictions set out in section 91 is fundamentally different: the wording of the section limits not the volume of ads but the veracity of their content, which presents arbiters with a far more subjective task.

Thus, the real question is not whether political speech has been encroached upon but whether such a violation is reasonably justified. How does section 91 of the *CEA* stand against the relevant case law? While the objective here is not to provide an exhaustive analysis, the relevant jurisprudence related to disinformation and misinformation does show why the government's task of defending section 91 was a difficult one.

Relevant Case Law: Disinformation and Elections

The Supreme Court dealt directly with the regulation of disinformation in *R. v Zundel* and recognized that those who deliberately publish falsehoods are protected by section 2(b) given that "false statements can sometimes have value and given the difficulty of conclusively determining total falsity."[25] The 1992 decision dealt with section 181 of the *Criminal Code*, which provided that "every one who wilfully publishes a statement, tale, or news that he knows is false and causes or is likely to cause injury or mischief to a public interest is guilty of an indictable offence and liable to imprisonment."[26] The Supreme Court struck down the provision, finding it violated section 2(b), with the majority ruling that it did not meet the threshold of pressing and substantial under section 1 of the *Charter*. In its decision, the Court noted as key considerations a lack of evidence of a social problem to justify its purpose, the section's infrequent use, the absence of a comparable law in another democratic country, and the labelling of the law as anachronistic by the Law Reform Commission of Canada.[27] The majority also concluded that the section was broader and more invasive than was necessary to achieve its aim, with the phrases "statement, tale, or news" and "injury or mischief to a public interest" singled out as being under-defined and overbroad.[28]

While *Zundel* deals directly with prohibitions on disinformation, the Supreme Court's approach to regulating speech during elections is also instructive for considering the CCF's challenge to section 91. In *R. v Bryan*, at question was whether section 329 of the *CEA*, which prohibits the transmission of election results in one electoral district to another electoral district before the close of all polling stations, was a justifiable encroachment on section 2(b). Because the closing times of polling stations are staggered across Canada, the regulation meant that election results from Atlantic Canada were effectively under an embargo for several hours until polling stations in British Columbia closed. The Supreme Court upheld the provision, with the majority focusing on the importance of ensuring "informational equality" to deal with possible negative effects to public confidence.[29] Concerns over public confidence focused on the fact that, without the provision, some voters would be able to access information that others could not, and furthermore, such information could affect voter participation or choices.

As the *Bryan* decision relates to the risk posed by content restrictions, the opinion of the dissenting judges is also informative. The minority argued that the publication ban imposed by section 329 was not justifiable under section 1's proportionality test. Citing the lack of social science evidence to sufficiently justify the harm caused by the ban, the justices refer to the prohibition as "an excessive response to an insufficiently proven harm" and cite only "speculative and unpersuasive evidence to support the government's claim that the information imbalance is of sufficient harm to voter behaviour or perceptions of electoral unfairness."[30] Here, the dissenting judges evoke concerns about tangible harms caused by informational prohibitions for voters and appear supportive of a more permissive policy approach where the justification for harm must be built upon credible material evidence by the government before a prohibition can be viewed as a reasonable restriction.

In *Thomson Newspapers Co. v Canada (AG)*, the Supreme Court struck down section 322(1) of the *CEA*, which prohibited the publication, broadcast, or dissemination of opinion surveys within the last three days of an election campaign. The purpose of the ban was to prevent inaccurate polling from influencing the choices of voters since there would arguably not be enough time to identify and correct inaccurate polls so close to election day. In ruling that section 322(1) was unconstitutional, the Court's analysis focused on the provision's failure to minimally impair voters' freedom of expression. In its reasoning, the majority placed importance on the intelligence of the Canadian voter, noting that "the presumption in this Court should be that the Canadian voter is a rational actor who can learn from experience and make independent judgments about the value of particular sources of electoral information."[31] The fact that the interests of voters and pollsters are seemingly not opposed (compared to political advertisers, whose aim is to persuade voters) and that Canadian voters are not a historically vulnerable or disadvantaged group were also mentioned by the majority.[32]

Questions Regarding the Constitutionality of Section 91 of the *Canada Elections Act*

In considering the constitutionality of section 91 of the *CEA*, there are some features of the relevant jurisprudence that appear to work in the government's favour. Section 91 is directed at a targeted harm – that of misleading the electorate during an election period – whereas in *Zundel*, the majority was concerned that the undefined phrase "injury or mischief to a public interest" could be "capable of almost infinite extension."[33] The harm of manipulating the public (see Moon, this volume) was emphasized in *Thomson Newspapers Co.*, as well, where the fact that polling firms do not overtly seek to manipulate the electorate was an important factor in the Supreme Court striking down the polling publication ban. On the other hand, the fact that section 329 of the *CEA* restricted the distribution of election results, which would permit the flow of additional (presumably correct) information to a geographically concentrated subset of voters, was not enough to persuade the majority in *Bryan* to strike down the legislation. While in these latter two cases, the information being shared is presumably truthful, in the instance of disinformation, the aim of those who are creating and distributing false information is clearly to manipulate the public, and there is a growing body of evidence confirming that disinformation campaigns can and do achieve this aim.[34] As noted by Michael Karanicolas, the threat posed by disinformation is further exacerbated by micro-targeting, which allows distributors of disinformation to tailor their messages in a manner that focuses on latent biases or the concerns of individual recipients.[35] In other words, section 91 addresses a specific and recognized harm to citizens' confidence in the integrity of Canadian elections.

A complicating factor in considering section 91's constitutionality is the notion of the informed voter. In *Harper*, the Supreme Court recognized that members of the public have a right to meaningful participation in the electoral process, including exercising their vote in an informed manner.[36] For a citizen to be an informed voter, the Court reasoned that they "must be able to weigh the relative strengths and weaknesses of each candidate and political party" and "to consider opposing aspects of issues associated with certain candidates and political parties where they exist."[37] As the Supreme Court noted in *Libman v Quebec (Attorney General)*, a case that dealt with campaign spending in referendums, "elections are fair and equitable only if all citizens are reasonably informed of all the possible choices."[38] In *Thomson*, the Supreme Court further affirmed the importance of the informed voter, stating that "the promotion of an informed vote over a misinformed vote" meets the purposes underlying freedom of expression.[39]

Given that the goal of disinformation is arguably to make a citizen less informed, section 91 works in service of promoting an informed vote by banning individuals and organizations from presenting false information about actors associated with political parties. However, the right of citizens to be reasonably informed must be considered alongside the presumption of their "maturity and intelligence."[40] In *Thomson*, the presumed maturity and intelligence of the voter meant that the Supreme Court dismissed the possibility that citizens could be so gripped by a poll result at the end of an election period as to forget the issues and interests that motivate them to vote for a particular candidate.[41] Surveys, however, seem to pose a different challenge for citizens in comparison to disinformation. Today, the sophistication of some disinformation campaigns means that even the most highly informed citizens are vulnerable to this type of political manipulation and deceit. It is therefore unclear how a court may eventually navigate the limits of the informed voter within the context of misinformation.

For section 91, what proved most vulnerable to constitutional challenge was that it applied to both misinformation and disinformation. The revisions brought in with the *Elections Modernization Act* removed the requirement that those who distribute disinformation must do so knowingly. The removal of intent resulted in section 91 capturing misinformation within its scope, potentially including journalists who report on incorrect information, as well as ordinary citizens who unknowingly share false information on social media. While the Office of the Commissioner of Canada Elections stated that it was unlikely to charge someone who unknowingly shared false information, Justice Davies, who heard the CCF's challenge, concluded that people who lacked *mens rea* could technically be punished under the provision.[42] Moreover, the language in section 91 provides no exceptions for satire or parody, making the kinds of speech potentially captured under the provision wide in scope. This seems especially problematic given that unlike false statements, which arguably undermine the objective of the informed voter, satire and parody can serve to foster political participation.

Altogether, the broad scope of section 91 opens up serious concerns about whether it minimally impairs section 2(b) under the reasonable limits test of section 1. While Justice Davies ruled section 91(1) does not meet the minimal impairment requirement under section 1, it was decided on quite narrow grounds and did not engage a full section 1 analysis. The attorney general argued that, despite the removal of the word "knowingly" from section 91(1), the *mens rea* of the offence still required an element of knowledge, capturing disinformation, but not misinformation. Interestingly, the attorney general conceded that if the Court determined section 91(1) could be contravened without proof of knowledge, then it was not a justifiable limit on freedom of expression.[43] The Court did indeed find that the "offense of contravening section 91(1) does not include an element of knowledge that the statement in question is false" and therefore ruled section 91(1) unconstitutional on section 2(b) *Charter* grounds.[44] With the attorney general's concession, none of the other issues raised by the CCF were considered. Thus, following *Canadian Constitution Foundation v Canada (Attorney General)*, section 91(1) is no longer in effect, but the limited scope of the decision means that it offers little instruction for balancing the regulation of disinformation with the protection of freedom of expression under section 2(b) of the *Charter*.

There is also the important question of whether or not section 91, as it was modified in 2018, can actually be effective in realizing its objective of combatting disinformation and misinformation during election periods. Canada is an outlier in using this regulatory approach to disinformation and misinformation,[45] the use of which has been discouraged by an increasing number of experts.[46] Interestingly, prohibiting disinformation does not appear to enjoy total support within Canadian government either. In December 2018, the House of Commons Standing Committee on Access to Information, Privacy and Ethics published a study on the risks posed by disinformation and data monopolies. While many of its recommendations focused on measures to enhance transparency around disinformation, none called for the regulation of speech comparable to what was included in section 91 of the *CEA*.[47]

This regulatory approach does not even appear to be preferred by the agency responsible for conducting federal elections. In Elections Canada's 2016 report *An Electoral Framework for the 21st Century*, from which many of the reforms implemented in the *Elections Modernization Act* were derived, the chief electoral officer recommended that section 91 be repealed, noting that "serious cases of defamation or libel can be dealt with through alternative civil or criminal legal mechanisms."[48] Given the questionable effectiveness of section 91 when it comes to actually minimizing the harms of disinformation versus its potential to chill political expression, the proportionate effects of the provision appear questionable.

When thinking about how the Supreme Court might address a broader challenge to the constitutionality of section 91, it is essential that we consider how to balance the preservation of a healthy informational environment and the practicalities of assessment and enforceability of a ban on false and misleading statements. Certainly, the Court has signalled, through *Thomson* and *Bryan*, the importance of information to the democratic process, and therefore attempts to preserve section 91 would fall to a section 1 proportionality challenge. The Court's previous jurisprudence in *Bryan* and *Harper* suggest that access to information and the prevention of an informational imbalance would meet the definition of a "pressing and substantial objective."[49] However, assessing the proportionality of a ban on false and misleading statements could plausibly threaten the prohibition. First, the nebulous nature of disinformation and questions about how to assess it, coupled with the aforementioned concern by key officials such as the chief electoral officer about enforcement and the inappropriate nature of mechanisms for sanction, suggest that attempting a ban on false and misleading statements may pose an uphill battle when it comes to establishing a rational connection. The ban itself may fail to be effective given the fast-changing nature of digital communications, and it would be all but inept against the wording of section 91 sanctioning not only the publication of misinformation but, more broadly, those who "make" a false statement during the campaign. With due consideration to the standard for minimal impairment set out in *RJR-MacDonald Inc. v Canada (Attorney General)*, the Court would also have to consider whether the law has been "carefully tailored so that rights are impaired no more than necessary" while still according "some leeway to the legislator."[50] While the aim of legislators may have been a precautionary move to stem a problem that has been recognized to have far-reaching effects internationally, section 91 might not only have had the effect of chilling democratic deliberation in the public forum but also serving as a remedy for what is, at present, "an undemonstrated problem and, as a result, an overbroad intrusion on a Charter right."[51] In other words, the Court may look for quantifiable evidence of substantial harm before permitting an override of section 2(b) rights. Finally, an outright ban on statements that cannot be fully substantiated in the relatively short duration of an election campaign may weigh against considerations of proportionality. Election campaigns, for all their high stakes, ultimately amount to short informational bursts. Subduing open conversation about issues that may influence voters' decision-making processes without giving them the time to receive irrefutable evidence may dampen public participation beyond the intent of section 91. In sum, even in the face of evidence of low-quality information in the campaign environment, a considerable number of countervailing considerations may undermine section 91's ability to withstand further *Charter* scrutiny.

Conclusion

This chapter focused on an attempt by the Canadian federal government to navigate the difficult regulatory waters of disinformation, misinformation, and the right to political expression. Section 91 of the *Canada Elections Act* prohibited the making or publishing of certain categories of false statements during the federal election campaign with "the intention of affecting the results" of an election. The 2018 revisions made to section 91 faced a near immediate constitutional challenge by the Canadian Constitution Foundation, which resulted in section 91(1) being struck down under section 2(b). While the judicial decision itself provides limited guidance, this episode illustrates the difficulties involved in addressing the threat of disinformation and misinformation while also respecting *Charter* freedoms. As the analysis in this chapter suggests, and the Ontario Superior Court of Justice confirmed, the broad scope of section 91, particularly its regulation of both disinformation and misinformation, means that it did not achieve this needed balance.

Regardless of the case's outcome, the more fundamental question is arguably whether banning certain types of speech based on content that otherwise does not infringe the law is a desirable approach to addressing the harms of disinformation and misinformation at all. One way or another, legislators and policymakers will have to address misinformation and disinformation in future federal elections. What might plausible solutions look like? Two pathways seem possible and are not mutually exclusive. First, the federal government may opt to modify section 91 so that its limitations on freedom of expression are not as broad. For example, reinstating the concept of intent in section 91 would capture explicit cases of disinformation. The fact that section 91 went unused while the criterion of intent was included, however, suggests that this threshold makes the provision largely ineffective as an enforcement tool. The second, and more commonly recommended pathway, focuses on education, information, and transparency to try to weaken the influence and effects of disinformation and misinformation during election campaigns. Embedded in this second pathway is an acceptance that misinformation cannot be eliminated and is unlikely to be deterred by prohibitions or sanction. This second pathway also requires a significant commitment of resources by the federal government if it is to be effective. This will have to be done with an eye to balancing legitimate third-party activity – some of which may be viewed as distasteful and/or incorporate poor-quality information, though not actual misinformation. As the public bears some of the responsibility for this approach, compliance can never be fully guaranteed. Working with digital communications companies such as Twitter (which Elections Canada has already done to some extent) to assess content may be useful, though it is unclear how far these organizations will want to intervene in the political realm. Some sort of cataloguing of misinformation that is searchable, as is done by the Canada Revenue Agency and other government bodies with respect to listing commonly used fraud scams, could be a useful tool, though it would, again, require citizens to be actively on guard for this type of content in their day-to-day communications.

The 2018 changes to section 91 of the *CEA* put Canada out of step with other democracies as well as recommended best practices. The 2021 decision by the Ontario Superior Court of Justice means that federal government must now decide on a new path forward. The risks of disinformation, particularly systematic disinformation campaigns, to democracy are real, which is why effective policy initiatives are so critical, especially during election periods. While the changes to section 91 may have been predicated on the desire to prevent harm, they fell short of this needed standard. If policy change is not brought about by legislators in a timely fashion, public opinion towards and levels of trust in legislators might be the catalyst that brings change. Hopefully, this comes before – not after – a major disruption to the Canadian electoral process.

NOTES

1 Emma McIntosh, "A Fake Justin Trudeau Sex Scandal Went Viral. Canada's Election-Integrity Law Can't Stop It," *National Observer*, 10 October 2019, https://www.nationalobserver.com/2019/10/10/news/fake-justin-trudeau-sex-scandal-went-viral-canadas-election-integrity-law-cant-stop.

2 Rapid Response Mechanism Canada, "Alberta Election Analysis," Government of Canada, last modified 3 August 2020, https://www.international.gc.ca/gac-amc/publications/rrm-mrr/alberta_elections.aspx?lang=eng.

3 Charelle Evelyn, "NDP to Support Liberal Election Bill, Tories Won't, after Committee Makes 73 Changes," *Hill Times*, 24 October 2018, https://www.hilltimes.com/2018/10/24/liberal-election-bill-better-nothing-says-ndp-critic-73-changes-c-76/173371; Marco Vigliotti, "Elections Bill Gets Royal Assent

after Fractious Path through Parliament," *iPolitics*, 14 December 2018, https://ipolitics
.ca/article/elections-bill-gets-royal-assent-after-fractious-path-through-parliament/.

4   Interestingly, provisions addressing misinformation are not even mentioned
    in the Charter Statement on Bill C-76 issued by the Department of Justice.
    See Department of Justice, "Charter Statement – Bill C-76: An Act to Amend
    the Canada Elections Act and Other Acts and to Make Certain Consequential
    Amendments," 8 May 2018, https://www.justice.gc.ca/eng/csj-sjc/pl/charter-charte
    /c76.html.

5   Canadian Constitution Foundation, "Canadian Constitution Foundation Launches
    Constitutional Challenge against Elections Censorship Law," 18 September 2019,
    https://theccf.ca/canadian-constitution-foundation-launches-constitutional
    -challenge-against-elections-censorship-law/.

6   *Canadian Constitution Foundation v Canada (Attorney General)*, 2021 ONSC 1224.

7   Elizabeth Thompson, "Trudeau Government Won't Appeal Ruling That Struck
    Down Part of Elections Law," *CBC News*, 23 March 2021, https://www.cbc.ca
    /news/politics/elections-law-misinformation-disinformation-1.5959693.

8   Canadian Internet Registration Authority, *Canadians Deserve a Better Internet*
    (Ottawa: Canadian Internet Registration Authority, 2019).

9   Elizabeth Thompson, "Poll Finds 90% of Canadians Have Fallen for Fake News,"
    CBC News, 11 June 2019, https://www.cbc.ca/news/politics/fake-news
    -facebook-twitter-poll-1.5169916.

10 Samantha Bradshaw and Philip N. Howard Howard, *The Global Disinformation
    Order: 2019 Global Inventory of Organised Social Media Manipulation* (Oxford:
    Oxford Internet Institute, University of Oxford, 2019).

11 Independent High Level Group on Fake News and Online Disinformation, *A
    Multi-Dimensional Approach to Disinformation* (Brussels: European Commission,
    2018).

12 Ibid., 5–6.

13 For a comprehensive review of measures designed to protect elections from
    disinformation, see Yasmin Dawood, "Combatting Foreign Election Interference:
    Canada's Electoral Ecosystem Approach to Disinformation and Cyber Threats,"
    Election Law Journal: Rules, Politics, and Policy 20, no. 1 (2021): 10–31.

14 Joan Bryden, "Several Tech Giants Sign onto Canadian Declaration on Electoral
    Integrity," *Global News*, 27 May 2019, https://globalnews.ca/news/5323084
    /tech-giants-electoral-integrity/.

15 Bernard Descôteaux and Colette Brin, "Funding for Canadian Media: The Who,
    What and How," *Policy Options*, 19 December 2019, https://policyoptions.irpp.org
    /magazines/december-2018/funding-for-canadian-media-the-who-why-and
    -how/; Bryden, "Several Tech Giants Sign onto Canadian Declaration on Electoral
    Integrity."

16 Canadian Heritage, "Backgrounder – Helping Citizens Critically Assess and
    Become Resilient against Harmful Online Disinformation," Government of

Canada, last modified 21 August 2019, https://www.canada.ca/en/canadian
-heritage/news/2019/07/backgrounder--helping-citizens-critically-assess-and
-become-resilient-against-harmful-online-disinformation.html.

17 Independent High Level Group on Fake News and Online Disinformation, *A Multi-Dimensional Approach to Disinformation*, 5.

18 Ibid., 30.

19 Under sections 486(4) and 500(5) of the *CEA*, any person who contravenes section 91(1) of the act is guilty of an offence, and may be sentenced (1) on summary conviction, to pay a fine of up to $20,000, to be imprisoned for up to one year, or both; or (2) on conviction on indictment, to pay a fine of up to $50,000, to be imprisoned for up to five years, or both.

20 The previous version of section 91 captured false statements "in relation to the personal character or conduct of a candidate or prospective candidate."

21 Canadian Press, "Scheer Accused of Breaking Law, Falsely Claiming He Was Once an Insurance Broker," *National Post*, 30 September 2019, https://nationalpost.com /news/politics/election-2019/scheer-accused-of-breaking-law-falsely-claiming-he -was-once-an-insurance-broker.

22 Canadian Constitution Foundation, Notice of Application: *Canadian Constitution Foundation v Attorney General of Canada* (Ontario Superior Court of Justice, 2019), 10.

23 Erin Crandall and Andrea Lawlor, "Third Party Policy and Electoral Participation after *Harper v. Canada*: A Triumph of Egalitarianism?," in *Policy Change, Courts, and the Canadian Constitution*, ed. Emmett Macfarlane (Toronto: University of Toronto Press, 2018), 210–29; Colin Feasby, "*Libman v. Quebec (AG)* and the Administration of the Process of Democracy under the Charter: The Emerging Egalitarian Model," *McGill Law Journal* 44, no. 1 (1998): 5–38; Andrea Lawlor and Erin Crandall, "Understanding Third Party Advertising: An Analysis of the 2004, 2006 and 2008 Canadian Elections," *Canadian Public Administration* 54, no. 4 (2011): 509–29.

24 With the rise of low-cost and free methods of communication, especially via social media, there are increasingly questions as to whether a simple equating of money with speech is still appropriate. Despite the importance of social media to political communication, however, spending on election advertising remains critical. See Tamara A Small, "Digital Third Parties: Understanding the Technological Challenge to Canada's Third Party Advertising Regime," *Canadian Public Administration* 61, no. 2 (2018): 266–83.

25 *R. v Zundel*, [1992] 2 SCR 731 at 733.

26 Section 181, *Criminal Code*, RSC 1985, c C-46.

27 *R. v Zundel* at 733.

28 Ibid. at 734.

29 *R. v Bryan*, [2007] 1 SCR 527, 2007 SCC 12 at paras 46–9.

30 Ibid. at paras 103 and 110.

31 *Thomson Newspapers Co v Canada (AG)*, [1998] 1 SCR 877 at para 112.

32 Ibid. at paras 114 and 117.

33 *Zundel* at 734.

34 David M.J. Lazer et al., "The Science of Fake News," *Science* 359, no. 6380 (2018): 1094–6.

35 Michael Karanicolas, "Subverting Democracy to Save Democracy: Canada's Extra-Constitutional Approaches to Battling 'Fake News,' " *Canadian Journal of Law and Technology* 17, no. 2 (2019): 212.

36 *Harper v Canada (Attorney General)*, [2004] 1 SCR 827 at para 71.

37 Ibid.

38 *Libman v Quebec (Attorney General)*, [1997] 3 SCR 569 at para 47.

39 *Thomson Newspapers Co. v Canada (AG)* at para 25.

40 Ibid. at para 101.

41 Ibid.

42 *Canadian Constitution Foundation v Canada (Attorney General)* at para 53.

43 Ibid. at para 10.

44 Ibid. at para 9.

45 Among consolidated democracies, France appears, as of January 2020, to be the only other exception. See, Daniel Funke and Daniela Flamini, "A Guide to Anti-misinformation Actions around the World," *Poynter*, accessed 24 January 2020, https://www.poynter.org/ifcn/anti-misinformation-actions/.

46 Independent High Level Group on Fake News and Online Disinformation, *A Multi-Dimensional Approach to Disinformation.*

47 House of Commons Standing Committee on Access to Information, Privacy and Ethics, *Democracy under Threat: Risks and Solutions in the Era of Disinformation and Data Monopoly* (Ottawa: Parliament of Canada, 2018).

48 Office of the Chief Electoral Office of Canada, *An Electoral Framework for the 21st Century: Recommendations from the Chief Electoral Officer of Canada Following the 42nd General Election* (Ottawa: Elections Canada, 2016), 71.

49 *R. v Bryan* at para 104; *Harper v Canada (Attorney General)* at para 132.

50 *RJR-MacDonald Inc. v Canada (Attorney General)*, [1995] 3 SCR 199 at para 60.

51 *R. v Bryan* at para 133.

5 Regulating Expression on Social Media

CARISSIMA MATHEN*

Since 2016, Western democracies have experienced a number of events that cast into stark relief the tenets, norms, and controls required for them to function. Election mischief, co-option of news-gathering, manipulation of information, increased levels of social alienation and polarization, and a hardening of attitudes against political opponents have become points of deep concern at all levels of government.[1] Many of the above concerns involve expression on social media,[2] contributing to the sense that the latter is a sinister force that threatens political stability and social cohesion.

In such an environment, previously sacred principles can appear out of step. One of those is the principle of free expression – especially as it operates in the ecosystem of the internet. There have been numerous calls to regulate either online expression itself or the powerful companies that control the platforms that give it scope and reach.

Even five years ago, such calls would have been fanciful. No more. In the European Union (EU), the General Data Protection Regulation (GDPR) has introduced unprecedented levels of monitoring, reporting of, and financial penalties for privacy and data-collection breaches.[3] Individual EU member states, like France and Germany,[4] have proposed or instituted aggressive laws intended to combat illegal hate speech. A 2019 United Kingdom white paper, if translated into legislation, would require platforms to identify and remove harmful material.[5] Even the United States has entertained discussions about content-based regulatory schemes,[6] usually considered anathema under the First Amendment.[7]

In Canada, political actors regularly emphasize the need for social media companies to cooperate and pull their weight, especially in relation to election security, "fake news," and political advertising. Non-governmental actors argue that present norms and practices are inadequate to deal with increasingly pervasive and complex forms of manipulation.[8] In the 2019 federal election, several political campaigns proposed or endorsed explicit content-related social media regulation.

This chapter sounds a cautionary note about much of this. I have watched with increasing disquiet the shift to greater acceptance of social media regulation that would capture far more expression than, for example, existing criminal prohibitions.[9] Advocates of regulation only occasionally acknowledge Canada's current constitutional commitments to freedom of expression, the limits of the *Charter*'s application, and the need to demonstrate that any actual or reasonably anticipated interference with expressive rights is justified.

Below, I offer two principal arguments about why caution is warranted. The first is that trying to regulate social media raises sobering problems of interpretation, effect, and scale. The second is that underlying the increasing attacks on social media platforms is an eagerness to shift responsibility for complex social dynamics away from the state and onto third parties. This privatizes the regulation of expression while expecting platforms to adopt public-interest frameworks that are probably at odds with their corporate missions and business interests. The most likely result is a chokehold on expression by means of prior restraint systems employed in an inherently risk-averse business mindset. I conclude that governments should refrain from seeking to control social media expression unless they are prepared to do so directly.

The Impact, and Challenge, of Social Media

Online expressive activity has had and continues to have an enormous impact on just about everyone. Of the world's more than 7 billion persons, 4.4 billion use the internet in some way. Just under 3.5 billion are active users of social media, and most have multiple online accounts. The scale of communication among those users is practically incomprehensible. Every day, 60 billion messages are sent using Facebook Messenger and WhatsApp; 95 million photos are uploaded to Instagram; 500,000 persons join Facebook; 500 million tweets appear on Twitter; and 1 billion hours of YouTube video is watched (and is added at the rate of 500 hours per minute). Google processes 100 billion search requests per month, or 40,000 per second. By 2014, it had indexed 130 trillion (130,000,000,000) web pages.[10]

The sheer scale of social media on the above platforms makes content moderation a significant challenge.[11] First, the volume of content posted or uploaded is too large for review by humans, so the platforms must rely, at least initially, on automated systems. Such systems may fail to detect and correct for relevant context (so that, for example, a Holocaust researcher is delisted because of a ban on "Nazis").[12] Second, the volume of content that *is* flagged for human review (either by automated systems or by the public) necessitates large armies of content moderators reviewing controversial material. That raises further concerns about the impact of such review on those moderators' health and well-being.[13] Third, the scale involved means that the smallest of policy changes can have profound impacts on communication and on communities. Even with near perfect certainty (say, 99.9999 per cent accuracy), any new scheme will produce many thousands of "false positives" or "false negatives."

The above figures tend to spur impatience from those advocating greater control of social media. Some express scepticism at the idea that the sheer volume of information and data transmission presents a barrier to the kind of regulation that ought to be carried out. The enormous wealth and resources of tech companies is assumed to come with limitless capacity to bring online communication to heel – at least if there is sufficient will (or state-backed imperatives) to apply the necessary resources. Such scepticism was in evidence when the *Canada Elections Act* introduced, in 2018, a new regime for online political advertising. Among other things, such advertising must be identified, recorded, and stored in retrievable databases.[14] Google determined that it could not comply with the regime's technical requirements in time for the October 2019 federal election. It decided, instead, to prohibit all paid political election advertising on its platforms.[15]

Reasoning that the fewer political ads, the better, many individuals greeted the news with indifference or enthusiasm. Others, though, including members of the federal cabinet, viewed Google's decision as dismissive of and insufficiently attentive to the underlying policy objectives. Underlying much of this was suspicion of Google's assertion that it could not easily track and index such advertising as the law required. A federal minister observed:

> We know that Google is enormously capable both technically and financially. It should apply these resources to producing a registry in Canada that complies with Canada's laws.[16]

And some scholars remarked:

> Google might have picked the market exit strategy because it genuinely cannot technically come up with a compliant registry in time. We find that surprising. There is no doubt that the new Canadian law is imperfect, but Google is likely capable of building a world-class searchable registry of political ads. One would assume a search-engine giant would be capable.[17]

The belief that technology companies can do just about anything asked of them is pervasive. But, to stay with online advertising, the ecosystem is both tremendously complicated and very different from broadcast and print media. In its testimony before a parliamentary committee,[18] Google stated that it allows advertisers to serve different types of ads on both Google and third-party sites. Advertisers bid for the opportunity to serve an ad to different users (in transactions lasting less than a second). The new regime requires any site running political ads to maintain a registry, but the technology powering the display of ads on third-party sites does not enable a site to obtain in a timely manner a copy of the ad it had displayed. This is very different from advertising on closed social networks, such as Facebook and Twitter, which explains why major social media platforms decided to accept the new rules, while most advertising networks (Google, Verizon Media) opted to prohibit advertising during the election.[19]

A different response is to turn the immense scope of online activities back on the companies. The mushroom-like growth of technology and social media is, to use a popular phrase, a feature, not a bug. That growth is directly responsible for the social media ills that societies now confront. The companies, on this view, can hardly plead innocence or impotence with regard to a problem of their own making. If the tech giants truly are unable to deal with the situation, they should be brought to heel regardless of the impact on their businesses (which critics view as having low social value anyway) or on how people interact with each other online (since such interactions tend to produce bad outcomes both for users and society as a whole).

A number of people, including US senator Elizabeth Warren, have taken direct aim at large tech companies, insisting that their market dominance raises legitimate anti-trust issues that could, eventually, support direct state action to break them up. Evaluating such arguments is beyond the scope of the present chapter, but their very existence indicates just how far the pendulum has swung. If law- and policymakers are willing to contemplate the dismantling of such iconic American companies, it is not a stretch to think that they would be willing to countenance specific action to curb perceived problematic speech.

First Principles

Freedom of expression is entrenched in the Constitution of Canada through section 2(b) of the *Charter of Rights*. Even prior to the *Charter*, enacted in 1982, a series of mid-twentieth-century cases articulated a theory that Canada had an "unwritten constitution," in which freedom of speech played a central role. For at least a century, then, Canada has had a strong tradition of respect for and promotion of free speech, particularly where that speech concerns "the freest and fullest analysis and examination from every point of view of political proposals."[20]

Expression is essential to the political governance of society and to individual searches for meaning. In the seminal case of *Keegstra*,[21] which concerned criminal laws against hate speech, the Supreme Court stated that the guarantee in section 2(b) enables Canadians to engage in democratic government, to determine truth in a variety of contexts, and to achieve self-fulfilment by creative, dialogic, and personal reflection. These are the underlying "core values" of the freedom, which, depending upon the context in which expression is engaged, are implicated in diverse ways and to different degrees.

Courts have interpreted the term "expression" broadly, extending it to any activity, short of physical violence, that is intended to convey meaning. Hate propaganda,[22] defamatory libel,[23] and publishing false news[24] have all been found to fall within the scope of the freedom. The Supreme Court has consistently recognized free expression as a pre-eminent right in the Canadian legal order, an "essential value of Canadian parliamentary democracy,"[25] and integral to "any system which values self-government."[26]

A law or state action can infringe freedom of expression by purpose or by effect. Purposeful interference is demonstrated where the state has restricted the *content* of expression by singling out particular meanings that are not to be conveyed; the *form* of expression in order to control access by others to its meaning; or the *ability* to convey meaning. A law that is neutral regarding expression will nonetheless have an infringing effect if it interferes with a person's attempt to express meaning, if their expression is in line with one of the core values described above.

Compared to the United States, the Canadian constitution grants the state more latitude to limit expression rights. That is because under section 1 of the *Charter*, rights and freedoms are subject to "reasonable limits": limits that are prescribed by law, and "demonstrably justified in a free and democratic society."[27] As a result, a number of laws that limit expression – criminal hate speech;[28] compelled health warnings on tobacco products;[29] prohibition on child-directed advertising[30] – have been upheld. For something to count as a reasonable limit, it must be animated by a "pressing and substantial objective" that is proportional to the rights limit in question. The limit must be "rationally connected" to the objective; minimally impairing of the *Charter* right; and must demonstrate proportionality between its salutary and deleterious effects.[31]

Because the *Charter*'s obligations extend principally to laws and state actors,[32] there might appear to be no *Charter* rights at issue when social media platforms decide what content to filter, prohibit, or amplify. It is true that so long as there is no actual legislative regime compelling them to do so, the actions of private companies that have the direct or indirect effect of limiting individuals' expression are immune from constitutional scrutiny. But many proposals (already enacted in some jurisdictions) include subjecting companies like Google, Facebook, and Twitter to specific regulatory control, or punishment, for content-related decisions. To the extent that such laws redound negatively to individual expressive rights, they would present at least a *prima facie* infringement of section 2(b). The government may not be targeting individual speakers directly, but if the effect of a law is to limit the full enjoyment of expressive freedom, it would be subject to constitutional scrutiny. Such a conclusion will be strengthened if there exists evidence that the government's purpose is to effect limits on what it considers harmful speech.

As well, governments increasingly apply informal pressure on companies to get them to "do the right thing and block, hinder, or take down content."[33] Governments buttress such requests by harnessing public anxieties to generate support, or they use the spectre of eventual regulation. This phenomenon has been called "jawboning."[34] Its relationship to freedom of expression is troubling, though somewhat under-explored in the Canadian context.[35] It is at least arguable that using the threat of regulation in order to effect certain content-related results implicates *Charter* rights as much as any subsequent regulation.

Finally, it is important to keep in mind the bearers of expression rights. Canadians are deemed capable of exercising political and personal judgment and applying discernment to what they read, write, record, watch, and listen to (see Moon, this volume). In the electoral context, the Supreme Court has affirmed that "the Canadian voter is a rational actor who can learn from experience and make independent judgments about the value of particular sources of electoral information."[36] There is little question that a similar presumption would apply to other contexts in which expression rights are threatened.

Attempts to regulate social media will not necessarily run afoul of the Canadian constitution. The government will have an opportunity to justify them as a reasonable limit on expression. But it should have to hand some evidence supporting a reasoned apprehension of harm, and some indication that it has appropriately balanced freedom of expression and its attendant principles against compelling state objectives. To date, there has been scant evidence of that sort of discussion in the context of social media.

Discomfiting Signals

On 15 March 2019, a white nationalist terrorist targeted a mosque in Christchurch, New Zealand, killing fifty-one people. For seventeen minutes, the killer broadcast the attack over Facebook Live, the platform's streaming service (according to Facebook, no complaints were received until twelve minutes after the livestream ended). Over the next twenty-four hours, the footage was shared in millions of additional videos. While Facebook acted expeditiously in removing at least 1.5 million of those videos, it admitted to facing a "whack-a-mole" problem: as material was pulled from one user account, new versions would surface.

The horrific event produced the "Christchurch Call" – "a commitment by Governments and tech companies to eliminate terrorist and violent extremist content online." The signatories expressed "the conviction that a free, open and secure internet offers extraordinary benefits to society" and that "respect for freedom of expression is fundamental," but stated that "no one has the right to create and share terrorist and violent extremist content online."[37]

The Christchurch principles are reflected in a number of laws. Both France and Germany threaten steep financial penalties for companies whose online sites and platforms host "hateful" content. Legal jeopardy kicks in very quickly – in some cases no more than twenty-four hours after a post. Australia has suggested that it is willing to imprison corporate officers.

In the United Kingdom, a 2019 white paper proposed a new regulatory framework wherein "a new duty of care towards users" would be overseen by an independent tribunal delegated to set "codes of practice" or to monitor tech companies to do the same. It urged that companies "be held to account for tackling a comprehensive set of online harms, ranging from illegal activity and content to behaviours which are harmful but not necessarily illegal," such as harassment, bullying, and promotion of certain ideas (like self-harm) that could present risks for vulnerable or young persons.[38]

To date, Canadian efforts to control or impose consequences on users or providers of social media content have been few. Exceptions include Nova Scotia's *Cyber-safety Act*[39] (struck down as unconstitutional in 2015);[40] the 2014 amendments to the *Criminal Code* prohibiting the electronic dissemination of intimate images (sometimes called "revenge porn");[41] and the 2018 changes to the *Canada Elections Act* regarding political and issue advertising. As discussed above, the latter include creating a registry on each platform that displays such ads, updated in real time, and that reveals their provenance, including who created and paid for them. In its 2019 federal election platform, the Liberal Party of Canada proposed instituting significant financial penalties for failing to remove hate speech, incitement to violence, exploitation of children, radicalization, and creation or distribution of terrorist propaganda.

In 2020, both the COVID-19 pandemic and the renewed attention to racism and police violence seem to have accelerated political interest in dealing with misleading or intolerant expression. It is not far-fetched to think that Canadian jurisdictions will seek to crack down on certain content on social media. Hate speech, violent extremism, and harassment are frequently cited as categories requiring oversight.

The proposals being discussed in Canada represent a worrisome development. The federal government has stated that it will seek to impose penalties for hosting expressive behaviour that society has not seen fit to punish directly. The penalties would fall not on the creators of such content, but on third parties. To be sure, the reality of modern communication is such that an individual speaker has relatively little power or ability to reach others. Very often, one's chances of exerting influence depend on harnessing technology to reach as many listeners or viewers as possible. Still, imposing intermediate liability constitutes a marked departure from the current framework, which has largely immunized third-party carriers for content that they neither create nor expressly endorse. Given the realities of social communication, it would represent a fundamental shift in how liberal societies conceptualize responsibility for expression writ large.

Traditionally, democratic societies have approached controls on free expression with caution, out of a belief that punishing or sanctioning any speech risks undermining essential features of the political and legal system. Core to these societies is the idea that citizens are entitled to interrogate essential moral questions, to question accepted wisdom, and to express their opposition to laws and policy without fear of reprisal.

To be sure, individual self-fulfilment cannot operate unbounded (see Bennett, this volume). As stated earlier, the Canadian constitution allows the state to subject expression to reasonable limits. Where speech is liable for the application of a criminal sanction, acceptable limits may include defining the offence to require proof of definitive, subjective *mens rea* (as opposed to an objective reasonableness standard of fault) and limiting its scope to extreme expression that society fears could lead to actual harm to individuals. In the context of state-enforced human rights codes, the *mens rea* requirement is absent but the content threshold for the expression is similarly stringent.[42] As well, the notion of "punishment" is largely absent, because the human rights context is meant to be educative and remedial.

Defending Free Expression in a Digital Age

Instituting greater controls on social media expression must reckon with the reaction of its millions upon millions of users. Recent dynamics suggests that that response is likely to be extremely negative. The negativity likely will not derive from a uniform hostility to greater control over expression, but from identity-based or partisan preferences over what, and whose, expression should be controlled (see Macfarlane, Moon, this volume). Individual users are also likely to believe that they are subject to greater controls than their rivals. Disputes often involve competing claims of moral and political wrong from separate marginalized groups. It is undesirable for the state to take a firm position where a conflict does not present an obvious and serious risk of harm or injury. For the state to put such an expectation on social media companies is an even worse proposition.

The public often construes expression as subject to less protection, and greater state control, than it actually is. Many people deem any speech that they find abhorrent as "hateful." No doubt, it is difficult to put aside one's personal reaction to offensive statements – particularly if those statements target a group or characteristic with which someone identifies – and apply the objective analysis that the law requires. Yet that objectivity is required as a matter of both statutory and constitutional obligation. Speech that engages in stereotype, descends into slurs, or is extremely caustic or aggressive may be deeply problematic without meeting the high legal threshold for hate speech.

Below, I discuss a few examples. While not all of the cited examples originated on social medial platforms, they quickly spilled onto them, and similar controversies erupt there regularly.[43] My purpose is to illustrate broader trends that redound negatively to free expression norms.

The first is the fight over gender pronouns waged by University of Toronto professor Jordan Peterson.[44] Peterson drew international attention in 2016 after publishing a series of videos objecting to the implications of greater recognition of the equality rights of transgender persons. Specifically, Peterson rejects the idea that society should change pronoun conventions – motivated by recognition and respect for gender nonconforming or non-binary persons – and call individuals who reject terms like "he" or "she" a word like "they." Peterson has a significant social media presence, including 1.5 million followers on Twitter and 2.78 million subscribers on YouTube.

Peterson's arguments are certainly open to critique. For example, he has made flatly incorrect predictions about federal laws that now recognize an individual's "gender identity." In 2018, the *Canadian Human Rights Act* and the *Criminal Code* were amended to include gender identity as a prohibited ground of discrimination, or a relevant personal characteristic. Peterson alleged that as a result he could face jail time for refusing to subscribe to new naming conventions in his university classes. The charge is inaccurate since Peterson's employer, the University of Toronto, is not subject to the federal human rights code, and there is no plausible argument that refusing to use someone's preferred pronouns would count as the "wilful promotion of hatred," as required by the criminal offence in question.

But Peterson's opponents likewise fall into error when they paint his provocative and occasionally disturbing statements as "hate speech."[45] The following excerpt from a 2016 discussion is representative:

PANELLIST #1: I think it's a common misconception about [the new federal law], that it's somehow going to make pronoun use into hate speech. If you actually look at the provisions, we're talking about very minor amendments to the Criminal Code ...

PETERSON: They're not minor. They put it into the hate speech category. They're not minor at all. That's a misstatement. Don't tell me they're minor. That's not right.
...

MODERATOR: [Panellist #2], can I be clear of something? You've accused him of abusing students by not using pronouns.

PANELLIST #2: That's how I see it.

MODERATOR: That is tantamount to abuse, in your view?

PANELLIST #2: Absolutely. Many ...

PETERSON: Is it tantamount to violence?

PANELLIST #2: Yes.

PETERSON: How about hate speech?

PANELLIST #2: Of course it's hate speech. You won't refer to [students] in a way that recognizes their humanity and dignity.[46]

Note that the first, more sober intervention by Panellist #1 (a law professor) was overshadowed by Panellist #2's dramatic claim that Peterson engages in abuse and hate. No one else on the panel challenged that claim. Not only was it unsupported as applied to Peterson's words (in my opinion), but in the specific context it played into Peterson's broader claim that much of transgender activism seeks merely to punish those who are "politically incorrect."

The second example concerns "gender critical" activists and scholars who argue that relying solely on a person's self-identification to determine their gender puts at risk legal protections for and, in some cases, the security of (cis) women and girls. They worry that self-identification will eliminate spaces (such as prisons or homeless shelters) created specifically to cater to women's needs. Transgender activists and supporters commonly describe such views as "hate speech." See, for example, the joint statement by Minorities and Philosophy UK and Minorities and Philosophy International protesting an appearance by philosopher Kathleen Stock at the Aristotelian Society;[47] the widely circulated online blog post titled "I Am Leaving Academic Philosophy Because of Its Transphobia Problem";[48] the objection to a speaker at the University of British Columbia;[49] and the outcry against the Toronto Public Library when it rented a room for a talk by feminist Meghan Murphy.[50]

The backlash against Murphy is particular interesting, since many who oppose her cite with approval the fact that she was banned from Twitter for mis-gendering a self-identified trans woman, Jessica Yaniv. Yaniv is herself notorious for repeatedly seeking out genital waxing services from racialized or immigrant women, and launching human rights complaints when refused. The BC Human Rights Tribunal dismissed the complaints in 2019, finding that they were made in bad faith.[51]

There is some irony in relying on Twitter to augment such a critique. Twitter's motivations for dealing with particular users are opaque and its commitment to equal application of its rules uncertain. Murphy's banishment from the platform is twinned with repeated characterizations of her views as hateful; her talk is alleged to expose trans persons to contempt and hatred, and to make them less safe.[52]

The debate over trans rights is difficult and painful. But we should not understate the allegation that a person is engaging in hate speech. Under the *Criminal Code*, the wilful promotion of hatred is a strictly indictable offence punishable by up to five years in prison. Calling someone a hate-monger implies that one finds their behaviour so egregious that they should be criminally punished, potentially including a jail sentence (it is possible to call someone out for hate outside a legal context, but the vast majority of persons do not make that distinction). It is for that reason, among others, that judicial interpretation of "hate propaganda" has stressed its exceptional nature, requiring proof beyond a reasonable doubt that the impugned expression reflects "detestation" and "extreme enmity" of targeted groups (see Macfarlane, this volume).[53]

One of the reasons that people seem more likely to perceive that controversial statements rise to the level of "hate speech" is that concepts like "harm," "safety," and "violence" have taken on ever-expanding meanings. For many, society has moved far beyond the idea that, sometimes, words can wound.[54] Today, persons regularly allege that they suffer grievous injury simply by the expression of controversial ideas, particularly if that expression is viewed as part of a debate putting into question a person or group's identity, status, rights, or privileges.

Numerous disciplines, including history, literature, and philosophy, have been called out for enabling academic discussion viewed as harmful to marginalized groups. In 2017, an article written by a feminist philosopher and published in the academic journal *Hypatia* interrogated the relevant distinctions between claims of being transgender and claims of being transracial, suggesting that those who advocate for social acceptance of the former may have few grounds to object to the latter.[55] Eight hundred persons signed a letter demanding the article's retraction. The signatories alleged that its many "failures of scholarship do harm to the communities who might expect better."[56] (While the *Hypatia* controversy involved a journal, the vast majority of it played out on social media, including Facebook, Twitter, and various academic blogs.[57]) After a *Hypatia* editorial subgroup appeared to agree with the critics, stating that the article should not have been published, the journal's editor intervened to defend both the article and the peer-review process through which it had passed. By that time, the author (who was untenured) had been subject to vitriolic criticism, both online and directly, including demands to her employer that she be fired.[58]

Some may not see the above examples as problematic because they agree with the criticisms voiced about the speakers or their positions. Others may concede that the rhetoric is troubling but deny that it indicates a broader problem. In my opinion, the examples are troubling to the extent that they reveal new expectations of tailoring speech to avoid social censure – speech that, even a few years ago, would have been accepted as part of legitimate debate.

The scale of social media greatly amplifies conflict. A single tweet can "go viral," attracting attention and condemnation from an audience limited only by the number of persons on the platform. The nature of the communication media itself seems to intensify conflict, raising the stakes for an unwise comment while also demanding simultaneous reply and response. After the open letter objecting to the *Hypatia* article came under stringent criticism, one of the signatories admitted that she felt great pressure to respond immediately because the article was causing so much pain to certain communities. That pain was expressed on platforms, such as Twitter and Facebook, where it could be easily and instantly shared with many thousands of people. Where, before, intense debate over a scholarly piece might have been hashed out in faculty lounges, conference panels, or reply essays, today they are likely to be waged on a global stage. (In some cases, to be sure, that very scale amplifies the negative consequences of ill-considered speech or invective.)

Privilege, and its corresponding social power, cuts across many lines: race, religion, sex, sexuality, gender, class, education, and professional status. Today, one might add to that "social media capital," or the degree to which someone already has a following, so that in a conflict they can expect support from thousands of people quite removed from the situation. This emergent factor affects the analysis of both individual vulnerability and problematic speech. A relatively obscure person might make an ill-advised, even intolerant, comment. If that comment is called out on social media by someone with tens of thousands of supporters, the negative effect on the "transgressor" may well be incommensurate with the original sin. And, of course, the tweet's initial "footprint" will be greatly magnified. Most people recognize the problem when someone like Donald Trump engages in such a tactic (in 2016, his tweets against a union organizer caused the person to experience extreme levels of harassment).[59] Even if the person doing the calling out is not as problematic as Trump – indeed, is otherwise admirable – social media presents a great temptation to rain down consequences on people out of all proportion to the ill effect of their words. If platforms are expected to police problematic expression, they may well respond more quickly and severely to speech called out by popular or powerful users, with profoundly unequal effects.

Choices for the State

Traditionally, free expression analysis has assumed a dyadic model: the individual citizens who engage in or are affected by speech acts, and the state that attempts to control, punish, or allocate their speech rights. Social media complicates the analysis. While there have always been intermediaries like publishers and other traditional media, tech companies represent an unprecedented change. Platforms have transformed the economy of speech – extending its possibilities to exponentially more speakers (and listeners), while also controlling much of the speech that actually takes place by creating networks dedicated to encouraging users to log on, click, download, watch, stream, and comment as much as possible. The cost to users and creators is not obvious: they make no, or minimal, direct financial contribution, but they attract immense advertising dollars, or provide to platforms the rich data of their personal information, activities, and tastes.

In dealing with the issue, governments confront at least two pressures. First, they cannot compete with the information array and user base that tech companies harness and make available. Certainly, governments have proved unwilling to devote the necessary resources to creating comparable digital infrastructure. And second, politicians themselves trade heavily on the benefits of social media. They stream town hall meetings and announcements on Facebook Live, they engage hundreds of thousands of people through Twitter, and they use Google to disseminate political advertising. They are, at least, as dependent upon social media as their constituents – even as they decry its ills.

The latter point may explain why political actors frequently speak out of both sides of their mouths: demanding greater controls on expression while simultaneously attacking platform decisions that they deem politically problematic. This is evident at parliamentary committees struck to examine issues like election interference or hate speech. At one meeting, Facebook might face criticism for its decision to not take down a manipulated video of Speaker of the US House of Representatives Nancy Pelosi (it instead labelled it as false).[60] One MP went so far as to state that the company was "claiming a sort of perverted defence claim of free speech."[61] But another member will upbraid YouTube for pulling down a constituent's video (most likely, for copyright infringement) without giving the user sufficient notice or an opportunity to appeal. Governments demand immediate and totalizing results yet strongly object (on constituents' behalf) to any perceived lack of due process. And, of course, they do not wish to be implicated in measures that might impose additional costs on voters.

Regulating expression highlights many tensions among competing values and goods. Providing an open and low-barrier platform risks exposing people to speech that is constitutionally protected but whose value is questionable. Ensuring the largest possible community for users (which goes some way towards mitigating the systemic obstacles to meaningful expression for marginalized groups) usually involves a trade-off with privacy. Control of speech that is considered harmful is extremely difficult to achieve at scale.[62]

The above factors may explain why the government response to concerns over social media has generally been to download responsibility for content moderation to the companies. The move sidesteps messy disputes that would implicate governments in decisions that might be unpopular with key constituents, and instead keeps the focus squarely on the platforms. Doing so, however, lodges responsibility for content moderation outside any public interest considerations. Instead, it overlays it with private corporate missions that, if they do not squarely contradict broader social goals, cannot be expected to reliably prioritize them either (see Moon, this volume).[63]

Given the above considerations, governments ought not to rely on third parties to both ensure access to the benefits of the internet (chiefly, by offering access to search engines and to browsing and social platforms for no direct cost) *and* police speech (such as material thought to be harmful, offensive, troll-ish, bullying, and inhibiting of others' expression) that falls outside the small category of materials that are actually illegal. If the state is unwilling to assume the responsibility for preserving and promoting digital infrastructure, then it would be best for it to refrain from imposing prior restraint systems upon non-state actors. While it would be ambitious for governments to take on the challenge of tending to digital infrastructure, I believe it strikes the most principled stance vis-à-vis the differing objectives in play.

Such a move would no doubt face objections from all sides of the free expression debate. One that dovetails with the general sympathies articulated in this chapter is that state involvement risks greater, and more problematic, infringements on speech. While that is a fair concern, it is quite possible that an entirely state-controlled social media would on balance produce less infringement on expression than would farming out the task to private actors. That is because, when private actors are subject to state sanction or penalty for the material they convey but have not created, their most likely response is to over-regulate through prior restraint – to set up *ex ante* guardrails *beyond* their rational calculation of what kind of speech is prohibited – in order to ensure the greatest certainty for themselves. In such an environment, individual tailoring is likely to go out the window, in part because of the scale issues discussed earlier, and in part because the companies will eschew taking on such a role openly.

The state, by contrast, is not in the same position when it both enacts standards and bears the primary responsibility for abiding by them. That certainly will not ease all the fears, nor will it avoid other problems, particularly as regards adverse effects caused by systemic inequality and implicit biases. Nevertheless, acknowledging that it is for the state to take greater control and responsibility for regulating content would be a more honest – if not necessarily easier – approach to a continued vexing problem.

NOTES

* I wish to thank three anonymous reviewers for their comments.

1 Robert S. Mueller III, *Report on the Investigation into Russian Interference in the 2016 Presidential Election*, vol. 1 (Washington, DC: Department of Justice, 2019), https://www.justsecurity.org/wp-content/uploads/2019/04/Muelller-Report -Redacted-Vol-I-Released-04.18.2019-Word-Searchable.-Reduced-Size.pdf; Sarmishta Subramanian, "Is Canada Broken?" *The Walrus*, 19 September 2019, https://thewalrus.ca/democracy-is-canada-broken/.

2 I use "social media" to encompass social networks, search engines, forums, messaging services, and, in the words of the UK white paper, any website allowing "users to share or discover user-generated content or interact with each other."

3 General Data Protection Regulation 2016/679.

4 For the French context, see "Loi no. 2020-766 du 24 juin 2020 visant à lutter contre les contenus haineux sur internet," *Journal officiel lois et décrets*, no. 0156 (25 June 2020), https://www.legifrance.gouv.fr/jorf/id/JORFTEXT000042031970, and Chloe Hadavas, "France's New Online Hate Speech Law Is Fundamentally Flawed" *Slate*, 26 May 2020, https://slate.com/technology/2020/05/france-hate-speech-law -lutte-contre-haine-sur-internet.html. For more on the German *Network Enforcement Act* (*NetzDG*), see "Inside Germany's Crackdown on Hate Speech," Mozilla, April 2019, https://internethealthreport.org/2019/inside-germanys -crackdown-on-hate-speech/.

5 Secretary of State for Digital, Culture, Media and Sport, and Secretary of State for the Home Department, "Online Harms White Paper: Full Government Response to the Consultation," 15 December 2020, Cmnd. 354, https://www.gov .uk/government/consultations/online-harms-white-paper/outcome/online-harms -white-paper-full-government-response.

6 See, for example, the bills proposed by Republican Senator Josh Hawley: *Social Media Addiction Reduction Technology Act*, S. 2314, 116th Congress (2019–20), https://www.hawley.senate.gov/sites/default/files/2019-07/Social-Media -Addiction-Reduction-Technology-Act.pdf; *Ending Support for Internet Censorship Act*, S. 1914, 116th Congress (2019–20), https://www.hawley.senate.gov/sites /default/files/2019-06/Ending-Support-Internet-Censorship-Act-Bill-Text.pdf. Senator Hawley has expressed disdain for social media, calling it "a parasite on productive investment, on meaningful relationships, on a healthy society." See Emily Stewart, "Josh Hawley's Bill to Limit Your Twitter Time to 30 Minutes a Day, Explained," *Vox*, 31 July 2019, https://www.vox.com/recode/2019/7/31/20748732 /josh-hawley-smart-act-social-media-addiction.

7 *Sable Communications v FCC*, 492 US 115 (1989); *RAV v City of St. Paul*, 505 US 377 (1992).

8 Public Policy Forum, "Poisoning Democracy: How Canada Can Address Harmful Speech Online," November 2018, https://ppforum.ca/wp-content/uploads/2018/11 /PoisoningDemocracy-PPF-1.pdf.

9 *Criminal Code*, RSC 1985, c C-46, s 318.

10 Kit Smith, "126 Amazing Social Media Statistics and Facts," *Brandwatch*, 30 December 2019, https://www.brandwatch.com/blog/amazing-social-media -statistics-and-facts/#section-15.

11 One critique of the platforms is that they behave like traditional media publishers to the extent that they exert any sort of content control and, therefore, should be subject to the same responsibilities. If that is indeed the correct approach, then a logical response would be to exert no control whatsoever, or to behave exactly like newspapers and pre-select *all* content. The sheer scale of the communications at issue, and the fact that it is generated by users, however, are salient differences between platforms and traditional publishers, with broad implications for free expression norms. No reasonable person would wish for a totally unregulated

internet. But subjecting all platform content to pre-vetting is equally as problematic.

12 Ari Feldman, "As YouTube Cracks Down on Holocaust Denial, It Deletes Anti-Semitism Researcher's Account," *Forward*, 6 June 2019, https://forward.com/fast-forward/425532/youtube-holocaust-denial-anti-semitism-researcher-account/.

13 Sarah T. Roberts, *Behind the Screen: Content Moderation in the Shadows of Social Media* (New Haven, CT: Yale University Press, 2019); Terry Gross, "For Facebook Content Moderators, Traumatizing Material Is a Job Hazard," *Fresh Air*, NPR, 1 July 2019, https://www.npr.org/2019/07/01/737498507/for-facebook-content-moderators-traumatizing-material-is-a-job-hazard.

14 *Election Modernization Act*, SC 2018, c 31.

15 Tom Cardoso, "Google to Ban Political Ads Ahead of Federal Election, Citing New Transparency Rules," *Globe and Mail*, 4 March 2019, https://www.theglobeandmail.com/politics/article-google-to-ban-political-ads-ahead-of-federal-election-citing-new/.

16 Ibid.

17 Elizabeth Dubois, Fenwick McKelvey, and Taylor Owen, "What Have We Learned from Google's Political Ad Pullout?," *Policy Options*, 10 April 2019, https://policyoptions.irpp.org/magazines/april-2019/learned-googles-political-ad-pullout/.

18 Canada, House of Commons Standing Committee on Access to Information, Privacy and Ethics (Meeting No. 148, 9 May 2019), 42nd Parl., 1st Sess., https://www.ourcommons.ca/DocumentViewer/en/42-1/ETHI/meeting-148/evidence.

19 But see the decision by Twitter on 30 October 2019 to ban all paid political and issue advertising on its platform: Associated Press, "Twitter Bans All Political Advertising on Its Service, Diverging from Rival Facebook," CBC News, 30 October 2019, https://www.cbc.ca/news/technology/twitter-bans-political-advertisements-1.5341655.

20 *Reference Re Alberta Statutes – The Bank Taxation Act; The Credit of Alberta Regulation Act; and the Accurate News and Information Act*, [1938] SCR 100 at 133.

21 *R. v Keegstra*, [1990] 3 SCR 697.

22 Ibid.

23 *R. v Lucas*, 1998 CanLII 815 (SCC), [1998] 1 SCR 439, [1998] SCJ No 28.

24 *R. v Zundel*, 1992 CanLII 75 (SCC), [1992] 2 SCR 731, [1992] SCJ No 70.

25 See *Keegstra*, *supra* note 21.

26 *Committee for the Commonwealth of Canada v Canada*, [1991] 1 SCR 139.

27 Occasionally the argument is made that the equal enjoyment of rights between male and female persons is absolutely guaranteed by section 28 (which is found among the *Charter*'s interpretative sections and therefore is not generally considered to have substantive effect). But Canadian courts have applied a section 1 analysis to sex-based equality claims without considering section 28. See *R. v Hess; R. v Nguyen*, [1990] 2 SCR 906 (minority opinion).

28 See *Keegstra*, *supra* note 21.

29 *Canada (Attorney General) v JTI-Macdonald Corp.*, [2007] 2 SCR 610, 2007 SCC 30.

30 *Irwin Toy Ltd. v* Quebec (Attorney General), [1989] 1 SCR 927.

31 *R. v Oakes*, [1986] 1 SCR 103.

32 *Charter*, section 32(1):
This Charter applies
(*a*) to the Parliament and government of Canada in respect of all matters within the authority of Parliament including all matters relating to the Yukon Territory and Northwest Territories; and
(*b*) to the legislature and government of each province in respect of all matters within the authority of the legislature of each province.
See also, *Eldridge v British Columbia (Attorney General)*, [1997] 3 SCR 624.

33 Jack M. Balkin, "Free Speech in the Algorithmic Society: Big Data, Private Governance, and New School Speech Regulation," *University of California Davis Law Review* 51 (2018): 1177

34 Derek E. Bambauer, "Against Jawboning," *Minnesota Law Review* 100 (2015): 51, 84–8.

35 But see Michael Karanicolas, "Subverting Democracy to Save Democracy: Canada's Extra-Constitutional Approaches to Battling "Fake News," *Canadian Journal of Law and Technology* 17, no. 2 (2019), https://papers.ssrn.com/sol3/papers .cfm?abstract_id=3423092.

36 *Thompson Newspapers Co. v Canada (Attorney General)*, [1998] 1SCR 877 at para 112.

37 The text of the Christchurch Call is available at https://www.christchurchcall.com/.

38 Gian Volpicelli, "All That's Wrong with the UK's Crusade against Online Harms," *Wired*, 9 April 2019, https://www.wired.co.uk/article/online-harms-white -paper-uk-analysis.

39 *Cyber-safety Act*, SNS 2013, c 2.

40 *Crouch v Snell*, 2015 NSSC 340.

41 *Criminal Code*, RSC 1985, c C-46, s 162.1; for discussion, see Carissima Mathen, "Crowdsourcing Sexual Objectification," *Laws* 3, no. 3 (2014): 529.

42 *Saskatchewan (Human Rights Commission) v Whatcott*, 2013 SCC 11, [2013] 1 SCR 467.

43 For a related controversy that arose on Twitter after this chapter was completed, see the reaction to tweets by author J.K. Rowling concerning whether people other than "women" can menstruate: Lisa Machado, "J.K. Rowling Muddied the Message about Lack of Hygiene Products," *Healthing.ca*, 9 June 2020, https://www.healthing .ca/opinion/j-k-rowling-shows-us-again-the-ease-of-social-media-hate.

44 See, for example, Senate of Canada, Standing Committee on Legal and Constitutional Affairs over *Bill C-16: An Act to Amend the Canadian Human Rights Act and the Criminal Code Evidence* (17 May 2017), 42nd Parl., 1st Sess., https:// sencanada.ca/en/Content/SEN/Committee/421/lcjc/53339-e.

45 Peterson is also frequently called "alt-right," a term he takes great exception to, going so far as to initiate defamation proceedings. See Peter Goffin, "Jordan Peterson Sues Wilfrid Laurier University for Defamation over Staff Remarks during Meeting," *Toronto Star*, 21 June 2918, https://www.thestar.com/news /canada/2018/06/21/jordan-peterson-sues-wilfrid-laurier-university-for -defamation-over-staff-remarks-during-meeting.html.

46 For video of the panel discussion, see "Genders, Rights and Freedom of Speech," *The Agenda with Steve Paikin*, TVO, 26 October 2016, https://www.tvo.org/video /genders-rights-and-freedom-of-speech. A transcript of the discussion is also available at https://www.tvo.org/transcript/2396103/genders-rights-and-freedom -of-speech. Panelist #1 was University of Ottawa law professor Kyle Kirkup. Panelist #2 was Nicholas Matte, a lecturer at the University of Toronto.

47 "Joint Statement in Response to the Aristotelian Society Talk on 3rd June 2019," *MAPUK*, 3 June 2019, is no longer on the organization's website. It was discussed in a blog post by Justin Weinberg, "Trans Women and Philosophy: Learning from Recent Events," *Daily Nous*, 5 June 2019, http://dailynous.com/2019/06/05/trans -women-philosophy-learning-recent-events/. Portions were also reproduced in Ophelia Benson, "They Would Do Well to Repudiate This Embarrassment from the UK Chapter," *Butterflies and Wheels* (blog), 4 June 2019, at http://www .butterfliesandwheels.org/2019/they-would-do-well-to-repudiate-this -embarrassment-from-the-uk-chapter/.

48 t philosopher, "I Am Leaving Academic Philosophy Because of Its Transphobia Problem," *Medium*, 30 May 2019, https://medium.com/@transphilosopher33/i-am -leaving-academic-philosophy-because-of-its-transphobia-problem-bc618aa55712. The article was retweeted and "liked" many hundreds of times, and was the subject of a post attracting over 250 comments on the influential online philosophy blog *Daily Nous*. See Weinberg, "Trans Women and Philosophy."

49 The talk was entitled "The Erosion of Freedom: How Transgender Politics in School and Society Is Undermining Our Freedom and Harming Women and Children." For a statement summarizing these objections, see Joey Hansen, "Memo to Members Regarding the Anti-SOGI Event at Point Grey Campus," accessed 30 April 2021, https://aaps.ubc.ca/member/news/memo-member-regarding -anti-sogi-event-point-grey-campus. Of particular note is the claim that "[the invited speaker] indicates that 'transgender politics' are harming women and children. He alleges that transgender individuals are mentally ill and that any attempts to educate children about the issues transgender individuals face is 'brainwashing.' I believe these comments are wilfully promoting hate against transgender individuals."

50 " 'I'm Not Going to Reconsider': Toronto's Top Librarian Refuses to Bar Speaker Critical of Transgender Rights," *As It Happens*, CBC Radio, 17 October 2019, https://www.cbc.ca/radio/asithappens/as-it-happens-thursday-edition-1.5324424 /i-m-not-going-to-reconsider-toronto-s-top-librarian-refuses-to-bar-speaker

-critical-of-transgender-rights-1.5324431; Gwen Benaway, "This Is What Happened When I Stood Up Publicly for Trans Rights in Toronto," *Flare Magazine*, 28 October 2019, https://www.flare.com/news/toronto-public-library -meghan-murphy-trans-rights/; Glad Day Bookshop, "Glad Day Statement on Transphobic Event at the TPL," Facebook, 29 October 2019, https://www .facebook.com/GladDay/posts/glad-day-statement-on-transphobic-event-at-the -tpltuesday-october-29-2019glad-da/2495308547172600/. Murphy is similarly concerned about some aspects of recognizing gender expression as a protected ground of discrimination; and she rejects the idea that there are no relevant differences between trans and cis women. See Meghan Murphy, "Bill C-16 Misunderstands What Gender Is and How It Harms Women under Patriarchy," *Feminist Current*, 11 May 2017, https://www.feministcurrent.com/2017/05/11 /bill-c-16-misunderstands-gender-harms-women-patriarchy/.

51 *Yaniv v Various Waxing Salons (No. 2)*, 2019 BCHRT 222, https://www.canlii.org/en /bc/bchrt/doc/2019/2019bchrt222/2019bchrt222.html?resultIndex=2 at para 134.

52 In fairness, it should be noted that the chief librarian, Vickery Bowles, has repeatedly cited as a reason for not cancelling the booking the fact that Murphy has never been charged with a hate crime (though she also offered that having reviewed Murphy's prior talks she did not find anything "hateful" in them). See "I'm Not Going to Reconsider," *supra* note 50.

53 See *Whatcott, supra* note 42.

54 Mari Matsuda, *Words That Wound: Critical Race Theory, Assaultive Speech, and the First Amendment* (New York: Routledge, 1993).

55 Rebecca Tuvel, "In Defence of Transracialism," *Hypatia* 32, no. 2 (2017): 263–78. I acknowledge that some transgender persons reject the term "transgenderism," but it was used in the article and offers the necessary comparison with transracialism.

56 The alleged failures were using "vocabulary and frameworks not recognized, accepted, or adopted by the conventions of the relevant subfields," such as "deadnaming" a trans woman (i.e., parenthetically referring to Caitlyn Jenner by her birth name of "Bruce"); mischaracterizing "various theories and practices relating to religious identity and conversion," most notably Judaism; misrepresenting "leading accounts of belonging to a racial group" and incorrectly citing a particular race theorist; and failing "to seek out and sufficiently engage with scholarly work by those who are most vulnerable to the intersection of racial and gender oppressions (women of color) in its discussion of 'transracialism.'" It should be noted that Tuvel apologized for "deadnaming" and requested that the article be amended to remove the reference to "Bruce Jenner." At the time of writing, the text of the open letter was available at https://docs.google.com/forms/d/1efp9C0MHch_6Kfgtlm0PZ76nirWtc EsqWHcvgidl2mU/viewform?ts=59066d20&edit_requested=true.

57 See Justin Weinberg, "Philosopher's Article on Transracialism Sparks Controversy (Updated with Response from Author)," *Daily Nous*, 1 May 2017, http://dailynous

.com/2017/05/01/philosophers-article-transracialism-sparks-controversy/. The post also includes several associated links pertaining to this controversy.

58 Interview with Rebecca Tuvel, *What Is it Like to Be a Philosopher?*, 5 October 2017, http://www.whatisitliketobeaphilosopher.com/#/rebecca-tuvel/; see also Weinberg, "Philosopher's Article on Transracialism Sparks Controversy."

59 Scott Horsely, "Trump Takes Aim at Union Official over Carrier Job Count," *NPR*, 8 December 2016, https://www.npr.org/2016/12/08/504815928/trump-takes -aim-at-union-official-over-carrier-job-count.

60 Donnie O'Sullivan, "Doctored Videos Shared to Make Pelosi Sound Drunk Viewed Millions of Times on Social Media," *CNN*, 24 May 2019, https://www.cnn.com /2019/05/23/politics/doctored-video-pelosi/index.html.

61 See the Honourable Peter Kent's comments (at 12:30) in Canada, House of Commons Standing Committee on Access to Information, Privacy and Ethics (Meeting No. 153, 28 May 2019), 42nd Parl., 1st Sess., https://www.ourcommons.ca /DocumentViewer/en/42-1/ETHI/meeting-153/evidence.

62 See Mike Masnick, "The Impossibility of Content Moderation: YouTube's New Ban on Nazis Hits Reporter Who Documents Extremism, Professor Teaching About Hitler," *Techdirt*, 7 June 2019, https://www.techdirt.com/articles/20190606 /14122842345/impossibility-content-moderation-youtubes-new-ban-nazis-hits -reporter-who-documents-extremism-professor-teaching-about-hitler.shtml.

63 See the response to Facebook CEO Mark Zuckerberg's speech insisting that Facebook cannot vet political speech, even to remove falsehoods in Steven Levy, "Zuckerberg Doubles Down on Free Speech – the Facebook Way," *Wired*, 17 October 2019, https://www.wired.com/story/zuckerberg-doubles-down -free-speech-facebook-way/#:~:targetText=Zuckerberg%20Doubles%20Down %20on%20Free%20Speech%E2%80%94the%20Facebook%20Way,the %20world%20a%20better%20place.&targetText=Essentially%2C%20he's%20saying %E2%80%94as%20he,that%20Facebook%20is%20essentially%20positive. See also Siva Vaidhyanathan, "Mark Zuckerberg Doesn't Understand Free Speech in the 21st Century," *Guardian*, 18 October 2019, https://www.theguardian.com /commentisfree/2019/oct/18/mark-zuckerberg-free-speech-21st-century.

6 The Right to Protest and Counter-Protest: Complexities and Considerations

CARA FAITH ZWIBEL[*]

Those who argue forcefully and sincerely for the robust protection of freedom of expression often say that the best response to speech you don't like is not censorship or silencing, but more speech. When faced with hateful and harmful rhetoric, the answer is not to turn away, but to step up, engage, and counter. Those who posit counter-speech as a "solution" often imagine a dialogue or, at a minimum, monologues taken in turns. But if the speech/counter-speech dynamic simply turns into a cacophony of voices where only the loudest or most visible wins, have the interests of free expression been served? Alternatively, if counter-speech functions in a way that effectively obliterates or renders invisible the initial message, is this the free speech that advocates have in mind?

This chapter probes whether there is a point at which speech and counter-speech – particularly in the context of protests and counter-protests – conflict in a manner that genuinely undermines expressive freedom. It begins with a brief discussion of the right to protest as protected by the *Canadian Charter of Rights and Freedoms*.[1] I argue that the *Charter* not only requires that state-imposed limitations on protest be held to a stringent justification standard, but also that there are times when the state may be required to take affirmative steps to facilitate the exercise of this right. In the next section, I consider some of the principles that Canadian courts have used in fashioning both the scope of freedom of expression and the contours of its limitations and consider how these principles function in the context of protests. In particular, I look at the exclusion of violence and threats of violence from the section 2(b) protection and the role that location plays in determining whether expression gets the benefit of *Charter* protection. I also scrutinize the role of the audience by discussing how courts have characterized the dynamics between speaker and listener.

I then touch briefly on the ways in which the right to protest can be limited and specifically examine the Supreme Court of Canada's recent consideration of a purported police power to arrest for an apprehended breach of the peace.[2] I argue that this decision may prove to be a significant step forward in affirming the right to protest and clarifying the limitations on police interference. Finally, I explore some of the situations where protesters and counter-protesters clash and address the post-secondary context in which such clashes may become the subject of regulation and discipline. In this section, I take a close look at a recent case from the Alberta Court of Appeal[3] that raises the competing rights of protesters and counter-protesters. I will conclude by briefly discussing the factors to consider in analysing instances where the expressive freedoms of two or more groups clash. My argument is that the state has an obligation to facilitate the exercise of free expression even in situations of competition. I recognize that there will be instances where efforts to protect the rights of one group may cross a line and unduly burden the rights of another. Attempting to draw this line is no easy task, but I contend that it is worth the effort to at least begin sketching its outlines in order to advance our thinking on both freedom of expression and its limits.

The Right to Protest

Freedom of expression is essential to a democratic form of government; the exercise of most other rights is dependent on its meaningful protection. The importance of this freedom was recognized long before the *Charter* entrenched its protection in 1982. In 1938 the Supreme Court was asked to consider whether Alberta could enact a statute requiring newspapers in the province to publish a government reply to any criticism of provincial policies.[4] Two of the judges recognized it as "axiomatic that the practice of this right of free public discussion of public affairs ... is the breath of life for parliamentary institutions."[5]

In the *Charter* era, the Supreme Court's early statements highlight the central role that freedom of expression plays in a democracy:

> Freedom of expression was entrenched in our *Constitution* and is guaranteed in the Quebec *Charter* so as to ensure that everyone can manifest their thoughts, opinions, beliefs, indeed all expressions of the heart and mind, however unpopular, distasteful or contrary to the mainstream. Such protection is, in the words of both the Canadian and Quebec Charters, "fundamental" because in a free, pluralistic and democratic society we prize a diversity of ideas and opinions for their inherent value both to the community and to the individual. Free expression was for Cardozo J. of the United States Supreme Court "the matrix, the indispensable condition of nearly every other form of freedom"; for Rand J. of the Supreme Court of Canada, it was "little less vital to man's mind and spirit than breathing is to his physical existence."[6]

Although freedom of expression is often conceived of as an individual right, its power can increase exponentially when combined with the freedom to peacefully assemble and associate.[7] This bundle of rights is what allows for collective action – including collective forms of expression – in order to pursue political and social goals. For reasons that are not obvious, there has been almost no meaningful independent jurisprudence developed under the *Charter's* protection of freedom of peaceful assembly,[8] and freedom of association case law has largely focused on collective action in the labour context. As a result, cases that implicate the rights of protesters tend to focus on freedom of expression and its limits, as well as common law and constitutional restrictions on police powers.

Without engaging in a debate about whether the *Charter* protects "positive rights," my contention is that the *Charter* does require state facilitation of the right to protest, simply by virtue of the nature of protest and of the public locales in which it is most likely to take place.[9] For example, Ontario's *Police Services Act*[10] recognizes in its Declaration of Principles the "importance of safeguarding the fundamental rights guaranteed by the *Canadian Charter of Rights and Freedoms* and the *Human Rights Code*."[11] Moreover, in a Joint Report on the Proper Management of Assemblies, two United Nations special rapporteurs noted that states should plan properly for assemblies, including the development of contingency plans and precautionary measures to de-escalate tense situations and reduce the risk of violence.[12]

Free Expression Fundamentals

There are a few fundamental principles and assumptions that need to be addressed before we consider whether or how protest and counter-protest can be reconciled in a way that best facilitates freedom of expression for all. First, we need to be mindful of the scope of protection for expressive freedom under the *Charter* and, in particular, the types of expression that, either because of content or location, are simply not protected by section 2(b) according to the current jurisprudence. Second, we need to consider the place of the audience or listener and how their role may impact which limits on expression may be deemed reasonable, and which may not.

Conflating Violence, Hate, and Fear

The Supreme Court has long recognized that, despite the breadth of section 2(b)'s protection, there are some *forms* of expression that are simply beyond its ambit. In particular, the Court has held that while violence may well have expressive content, it is not protected by section 2(b).[13] The Court has also made plain that the violence exception includes "threats of violence" since both categories "undermine the very values and social conditions that are necessary for the continued existence of freedom of expression."[14] (For a more fulsome discussion of whether the values and social conditions necessary for free expression are eroding in the modern era, see Moon, this volume).

While hateful or extremely offensive speech may be experienced by its targets as a form of violence, this does not mean that it "qualifies" as violence for the purposes of a *Charter* analysis under the existing case law. Debates about the evidentiary threshold for establishing harm raise important questions for the purposes of a legal analysis, but there seems little reason to doubt that some messages hurt (on the strength of the evidence of harm, see Macfarlane, this volume). A group of protesters that show up at a Pride parade and say that celebrants will "burn in hell" may reasonably be perceived as engaging in acts of violence (or threats) against the community. Such a perception is fostered not only by the specific words used, but also by the decision of protesters to communicate their message on a day that is meant to be about celebrating and taking pride in your identity. Similarly, anti-immigrant rhetoric that urges people to "go back" where they came from may also be experienced as a form of violence; the perception of this message as a threat may be heightened depending on the time, place, and manner in which the view is expressed.

Those who have had the unfortunate experience of facing these and other messages may well experience them as acts of violence, but the current jurisprudence takes a much more literal approach to the term's meaning. Moreover, as offensive as these types of "counter-protests" may be to their targets, they will not always place an undue burden on expressive freedoms. Putting up with those who take issue with – and seek to counter – your message is part of living in a free society. As a result, such messages do benefit from section 2(b) protection and any limitations will have to be justified under section 1, the *Charter*'s reasonable limits clause.

This point is significant in the protest context, because tensions and emotions tend to be high in these situations, particularly if there is a competition between protesters and those wishing to counter their message. The Ontario Court of Appeal recently highlighted the issue in *Bracken v Fort Erie*.[15] It held that a municipality had unlawfully issued a trespass notice against an individual protester. Rather than involving a minority group being targeted with hateful expression, *Bracken* concerned an arguably much easier and more mundane case – a disgruntled citizen unhappy with the actions of his municipal government. He mounted a protest – consisting only of himself and a megaphone – outside of city hall prior to a public meeting.[16] Because of previous interactions with some municipal staff when Mr. Bracken was angry, the staff argued that they felt fearful and intimidated by his protests outside of city hall, so they contacted the police and issued a trespass notice. In a shocking decision, the Superior Court judge who first heard Bracken's challenge to the notice held that his expression was not protected under section 2(b) because of the exclusionary rule against violence.[17] The Court of Appeal took special care to correct this error. After pointing out the paucity of evidence about the supposed danger posed by the lone protester (observed by all staff from a safe distance on the day in question),[18] the Court noted that

> Violence is not the mere absence of civility. The application judge extended the concept of violence to include actions and words associated with a traditional form of political protest, on the basis that some Town employees claimed they felt "unsafe." This goes much too far. A person's subjective feelings of disquiet, unease, and even fear, are not in themselves capable of ousting expression categorically from the protection of s. 2(b).
>
> The consequences of characterizing an act as violence or a threat of violence are extreme: it conclusively defeats the *Charter* claim without consideration of any other factor. Accordingly, courts must be vigilant in determining whether the evidence supports the characterization, and in not inadvertently expanding the category of what constitutes violence or threats of violence.
>
> ... A protest does not cease to be peaceful simply because protestors are loud and angry. Political protesters can be subject to restrictions to prevent them from disrupting others, but they are not required to limit their upset in order to engage their constitutional right to engage in protest.[19]

While the point may seem obvious, it is worth emphasizing at a time when popular discussion of "safe spaces" seems to suggest to some that barriers to free expression can be easily erected and justified. Very often the primary purpose of a protest is to disrupt and disturb. The fact that messages may incite fear or discomfort in some does not eliminate or lessen the need to ensure that any restriction on expressive freedom is reasonable and demonstrably justified.

Location as a Proxy for Reconciling Competing Rights

Another important consideration relevant to the protest/counter-protest dilemma is location. While it is said that a private property owner may exclude the public (and thus the public's expressive activity) from his or her property, the more difficult question involves how to draw lines in what are traditionally considered public spaces. The dividing line between public and private spaces may also not be as clear as it once was. There are many privately owned spaces that effectively function (or may even be designated) as public spaces.[20]

Canadian case law considers the historical and actual function of the location where the expressive activity occurs and asks whether these are "incompatible with expression or suggest that expression within it would undermine the values underlying free expression."[21] As Chief Justice Lamer in *Committee for the Commonwealth of Canada v Canada* stated,

> The fact that one's freedom of expression is intrinsically limited by the function of a public place is an application of the general rule that one's rights are always

circumscribed by the rights of others. In the context of expressing oneself in the places owned by the state, it can be said that, under s.2(*b*), the freedom of expression is circumscribed at least by the very function of the place.[22]

While location is here characterized as a factor that defines the scope of 2(b) protection, it also feeds into a section 1 analysis. Government objectives associated with particular public spaces, and the various uses to which those spaces may be put, will inform the analysis under rational connection, minimal impairment, and proportionality. In these cases, location may function, at least in part, as a proxy for the reconciliation of competing interests.

Some of the case law that came out of the Occupy protests that took place across Canada in 2011 help to highlight the point. In these cases, courts were asked to consider the rights of the Occupy protesters, who typically brought their movement to public parks with no concrete plans to leave. The act of occupying the space by camping overnight was seen as an essential part of the message that the protesters wanted to communicate. Since expression in a public park cannot be said to be incompatible with the purposes underlying free expression, attempts to evict the protesters infringed section 2(b) and had to be justified under section 1.[23] At the same time, some of these public spaces had arguably ceased to operate as they were intended to, and the broader public (i.e., those not involved in Occupy) argued they were being denied access to and use of the space. In assessing whether the eviction of protesters could be justified under section 1, courts considered the government objective of regulating the use of parks for the benefit of the public and determined that restricting certain activities (e.g., camping) and access to the park at certain times (e.g., overnight) was reasonable.[24]

The Significance of an Audience

Even if a particular location is compatible with expressive activity and may be an obvious site for protest, the goals of the speaker may not be achieved if confined to these spaces. Freedom of expression may in part be about self-fulfilment, but the goal of a speaker is usually to be heard, at least by someone. Freedom of expression could hardly be considered meaningfully protected if the state could relegate expression to venues where no audience could or would attend.

During the Toronto G20 in the summer of 2010, the police urged those who intended to protest to exercise their rights in a "designated speech zone" at Queen's Park.[25] The venue is clearly an appropriate site for protest, but it was also nearly three kilometres away from the site of the summit at the Metro Toronto Convention Centre. For those protesters who wanted the world leaders in attendance to be aware of their message, this distance completely undermined their expressive goals. Even if it may be reasonable to keep protesters at some distance to ensure that summit participants were not prevented from conducting their business, this should not require a distance where protesters can be neither seen nor heard.[26]

The other side of the coin is that Canadian law recognizes that there is no right to a captive audience. Just as the *Charter* protects the right to speak and to choose not to speak, it also protects the right to listen and to choose not to listen. In *Ontario (Attorney General) v Dieleman*,[27] Ontario's Superior Court considered whether to grant the provincial government an injunction restraining protesters from engaging in certain activities within zones close to abortion clinics and the residences of abortion providers. Relying on Canadian and American jurisprudence, Justice Adams wrote the following:

> The principle behind a constitutional aversion to "captive audiences" is that forced listening "destroys and denies, practically and symbolically, that unfettered interplay and competition among ideas which is the assumed ambient of the communication freedoms"... Free speech, accordingly, does not include a right to have one's message listened to. In fact, an important justification for permitting people to speak freely is that those to whom the message is offensive may simply "avert their eyes" or walk away. Where this is not possible, one of the fundamental assumptions supporting freedom of expression is brought into question.[28]

This concern about a captive (and potentially vulnerable) audience has come to a head in many other cases. In a recent series of decisions dealing with graphic anti-abortion ads on public buses,[29] courts expressed particular concern about the impact of the message on young children. Implicit in some of these cases is the assumption that an audience will either listen to a speaker or choose not to. There are, of course, other possible audience responses that must be considered. While Canadian case law that squarely addresses audience reaction is thin, the American jurisprudence that speaks to the problem of the "hostile audience" and the "heckler's veto" is fairly well developed.

The early American cases seemed to accept that restrictions could be placed on expression because of the potential for a negative audience reaction. Thus, in the early 1950s, the US Supreme Court upheld a disorderly conduct conviction against Mr. Feiner, who had given a speech that the police feared would lead to a fight.[30] A majority of the Court said that Feiner was arrested not for the content of his speech, but rather "the reaction which it actually engendered."[31] Justice Black's dissenting opinion pointed out the problems with such an approach, arguing that the police had an obligation to protect Feiner's constitutional "right to talk."[32] He held that "if, in the name of preserving order, [the police] ever can interfere with a lawful public speaker, they first must make all reasonable efforts to protect him."[33]

By contrast, in *Forsyth County v Nationalist Movement*,[34] the US Supreme Court struck down a county permitting procedure that it held afforded too much discretion to a county administrator in setting a permit fee for a public demonstration. In effect, the permitting scheme asked the administrator to consider the content of the demonstration, to try to predict what the public reaction to it would be, and to assess a fee on that basis. The Court stated the principle plainly: "Listeners' reaction to speech is not a content-neutral basis for regulation."[35]

Thus, in the United States at least, it is clear that the rights of speakers cannot be limited based on the fact that their speech may invite a strong – and negative – audience reaction. While explicit discussion of audience reaction in Canadian cases is less common, the approach to balancing rights and interests under section 1 of the *Charter* would seem to allow this factor to play a larger role and would likely countenance more restrictions on expression. Fortunately, as discussed further below, our Supreme Court has recognized some of the dangers of punishing the speaker for the expected reaction of the audience.

State Tools to Restrict Protest

It is perhaps obvious that expressive freedom can be curtailed by the state in a wide variety of ways. Restrictions or limits in the protest context may take the form of advance notice requirements, permit fees, and minimum insurance coverage prerequisites. Restrictions may be built into municipal by-laws that prohibit noise and nuisance or restrict the distribution of literature or the placement of signage. Traffic and trespass laws have also been used to restrict protest activity. In the absence of a clear statutory basis that can be relied upon to limit protests, police may rely on their ancillary powers. Finally, the state and private actors alike may seek injunctive relief from the courts to put an end to disruptive protests.

The police power to arrest for a breach of the peace is a tool commonly employed to clamp down on protesters. These arrests allow for the temporary detention of an individual without a criminal charge.[36] During the Toronto G20, hundreds of people were arrested using this power; they were ultimately released without charge, but their ability to exercise their freedom of expression and assembly were curtailed in a manner that was immediate and, at least insofar as it concerned that year's G20 conference, final.[37]

As others have argued, the boundaries of the power to arrest for breach of the peace are not clear because the very term "breach of the peace" can give rise to a wide variety of interpretations.[38] There are a few unique aspects of this arrest power that are worthy of note. First, an arrest for breach of the peace does not presuppose any unlawful activity. Police have the power to effect an arrest in the absence of any law being broken. Second, because criminal charges do not generally flow from these arrests, they are evasive of judicial review. A protester would have to take affirmative steps to challenge their detention, something that is costly, time-consuming, and may not result in any meaningful remedy.

Our courts have attempted to narrow the potential breadth of the power by requiring that the breach of the peace be imminent and the risk substantial before the police power may be exercised. As the Ontario Court of Appeal held in *Brown v Durham Regional Police Force*,[39] a breach of the peace

> does not include any and all conduct which right-thinking members of the community would regard as offensive, disturbing, or even vaguely threatening. A breach of the peace contemplates an act or actions which result in actual or threatened harm to someone.[40]

The Supreme Court of Canada had an opportunity to consider the scope of this power in a recent decision arising out of a protest. In *Fleming v Ontario*,[41] the Court was faced with the rare case where an individual arrested but not charged chose to pursue a civil claim against the police.

Mr. Fleming had planned to take part in a peaceful protest and display a Canadian flag. The protest was to take place near the Douglas Creek Estates (DCE), territory in Caledonia, Ontario, that has, for many years, been the subject of a land dispute between the Six Nations of the Grand River and the Crown. The long-standing occupation of the DCE by Indigenous protesters and the Province's decision to allow them to continue to occupy the land was the subject of significant criticism, litigation, and protest activity.[42] Mr. Fleming was among those who were opposed to the occupation of the DCE and planned to be part of a flag march. The Ontario Provincial Police (OPP) was aware of the planned flag protests and they feared that violence could result if the protesters entered onto the DCE land; the plan was to arrest any protesters who did so. Mr. Fleming ultimately did step onto the DCE land and some of the Indigenous protesters began to approach him. He was then arrested by the OPP, who claimed the arrest was justified on the basis of the "ancillary powers doctrine."

The Superior Court judge that first heard Mr. Fleming's claim found that his arrest was unlawful and awarded him over $100,000 in damages. A majority of the Ontario Court of Appeal overturned the decision, with a strong dissent.[43] At the Supreme Court of Canada, Mr. Fleming's appeal was allowed and the trial decision restored. The Court summarized the police power being claimed as one "to arrest individuals who have not committed any offence, who are not about to commit any offence, who have not already breached the peace and who are not about to breach the peace themselves."[44] In a strong rebuke of the arrest power the police relied on, the Court found that

> no such power exists at common law. The ancillary powers doctrine does not give the police a power to arrest someone who is acting lawfully in order to prevent an apprehended breach of the peace. A drastic power such as this that involves substantial interference with the liberty of law-abiding individuals would

not be reasonably necessary for the fulfillment of the police duties of preserving the peace, preventing crime, and protecting life and property. This is particularly so given that less intrusive powers are already available to the police to prevent breaches of the peace from occurring.[45]

The Supreme Court also highlighted that when he was arrested, Mr. Fleming was engaged in constitutionally protected expression. It agreed with the trial judge that the police actions had infringed Mr. Fleming's rights under section 2(b) of the *Charter*, stating that freedom of expression was implicated "where a police action prevents individuals from lawfully expressing themselves because their expression might provoke or enrage others."[46]

The *Fleming* decision is a significant right-to-protest case insofar as it affirms that police powers must be curtailed so as not to significantly intrude upon individual liberty. Its holding also suggests that the police have a duty to facilitate the exercise of the right to protest. It is therefore worth considering how this principle operates in cases involving direct and significant confrontations between protesters and counter-protesters. In the section that follows, I will offer some thoughts on the complexities that arise when competing free speech interests are at stake.

Competition in the Marketplace of Ideas

My interest in attempting to reconcile competing freedom of expression interests has grown out of a recognition that a focus on counter-speech or "more speech" may not adequately account for the complications that arise when speech and counter-speech clash in the real world. There are instances where the expressive activities of two or more groups have clashed in ways that call into question the viability of counter-speech as a "solution" to the problem of censorship. For example, at a Pride festival in Hamilton, Ontario, in the summer of 2019, anti-gay protesters attended the park where the festival took place holding signs and chanting. In response, counter-protesters erected a physical barrier (a large black curtain) designed to shield Pride participants from the messages of protesters.[47] This shielding tactic is not new; it can and has been used in powerful ways. For example, when members of the US-based Westboro Baptist Church showed up at the funerals of victims of the 2016 Pulse nightclub shooting, in Orlando, Florida, with hateful signs and messages, counter-protesters dressed as angels with large wings to shield the grieving families.[48]

The Consequences of Competition

A case recently decided by the Alberta Court of Appeal raises some difficult questions about how to reconcile competing free speech interests. In *UAlberta*

ProLife v Governors of the University of Alberta,[49] an anti-choice[50] registered student group held an on-campus event in which they included a large display, approximately 700 square feet in size, that purported to include photos of whole and dismembered fetuses at various stages of development. In response, a large group of students, faculty, staff, and members of the general public attended and stood side by side, holding signs and banners to block the display while cheering and chanting. The University was aware that there was a counter-protest planned and had designated a nearby area for counter-protesters. They refused to move to this spot, however, since one of the purposes of their protest was to shield passers-by on campus from having to view the graphic images.

The anti-choice group complained that the counter-protesters had violated the school's Code of Conduct, but the University declined to take disciplinary action.[51] The following year, when the same student group sought to have a similar display on campus, the University took the position that they were required to pay security costs in order to hold the event, with a price tag of $17,500. Needless to say, the student group could not afford this cost and therefore could not hold the event.

The anti-choice group sought judicial review of both the University's decision not to discipline the counter-protesters and the security costs decision. The Alberta Court of Queen's Bench found that the counter-protesters "significantly" obstructed the display and failed to comply with the University of Alberta's Protective Services' direction to stay in the space designated for them.[52] Nevertheless, based on the standard of review and the broad discretion afforded to the University in matters of discipline, the judicial review of the failure to discipline was dismissed. Applying a reasonableness standard, and informed by a *Doré*-style *Charter* analysis, the Court also upheld the security costs decision, finding that it was justified based on the events of the prior year and the need for security/police presence.[53]

Significantly, while the Court of Queen's Bench clearly recognized that the security costs impact expressive freedom, it considered it eminently reasonable to expect individuals to pay in order to exercise this freedom based on how others may react to the message conveyed. On this logic, the more controversial or unpopular the speech, the more costly it will be to express it. The Court of Queen's Bench chalked this up to "proportional balancing" with no rigour or meaningful discussion of the implications. The judge acknowledged that it may have also been reasonable "to require [that] UAlberta Pro-Life be responsible for only a portion of the costs, since the anticipated counter protesters contribute to the risk identified in the assessment,"[54] but was nevertheless satisfied that requiring that the student group bear the full costs fell within the range of reasonable outcomes. There is no discussion of the "heckler's veto" problem (manifested in the form of fees in this instance) or how it can be addressed using Canadian freedom of expression doctrine.

The Alberta Court of Appeal took some steps to address these flaws in reasoning. It dismissed the discipline appeal[55] but did allow the appeal on security costs.[56] According to the Court of Appeal, the lower court erred in its application of the *Doré*-style analysis and watered down the justification required where *Charter* rights are implicated. The Court of Appeal held that the judge below

> essentially applied a utilitarian approach that did not recognize the onus on the University, and did not apply the correct criteria. Even if *Doré* opened a form of *Charter s 1 analysis to fit with administrative law principles about deference, Dore* did not, in my view, substitute a test of mere arguable reasonableness for demonstrable justification in a free and democratic society as adapted under *Dore*. This error cut both ways. Both Pro-Life's position and that of the University did not get the complete evaluation which was necessary under the proper test with the burden properly allocated.[57]

The Court of Appeal also grappled with questions about how to address concerns related to "involuntary audience," holding that such concerns – which may cut two ways – must be considered in any analysis seeking to justify restrictions on freedom of expression.[58] Since the issue before the Court was moot (the time when the group wanted to hold the event had long since passed), the Court of Appeal's decision only provides some guidance to other decision makers in addressing security costs in controversial protest cases. Nevertheless, the Court's characterization of the groups of speakers and how it treats their competing free expression interests for the purposes of its analysis may prove to be important jurisprudential building blocks in the cases to come.[59]

Regulating the Marketplace

Ideally, protests and counter-protests coexist in a manner that does not require state intervention and where expressive rights are not unreasonably limited. In other words, the marketplace operates without regulation. Where concrete realities render this impossible, however, how can free expression interests be reconciled?

This issue has become relevant in the university context, particularly in Ontario and Alberta, where provincial governments are requiring post-secondary institutions to implement free speech policies in line with the "Chicago Principles."[60] These principles state that "while members of the university/college are free to criticize and contest views expressed on campus, they may not obstruct or interfere with the freedom of others to express their views." Moreover, Ontario has also said that the policies must confirm that "existing student discipline measures apply to students whose actions are contrary to the policy (e.g., ongoing disruptive protesting that significantly interferes with the ability of an event to proceed)."[61] This suggests that counter-protests may be significantly restricted in the name of free expression – a troubling proposition.

Putting aside questions about the wisdom of a government requiring post-secondary institutions to implement a particular form of free speech policy, consider the significant practical difficulties that will come with implementing the "counter-protest" aspect of these policies. When will a counter-protest be said to "obstruct or interfere" with the freedom of others, and what happens if we set the bar too low? What constitutes "significant" interference with an event? The policy requirement does nothing to address the reality that post-secondary institutions seeking to facilitate free speech are likely to incur significant security costs as a result – and may seek to pass those costs on to students. It also ignores the reality that post-secondary institutions have to face in the realm of student discipline. As highlighted in the *UAlberta Pro-Life* case, institutional resources available for a disciplinary system may be limited, and institutions will have to prioritize how they expend such resources.[62] When compared with serious issues of sexual assault or acts of violence on campus, it is reasonable that discipline for "obstructing an event" would take a back seat.

As with most freedom of expression issues, there are no easy answers. I propose, however, some questions to help reconcile competing free expression interests:

1. What are the purposes of the protest and the counter-protest?
2. What is the effect of the counter-protest?
   - Is it trying to "free" an otherwise captive audience from a message they likely don't care to hear?
   - Is it providing a warning about the nature of the protest?
   - Is it shielding some from exposure to the protest?
   - Does it eliminate the audience's choice to engage with protesters by rendering their message invisible?
3. How is public space being used and shared?

In the Pride example, those who attended the festival in order to "protest" against Pride appear to have been expressing their displeasure that a public space was being used to celebrate LGBTQ+ rights. There is a clear expressive purpose here. As mentioned above, those who attended to "counter" those protests erected large black curtains to shield Pride celebrants from the messages of protesters. The counter-protesters' purpose appears to have been directed more at limiting the reach of the protesters' messages and less at articulating any independent message of their own.[63] The effect of the counter-protest was certainly to shield some Pride celebrants from the messages of the protesters or, viewed from a different perspective, prevent the protesters from effectively communicating their message. At the same time, it is likely that those who saw the large black sheets were aware of the kinds of messages that lay beyond.

The *UAlberta* example is a little more nuanced. To start, the anti-choice student group was arguably not actually engaged in a protest at all; their display was certainly expressive in nature, and while it might be characterized as protesting Canada's policies on reproductive rights, the group would likely claim that they were simply seeking to engage individuals in discussion on this issue and/or provoke strong emotions in those who passed by the display. Indeed, in their factum before the Alberta Court of Appeal, UAlberta Pro-Life states:

> The Appellants [UAlberta Pro-Life] are not "protesters." The Appellants are, and were at the 2015 Event, students who are authorized by [the] University to hold a University function in accordance with the rule of law, to express their opinions on campus in a peaceful manner.[64]

The factum also takes issue with the characterization of the other students as "counter-protesters," referring to them instead as "blockaders" and "obstructers" and arguing that they were not engaged in protected expression but were instead violating the University's Code of Conduct. There was some evidence before the Court that the counter-protesters had communicated through social media about their plans to blockade, obstruct, and interrupt the UAlberta Pro-Life event. However, the evidence of what took place at the relevant time suggests a more complicated picture. As the Alberta Court of Queen's Bench noted,

> The March 3–4 event was indeed the subject of a counter-demonstration. Photographs put in evidence by the Applicants clearly show that dozens of other individuals formed a human barrier in front of the large displays which Pro-Life had erected, and hoisted large banners of their own. Because Pro-Life's signs were *mostly obscured* by the counter-demonstrators, it is difficult, *but not impossible*, to discern their message. However, *portions of the graphic images can still be seen.*[65]

Thus, the evidence is that the message of the anti-choice group was not fully obstructed. What is unclear is whether students who did have an interest in engaging with the graphic display were prevented from doing so. In other words, could they pass through the "blockade" and view the images if they so chose?

There was also evidence that the counter-demonstrators erected their own signs with messages, some of which expressed their view on the abortion issue (e.g., "Don't Like Abortion, Don't Have One," "No Shame," and "We Demand Safe Spaces"), while others sought to warn passers-by of what lay beyond their signs (e.g., "Trigger Warning" and "Beware Graphic Anti-Choice Solicitation"). In the *UAlberta* case, it thus appears that the counter-protesters may have had multiple purposes and effects, which included shielding passers-by from graphic images, warning them about the images so they could decide for themselves whether to engage, and expressing their own views.

Concluding Thoughts

This examination of counter-speech, particularly in the protest context, has sought to highlight some of the complexities inherent in modern free speech debates, recognizing that there are rarely simple answers to complex questions. Robust protection of freedom of expression requires that we hold state actors seeking to restrict it to stringent standards and, in some cases, hold them accountable for the meaningful facilitation of the right to protest. I remain convinced that censorship and content-based restrictions on speech should not be countenanced. However, the common response of free speech advocates that "more speech" is better has perhaps oversimplified what "more speech" might really mean.

As discussed in some of the examples above, counter-speech can take different forms, and not all will meaningfully further the objectives of free expression. Moreover, to the extent that state actors, police, and, increasingly, post-secondary administrators, have to make calls about how to manage competing free expression interests, there are a number of factors that will have to be carefully canvassed and considered, and the framework of questions proposed may well lead in a variety of directions. There is a need to engage in the context-specific analysis that is typically required in free expression cases, while aiming to provide fair rules that can be applied consistently and with some predictability. It is a work in progress, but one worth pursuing.

NOTES

* LLB, LLM, Director, Fundamental Freedoms Program, Canadian Civil Liberties Association. The views set out in this chapter are my own and do not necessarily reflect the position of the CCLA.

1 *Canadian Charter of Rights and Freedoms*, Part 1 of the *Constitution Act, 1982*, being Schedule B to the *Canada Act 1982* (UK), 1982, c 11 [*Charter*].

2 *Fleming v Ontario*, 2019 SCC 45 [*Fleming*].

3 *UAlberta Pro-Life v Governors of the University of Alberta*, 2020 ABCA 1 [*UAlberta Pro-Life*].

4 *Reference Re Alberta Statutes – The Bank Taxation Act; The Credit of Alberta Regulation Act; and the Accurate News and Information Act*, [1938] SCR 100.

5 Ibid. at 133.

6 *Irwin Toy Ltd. v Quebec (Attorney General)*, [1989] 1 SCR 927 at 968–9 (citations omitted).

7   Section 2(c) of the *Charter* protects freedom of peaceful assembly. Freedom of association is protected pursuant to section 2(d).

8   See Basil S. Alexander, "Exploring a More Independent Freedom of Peaceful Assembly in Canada," *Western Journal of Legal Studies* 8, no. 1 (2018): 1–18.

9   Police are responsible for guarding public safety and maintaining public order. Where protest activities take place in public spaces, police services will often be required to mediate competing interests.

10 *Police Services Act*, RSO 1990, c P. 15.

11 Ibid., s 1.

12 United Nations General Assembly, Human Rights Council, *Joint Report of the Special Rapporteurs on the Rights to Peaceful Assembly and Extrajudicial, Summary or Arbitrary Executions and the Proper Management of Assemblies*, para 52, UN Doc. A/HRC/31/66 (4 February 2016).

13 *Irwin Toy Ltd. v Quebec (Attorney General)*, [1989] 1 SCR 927.

14 *R. v Khawaja*, 2012 SCC 69 at para 70.

15 *Bracken v Fort Erie (Town)*, 2017 ONCA 668 [*Bracken* ONCA].

16 Ibid. at paras 8–10.

17 *Bracken v Fort Erie (Town)*, 2016 ONSC 1122 at paras 95–7. The Superior Court judge stated that while the content of Mr. Bracken's speech was protected, "What is objectionable and not protected by the *Charter* is the erratic, confrontational behaviour with which Bracken acted on that day, particularly to the detriment of the staff of the Town and members of the public."

18 *Bracken* ONCA, *supra* note 15, para 37.

19 Ibid. at paras 49–51.

20 My discussion in this chapter is based on the assumption that protests take place where there is some connection to government or state action such that the *Charter* is indeed engaged. As will be discussed *infra*, freedom of expression in a university setting raises some complications. Canadian universities typically have some statutory foundation and many receive substantial government funds. At the same time, these institutions must also operate independent of government to adequately protect academic freedom. At the moment, the Canadian jurisprudence suggests that a university may be considered "government" for *Charter* purposes in some of its functions, but not in others.

21 *Greater Vancouver Transportation Authority v Canadian Federal of Students – British Columbia Component*, 2009 SCC 31 at para 42.

22 *Committee for the Commonwealth of Canada v Canada*, [1991] 1 SCR 139 at 157.

23 In *Batty v City of Toronto*, 2011 ONSC 6862 at para 70, Brown J. stated: "I do not accept the City's argument that the Protesters' act of camping out and, in effect, taking over a public park is not activity which engages s. 2 of the *Charter*. The current approach of the Supreme Court of Canada to the issue of the mode of expression is not whether the form of the expression is compatible with the function of the public space, but whether free expression in the chosen form would

undermine the values the guarantee is designed to promote. Shelters have been held by other courts to constitute a mode of expression which falls within the guarantees of s. 2, especially s. 2(b) of the *Charter.*"

24 See *Calgary (City) v Bullock (Occupy Calgary)*, 2011 ABQB 764. Note that in *Batty, supra* note 23, the Court rejected the argument that the restrictions were not minimally impairing because they effectively constituted an absolute ban on certain expressive activities and because the City had failed to demonstrate that they had considered alternatives to the eviction of protesters.

25 "G20 Protest Area Moved by Toronto Police," *CBC News*, 6 May 2010, https://www .cbc.ca/news/canada/toronto/g20-protest-area-moved-by-toronto-police-1.885068.

26 This concern was raised by the Canadian Civil Liberties Association (CCLA) in a Statement of Concerns presented to law enforcement prior to the summit. For a summary of the concerns, see Brent Patterson, "News: Canadian Civil Liberties Association Raises Concerns about G8/G20 Security Measures," Council of Canadians, 23 May 2010, https://canadians.org/fr/node/5585.

27 *Ontario (Attorney General) v Dieleman,* 1994 CanLII 7509 (ONSC).

28 Ibid. at para 641 (citations omitted).

29 *The Canadian Centre for Bio-Ethical Reform v South Coast British Columbia Transportation Authority*, 2018 BCCA 344, overturning 2017 BCSC 1388; *Canadian Centre for Bio-Ethical Reform v Grande Prairie (City)*, 2018 ABCA 154, affirming 2016 ABQB 734.

30 340 US 315 (1951).

31 Ibid. at 319–20.

32 Ibid. at 326.

33 Ibid.

34 505 US 123 (1992).

35 Ibid. at 134.

36 Section 31(a) of the *Criminal Code*, RSC 1985, c C-46 provides: "Every peace officer who witnesses a breach of the peace and every one who lawfully assists the peace officer is justified in arresting any person whom he finds committing the breach of the peace or who, on reasonable grounds, he believes is about to join in or renew the breach of the peace."

37 "G20 Accountability ... By the Numbers ...," Canadian Civil Liberties Association, December 2012, https://ccla.org/cclanewsite/wp-content/uploads/lg_img/G20 -infographic-large-final.png.

38 Jackie Esmonde, "The Policing of Dissent – The Use of Breach of the Peace Arrests at Political Demonstrations," *Journal of Law and Equality* 1 (2002): 248.

39 (1998), 43 OR (3d) 223.

40 Ibid.

41 *Fleming, supra* note 2.

42 See, for example, *Henco Industries Ltd. v Haudenosaunee Six Nations Confederacy Council* (2006), 82 OR (3d) 721.

43 2018 ONCA 160. The dissent of Huscroft J.A. at paras 100–2 makes particular reference to the American "hostile audience" doctrine, arguing that police have an obligation to take "all reasonable steps before resorting to control of the speaker."

44 *Fleming, supra* note 2, at para 6.

45 Ibid. at para 7.

46 Ibid. at para. 66.

47 See, for example, Adam Carter, " 'Hateful' Protest at Hamilton Pride Event Condemned," *CBC News*, 15 June 2019, https://www.cbc.ca/news/canada/hamilton /hamilton-pride-festival-altercation-police-1.5177439.

48 See, for example, Tim Stelloh, "Angels Quietly Block Westboro Protesters at Orlando Funeral," *NBC News*, 19 June 2016, https://www.nbcnews.com /storyline/orlando-nightclub-massacre/angels-quietly-block-westboro-protesters -orlando-funeral-n595311.

49 *UAlberta Pro-Life, supra* note 3.

50 While the group characterizes itself as pro-life, I have chosen to use the language of "anti-choice" when referring to the group in generic terms. This reflects my rejection of the pro-life language, which, in my view, suggests that those who believe in the right to choose to terminate a pregnancy are "anti-life." It further reflects my view that those who argue that access to abortion must be restricted or eliminated do effectively deny that a person carrying a child has the right to choose to terminate. Notwithstanding my own views on the substantive issue of abortion, I believe anti-choice groups share the same expressive freedoms as anyone else and that attempts to restrict or limit their expression must be held to a stringent justification standard.

51 The group organizing the anti-choice protest were also the subjects of complaints. See Justice Centre for Constitutional Freedoms, Written Submissions of the Respondent, 4 February 2016 Decision, accessed 4 May 2021, https://www.jccf.ca /wp-content/uploads/2013/02/U-of-A-response-re-condoning-mob-behaviour .pdf, para 20.

52 *UAlberta Pro-Life v Governors of the University of Alberta*, 2017 ABQB 610 [*UAlberta Pro-Life* QB], at para 5.

53 Ibid. at paras 66–7.

54 Ibid. at para 68.

55 The decision on discipline grapples with the protest and counter-protest dynamic to a limited degree, referencing the original discipline decision. See in particular *UAlberta Pro-Life, supra* note 3, at paras 97–9.

56 The appeal on this ground was allowed, but given the mootness of the issue, no other remedial orders were made.

57 Ibid. at para 159.

58 Ibid. at paras 171–5.

59 Although not relevant to this discussion, the Court of Appeal's decision is perhaps most notable for the fact that it finds that, in the context of the judicial review

before it, the University is bound by the *Charter* and held to the same standards of justification as any government/state actor.

60 See University of Chicago, "Report of the Committee on Freedom of Expression," accessed 4 May 2021, https://provost.uchicago.edu/sites/default/files/documents/reports/FOECommitteeReport.pdf.

61 "Backgrounder: Upholding Free Speech on Ontario's University and College Campuses," Office of the Premier, 30 August 2018, https://news.ontario.ca/opo/en/2018/08/upholding-free-speech-on-ontarios-university-and-college-campuses.html.

62 *UAlberta Pro-Life* QB, *supra* note 52, at para 32.

63 I acknowledge that the act of seeking to shield Pride celebrants from the messages of the protesters sends a message and certainly has expressive content. Nevertheless, I maintain that the counter-protesters in this example did not truly seek to "counter" the messages conveyed, but instead sought to render those messages invisible, at least for those celebrating Pride.

64 Justice Centre for Constitutional Freedoms, Factum of UAlberta Pro-Life, accessed 4 May 2021, https://www.jccf.ca/wp-content/uploads/2018/07/Filed-Factum-UAlberta-Pro-Life-Appeal-1.pdf, para 48.

65 *UAlberta Pro-Life v University of Alberta*, 2015 ABQB 719 at para 12 (emphasis added).

7 Positive Rights, Negative Freedoms, and the Margins of Expressive Freedom

BENJAMIN J. OLIPHANT

After nearly four decades of judicial interpretation, it is reasonably clear that freedom of expression under section 2(b) of the *Canadian Charter of Rights and Freedoms* is treated primarily as a "negative" entitlement. By that I mean the state is generally prohibited from interfering with, but is generally not required to "positively" facilitate or support, expressive activities.[1] The vast majority of freedom of expression cases fall comfortably within this general rule, as they involve various forms of government restrictions or limitations on expressive activities in which individuals are otherwise free and able to engage.

However, there are a range of circumstances on the margins of the section 2(b) case law that complicate any bright line distinction between so-called positive and negative rights in this context, and a number of recent controversies in Canada provide a useful opportunity for a discussion and clarification of these issues. While these circumstances may involve some element of "positive" state action, they are not necessarily excluded from consideration under section 2(b) as a result. Rather, as I hope to show, different categories of cases raise different concerns with respect to whether a breach of freedom of expression has been established, and each calls out for discrete treatment on its own terms.

The Key Concepts

The distinction between "positive" and "negative" rights, and the closely related question as to whether the government has engaged in "state action" sufficient to attract constitutional liability, have bedevilled courts and commentators for some time. For the purpose of this chapter, we should briefly attempt to explore why these concepts tend to be unhelpful unless viewed through the lens of a particular constitutional guarantee.

The problem with a general "state action" requirement is not that it is wrong but rather that it does little work as a stand-alone, abstract principle. In our modern regulatory state, it is nearly always possible to point to *some* state action that is alleged to be constitutionally deficient. This is especially the case once we conclude that, in at least some circumstances, statutes may be constitutionally vulnerable on the basis that they are *under-inclusive*; in other words, that the state has improperly *failed* to act in some respect.[2] Moreover, even in the absence of a statute governing the matter in question, there is always the common law, the creation and enforcement of which is no less a matter of state action than the is creation and enforcement of statute law.[3] The question in every difficult case is not *whether* there is state action in some abstract sense, but whether the particular state action *in question* is consistent with the particular constitutional guarantees relied upon.

The answer to that question may well be, with respect to certain *Charter* provisions, that they can only be engaged by the active conduct of state actors, and not by what might be better characterized as state *inaction*. To use an easy example, the legal rights set out in section 11 are only triggered upon a person being "charged with an offence." As this only applies to the charging of criminal and certain quasi-criminal offences, the section 11 rights can only be infringed by state actors, and only in relation to a specified type of state action: charging someone with an offence. But that legal reality is primarily a function of the nature of the specific rights in question, rather than a function of the presence or absence of "state action" as a more general proposition.

Other *Charter* provisions, however, are more broadly conceived and more readily lend themselves to legal implications that arise out of what we might call a state omission or inaction, rather than state action. For instance, section 15 guarantees that persons are not only "equal before and under the law," but that they also have the right "to the equal protection and equal benefit of the law." If a law benefits or protects some people and not others in a discriminatory fashion, the *failure* to confer the benefit on or extend the protection to others can clearly run afoul of section 15.

In short, once we hold that the common law can be subject to some form of constitutional scrutiny, and that statutes may fail to adequately protect constitutional rights, there is little left that is categorically beyond the reach of the *Charter*.[4] This does not mean that it will be easy to determine when a particular right or freedom is abridged, nor does it mean that the proximate source of a deprivation (i.e., governmental or private actors) or the nature of the state action (i.e., action or inaction, statutory or common law) in question are irrelevant. It is just to say that the debate is internal to the understanding of the specific *Charter* right in question, not something that is resolved by some uniformly applicable "state action" requirement.

Similar observations can be made with respect to the closely related distinction between so-called positive and negative rights. These are notoriously slippery concepts, but I will use the terms rather simplistically to describe circumstances where the state has, vis-à-vis the rights holder, an affirmative duty to act to secure for them a particular entitlement (i.e., *positive* rights), on the one hand, and a duty to not act or not interfere with a person's independent ability to act in a certain manner (i.e., *negative* rights), on the other. In the former case we seek the state's assistance in the form of positive action, and in the latter only its forbearance in the form of state inaction.

Understood in this way, there is no general rule that all provisions found in the *Charter* contain a particular juridical structure, either positive or negative. Some provisions of the *Charter* are primarily if not exclusively "negative";[5] others are quite clearly "positive";[6] some contain elements of both.[7] The fact some *Charter* guarantees entail positive obligations does not mean that all do, or that all do to the same extent; nor does it mean that the concepts are necessarily useless or should be abandoned.[8] It simply means that, as with our state action problem, we have to look closely at the particular constitutional provision in question and how it operates. I turn to that issue now with respect to freedom of expression.

The "Problem" in the Context of Freedom of Expression

Primarily "Negative"

The orthodox view in Canada is that freedom of expression, like the other fundamental freedoms, is primarily a negative entitlement, in that it typically only places the state under an obligation to not interfere with the exercise of those freedoms. In their core application, they do not place the state under a constitutional obligation to fund, support, or otherwise actively facilitate the exercise of those freedoms.[9]

This orthodox view was set out in *Haig v Canada*, a case involving the government excluding persons from voting in a referendum due to their fluid residency status. In that case, L'Heureux-Dubé J. noted that "case law and doctrinal writings have generally conceptualized freedom of expression in terms of negative rather than positive entitlements," with the "traditional view" of freedom of expression being that it "prohibits gags, but does not compel the distribution of megaphones."[10] While the referendum at issue in *Haig* was clearly a platform for expression in some sense, section 2(b) does not impose "any positive obligation" on governments to offer such a platform "to anyone, let alone to everyone."[11] Therefore, the government could choose to extend this opportunity for expression to some, and not others, without impacting the freedom of expression of the latter. On this same logic, the Court has rejected various constitutional challenges where the claimant sought state assistance or access to a certain "platform" to facilitate their expression, which has generally been classified as seeking a positive right beyond the scope of section 2(b).[12]

While this was at one time the default assumption that applied to all of the fundamental freedoms, the Supreme Court has been cautious to never say never,[13] and it has since departed from this posture significantly in one particular context – freedom of association as protected through labour relations statutes.[14] However, outside of this context, the Court has generally hewed closely to the orthodox distinction in the context of the fundamental freedoms, and freedom of expression in particular.[15] As such, I take it to be the *general* rule under section 2 that the state may not act to impede religious belief or practice, expression, assembly, or associational activities, but it need not actively facilitate, promote, enhance, or assist those activities.

The Justifications for the General Rule

Before discussing the exceptions or qualifications to the rule in the context of freedom of expression, it is worth briefly acknowledging the various rationales for the general rule itself. The first is the idea that inherent in the notion of a constitutional "freedom," at least as "traditionally understood," is that it compels government inaction rather than action.[16] As the Court held in *Delisle*, "it is because of the very nature of freedom that s. 2 generally imposes a negative obligation on the government and not a positive obligation of protection or assistance."[17] This notion of a negative liberty from government restraint is perhaps best captured by Isaiah Berlin, who defines political liberty as "simply the area within which the subject – a person or group of persons – is or should be left to do or be what he is able to do or be."[18]

Second, the implications of a broadly understood state obligation to actively ensure or promote a right to expression would be difficult if not impossible to cabin on a principled basis, and would seem to require results that go well beyond the purpose of the guarantee. This flows from the fact that our real, practical ability to engage in expressive activities is constantly limited by private actors and private actions, and the government could always step in to assist the speakers in their expressive endeavours. The decision of parent or teacher to discipline a child for using foul language, a private employer's requirement for certain speech and prohibition of other speech, or even critical speech that dissuades the subject of criticism from continuing their expression, could all hypothetically become subject to constitutional scrutiny. Perhaps even more significantly, the extent to which individuals are practically able to effectively or meaningfully exercise their fundamental freedoms will also correspond to a large extent with their social standing, education, abilities, free time, and perhaps most of all, material resources.[19]

Again, governments can (and sometimes do) act positively to enhance the opportunities for and effectiveness of a person's expression, or they may restrict the speech of some in order to ensure a measure of equality in the context of particular expressive opportunities.[20] Generally, however, the courts have not required governments to do so as an incident of freedom of expression.

Treating freedom of expression as a general, positive entitlement to "meaningful" or "effective" expression would not only risk embroiling the courts in an infinite range of private squabbles, but would seem to require them to identify a minimum distribution of material, educational, and social resources necessary to meaningfully or effectively exercise freedom of expression, and to then require the government to distribute at least that amount of these resources to everyone. To use freedom of expression as a means of requiring the government to police purely private interactions or a vehicle for the broad redistribution of resources in this way would be, by most accounts, to exceed the purpose of the guarantee.

Cases on the Margin of Freedom of Expression

As neat as the positive vs. negative right distinction might seem in theory, and that itself is disputed, it is considerably messier in practice. There are a number of circumstances appearing to involve some element of "positive" government action that are different – or at least are treated differently – from a mere unwillingness of state actors to "support" or "facilitate" a particular exercise of freedom of expression. Typically, they arise in contexts where the government marshals its own powers and resources – over property it holds, over benefits it distributes, over funding choices it makes – to effectively punish, coerce, or restrict expression with which it disagrees, or to otherwise unduly limit the expressive opportunities already available to members of the public.

In these types of situations, a strict application of the orthodox conception of freedom of expression – that the government has no obligation to confer a benefit, platform, or opportunity – is often understood to be inadequate. We have moved past Justice Holmes's dictum that "the petitioner may have a constitutional right to talk politics, but he has no constitutional right to be a policeman."[21] While this statement remains true in the abstract, the implication of it – that the state can freely condition access to important government opportunities or benefits on speech-related grounds – is not true, or at least not always true.

There is no definitive list of circumstances in which these claims properly arise, and there is often considerable overlap between the categories proposed below. However, I focus on four specific circumstances that arise with some regularity, and seek to highlight their constitutional implications with reference to recent Canadian controversies.

The Meaningful Expression Cases

GENERAL
The first category – which I will call the "meaningful expression" cases – are those involving some sort of state action that (indirectly) limits the effectiveness

or intended impact of a person's past or future speech. In my view, while these cases typically arise out of state action, we should be cautious before accepting that such claims rise to the level of a limitation on freedom of expression in the first place.[22]

The need for caution stems from the recognition that nearly everything a government does can, in some derivative or indirect sense, impact the "meaningfulness" or "effectiveness" of a person's expression. Every tax dollar taken away from individuals is one less that they can spend on speech-related activities; every dollar of government benefits achieves the opposite. A government scandal may "encourage" expression, in the sense of leading to an outpouring of critical speech, while sound fiscal management might "discourage" it. Any change in government policy may make certain expression irrelevant, and other expression more salient moving forward. And so on. As Justice LeBel noted in *Baeir*, "nearly everything people do creates opportunities for expression if 'expression' is viewed expansively enough."[23]

For instance, if the government decided to turn a public park into a private parking lot (or refused to turn a private parking lot into a public park), a "platform" for expression would be diminished (or not expanded). However, even the most ambitious court would likely balk before suggesting that the constitution guarantees a particular placement or volume of expressive greenspace on freedom of expression grounds. Similarly, if I campaign vigorously against a particular policy, and the government nevertheless enacts that policy into law, the relevance or impact of my past campaigning has been undermined moving forward, and the potential impact of any future expression on the subject diminished, at least to some extent. But that alone does not create a section 2(b) issue.

In other words, merely identifying some remote train of causation whereby the ultimate outcome of a government decision is to impact or affect the meaningfulness, effectiveness, or relevance of expression is not, in my view, sufficient in itself to demonstrate a breach of freedom of expression. This does not mean that only those government regulations that deliberately prohibit or inhibit speech are constitutionally vulnerable; having that effect, regardless of the purpose, will often suffice. However, it means that we should look carefully at claims that purport to be derived exclusively from the "meaningfulness" or "effectiveness" of expression in which an individual is perfectly free to engage, rather than claims that expressive activities themselves are (directly or indirectly) prohibited, limited, or inhibited.

Take, for instance, the *Baier* case, which involved a challenge to legislation that excluded school employees from running to become school trustees. While being a trustee *involves* expressive activities, so does every other job I can think of. Perhaps more to the point, access to the trustee position may amplify the *impact* or *meaningfulness* of an individual's expression as compared to someone who is not a trustee, but again, so does any high profile government position, any access to additional time or resources that can be spent on expression, and so on. In my view, the trustee position itself is not created as a "platform" *for* expression, in the relevant sense discussed below; nor is there reason for assuming that the government's purpose in restricting access to the position was to somehow burden expressive activities generally, much less the expression of certain substantive viewpoints which, as will be discussed, is a particular red flag in this context.

Although the majority in *Baier* ultimately held that the claim fell outside the scope of section 2(b) following a somewhat involved "positive rights" analysis,[24] I tend to agree with the concurring judgment of LeBel J. that the impugned measures simply did not implicate freedom of expression in the first place, and the claim was better characterized as one seeking "a right to participate in a political and managerial function in a democratically elected public body."[25] In order to engage section 2(b), I suggest that there must be some more proximate connection to restrictions or burdens on expressive activities beyond the fact that those activities may be less effective at achieving the speaker's ultimate objectives than they otherwise would be.

MEANINGFUL EXPRESSION AND TORONTO CITY COUNCIL

The "meaningful expression" issue is aptly demonstrated in the recent *Toronto City Council* case, which involved a challenge to the provincial government's decision – in the midst of a municipal election – to change the number of city council seats from 47 to 25. Predictably, this created some degree of chaos in terms of the ongoing election.[26] The difficulty for those who opposed the redistricting was that municipal elections are clearly excluded from the scope of the "right to vote" in section 3, which has been read broadly to protect a range of democratic rights, but only in the context of provincial and federal elections. As in the *Baier* case, the claimants were effectively boxed out of a section 3 challenge, and so relied on section 2(b).

The Superior Court found that section 2(b) was violated in two ways, although I will only focus on the first: the finding that changing the ward structure retroactively rendered previous expression by candidates ineffective or meaningless, and required candidates to spend time, money, and effort addressing the implications of the redistricting, which they may rather have spent discussing their campaign platforms. Taken together, the Court held that this "substantially interfered with the candidate's ability to effectively communicate his or her political message to the relevant voters."[27] Or, as the Court of Appeal described it, the applicants claimed that the redistricting "made prior messages irrelevant to the voters, and subsequent messages inaudible."[28]

Although the distinction between positive and negative rights was relied on by the Court of Appeal in resolving the case, I am not convinced it actually involved any request for positive state action or "a claim to a particular platform," as such.[29] A particular ward structure is not a "platform" for expression so much as it is simply a fact in the world that may impact what people may choose to talk about. I think the essence of the claim was "negative" in orientation: that by *actively changing* the structure mid-election, whatever it was at the outset and whatever it had become, the provincial government diminished the effectiveness, relevance, or intended impact of expressive activities.

While I do not think that the positive vs. negative rights distinction is directly engaged in this context, the "meaningful expression" issue discussed above is. In this respect, I think the Court of Appeal came to the right conclusion for the right reasons earlier in the judgment. As it explained in a key passage, section 2(b)

> protects against interference with the expressive activity itself, not its intended result. Put another way, freedom of expression does not guarantee that government action will not have the side-effect of reducing the likelihood of success of the projects or joint enterprises that any person is working to achieve.[30]

In this case, the impugned change "did not, and could not, erase the messages that had already been communicated," and it did not prevent any candidate "from saying anything he or she wished to say on any subject" or "prescribe or proscribe any future messaging."[31] Rather, it was a claim that "prior expressive activity by the candidates would not in fact contribute to the project of securing their election, and that additional, different campaigning would now be required."[32] To the extent that this claim was grounded solely in the efficacy or substantive meaningfulness of the expression to accomplish a particular end, I think that it was properly treated as beyond the protections afforded by freedom of expression under the *Charter*.[33]

Public Forum Cases

GENERAL

A second category of cases on the margins of section 2(b) is what I will call "public forum" cases. In this context, the positive vs. negative rights issue arises from the government's control over the physical space necessary for many expressive activities, and the claim that such access is contingent on establishing a "positive right" to engage in expression in that state-controlled forum. However, characterizing the access to public space as a discretionary privilege, and hence prohibitions on access to that space implicating only an unprotected "positive right," seems entirely inadequate.

While the "public forum" doctrine as such is a unique feature of US constitutional law,[34] Canadian courts have grappled with similar issues, and reached similar conclusions. For instance, in *Greater Vancouver*,[35] the Supreme Court held that a publicly run bus service that provided advertising space could not prevent individuals from advertising on the bus without a compelling section 1 justification. According to the Court, the "very fact that the general public has access to the advertising space on buses is an indication that members of the public would expect constitutional protection of their expression in that government-owned space." The Court likened it to a "city street," in that it is a "public place where individuals can openly interact with each other and their surroundings."[36] Canadian cases have extended this type of protection to other public forums owned or controlled by governments, such as sidewalks, airports, marketplaces, and parks.[37]

In my view, the justification for this approach is that protecting access to public forums does not cause the same concerns as many positive rights cases. The claimant is not seeking a positive entitlement – in the sense that the government must *create* an opportunity for speech that does not already exist or fund the distribution of a particular message – as a stand-alone proposition, but is, rather, seeking to be left alone to exercise the freedom in a public space that already exists. Once the public forum has been created, the government generally need not do anything but refrain from restricting individuals from exercising their freedoms in that venue as they see fit.[38] The same can generally be said for public protests. While certain gatherings may sometimes require a degree of additional security, the participants are not seeking funding, support, or access to which they would otherwise not be entitled. They are just seeking to be protected in the course of living their lives and lawfully exercising their freedoms, as we all are entitled to expect, all of the time (see Zwibel, this volume).

In effect, by creating a public forum compatible with expressive activities, the constitutional baseline has been shifted, such that access to the (government-controlled) property is presumptively permitted, and restrictions on that access tied to expressive activities are treated as restrictions on freedom of expression. What in one sense could be characterized as a "positive" entitlement to access a platform has instead become understood or treated as a "negative" entitlement to be free to engage in expression using the pre-existing forum.[39]

PUBLIC FORUMS AND TWITTER BLOCKING

A modern example of the challenge of defining a public forum is the question of blocking certain individuals from seeing and commenting directly in response to the Twitter posts ("tweets") of governments or public officials, which has been the source of numerous recent controversies in Canada.[40] The basic question in this context is this: Is a public official's or government-run Twitter feed, which they use to announce government policies and provide information in relation to their public duties, properly considered a public forum of some sort, akin to a public park, square, or sidewalk, subject to constitutional protections as described above? Or is it more akin to "private property" that just happens to be owned or controlled by a public official, like the front lawn of a politician's home or a campaign office, access to which they can control as they see fit?

While I cannot delve deeply into the nuances here,[41] my view is that the former is the better analogy in this context. Government social media accounts can constitute a type of "modern public square,"[42] to the extent they are controlled and maintained by government actors and compatible with commentary from the public. Moreover, unlike some of the specific platforms discussed below, one person's ability to see and respond to a government tweet is not limited by time or funding restrictions (as in holding face-to-face consultations) or physical limitations (as in a conference room) that make at least some exclusions necessary.

I think we would consider it a rather intolerable intrusion on freedom of expression if a public official, in a public forum ostensibly available to all members of the public, sent around police officers or security guards to evict those who do not seem to support the public official or their message. It is true that, in such situations – as in the context of a Twitter blocking – the individuals excluded from the public venue can express themselves elsewhere. They can go down to another public area or find a private one, where no one is actually located to hear the dissenting message. But in my view, that does not eliminate the constitutional concern. The key features and logic of public forums is that they are pre-existing venues, publicly owned and controlled, compatible with expressive activities, and thus represent a particularly effective venue for communication that is ostensibly available to the entire community. The ability to see and respond to the posts on government Twitter accounts, and to do so directly below the tweets in question, would seem to check all of these boxes.

Public officials can of course avoid this issue entirely by not creating an online public forum in the first place. In the Twitter context, they can create a personal Twitter account that is not associated with their public role or functions, in which case I would think it would be immune from constitutional scrutiny, in the same way I cannot rely upon my freedom of expression to give an unsolicited speech in the prime minister's kitchen. They can also "mute" users, which strikes me as akin to merely ignoring critical speech, as they are entitled to do in any context. While I might go to a public rally to hold up a sign, I cannot make anyone – including government officials – read it. However, having chosen to create or utilize a public forum directly associated with official government functions, in order to reach and engage with the widest possible audience, it strikes me as constitutionally problematic for a public official to require that expressive forum to be used only to praise, but not criticize or question, the public official or government policies.

For all its incurable faults, the great promise of social media is that it can open up new and uniquely democratic forums for public engagement, including public dissent and criticism. Unlike stump speeches that are only available to those living nearby, or news releases and no-questions press conferences that are decidedly unidirectional, forums like Twitter create opportunities for constant engagement, debate, interaction, and feedback. It provides individuals – particularly those with relatively little political, economic, or social power – a meaningful opportunity to have their views broadcast and heard, in nearly equal measure to the public figures they support or denounce. This can only occur if they are able to see and respond directly to the tweets of public officials, rather than being left alone in the wilderness of their own feeds and followers. In my view, excluding people from that conversation on the basis of their political opinions or substantive viewpoints, in a modern forum designed deliberately for the purpose of fostering that type of dialogue, is properly scrutinized through a constitutional lens.

Specific Platforms

GENERAL

The third category of cases are those in which the government creates specific opportunities for specific types of expression, which I will call the "specific platform" cases. The specific platform cases are not ones in which we can presume the pre-existence of a physical or digital "place," compatible with expressive activities, in which persons can be left alone to express themselves as they please, as in the public forum cases. Rather, it involves the government establishing particular expressive opportunities, typically for a specific or narrow purpose, such as in the case of referenda, plebiscites, consultations, or conferences.

As the cases cited above suggest, granting this opportunity to some, but not all, will not easily lead to a finding that 2(b) has been breached.[43] By and large, access to such specific platforms is treated as a "positive right" that does not call out for judicial correction or scrutiny. As Justice Bastarache observed in *Delisle,* were it otherwise, "the state could not financially support the theatre because that would violate the freedom of expression of musicians; it could not help charitable organizations without violating the freedom of association of chess clubs."[44] A related concern was identified in *NWAC,* where the Court characterized as "untenable" the position that "if the Government chooses to fund a women's organization to study the issue of abortion to assist in drafting proposed legislation," it would be "bound by the Constitution to provide equal funding to a group purporting to represent the rights of fathers."[45]

These statements suggest that governments must be able to choose to survey views of some people on some topics and not others, or to hold public hearings or consultations for this purpose and not that one, and so on. In addition, the creation and use of these specific platforms are typically limited by time, resources, or physical space, if not all three, such that it is not possible to extend the same opportunity all individuals, groups, views, and subject matters.

While overt *restrictions* on expression in connection with these opportunities are properly scrutinized under section 2(b),[46] the failure of the government to *more broadly extend* these specific platforms or opportunities is typically not.

Notably, unlike the general public forum cases, the specific platform cases typically would require the state to actively do something – to solicit certain views or promote certain speech, whether by means of additional topics, additional participants, additional funding, or additional platforms for expression. It seems to be this element of additional state action – beyond the initial choice to create the forum in the first place – which has led the courts to treat these as "positive rights" claims, and with corresponding scepticism.

Similarly, unlike a decision to exclude a person from a true public forum – which all members of the public are presumptively entitled to use to express their views and opinions with those willing to listen – the failure to extend a specific platform does not deprive anyone of an expressive opportunity or ability they otherwise had prior to the impugned government action. In short, while these types of selective funding or platform decisions might, in appropriate cases, raise constitutional *equality* problems, which more readily lend themselves to the imposition of a positive obligation on the government,[47] they generally are not seen as resulting in a breach of section 2(b).

SPECIFIC PLATFORMS AND ELECTION BALLOTS

A recent example of the specific platforms controversy arose in a case called *Rodriguez*, where the claimant challenged the fact that the options on the provincial election ballot did not include a none-of-the-above option, alleging that this infringed his freedom to express his dissatisfaction with all available candidates.[48] The Nova Scotia Supreme Court observed that the claimant was not in any way restricted from expressing himself in relation to the election, nor excluded from participating in the opportunity to do so by voting for candidates. Rather, the claimant's "only complaint is that the government has not designed the voting process in a way that permits him to express a particular opinion by a particular means." The Court held this was "necessarily ... a positive right claim," as it "depends on the premise that the government is under a positive obligation to act in a certain way to facilitate the expressive activity in which he wishes to engage."[49]

This would seem to fit nicely into our category of specific platform cases, in both structure and result. Nothing about the government's conduct deprived the individual in question of the full scope of freedom to which he or she would otherwise have been entitled. Moreover, accepting the conclusion that the government was positively obliged to include on the ballot some options for expression beyond those necessary for the purpose of the ballot would seem to set off an unending chain of demands for each person to express themselves however they see fit through this particular platform.

Benefit Cases – Unconstitutional Conditions

GENERAL

The fourth category I will call the "benefits" cases, which again raise a unique set of issues, albeit ones that often overlap with the forum/platform cases just discussed. The primary concern in the benefits cases derives from the risk that the government will use its spending power to systematically favour viewpoints with which it agrees, or to seek to restrict the views of those with whom it disagrees. We can imagine particularly egregious examples to establish the basic category, such as conditioning access to public health-care coverage upon recipients sharing or expressing certain substantive viewpoints (or not expressing others). Limiting a critically important and generally available government benefit on the basis of a requirement to publicly praise the government, or to refrain from criticizing the government, strikes me as self-evidently intolerable on freedom of expression grounds.

These types of *general* benefit cases share with the public forum cases an important characteristic – that they are general and largely unconditional benefits conferred equally as a right of citizenship or residency. The ultimate claim is not that the government must actively do something – such as create a public park, offer a public health-care or employment insurance program, or confer any other benefit available to the population in general. Rather, the claim is that *once* these benefits or opportunities are conferred on a broad and generalized basis, it effectively shifts the constitutional baseline, after which the state is restricted in its ability to take those benefits away on the basis of expression. In this sense at least, the claimants are not seeking a positive entitlement, as such, but rather to restrict the government from interfering with the pre-existing state of affairs on grounds tied to the exercise of a fundamental freedom.

As in the forum/platform cases, the difficulty in the benefits context tends to be distinguishing between those types of *general* benefits that are properly considered an entitlement of residency or citizenship, and those types of *specific* benefits that – like specific platforms – can be restricted, at least based on the purpose of their conferral. Just as the government may create specific expressive platforms for specific expressive purposes and not others, it may confer specific benefits for specific purposes that could have speech-related implications where doing so is integral to the program itself.

For instance, while most would agree that the government cannot deprive you of health care or access to public parks for criticizing the government or expressing a particular viewpoint, most would also agree that the government can generally choose to subsidize artists and not musicians, or to commission studies addressing substantive racial inequality and not "reverse discrimination." The difficult question, as in the forum/platform cases, is what to do between these extremes.

I am not aware of many Canadian cases addressing this issue directly, except to the extent that they overlap with the public forum and specific platform cases described above (and the overlap is not insignificant). However, there is some guidance in the US case law, where the general rule applied is consistent with the orthodox "negative freedom" position stated above. As outlined in *AID v Alliance for Open Society Intern*:

> As a general matter, if a party objects to a condition on the receipt of federal fund-
> ing, its recourse is to decline the funds. This remains true when the objection is
> that a condition may affect the recipient's exercise of its First Amendment rights.[50]

One of the cases cited in *AID* for the general rule, *Regan v Taxation With Representation of Wash*, dealt with restrictions on charitable tax status on the basis of expressive activities (namely, engaging in political lobbying activities). In *Regan*, the US Supreme Court rejected the premise that freedom of expression requires the government to extend state subsidies in the form of tax breaks, stating that while the claimant "does not have as much money as it wants, and thus cannot exercise its freedom of speech as much as it would like, the Constitution 'does not confer an entitlement to such funds as may be necessary to realize all the advantages of that freedom.' "[51]

However, sorting out a stable and principled line to distinguish between those cases infringing freedom of expression and those merely involving an unwillingness to extend a positive benefit has proven elusive in the US context.[52] Attempting to achieve perfect analytical consistency in this context – whether in relation to "unconstitutional conditions" generally, or in relation to conditions relating to expression specifically – may not be possible.[53]

Nevertheless, the US courts seem to have come up with a few subsidiary doctrines to deal with borderline cases, in an attempt to discern where such selective benefit cases in fact run afoul of the First Amendment. For instance, in the *AID* case quoted above, the Court found that the government could not make federal funding for a program contingent on expressive activities that are in some sense beyond the scope or "contours" of the program or benefit itself.[54] In a similar vein, others suggest that the dividing line is whether the impugned conditions are "relevant" or "germane" to the purposes of the program.[55]

While each of these approaches are imperfect, their ultimate objective is sound: to ensure that governments are genuinely seeking to achieve valid government ends, rather than attempting to leverage government resources to unduly discourage, punish, or otherwise coerce speech with which the government disagrees. The latter circumstance strikes at a core tenet of freedom of expression, as articulated by Justice Jackson in terms that are equally applicable in the Canadian context: "If there is any fixed star in our constitutional constellation, it is that no official, high or petty, can prescribe what shall be orthodox in politics, nationalism, religion, or other matters of opinion or force citizens to confess by word or act their faith therein."[56]

CHARITY CASE AND SUMMER JOBS PROGRAM

There are two recent Canadian cases that I hope can shed some light on this selective benefits issue. First, in *Canada Without Poverty*, the Ontario Superior Court addressed the same issue addressed in *Regan*, but reached the opposite conclusion.[57] The impugned provision of the *Income Tax Act* limited charitable tax status to organizations who devote "substantially all" of their resources to "charitable" as opposed to "political" activities, which had been interpreted by the Canadian Revenue Agency to limit charitable status to those organizations whose public advocacy and expression made up less than 10 per cent of their overall budget. Although the claimant could – like any other private citizen, organization, or corporation – express itself freely in the absence of charitable status, it claimed that being forced to forgo charitable tax status on the basis of its expressive activities placed an unconstitutional restriction on freedom of expression.

The Ontario Superior Court agreed. Most relevant for our purposes, the Court held that because the charitable entity wanted to use preferable tax status to engage in expressive (albeit "political") activities closely tied to its charitable purposes, this meant that restrictions on access to charitable tax status constituted a "state-imposed *burden*" on expressive activities that "*prevents* or *impairs* the right holder from taking advantage of a state-supplied platform that it could otherwise freely access were it not for its insistence on exercising that right."[58] In my view, and with respect, the conclusion that this arrangement constitutes a burden on or impairment of free expression is not self-evident, and there seems to be some reason to doubt it in this context.

In particular, the charities were not seeking treatment equivalent to everyone else – as in the public forum cases or the general benefit cases. They were seeking a special and limited entitlement that is not available to others (charitable tax status), which the government had created for certain limited (non-political) purposes, and not other (political advocacy) purposes. Although perhaps not the most sensible policy available, there seems to be a rational reason for the government to want to subsidize those seen to be providing politically neutral charitable benefits (such as food, housing, clothing, and the like), but not those whose work primarily involves active political advocacy or overt attempts to influence public policy. And the groups affected were not self-evidently "impaired" in engaging in public policy advocacy, any more than the rest of us ineligible for preferable tax status are similarly "impaired" in engaging in our own public policy advocacy. Therefore, while the Court described the purpose of the measure as "to limit political expression,"[59] it could be equally described as "to not subsidize political expression."

Accepting the Court's conclusion on this issue also leads us to a number of uncomfortable questions. Does the fact that charitable tax status is limited to organizations with specific charitable purposes, or to charitable purposes at all, not raise the very same issue – once we assume that the denial of advantageous tax status constitutes a presumptive state-imposed burden on expression? What about other non-profit groups – anti-abortion advocates, for instance – who see their expressive activities as advancing the public welfare, as they view it to be? Is their ineligibility for charitable status not equally a "state-imposed burden" on their expressive activities? Even if we assume that the government can favour certain purposes, such as the alleviation of poverty, over others, what about groups – for instance, economic libertarians – who think that poverty is best alleviated through the absence of government interference, and who could benefit from tax exemptions to better express those views? Once we start going down this track, how do we avoid forcing the government to actively fund all sides of a controversial public policy debate, as a constitutional imperative?

On the other hand, the Court's conclusion can be defended in terms similar to those suggested above. In particular, the conclusion that section 2(b) had been breached turned in part on the Court's conclusion as to the "germaneness" of the condition (restrictions on political advocacy) to the overall purposes of the program (supporting charitable works). The Court effectively concluded that the condition was unrelated to the purposes of conferring charitable status, and indeed undermined those purposes, given that charitable purposes are often advanced through political advocacy as much as through the more direct provision of assistance.[60] In that sense, it could be argued that the condition tied to expressive activities was unconnected to the overall purpose of the program, as the Court viewed it to be. This highlights one of the difficulties with a germaneness consideration, which, perhaps unavoidably, turns on how specific (e.g., to support *non-advocacy based* charitable activities) or abstract (e.g., to advance charitable purposes *generally*) the Court's description of the purpose of the program is.

Overall, and while the point is certainly not beyond dispute, I think the case might have been better viewed as a specific benefits case, in which the government has considerable leeway to fund some activities and not others on various grounds relevant to the government's objectives, particularly given that the criteria used were not designed to privilege the substantive views of certain groups and not others. By contrast, charitable tax status (or any other specific benefit) contingent on expressing views favourable to or supported by the current government would tend to raise greater freedom of expression concerns.

The second case in this category arguably raises just those types of concerns. In 2018, it was announced that the federal government intended to restrict access to its summer jobs program based on the views or expression of particular groups; more specifically, the government said that no funding would be provided to organizations that refused to complete an attestation indicating their support for, among other things, reproductive freedom and access to abortion.[61] This was seen by some as an attempt to simply punish or coerce those who would otherwise be entitled to the benefit, on the basis of expression tied to their substantive world views, and in a way not rationally connected or germane to the policy itself (see Sirota, this volume).

In assessing this argument, we cannot ignore a number of clear similarities between the summer jobs controversy and the charitable tax status case. As with charitable tax status, no one is deprived of their ability to hold or express their opinions by the existence of the summer jobs program, or their ineligibility for it. The primary difference is that the condition in the charitable tax status case was both viewpoint-neutral[62] and (at least arguably) directly tied to the government's objectives in creating the benefit in question, while in the summer jobs case, a benefit ostensibly available to organizations generally was conditioned upon the expression of views deemed appropriate by the government, and without any close or obvious connection to the purposes of the program itself. If this characterization is correct, one can argue that the latter calls out for a constitutional justification in a way that the former does not.

Conclusion

As can be seen, the above discussion does not lead to any clearly defined rules or pristine, watertight categories. Some of the assumptions or perspectives endorsed above are disputable on any number of grounds, and this discussion only starts to scratch the surface in terms of the nuances these types of cases often present and the arguments in either direction. My primary goal has been to highlight the types of cases in which our "positive" vs. "negative" rights issue tends to arise in the context of freedom of expression, and to start to think about the different considerations that apply in each type of case, controversial and nebulous as the categories may be.

Adhering to the above categories will certainly create some difficulties in terms of the proper characterization in specific circumstances, as the government benefits cases demonstrate in particular, and ultimately this may require some degree of value judgments around the margins of each. However, in my view, seeing these categories of cases as being distinct in meaningful ways is better than attempting to achieve a degree of consistency or a uniform "test" across constitutional entitlements that is nearly impossible to maintain. The difficulty with general "positive" vs. "negative" rights analyses – or with the "unconstitutional conditions" subject matter more broadly – is that they often seek to combine too many disparate types of cases into a single framework, where there are degrees of nuance that may need to be attended to in light of the particular right or freedom at issue or the particular circumstance at hand. I hope that by attending to the above categories in the specific context of freedom of expression, at least as a starting point, we can avoid offering simplistic answers to inherently difficult questions and give these types of cases the careful attention they deserve.

NOTES

1   Among recent cases confirming this general principle, see, for example, *UAlberta Pro-Life v Governors of the University of Alberta*, 2020 ABCA 1 at paras 208–14; *Toronto (City) v Ontario (Attorney General)*, 2019 ONCA 732 [*Toronto (City) (ONCA)*] at paras 41–2, 47–8.

2   See, for example, *Vriend v Alberta*, [1998] 1 SCR 493; *Dunmore v Ontario (Attorney General)*, 2001 SCC 94.

3   Albeit subject to a different analysis than a direct challenge to a statute. See, for example, *RWDSU, Local 558 v Pepsi-Cola Canada Beverages (West) Ltd.*, 2002 SCC 8.

4   See Brian Langille and Benjamin J. Oliphant, "The Legal Structure of Freedom of Association," *Queen's Law Journal* 30 (2014): 262–5, and the sources cited therein.

5   As I will argue below is the case with respect to the fundamental freedoms, at least in their core application.

6   The section 23(3) obligation on the state to provide minority language schooling "where numbers warrant" is a quintessential "positive" obligation.

7   As noted, section 15 contemplates both negative rights (i.e., that individuals will not be punished or burdened by state action in a discriminatory manner) as well as positive rights (i.e., that individuals may be entitled to certain state benefits or protections given to others if their exclusion is discriminatory).

8   Indeed, I think taking care in this type of categorization is often critically important. See generally Langille and Oliphant, "Legal Structure."

9   See Benjamin J. Oliphant, "The Nature of the Fundamental Freedoms and the *Sui Generis* Right to Collective Bargaining: The Case of Vulnerable and Precarious Workers," *Canadian Labour and Employment Law Journal* 21 (2019): 322–38.

10   *Haig v Canada; Haig v Canada (Chief Electoral Officer)*, [1993] 2 SCR 995 [*Haig*] at 1035.

11   Ibid., at 1041.

12   *Native Women's Assn. of Canada v Canada*, [1994] 3 SCR 627 [*NWAC*] at 654–6; *Siemens v Manitoba (Attorney General)*, 2003 SCC 3 [*Siemens*] at paras 41–2; *Baier v Alberta*, 2007 SCC 31 [*Baier*] at paras 21–6.

13   See, for example, *Haig, supra*, at 1039; *Delisle v Canada (Deputy Attorney General)*, [1999] 2 SCR 989 [*Delisle*] at paras 25, 26, 33.

14   See generally Oliphant, "Fundamental Freedoms."

15   See *Haig, NWAC, Siemens, Baier, supra*. See also the cases cited in *supra* note 1.

16   See generally Oliphant, "Fundamental Freedoms," 330–8.

17   *Delisle, supra*, at para 26. The Court has at times implied that there is no meaningful distinction between rights and freedoms, and that the "freedom to do a

thing, when guaranteed by the Constitution interpreted purposively, implies a right to do it." See *Ontario (Attorney General) v Fraser*, 2011 SCC 20 t para 67. While I would agree that the mere use of the terms "freedom" or "right" is not dispositive, I think the suggestion that there is no distinction between the terms is overstated. See, for example, Langille and Oliphant, "Legal Structure," 266–8.

18 Isaiah Berlin, "Two Concepts of Liberty," in *Liberty: Incorporating Four Essays on Liberty*, edited by Henry Hardy (Oxford: Oxford University Press, 2013), 169. And see Oliphant, "Fundamental Freedoms," 323–38.

19 See, for example, the discussion in Oliphant, "Fundamental Freedoms," 333–7.

20 Such as in the context of elections. See, for example, *Harper v Canada (Attorney General)*, 2004 SCC 33.

21 Frederick Schauer, "Too Hard: Unconstitutional Conditions and the Chimera of Constitutional Consistency," *Denver University Law Review* 989 (1994–5): 992–3; Cass Sunstein, "Why the Unconstitutional Conditions Doctrine Is an Anachronism (with Particular Reference to Religion, Speech, and Abortion)," *Boston University Law Review* 70 (1990): 597–9.

22 A more complete discussion of this issue can be found in Oliphant, "Fundamental Freedoms," 330–40.

23 *Baier, supra*, at para 76.

24 Although a thoughtful attempt to square the freedom of expression case law with the exceptional imposition of positive obligations in the context of freedom of association, there is some dispute as to how helpful the analysis is in this context. See, for example, Robert E. Charney, "The Shaky Foundation of 'Statutory Platforms': A Comment on *Baier v. Alberta*," *Supreme Court Law Review* 42 (2008): 116.

25 *Baier, supra*, at paras 72–7. The fact that the claim did not properly fall within section 2(b) does not necessarily mean it should have been excluded from constitutional scrutiny altogether. See generally Robin Elliot and Michael Elliot, "The Addition of an Interest-Based Route into Section 15 of the Charter: Why It's Necessary and How It Can Be Justified," *Supreme Court Law Review* 64 (2d) (2014): 461.

26 *City of Toronto et al v Ontario (Attorney General)*, 2018 ONSC 5151 [*Toronto City Council*] at para 30.

27 Ibid., at paras 27–39.

28 Ibid., at para 58.

29 Ibid., at paras 52–61. On this point, see the analysis in Jamie Cameron and Bailey Fox, "Toronto's 2018 Municipal Election, Rights of Democratic Participation, and Section 2(b) of the Charter," *Constitutional Forum* 30, no. 1 (2021): 1–18.

30 *Toronto (City) (ONCA), supra*, at para 41.

31 Ibid., at paras 58–9.

32 Ibid., at para 59.

33 A more generous reading of the section 2(b) case law in the context of the Toronto
    City Council case can be found in Cameron and Fox, "Toronto's 2018 Municipal
    Election," where they make a strong argument that, on an orthodox section 2(b)
    analysis, the legislation in question had the effect of interfering with free expression.
    This is, I agree, the proper question in this case, rather than framing it as a matter
    of positive or negative rights. Where I depart from these learned authors is in the
    suggestion that government action "affecting" expressive activities is per se a breach
    of section 2(b) (see Cameron and Fox, "Toronto's 2018 Municipal Election," 12, 15).
    As noted above, in my view, there must be some dividing line here, because almost
    all government activity of any consequence has at least some derivative "effect" on
    expression, if that term is viewed widely enough. The question is whether the type
    of "effect" occasioned here constitutes a limitation on expression sufficient to estab-
    lish a breach, and how to distinguish this case from the multitude of other govern-
    ment actions that indirectly impact or affect the content, relevance, or effectiveness
    of past or future speech, without actually limiting or inhibiting that speech as such.

34 See, for example, *Minnesota Voters Alliance v Mansky*, 138 S Ct 1876 (2018), at
    1885–8.

35 *Greater Vancouver Transportation Authority v Canadian Federation of Students –
    British Columbia Component*, 2009 SCC 31 [*Greater Vancouver*].

36 Ibid., at para 43.

37 See, for example, *Bracken v Niagara Parks Police*, 2018 ONCA 261 at paras 39–44,
    and the cases cited therein.

38 *Greater Vancouver, supra*, at para 35.

39 As in any other *Charter* context, this does not mean that anyone can use such pub-
    lic forums unconditionally. See, for example, *Montréal (City) v 29521366 Québec
    Inc.*, 2005 SCC 62; *Canadian Broadcasting Corp. v Canada (Attorney General)*,
    2011 SCC 2.

40 See, for example, Joan Bryden, "Test Case Challenges a Politician's Right to Block
    People from Twitter Account," *Globe and Mail*, 17 October 2018, https://www
    .theglobeandmail.com/canada/article-test-case-challenges-a-politicians-right
    -to-block-people-from-twitter-2/. In the US context, see *Knight First Amendment
    Inst. v Trump*, 928 F 3d 226 (2d Cir 2019).

41 My views are developed more fully elsewhere, from which some of this text was
    borrowed: Benjamin Oliphant, "Twitter Blocking, Freedom of Expression, and
    Public Forums," *Double Aspect Blog*, 17 October 2018, https://doubleaspect
    .blog/2018/10/17/twitter-blocking-freedom-of-expression-and-public-forums/.

42 See *Packingham v North Carolina*, 137 S Ct 1730 (2017), at 1737.

43 See *supra* notes 10–16 and surrounding text.

44 *Delisle, supra*, at para 29.

45 *NWAC, supra*, at 655–6.

46 See, for example, *Libman v Quebec (Attorney General)*, [1997] 3 SCR 569.

47 Cases like *NWAC, supra,* may be a good candidate for more robust scrutiny in this respect. And see also Elliot and Elliot, "Interest-Based Route into Section 15."

48 *Rodriguez v Canada,* 2018 FC 1125 [*Rodriguez*].

49 Ibid., at para 43.

50 *AID v Alliance for Open Society Intern,* 133 S Ct 2321 (2013) [*AID*] at 2328.

51 *Regan v Taxation with Representation of Washington,* 461 US 540 (1983) [*Regan*] at 549.

52 For a helpful discussion of the inconsistencies, see Elena Kagan, "The Changing Faces of First Amendment Neutrality: *R.A.V. v. St. Paul, Rust v. Sullivan,* and the Problem of Content-Based Underinclusion," *Supreme Court Review* 1992 (1993): 29.

53 See, for example, Schauer, "Constitutional Consistency"; Sunstein, "Unconstitutional Conditions Doctrine."

54 *AID, supra,* at 2328–32, per Roberts CJ.

55 See, for example, K Sullivan, "Unconstitutional Conditions," *Harvard Law Review* 102 (1989): 1456–75.

56 *West Virginia Bd of Ed v Barnette,* 319 US 624 (1943) at 642. And see also Sunstein, "Unconstitutional Conditions Doctrine," 611–15.

57 *Canada Without Poverty v AG Canada,* 2018 ONSC 4147 [*CWP*].

58 Ibid., at paras 47–8 (emphasis added); see also paras 44–6.

59 Ibid., at para 57.

60 Ibid., at paras 41–3.

61 Brian Platt, "How the Canada Summer Jobs Program Became a Freedom-of -Religion Controversy," *National Post,* 21 January 2018, https://nationalpost.com /news/politics/how-the-canada-summer-jobs-program-became-a-freedom-of -religion-controversy. A slightly more nuanced version of the policy was subsequently adopted; see Jordan Press, "Liberals Drop Contentious Anti-abortion Test for Summer Jobs Funding," *CBC News,* 6 December 2018, https://www.cbc.ca /news/politics/liberals-summer-jobs-program-changes-1.4934674.

62 By "viewpoint-neutral" I mean that while the impugned measure clearly drew distinctions between the functions or activities of different charities – based on whether they sought to fulfil their purposes through political advocacy – it did not draw the distinction based on the substantive viewpoints of the charity (e.g., politically progressive or conservative, for or against a particular policy, etc.).

8 Compelled Speech: A Conscience- and Integrity-Based Approach

LÉONID SIROTA

Compelled speech – speech whose subject, and sometimes content, is dictated to a greater or lesser extent by law – is at once routine and dramatic. We encounter it every time we go to the grocery store, in the form of "nutritional information" required to be disclosed by anyone who sells us food or drink, and think nothing of it. The legal system, one might say, runs on compelled speech, in the shape of prescribed forms to be filed, documents to be disclosed, and witness testimony to be offered. At the other end of the spectrum, instances of compelled speech, such as Galileo's abjuration of the Copernican theory at the Inquisition's command or Henry VIII's unsuccessful attempt to extract an oath from Thomas More, live in historical and literary infamy.

It thus seems that, while some – perhaps a good deal of – speech compulsion is generally acceptable in a free and democratic society, other cases are beyond the pale. Yet the location of the dividing line between these two categories is difficult to ascertain.[1] In Canada, there are few Supreme Court cases on point (I will return to them below). In the United States, there are more, but their coherence leaves much to be desired.[2] Moreover, cases that involve compelled speech are not always litigated under the constitutional provisions explicitly protecting the freedom of speech or expression (in Canada, section 2(b) of the *Canadian Charter of Rights and Freedoms*).

This chapter endeavours to sketch a framework for thinking about compelled speech that could be used by a principled court. (The chapter makes no attempt to persuade courts to be principled, which they often are not.) It seeks to substantiate the intuition that, at least in some cases, speech compulsion is deeply disturbing, while eschewing the implausible "absolutist position that compelled noncommercial speech" – let alone the commercial sort – "is always unconstitutional."[3] It also takes into account the close, although often murky, relationship between the freedoms of expression and conscience that exists in cases of compelled speech.

The chapter sets out some examples of controversies surrounding compelled speech, most of them cases decided by the courts, but also some ongoing disputes. The focus is on Canada, but I briefly mention some American cases too. A subsequent section draws on these examples to point out that, while they involve a number of different constitutional rights, the underlying interests at stake in difficult compelled speech cases are those of conscience and integrity. Finally, the chapter proposes a framework for deciding compelled cases with these interests in mind before ending with a brief conclusion.

Some Examples

As mentioned at the outset, instances where individuals or organizations are required to engage in particular kinds of expression are very common. These include all manner of disclosure and reporting requirements, as well as process compelling witness testimony and the production of documents for the purposes of litigation. Most of these speech compulsions are perceived as unproblematic. Some may be objectionable on the grounds that they are unnecessarily cumbersome or invasive, but criticism along these lines goes to the detail rather than the principle of the speech compulsions at which it is aimed. Other objections, however, are more fundamental. In this section, I review a number of examples, starting with those that produced the few Supreme Court of Canada decisions on compelled speech and some other Canadian judicial decisions, as well as some well-known American cases and some ongoing controversies.

Supreme Court of Canada

The Supreme Court of Canada first engaged with compelled speech well before the enactment of the *Charter*. One of the statutes enacted as part of Alberta's attempt to implement social credit policies, and subsequently declared invalid by the Supreme Court,[4] would have required newspapers to publish the government's statements about its policies and also to disclose the identity of its sources to the government. The majority of the Court found that this legislation was part of and ancillary to the overall Social Credit legislative scheme and that it was invalid along with the rest of that scheme. However, Duff C.J. (with the agreement of Davis J.), without expressing a definitive opinion on the matter, suggested that the statute in question set up "autocratic powers which, it may well be thought, could, if arbitrarily wielded, be employed to frustrate" the freedom of public discussion.[5] Cannon J. was rather more categorical, writing that the legislation was based on the policy that "[t]he Social Credit doctrine must become, for the people of Alberta, a sort of religious dogma of which a free and uncontrolled discussion is not permissible," which would be achieved by "reducing any opposition to silence or bring[ing] upon it ridicule and public contempt."[6] Cannon J. added that the "right of the people to be informed through sources independent of the government concerning matters of public interest"[7] was essential to the operation of a democratic political system.

In another case decided with only minimal reference to the then just enacted *Charter*, the Supreme Court considered a labour arbitrator's order that an employer send its employees a letter stating, notably, that it approved of the labour legislation that applied to it.[8] The order was unanimously invalidated on grounds not directly connected to freedom of expression. However, a majority of the Court joined a brief concurring opinion by Beetz J., which rejected the order on the additional ground that "[t]his type of penalty is totalitarian and as such alien to the tradition of free nations like Canada, even for the repression of the most serious crimes."[9] Citizens are not required to approve of legislation – only to comply with it – and they cannot be made to voice approval where none exists. Beetz J. added that the *Charter*'s guarantee of the "freedom of thought, belief, opinion and expression" (section 2(b)) protects not only a person's "right to express the opinions he may have: a fortiori [it] must prohibit compelling anyone to utter opinions that are not his own."[10]

However, the Supreme Court soon qualified this view in the first fully *Charter*-based case on compelled speech. This time, it upheld another labour arbitrator's order that an employer provide an unfairly dismissed employee with a reference letter setting out the arbitrator's findings about the employee's performance.[11] Speaking for the majority on this point, Lamer J. (as he then was) found that, while a limitation of the employer's freedom of expression, the order was justified under section 1 of the *Charter*. It was a remedy for the employer's prior breach of the law, "limited to requiring that the employer state 'objective' facts which, in the case at bar, are not in dispute," and thus "not [a] very serious" imposition.[12] The majority of the Court went further and upheld an additional order prohibiting the employer from supplementing the letter dictated by the arbitrator. Lamer J. dissented on this point, on the ground that this had the effect of transforming a factual statement into an implicit expression of opinion endorsing this statement.

Meanwhile, Beetz J. dissented with respect to both orders. In particular, he rejected the distinction with *National Bank* based on the argument that the employer in *Slaight* was merely ordered to provide a true statement of facts:

> The former employer cannot be forced to acknowledge and state [these facts] as the truth apart from his belief in their veracity. If he states these facts in the letter, as ordered, but does not believe them to be true, he does not tell the truth, he tells a lie ... There may be a distinction, somewhat difficult to apply, between being forced to express opinions or views which one does not necessarily entertain, and being compelled to state facts, the veracity of which one does not necessarily believe; but, in my opinion, both types of coercion constitute gross violations of

the freedoms of opinion and expression or, at the very least, of the freedom of expression ... [S]uch a violation is totalitarian in nature and can never be justified under s. 1 of the *Charter*. It does not differ, essentially, from the command given to Galileo by the Inquisition to abjure the cosmology of Copernicus.[13]

That said, Beetz J. would have approved of an order requiring the employer to set out the arbitrator's findings, provided that they were clearly identified as such.

Finally, the Supreme Court has unanimously upheld the requirement that government-designed health warnings occupy at least 50 per cent of cigarette packaging.[14] The warnings were presented as the government's messaging, but the Court found that they limited the freedom of expression. However, the limitation was easily justified, being reasonably regarded as necessary to inform consumers of the effects of the product they were about to purchase, and creating large benefits at a small cost to the tobacco manufacturers' "expressive interest in creative packaging."[15]

Some Other Canadian Cases

Some lower court decisions are worth briefly discussing here. In the first, the Court of Appeal for Ontario upheld the requirement that applicants for Canadian citizenship swear an oath to, notably, "be faithful and bear true allegiance to Her Majesty Queen Elizabeth the Second, Queen of Canada, Her Heirs and Successors."[16] The Court found that this requirement did not limit the prospective citizens' rights under section 2(b) of the *Charter*, on the basis that "[r]ather than undermining freedom of expression, the oath amounts to an affirmation of the societal values and constitutional architecture of this country, which promote and protect expression."[17] Furthermore, while "[t]he oath has an incidental effect on expression ... this effect is not worthy of constitutional disapprobation."[18] The Court also rejected the claim that the oath requirement infringed the freedom of religion of those who objected to the monarchy's association with the Church of England.

The Court of Appeal also rejected a challenge to the constitutionality of the requirement that medical professionals who object, on conscientious grounds, to providing certain services such as abortion and medical assistance in dying provide "effective referrals" to allow patients seeking these services to obtain them elsewhere.[19] The Court found that the requirement limited the objecting physicians' freedom of religion, but upheld it as justified under section 1 of the *Charter* on the basis, notably, that no alternative approach could provide timely access to the medical procedures desired by vulnerable patients. Although asked to address freedom of conscience in addition to freedom of religion, the Court did not do so, reasoning that "[t]o the extent the individual appellants raise issues of conscience, they are inextricably grounded in their religious beliefs."[20]

Most recently, however, Ontario's Superior Court of Justice struck down a provincial statute requiring gas stations to display stickers advising all and sundry of the provincial government's views about the effect of the federal carbon tax.[21] Morgan J. found that this requirement, in contrast to the citizenship oath, did not promote democracy and the rule of law, or even convey true information. Instead, it was purely partisan and misleading, and, as such, lacked a pressing and substantial objective, which is necessary for a limitation on the freedom of expression to be justified under the *Charter*.[22]

Ongoing Controversies

A number of recent or ongoing controversies, some of which could yet produce judicial decisions, also involve compelled speech. I review them briefly here, because they show that the issue of compelled speech is pressing. Indeed, it appears to be becoming more so.

In 2016, the Law Society of Upper Canada (since renamed the Law Society of Ontario) adopted a requirement that each of its licensees create and abide by a "Statement of Principles" acknowledging a purported "obligation to promote equality, diversity and inclusion generally, and in their behaviour towards colleagues, employees, clients, and the public."[23] Initially described as intended "to demonstrate a personal valuing of equality, diversity, and inclusion with respect to the employment of others, or in professional dealings with other licensees or any other person,"[24] the Statement of Principles was then said to do no more than restate licensees' existing obligations under anti-discrimination laws. Many of those subject to the Statement of Principles requirement, including the present author, remained unpersuaded,[25] especially since the Law Society refused to be legally bound by this interpretation of the requirement. The Statement of Principles requirement was repealed in 2019, following the election of benchers (members of the Law Society's governing board) who campaigned against it.[26] A legal challenge to the requirement, alleging *inter alia* that it breaches the *Charter*'s guarantees of freedom of thought, belief, opinion, and expression and freedom of conscience, had been launched, but it is likely moot now that the requirement is no longer in effect.

In 2017, the federal government required applicants for funding under the Canada Summer Jobs Program to attest, notably, that the applicant "organization's core mandate respect[s] individual human rights in Canada, including the values underlying the Canadian Charter of Rights and Freedoms as well as other rights. These include reproductive rights and the right to be free from discrimination on the basis of sex, religion, race, national or ethnic origin, colour, mental or physical disability, sexual orientation or gender identity or expression."[27] The constitutionality of this requirement was challenged by groups that regard it as a violation of their freedoms of conscience and expression. In late 2018, the government substantially modified the attestation requirement. Its relevant part is now limited to a statement that "[a]ny funding under the Canada Summer Jobs program will not be used to undermine or restrict the exercise of rights legally protected in Canada."[28] However, the constitutional challenge to the previous version of the attestation is still ongoing, and the new version has been criticized as a flawed attempt to invoke the constitutional rights of some individuals to limit those of others.[29]

Some US Cases

A brief consideration of some cases decided by the Supreme Court of the United States is also instructive. To be sure, that court is generally more solicitous of the freedom of expression than Canadian courts are, and Canadian courts have sometimes found American precedents in this area unpersuasive.[30] That said, the Supreme Court of Canada has not considered First Amendment jurisprudence in its few compelled speech cases.

Perhaps the most famous American decision on compelled speech is *West Virginia State Board of Education v Barnette*.[31] In a stirring opinion by Jackson J., a majority of the Supreme Court held that school authorities could not require objecting children to salute the American flag, concluding that

> freedom to differ is not limited to things that do not matter much. That would be a mere shadow of freedom. The test of its substance is the right to differ as to things that touch the heart of the existing order. If there is any fixed star in our constitutional constellation, it is that no official, high or petty, can prescribe what shall be orthodox in politics, nationalism, religion, or other matters of opinion or force citizens to confess by word or act their faith therein.[32]

The US Supreme Court has found to be unconstitutional a number of other speech compulsions. For example, it struck down a statute requiring newspapers to publish a reply by a candidate for office to any criticism made by the newspaper.[33] It also invalidated a statute making it illegal to obscure the state motto on car licence plates, which had the effect of forcing motorists to display the motto on their vehicles.[34] (The motto in question, paradoxically, was New Hampshire's "Live Free or Die.") For the Court, the state could not make a citizen "participate in the dissemination of an ideological message by displaying it on his private property."[35] Most recently, it invalidated, as a violation of the freedom of speech, a statute requiring providers of services to pregnant women – including providers opposed to abortion – to communicate certain information about the availability of abortion services funded in whole or in part by the state government.[36]

What Is at Stake

Complementary Rights

One point that should be apparent from the foregoing review of cases and controversies related to compelled speech is that they involve claims based on a number of different, but related and even overlapping, rights. Most involve the freedom of expression (as it is termed under the *Charter*) or of speech (under the First Amendment). The freedoms of thought, belief, and opinion, which are protected by section 2(b) of the *Charter*, the same provision that guarantees the freedom of expression, and which have seldom been given independent consideration,[37] are sometimes referred to as well. (This is notably the case in Beetz J.'s opinion in *National Bank*; in *Slaight*, which was actually argued as a *Charter* case, Beetz J. only mentioned the freedom of opinion, and more tentatively than in *National Bank*.) *Miami Herald* was a freedom of the press case, and it seems logical to suppose that this right – also protected by section 2(b) – would have been argued had the *Charter* been in place when the *Alberta Statutes Reference* was decided.

But the arguments about compelled speech also feature other rights, which have a content quite independent from the freedom of expression. Notably, the freedoms of conscience and religion are raised in some cases, together with or even as an alternative to freedom of expression. *McAteer* featured both expression and religion claims. *CMDSC* was argued as a freedom of religion and freedom of conscience case, although the Court of Appeal only addressed freedom of religion. The case against the Law Society of Ontario's Statement of Principles requirement invoked both the freedom of expression and the freedom of conscience.

And even cases that present themselves as being about freedom of speech or expression sometimes involve elements of freedom of conscience or of religion. Some involve religious objectors: both *Barnette* and *Maynard*, for example, were brought by Jehovah's Witnesses. But it is telling that, in *Slaight*, which on its face had nothing to do with religion, Beetz J. invoked the example of "the command given to Galileo by the Inquisition to abjure the cosmology of Copernicus."[38] *That*, of course, was an example of religious persecution. It is telling, too, that in the *Alberta Statutes Reference* Cannon J. compared the inculcation of the Social Credit doctrine to that of "religious dogma."

Indeed, the choice of the particular right on which arguments against compelled speech are based sometimes seems to be dictated more by litigation strategy than by the nature of the case. Lack of precedent related to freedom of conscience may explain why this right was not emphasized in *McAteer* – as perhaps it ought to have been.[39] The Canadian courts' relative lack of solicitude for freedom of expression, or at least their willingness to uphold restrictions on it, may explain why *CMDSC* was presented as a case about religion and conscience rather than expression – while the situation in the United States is the opposite, and so *NIFLA*, arising out of similar facts (albeit that the regulation invalidated there was less onerous than that upheld in *CMDSC*) was a free speech case.

Conscience and Integrity

The multiplicity of rights involved in controversies involving compelled speech obscures an important and under-appreciated reality. Whether they are presented as being about freedom of expression, freedom of the press, or freedom of religion, many of these controversies centre around the ability of the persons whose speech the government wants to compel to act, and to present themselves as acting, in accordance with their own moral judgments and with integrity. Understanding that what is at stake in these cases are integrity and moral freedom, or, in other words, the freedom of conscience, is key to developing a principled way to resolve them, regardless of the contingent choices about litigation strategy and tactics.

The underlying claim or concern in many – but by no means all – cases involving compelled speech is that it would be *wrong* for the persons being targeted by the speech compulsion to speak as the government wishes them to. This wrongfulness may result from two main causes. First, the content of the speech being compelled may itself be morally problematic for the persons targeted by the compulsion. This may be because the ideas or opinions being communicated or suggested contradict some rule about right and wrong to which they subscribe. This is, for example, the issue in *Barnette* and *Maynard*. The moral issue can also arise, as Beetz J. suggested in *Slaight*, if one is being made to state purported facts that one does not believe to be true, in which case one is required to engage in conduct most people regard as morally wrong: lying.

When the state forces persons to speak or act in a way that they regard as morally prohibited, it commits a wrong of its own against them by interfering with their conscience, understood as an internal "moral judge or a faculty that signals what one ought to do (or not do),"[40] or passes judgment on one's actions.[41] This interference infringes the constitutional protection of freedom of conscience, which "protects moral judgments regardless of their source," on the basis that "moral reasoning is central to the human experience."[42] The state is not authorized to meddle with an individual's moral reasoning, or to deny its efficacy by ordering a person to disregard the commands of his or her conscience. In Lord Acton's words, the protection of the freedom of conscience rests on the recognition that "[t]he knowledge of good and evil [is] not an exclusive and sublime prerogative assigned to states, or nations, or majorities,"[43] but is within the capabilities, and responsibility, of individual persons.

Conscience can, but need not, be guided by religious considerations. For a religious person, it may be, in Abraham Lincoln's words, "the right as God gives us to see the right,"[44] while for a non-believer it may be something akin to an internal voice, but one that is entitled to the same sort of deference, and obedience, as God would be. Given the universality of moral reasoning in human experience, the torment of a person who has acted against the commands of his or her conscience is something that another human being ought to be able to understand and empathize with regardless of whether that conscience was religiously guided.[45] In any case, "[t]he experience of self-betrayal in matters of what is morally right and wrong – in matters of conscience – differs qualitatively from an inability to live in accordance with other matters such as personal preferences and tastes."[46]

Related to but somewhat distinct from a person's interest in safeguarding the autonomy of his or her conscience is that in protecting his or her integrity. While a complex notion,[47] integrity refers in part to "a certain concentration or purity or consistency," including "act[ing] as oneself only, rather than unconsciously or thoughtlessly mixing in with oneself the attitudes or habits of others," or, indeed, "standing alone for the sake of some commitment or other and refusing to go along with others or be incorporated in their plans or deeds."[48] In other words, persons of integrity follow through on their moral judgment, including when doing so is difficult or costly. But even without having come to conclusive moral judgments of their own, such persons refuse to allow themselves to be defined by the moral judgments of others, including "states, nations, and majorities." Kateb argues that Socrates is a model of moral of integrity in just this sense.

Interference with the integrity of those subject to compulsion is the second way in which compelled speech may be a wrong. Those who are speaking under government dictation are not speaking for themselves, and are therefore not acting with integrity, regardless of whether they regard the contents of what they are made to say as morally or factually misguided. To be made to do so is, as Richard Moon argues, an "indignity."[49] But the ability to refrain from expressing a view is also an important part of integrity, which is why it is not necessarily the case that, as Professor Moon suggests, "silence is [not] as valuable to the individual as expression."[50] Moreover, the view required to be communicated may contradict or undermine some other message that the person subject to the requirement may wish to communicate or some other aspect of the person's self-presentation,[51] undermining the speaker's integrity in the sense of purity or consistency of purpose. This was part of the issue in press freedom cases (the *Alberta Statutes Reference*, according to Cannon J., and

Miami Herald), and is the objection that a number of people, the present author included, had to the Law Society of Ontario's Statement of Principles.[52]

As Bird notes, conscience and integrity are very closely linked, because "[c]onscience points to moral judgments, and living in alignment with these judgments (or not) affects our integrity."[53] Indeed, "[i]ntegrity can be understood as the fruit of forming and following conscience."[54] Conversely, as Shapiro and Adams note, "one is hard-pressed to imagine a person feeling compelled to ignore her sense of what integrity requires to remain faithful to her conscience."[55] In respecting freedom of conscience, the state will also thereby make room for individuals to live with integrity (whether or not they take advantage of the opportunity). Conversely, state interference with a person's integrity, at a minimum, calls into question the state's commitment to freedom of conscience, because it evinces a lack of respect for the person's endeavour to live conscientiously.

Conscience and integrity share two very important characteristics. First, both are inherently subjective. As already noted, moral beliefs are personal; they are not to be dictated by state authorities. Similarly, what a person considers to be compatible with following his or her conscientious beliefs and self-presentation cannot be decided by others. Of course, the judgments on matters of morality and integrity of most members of a given community at a given time are likely to overlap. On some points at least, the consensus may be much more widespread. But that does not obviate the principle that the prerogative, and the responsibility, to judge these issues belongs to the individual. As a result, in cases implicating conscience and integrity "the essential question" is "whether the claimant sincerely believes that a certain course of action would cause her to commit, collaborate, or cooperate with immorality – with something that she considers morally wrong or evil."[56]

Second, and relatedly, the rightness or wrongness of the conscientious precepts a person holds, or "the pursuits that a person believes to constitute a life of integrity,"[57] are not relevant to the state's responsibilities in this realm. Of course, once one leaves the realm of pure belief and enters that of action, the state may be justified in intervening to prevent one from interfering with the rights of others. But that intervention can only properly be directed at securing these rights, and not on imposing a belief that the state believes to be correct, appropriate, or beneficial.

Proposed Approach to Compelled Speech

Recognizing that conscience and integrity are what is really at stake in compelled speech cases helps explain why any number of mundane speech compulsions are intuitively unproblematic. Most cases of compelled speech involve the disclosure of information in one form or another – whether on packaging of goods offered for sale, in various forms one is required to file with the government, including tax returns, or as witness testimony. I use the term "disclosure" to highlight the fact that the information required to be communicated in such contexts ought to be true, so far as the person required to provide it can tell, and that it is something already in the possession of the person in question, rather than being dictated by the state. The oath witnesses are required to swear enjoining them to tell "the truth, the whole truth, and nothing but the truth" illustrates this principle. Different considerations will apply to cases where persons targeted by speech compulsions are made to say something they do not believe to be true.

Generally speaking, the objections one might have to disclosures of information one believes to be true are not related to conscience and integrity. One might find such disclosures cumbersome or injurious to one's economic interests, of course. But there is, generally, no moral requirement preventing persons from telling what they believe to be true, and they will not normally be compromising their integrity, in the sense of self-contradiction, by supplying true facts in their possession. Thus, compelled disclosures are often justifiable, although they must remain subject to review to ensure that they are not unreasonably onerous in relation to their purposes. Electoral law provides a ready example of excessively burdensome disclosures in the shape of registration and reporting requirements imposed on individuals and organizations who seek to communicate with the public on matters of electoral concern in the period immediately preceding an election.[58]

It should be noted that there are some concerning cases even in the category of compelled disclosures of information. One, to which I turn below, concerns testimony that a person may have reasons of conscience for refusing to provide. Another concerns speech compulsions that are ostensibly disclosures of information but are really intended to convey a negative, and quite possibly misleading, impression to the recipients of the information at issue. Unless they are related to a public concern that can be demonstrably justified (that is, supported by evidence) by the government, such requirements may well interfere with the integrity of those subject to them by making them present themselves or their products or services as more dangerous or harmful than they believe them to be. Requirements that food containing genetically modified organisms (GMOs) be identified as such are perhaps the most obvious example. So long as there is no actual evidence of GMOs' harmfulness, the mandatory disclosure likely makes such food appear more suspicious than its makers think it to be.

At the other end of the spectrum of justifiability of speech compulsions, compelled statements of opinion, as well as compelled statements of alleged facts that the person required to make the statement does not believe to be true, are (virtually[59]) never justifiable. They replace the judgment of individuals as to what is right or true with that of the authorities, and are, as Justice Beetz said in *National Bank*, "alien to the tradition of free nations like Canada." When the state dictates, to a greater or lesser degree, the content of the opinions or facts to be affirmed, the speech compulsion amounts to the imposition of an official ideology. But even if the targets of the speech compulsion are left entirely free as to the content of their statement (a prospect that seems, in any event, illusory), the requirement to express an opinion on an issue on which one would rather remain silent interferes with the integrity of one's self-presentation.

In particular, it is important to stress that speech compulsions cannot be justified by widespread or official disagreement with the moral precepts on which a person refusing to speak in accordance with the wishes of authority may be acting. Conscience is inherently individual and therefore subjective. To say that the determination of the state (whether represented by a legislature, an administrative decision maker, or a court) regarding a moral issue can trump that of an individual defeats the point of protecting freedom of conscience.[60]

There is, finally, a middle category of cases where speech compulsions, while troubling because they interfere with conscience and integrity, may nevertheless be justified. While disagreement or disapproval do not warrant the state's compelling of speech, the need to protect the rights of others may do so. It is for this reason that the state can often compel the testimony that a witness regards as wrongful because it, for example, implicates friends, family members, co-religionists, or journalistic sources. The right of an accused or a party to a civil trial to a fair trial or to due process of law – a right that is especially, but by no means only, implicated where a person is faced with deprivation of liberty – would be compromised in the absence of such testimony.

Even when upholding such speech compulsions, however, courts should be sensitive to the objectors' qualms and recognize the seriousness of the imposition on their autonomy. The Court of Appeal for Ontario did this well in *CMDSC*, whatever one might think of the conclusion it ultimately reached. This recognition requires a balancing between the interests at stake. This means primarily the interests of the party seeking the compulsion and the one whose speech would be compelled. However, in some cases, relevant interests include those of people who may wish to confide in potential targets of speech compulsions, such as religious figures, health professionals, or journalists. People's ability to take such figures into their confidence for purposes ranging from spiritual welfare (or indeed compliance with religious requirements), to treatment, or to the advancement of the public interest would be impaired if they were readily amenable to speech compulsion.

There will not be many areas where the state will need to compel speech in order to secure the rights of others. Generalizing from the examples outlined above – witness testimony and, perhaps, the communication of information about medical procedures seen as constitutional entitlements by the law but as moral wrongs by some individuals – we might imagine a category of cases where a person possesses information to which another has a right and yet regards disclosure of this information (generally or for the specific purpose for which disclosure is being sought) as morally wrong. Perhaps there are other examples in this category, in addition to those already mentioned, but they do not readily come to mind. And it is still more difficult to think of other cases not having the same structure where speech compulsions would be necessary.

In particular, professions of adherence to a doctrine or statements of fact dictated to a speaker who does not believe them to be true are not analogous to mandatory disclosures of information in the exclusive possession of a person. No one's rights are being infringed by another person's failure to publicly subscribe to a particular set of beliefs. Justice Jackson recognized this in *Barnette*, pointing out that the case involved no conflict among the rights of different citizens or groups. On the contrary, he wrote, "[t]he sole conflict is between authority and rights of the individual."[61]

This is so even when the beliefs required to be professed are supposed to be conducive to greater respect of the rights of others. Even if the supposition is warranted, no one has an actual right, as opposed to, at most, a reasonable desire, to have others hold beliefs that make them more likely to uphold one's rights. It is only actions, not attitudes, that law – including constitutional and human rights law – controls. For example, the Law Society of Ontario's Statement of Principles was said to foster a climate of greater respect for the equality rights of groups historically marginalized in or by the legal profession. Such groups certainly have the right not to be subject to discriminatory *treatment* by the state (under both the *Charter* and provincial and federal anti-discrimination legislation) and by various individuals and organizations (under anti-discrimination legislation). Yet this law demands only compliance, not approval – like all other law, as Beetz J. pointed out in *National Bank*. Demands for approval, whether of the law or of the principles and ideals to which it gives effect, are totalitarian and incompatible with political liberty.

A further difficulty concerns not a specific type of compelled speech but a category of target for speech compulsion: corporations. Professor Moon argues that corporations generally, or perhaps "large" corporations specifically, can be compelled to speak. This is because "[i]f compelled expression ... is experienced as an invasion of one's personal sphere, or an interference with one's 'freedom of mind,' " corporations cannot be said to suffer from such invasions or interferences in the same way as individuals.[62] And, as a matter of positive law, the question of whether corporate entities are entitled to the freedom of religion and, arguably, conscience, remains unresolved,[63] although it is well established that corporations can assert violations of these (or any other) rights to establish the unconstitutionality of any statute they are charged with infringing.[64]

In my view, however, the objections to recognizing that corporations have integrity, and arguably even conscience, interests are not compelling. Corporations are certainly expected to act with integrity: not only to refrain from fraud and not mislead consumers, but, crucially for my argument, to have and carry out values and mission statements, to be aware of and fulfil a "social responsibility." No doubt a great deal of cynical or at least self-serving behaviour is undertaken in furtherance of corporate "values," but the demand for corporations to announce and act on moral principles is too widespread for the law to deny that they can ever do so. And while I cannot fully make this argument in the limited space available here, I believe that Thoreau was right that while "a corporation has no conscience ... a corporation of conscientious men is a corporation *with* a conscience."[65] It is worth noting, too, that corporations include not only cigarette manufacturers, on which Professor Moon's argument is focused, but also a variety of non-profits and NGOs that have taken on a corporate form, and are even more clearly defined by a sense of mission and purpose. To deny them the right to carry out this purpose with integrity would be quite wrong.

Conclusion

Applying the framework outlined above would not require many changes in existing law. For example, the law surrounding witness testimony already largely aligns with it. Witnesses can be compelled to speak, but generally only to facts in their personal knowledge. They are not required, or even permitted, except in the case of experts, to venture opinions, and are enjoined to tell what they think is the truth. Limited exceptions exist to balance the conscience and integrity interests of witnesses and the right of those seeking their testimony to a fair trial. Other commonplace disclosure requirements similarly aim at factual information, and do not seek to dictate the content of the compelled statements, beyond requiring them to be true. Conversely, the law generally avoids requiring people to lie, to express opinions dictated by the state, or to otherwise compromise their integrity.

Unfortunately, however, recent attempts to expand the state's role, and to enlist its coercive powers to ensure that individuals not only act in accordance with certain rules, as the law always has done, but subscribe – or at least affirm that they subscribe – to certain doctrines, break with the tradition of respect for individual conscience and integrity. They are innovations, or rather attempts to return the law to a past that it had left behind, albeit in the service of new ideals. The ideals may be better than those served by Henry VIII's oaths of supremacy or the Inquisition's pursuit of heretical astronomers, but the means taken to pursue them are no more respectful of human beings. They degrade the ideals they ostensibly pursue and should be renounced.

Even a good-faith commitment to respecting conscience and integrity will not prevent all disputes about compelled speech. There will be difficult cases to address in the middle category outlined above, where conscience and integrity claims must be set against the rights of other persons. However, while my proposed approach does not fully guide the courts in resolving such disputes, it may at least ensure that their decisions, however morally and factually fraught, will be *more* – if never *completely* – acceptable to the losers, by ensuring that they see their rights and scruples taken seriously and given consideration.

NOTES

1 Larry Alexander, "Compelled Speech," *Constitutional Commentary* 23, no. 1 (2006): 147.
2 Eugene Volokh, "The Law of Compelled Speech," *Texas Law Review* 97, no. 2 (2018): 355–95; Martin H. Redish, "Compelled Commercial Speech and the First Amendment," *Notre Dame Law Review* 94, no. 4 (2019): 1750.
3 Redish, ibid., 1771.
4 *Reference re Alberta Statutes*, [1938] SCR 100.
5 Ibid., 135.
6 Ibid., 144–5.
7 Ibid., 146.
8 *National Bank of Canada v Retail Clerks' International Union*, [1984] 1 SCR 269.
9 Ibid., 296.
10 Ibid.
11 *Slaight Communications Inc. v Davidson*, [1989] 1 SCR 1038.
12 Ibid., 1083.
13 Ibid., 1061 (paragraph breaks removed).
14 *Canada (Attorney-General v JTI-Macdonald Corp.*, 2007 SCC 30, [2007] 2 SCR 610.
15 Ibid., at para 139.
16 *Citizenship Act*, RSC 1985 c C-29, s 3(1) and Schedule.
17 *McAteer v Canada (Attorney General)*, 2014 ONCA 578, 121 O.R. (3d) 1, at para 74.
18 Ibid., at para 75.
19 *Christian Medical and Dental Society of Canada v College of Physicians and Surgeons of Ontario*, 2019 ONCA 393.
20 Ibid., at para 85.
21 *CCLA v Ontario (Attorney General)*, 2020 ONSC 4838, striking down the *Federal Carbon Tax Transparency Act*, 2019, SO 2019, c 7, Sch 23.
22 For a comment on this decision, see Leonid Sirota, "Unstuck," *Double Aspect* (blog), 8 September 2020, https://doubleaspect.blog/2020/09/08/unstuck/.
23 See Arthur J. Cockfield, "Limiting Lawyer Liberty: How the Statement of Principles Coerces Speech," *Queen's Law Research Paper Series no. 2018-100*, https://papers.ssrn.com/abstract=3141561, for a description of the "Statement of Principles," its background, and its history.

24 Ibid., 5.

25 Cockfield's article, ibid., makes this argument in detail.

26 Adrian Humphreys, "Ontario's Law Society Ditches Controversial Statement on Diversity but Loses None of its Acrimony," *National Post*, 11 September 2019, https://nationalpost.com/news/ontarios-law-society-ditches-controversial -statement-on-diversity-but-loses-none-of-its-acrimony.

27 See, for example, *Right to Life Association of Toronto and Area v Canada (Employment, Workforce and Labour)*, 2018 FC 102 at para 3.

28 Employment and Social Development Canada, "Canada Summer Jobs 2021: Providing Youth with Quality Work Experiences Applicant Guide" (2019), https:// www.canada.ca/content/dam/canada/employment-social-development/services /funding/CSJ2021_Applicant_Guide.pdf, 38.

29 Kristopher Kinsinger, "The Government's New Criteria for Summer Jobs Funding Suffer from the Same Defining Flaw as the Old," *CBC News*, 31 December 2018, https://www.cbc.ca/news/opinion/summer-jobs-funding-1.4961959.

30 See especially *R. v Keegstra*, [1990] 3 SCR 697 at 738–44.

31 319 US 624 (1943).

32 Ibid., at 642 (paragraph break removed).

33 *Miami Herald Publishing Co. v Tornillo*, 418 US 241 (1974).

34 *Wooley v Maynard*, 430 US 705 (1977).

35 Ibid., at 713.

36 *NIFLA v Becerra*, 138 S Ct 2361 (2018). It is worth pointing out that in *Planned Parenthood of Southeast Pennsylvania v Casey*, 505 US 833, 884–85 (1992), the Court upheld a requirement that doctors provide a range of information about the foetus, the abortion procedure, and support available to mothers. For a discussion of the tension between this holding (and subsequent lower-court jurisprudence based on it) and the subsequent one in *NIFLA*, see Volokh, "The Law of Compelled Speech," 389–91.

37 But see Dwight Newman, "Interpreting Freedom of Thought in the Canadian Charter of Rights and Freedoms," *Supreme Court Law Review (2d)* 91 (2019): 107–22.

38 *Slaight* at 1061.

39 See Léonid Sirota, "True Allegiance: The Citizenship Oath and the *Charter*," *National Journal of Constitutional Law* 33, no. 2 (2014): 137–68.

40 Brian Bird, "The Call in *Carter* to Interpret Freedom of Conscience," *Supreme Court Law Review (2d)* 85, no. 2 (2018): 119.

41 Thomas E. Hill, "Four Conceptions of Conscience," in "Integrity and Conscience," edited by Ian Shapiro and Robert Merrihew Adams, special issue, *Nomos* 40 (1998): 32.

42 Bird, "The Call in *Carter*," 117–18.

43 John Emmerich Edward Acton, *Lectures on Modern History*, edited by John Neville Figgis and Reginald Vere Laurence (London: Macmillan, 1906), 31.

44 "Lincoln's Second Inaugural Address" (4 March 1865), National Park Service, accessed 11 May 2021, https://www.nps.gov/linc/learn/historyculture/lincoln-second-inaugural.htm.

45 Leonid Sirota, "Ach, Mein Sinn," *Double Aspect* (blog), 30 March 2018, https://doubleaspect.blog/2018/03/30/ach-mein-sinn/.

46 Bird, "The Call in *Carter*," 124.

47 Damian Cox, Marguerite La Caze, and Michael Levine, "Integrity," *Stanford Encyclopedia of Philosophy* (Spring 2017 Edition), last modified 20 February 2017, https://plato.stanford.edu/archives/spr2017/entries/integrity/.

48 George Kateb, "Socratic Integrity," in "Integrity and Conscience," edited by Ian Shapiro and Robert Merrihew Adams, special issue, *Nomos* 40 (1998): 77.

49 Richard Moon, *The Constitutional Protection of Freedom of Expression* (Toronto: University of Toronto Press, 2000), 184.

50 Ibid., 182.

51 Redish, "Compelled Commercial Speech," 1756.

52 Leonid Sirota, "Affidavi," *Double Aspect* (blog), 29 January 2019, https://doubleaspect.blog/2019/01/29/affidavi/.

53 Bird, "The Call in *Carter*," 124.

54 Ibid., 125.

55 Ian Shapiro and Robert Merrihew Adams, "Introduction," in "Integrity and Conscience," edited by Ian Shapiro and Robert Merrihew Adams, special issue, *Nomos* 40 (1998): 1.

56 Bird, "The Call in *Carter*," 123.

57 Ibid., 129.

58 Leonid Sirota, "The System Is Working," *Double Aspect* (blog), 23 August 2019, https://doubleaspect.blog/2019/08/23/a-chill-on-global-warming/.

59 The one narrow exception to the general rule against compelled statements of opinion concerns expert testimony: once one volunteers (or, more often, accepts for a hefty fee) to provide opinion statements on behalf of a party to a judicial proceeding, one should accept being cross-examined, including on questions of opinion related to one's statement. Importantly, however, unlike ordinary witnesses who can be forced to testify, but only to factual issues within their personal knowledge, experts are not compellable, as an initial matter.

60 See Acton, *Lectures on Modern History*, 31; Bird, "The Call in *Carter*," 126–9.

61 *Barnette* at 630.

62 Moon, *Constitutional Protection*, 190.

63 *Law Society of British Columbia v Trinity Western University*, 2018 SCC 32, [2018] 2 SCR 293 at para 61.

64 *R. v Big M Drug Mart Ltd.*, [1985] 1 SCR 295.

65 Henry David Thoreau, "Civil Disobedience," in *Anti-Slavery and Reform Papers*, ed. H.S. Salt (London: Swan Sonnenschein and Co., 1890), 23 (emphasis in the original).

9 Balancing Freedom of Expression and Access to the Courts: Assessing Ontario's Anti-SLAPP Legislation

BYRON M. SHELDRICK

In 2015 the Ontario government passed the *Protection of Public Participation Act*, thereby creating section 137 of the *Courts of Justice Act*. This new provision restricts and regulates lawsuits that threaten freedom of expression or limit debate on issues of public importance. In doing so, Ontario became only the third jurisdiction in Canada to have successfully implemented restrictions on so-called strategic litigation against public participation (SLAPP).[1] The passage of this law was controversial, with environmental organizations and activist groups largely supportive but many business associations and developers opposed. The fear was that the operation of the legislation would prevent legitimate claims for damages from being brought to the courts, and that protest would effectively become a form of immunity from lawsuits. Some argued that the legislation lacked clear guidelines to operationalize the tests contained therein.[2] This chapter argues that, overall, the courts has delicately and appropriately balanced the need for regulation of strategic litigation while at the same time respecting the importance of access to courts.

Strategic litigation against public participation refers to a category of lawsuits that are launched to "silence" or curtail the expression of political opponents.[3] As such, they are inherently political in nature. SLAPPs operate to enmesh the target in expensive and lengthy litigation, draining them of resources. They operate to effectively punish individuals and groups for political engagement. They often use allegations of defamation as the vehicle for doing this. Accordingly, SLAPPs also generate a political chill, as others beyond those directly sued may be dissuaded from political engagement.

As a political tool SLAPPs can be very successful. Their power lies in the fact that a political strategy is dressed in the clothes of a real private law cause of action. They make use of the courts, and the procedural rules that operate to ensure due process and fairness, to advance a political agenda. As such, they operate to reframe the political issue that is at the heart of the dispute into a much narrower set of private law legal issues.[4] Consequently, broad public issues are diverted into the courtroom, where a much narrower set of issues are adjudicated.[5] The inherently political nature of these cases is reinforced by the fact that very few SLAPP lawsuits, if carried through to trial, are successful.

SLAPPs have been the subject of numerous studies, and the broad parameters of this sort of litigation has been well documented. It is not my intention to revisit those arguments. Rather, my aim is to provide an assessment of the effectiveness of the recent Ontario legislation restricting SLAPPs. Legislation governing SLAPPs needs to be very carefully drafted to balance access to the courts with protecting and preserving public discourse and public debate. At the end of the day, the effectiveness of the legislation will be determined by how it is applied and interpreted by the courts.

The Ontario Court of Appeal released a series of unanimous decisions interpreting the legislation on 30 August 2018. Those decisions, written by Mr. Justice Doherty, applied section 137 of the *Courts of Justice Act* across a diversity of factual contexts. This creates a unique opportunity to assess the application of the legislation. My argument is that the Court of Appeal has largely "gotten it right" in its interpretation of the legislation. The decisions reflect a sensitivity and understanding of the democratic implications of expression. The Court has shown a willingness to allow litigation to proceed where constraining expression involves limited or no threats to democratic values but has been quite prepared to halt litigation where expression is more deeply linked to democratic values and practices.

This chapter is divided into three sections. The first section outlines the provisions of the *Protection of Public Participation Act* and how it changed Ontario's judicial processes. The second section examines the decisions of the Ontario Court of Appeal. The third section provides a framework for analysing the reasoning employed by the Court and assessing the appropriateness of the judicial outcomes in the six cases. The chapter concludes by considering the implications of future appeals of these cases to the Supreme Court of Canada.

The *Protection of Public Participation Act*

The *Protection of Public Participation Act* was enacted in 2015 and contains a number of provisions that operate to reverse the logic of a typical SLAPP lawsuit. As discussed, it is generally in the interests of SLAPP plaintiffs to pursue a lengthy lawsuit, despite the likelihood of losing, precisely because the purpose of the lawsuit operates outside the "four corners" of the legal dispute. The *Protection of Public Participation Act*, through the creation of section 137.1 of the *Courts of Justice Act*, reverses the incentives for the plaintiff to delay and drag out a proceeding through a series of interrelated procedures. These provisions provide for (a) an early determination of whether a case is a SLAPP lawsuit; (b) an onus shift that requires the plaintiff to justify the merits of their case; and (c) cost provisions that make it less advantageous for SLAPP plaintiffs to file these suits. For the purposes of this chapter we will focus on the first two of these measures.

Section 137.1 creates an expedited hearing process for determining whether or not a case constitutes a SLAPP. The defendant can move to have a case dismissed for being a SLAPP any time after the initial claim has been filed. Success on a motion filed pursuant to section 137.1 results in the entire case being dismissed. The provision attempts to ensure that cases involving legitimate grievances are able to proceed to trial. It does this through the preliminary definition of a case as a SLAPP, along with a careful shifting of onus between the SLAPP defendant and the SLAPP plaintiff as the Court makes its determination. This shifting of onus allows the courts to consider the merits of the case, something that traditionally is not done on preliminary motions. Cases that raise legitimate claims are allowed to proceed, while cases that represent an unwarranted infringement on debate and expression are terminated.

Once a moving party makes an application under section 137.1 the Court engages in a three-step analysis involving:

1. a threshold test to determine that the lawsuit impacts public expression;
2. a merits-based assessment to determine whether the plaintiff's case has sufficient merit/legitimacy;
3. a public interest assessment.

It should be noted that the onus is on the moving party (the defendant) in part 1 to establish that their capacity to express themselves has been compromised by the lawsuit. If the defendant fails, the lawsuit will be allowed to proceed. In part 2, however, the onus shifts to the respondent (plaintiff) to establish the merits of their case. This involves both a consideration of the merits of the plaintiff's claim, but also whether or not the defendant has any reasonable defences to the lawsuit. If the plaintiff fails at this stage, the lawsuit will be dismissed. A public interest assessment is only necessary when both parties have succeeded in discharging their burdens under parts 1 and 2. Under this part of the test, the onus is on the plaintiff to establish that the harm suffered is sufficiently great that the public interest warrants overriding the interests in public discourse and permitting the case to continue.

The Threshold Requirement

Section 137.1(3) requires that the moving party establish that the lawsuit arises from an exercise of public expression. The section provides the following:

137.1(3) On a motion by a person against whom a proceeding is brought, a judge shall, subject to subsection (4), dismiss the proceeding against the person if the

person satisfies the judge that the proceeding arises from an expression made by
the person that relates to a matter of public interest. 2017, c. 3, s.3.

It is worth noting that expression is defined very broadly in section 137.1(2)
to include "any communication, regardless of whether it is made verbally or
non-verbally, whether it is made publicly or privately, and whether or not it is
directed at a person or entity." For the case to be dismissed as a SLAPP, the case
must arise from the defendant's expression about a "matter of public interest."

The question of defining the scope of "public interest" is not without some
difficulties. In the cases decided by the Ontario Court of Appeal, Mr. Justice
Doherty has provided some guidance. First, he makes it very clear that the
question of what constitutes expression in the public interest is not subject to
any sort of definitive list. The question of public interest will always, at a certain
level, be contextual and may vary depending on the facts of a particular case.
He does, however, state that certain types of issues will always fall within the
scope of the public interest. In particular, commentary about the conduct of
governmental affairs or the operation of the courts are, he states, always matters of public interest. This makes sense, as it would be hard to imagine that
expression related to key institutions of democratic practice and accountability
would fall outside of the public interest. At the same time, however, Doherty
makes it clear that the "public interest" is more than just a popularity contest.
He states that the public interest goes beyond issues in which the public is interested in a merely curious or prurient way.[6] The expression must relate to an
issue that, from a reasonable standpoint, has public implications. There may
very well be issues that most people are either unaware of, or disinterested in,
but nevertheless remain "of public interest." Similarly, there may be issues that
people are very much interested in, or even exorcised about, but which do not
fall within the scope of the public interest. Celebrity gossip, for example, may
be something the public is interested in, yet is not a matter of public interest.

Finally, Mr. Justice Doherty also emphasized that the existence of expression related to the public interest is sufficient to trigger the operation of section
137.1. The lawsuit merely needs to arise from that expression. The motives and
intentions of the speaker are not relevant to a determination of whether or not
the expression is in the public interest. Nor is the Court to engage in an assessment of the "merits" of the speech nor of the size of audience. So, an issue may
still be of public interest even if it is of concern to a relatively small group of
people. It may also be of public interest even if the position advanced is one
with which many, or even most people, would disagree.

In general, the threshold requirement will likely be a relatively easy hurdle
for a SLAPP defendant to overcome. However, it does serve as a critical step in
the process. It provides the Court with a vehicle for quickly weeding out cases
where the dispute between the parties is purely of a private nature and raises no

broader issues of public interest. One can readily imagine cases that might fall along a continuum of purely private, and appropriate for the Court to deal with as a matter of private law, and those where a broader set of public questions are at play. A property dispute between two neighbours, for example, may be a purely private matter. However, if that dispute raises broader issues related to the character of a neighbourhood, local zoning issues, or environmental concerns, what began as a private dispute might become a matter of public interest.

The Merits Test

If the defendant is successful in establishing that the litigation impacts expression related to the public interest, the onus shifts to the plaintiff to demonstrate that the lawsuit has merit and should be allowed to continue. Section 137.4 provides the following:

> (4) A judge shall not dismiss a proceeding under subsection (3) if the responding party satisfies the judge that,
> (a) there are grounds to believe that,
> (i) the proceeding has substantial merit and
> (ii) the moving party has no valid defence in the proceeding

This provision marks an important shift from the traditional common law approach to determining whether or not a cause of action should be struck out and a lawsuit dismissed by the courts on a preliminary motion. It requires the plaintiff to demonstrate the merits of their case before any evidence has been presented. It also requires the plaintiff to comment on the potential defences that might be brought forward by the defendant. This responds to two important elements that have traditionally characterized SLAPP lawsuits. First, in most cases SLAPP suits are not meritorious but rather involve trumped-up allegations of damages. Second, the common law rules for dismissing a case have generally erred on the side of allowing lawsuits to continue to trial. At common law the preference has been to permit a full trial of issues, allowing each party to present their evidence, rather than dismissing a claim based on the limited evidentiary record that exists on a preliminary motion. Most SLAPP lawsuits are unsuccessful because either the plaintiff was unable to establish their case on a balance of probabilities, or the defendant was able to bring forward a successful defence. Section 137.4 asks the Court to assess these two possibilities at a preliminary stage.

In assessing how the merits test should operate, Mr. Justice Doherty emphasized that the provisions of section 137.1(4) should be treated as a screening mechanism. It is not a process for summary judgment.[7] The Court is not deciding the merits of the case or the likelihood of either party's success. Given the preliminary nature of the motion the Court is not in a position to make findings of fact, assess the credibility of witnesses, or make a final determination about the issues in dispute. Rather than simply assuming everything in a statement of claim is true, as is the case in a traditional motion to dismiss, the Court must now assess whether there is a reasonable basis for the trial judge to accept the evidence available on the motion record. The Court is being asked to assess whether the litigation has substantial merit, in the sense that it is litigating a "real issue," rather than making a determination that the case is, in fact, meritorious. Ultimately, the Court is attempting to determine the likelihood of a case succeeding if it goes to trial. This requires not only a careful consideration of both the merits of the plaintiff's case, but also the possibility of the defendant raising a successful defence. Only if the plaintiff can establish both that the case has merit and that there are no reasonable defences will the case be allowed to proceed.

The Public Interest Hurdle

Even if the plaintiff is able to demonstrate that her case has substantial merit and the defendant has no defences (in other words, that there are good reasons to believe the plaintiff would be successful), there is one more hurdle that must be overcome. This requirement is contained in section 137.1(4)(b) and requires an assessment of overarching public interest in free expression. It is at this stage that the Court is asked to balance the importance of the public expression and the harm suffered by the plaintiff. Section 137.1(4)(b) requires the Court balance these two competing interests. The provision states:

> (b) the harm likely to be or have been suffered by the responding party as a result of the moving party's expression is sufficiently serious that the public interest in permitting the proceeding to continue outweighs the public interest in protecting that expression. 2015, c. 23, s. 3.

This provision assumes the importance of public expression. The onus is on the plaintiff to demonstrate that the harm they suffered warrants overriding that expression. It is not for the defendant to demonstrate that their expression warrants overriding the plaintiff's right to seek redress in the courts. Moreover, this provision does not ask the Court to consider these factors in an abstract fashion. Rather, the plaintiff's actual harm must be assessed. This provision reflects the fact that in SLAPP lawsuits the damages suffered by the plaintiff are slight or nominal, despite damage claims that typically seek millions of dollars.[8]

In interpreting this provision, Mr. Justice Doherty characterized section 137.1(4)(b) as the "heart of the legislation" and argued that courts should look for indicators that cases fit the classic definition of a SLAPP suit. In other words,

while the Court might not be looking for a complete breakdown and categorization of damages incurred, the plaintiff will have to do more than simply
assert damage. The Court, according to Mr. Justice Doherty, should be open to
indications of the following:

- History of plaintiff using litigation as a threat
- Financial or power imbalance favouring the plaintiff
- Punitive or retributory purpose behind the claim
- Minimal or nominal damages suffered by the plaintiff

The significance of this public interest balancing has led some courts to skip the
earlier analysis of the merits of the plaintiff's case. Instead, having determined
that the case arises out of public interest expression, the Court simply moves
to the balancing test. If the plaintiff fails this test, the case will be dismissed
regardless of an assessment of the merits. Obviously, however, if the Court determines that the public interest does not favour dismissing the case, the Court
will still have to conduct a merits analysis.

The appropriate and effective operation of a legislation scheme will ultimately depend on its application to specific factual situations. Assessing how
the legislation is actually applied by the courts also permits us to draw normative conclusions as to how the courts interpret the relationship between expression, its limitation, and broader democratic values.

The Cases

Cases Allowed to Proceed

Of the six cases heard by the Ontario Court of Appeal, two cases, *Veneruzzo v
Storey* and *Platnick v Bent*, were allowed to proceed. Both of these cases very
much appear to be private matters, with limited implications of a broad public
nature. *Veneruzzo v Storey* involved civil litigation that arose out of a motor
vehicle accident. The Court easily concluded that the expression involved did
not meet the public interest threshold and allowed the litigation to proceed.
Platnick v Bent is a more interesting case, in that the Court found that the expression involved was of public interest, but that the litigation was nevertheless
meritorious and should be permitted.

Platnick v Bent

In this case, Platnick, a medical doctor, sued Bent, a lawyer, for defamation,
claiming $15 million in damages. The defendant moved to have the litigation
dismissed as a SLAPP. They were successful on the initial motion, and the

plaintiff appealed. The Court of Appeal overturned the motions judge and the litigation was allowed to proceed.

The case focused on statements made by Bent that were critical of how the plaintiff prepared medical assessments of motor vehicle injuries for insurance companies. In a series of posts to the Ontario Trial Lawyers Association LIST-SERV, she implied that Platnick had deliberately misrepresented medical findings. The email was subsequently leaked to an advocacy organization and to the press. It was at this point that Dr. Platnick demanded an apology and retraction. When Bent refused, he commenced his lawsuit.

The Court of Appeal agreed with the motions judge that the litigation arose out of comments that related to a matter of public interest. The issue at stake was the proper administration of justice and the integrity of the process put in place by the government for determining motor vehicle accident claims. According to Mr. Justice Doherty, the email raised important questions about the honesty and reliability of medical reports filed as part of arbitration processes. In coming to this conclusion, however, Mr. Justice Doherty emphasized that finding the litigation related to a matter of public interest did not determine the merits of the libel claim. As Mr. Justice Doherty states, "an expression may be defamatory, false, and malicious, and still relate to a matter of public interest."[9]

In terms of the merit assessment, the Court of Appeal found that Platnick established that his case had merit. There was clear evidence that the elements of a defamatory statement were present. In this regard the case differs from those where there is no strong evidence that the plaintiff had been defamed. In terms of defences, however, the Court of Appeal disagreed with the motions judge. The motions judge had determined that the plaintiff had failed to establish on reasonable grounds that Bent had no defences to the allegation. The Court of Appeal, however, found that the defences Bent had raised to the allegations of defamation were all relatively weak, and likely to be unsuccessful at a full trial. Given the merits of the substantive allegations, combined with the weakness of any defences the defendant could put forward, the Court of Appeal found that the plaintiff had succeeded in discharging their burden under the merits portion of the test for a SLAPP.

The last issue to be addressed was the balance to be struck between the defendant's freedom of expression and the injury suffered by the plaintiff. In this assessment, the Court of Appeal also sided with the plaintiff. The Court accepted that the injury to the plaintiff's reputation and his future livelihood was significant. The defendant's free speech interests, by contrast, while relating to a matter of public interest, were more limited. The Court did not find that the lawsuit could be characterized by any of the indicia of a classic SLAPP lawsuit. In particular, there was no power imbalance between the parties (doctor vs. lawyer) and there was no evidence that the plaintiff routinely used litigation as a means of silencing critics. It was also not a case where the damages issued, if any, would be minimal or nominal. Given the nature of the case, and the indication of real damage to the Platnick's livelihood, the Court found that there would likely be potentially significant damages awarded by a court.[10] Accordingly, the Court of Appeal allowed the litigation to continue.

Cases Dismissed as SLAPPs

The Court dismissed four cases as SLAPPs. For our discussion we will focus on three cases that particularly highlight the interrelationship between expression, the courts, and democratic institutions.

1704604 Ontario Ltd. v Pointes Protection Association

The plaintiff 1704604 Ontario (170 Ontario) was proposing to build a new subdivision in Sault Ste. Marie and was opposed by the Pointes Protection Association (Pointes), a community-based residents' association. The plans for the subdivision needed approval from both the Sault Ste. Marie Region Conservation Authority (SSMRCA) and the Sault Ste. Marie City Council. The parties were embroiled in a complicated series of cases before several administrative and judicial bodies.

The SSMRCA granted 170 Ontario approval for the project and Pointes sought judicial review of that decision, arguing that the SSMRCA had exceeded its jurisdiction and its approval was, therefore, "illegal." The plaintiff also sought City Council approval but was turned down; 170 Ontario then appealed that decision to the Ontario Municipal Board (OMB). Pointes was granted standing to participate in the OMB hearing.

Pointes and 170 Ontario reached an agreement that settled the judicial review. The agreement provided for the case to be dismissed without costs, and Pointes agreed that they would not pursue future litigation requesting the same or similar relief sought in the judicial review.[11] They also undertook that in the proceedings before the OMB they would not argue that the SSMRCA resolutions were "illegal, invalid, or contrary to the relevant environmental legislation." They agreed, moreover, not to make the argument that the SSMRCA had exceeded its authority or that it had acted without "reasonable evidence."

During the OMB hearings the president of Pointes, Peter Gagnon, testified that the development would result in a loss of coastal wetlands and significant environmental damage, which was similar to his evidence to SSMRCA. The OMB dismissed 170 Ontario's appeal, with one board member indicating he preferred Mr. Gagnon's evidence to that of the expert called by 170 Ontario. As a result, the development was halted. Six months later 170 Ontario sued the defendants, arguing that Gagnon's testimony violated the agreement settling the judicial review.

The defendants brought a motion under section 137.1 for an order dismissing the claim. The motions judge agreed that Gagnon's testimony related to a matter of public interest but found that 170 Ontario had met its burdens under the merits and public interest sections of the legislation. The motion was dismissed, and the litigation allowed to proceed. On appeal, the Court of Appeal reversed this decision, and found that the case should be dismissed as a SLAPP.

On appeal, the public interest nature of the defendant's statements was not contested. The arguments focused on the application of sections 137.1(4)(a) and (b) to the case. Regarding section 137.1(4)(a), the motions judge had focused on the importance of the settlement agreement and the finding that the courts should view the enforcement of agreements as meritorious. Mr. Justice Doherty ruled that this was too narrow an approach and that the motions judge had focused on the subject matter of the case rather than the merits of the claim. He found that, while the enforcement of agreements might be important, the argument that the defendants breached the agreement was weak. A serious matter does not necessarily equate with a meritorious claim. Mr. Justice Doherty found that the issues raised by the defendant in his testimony to the OMB had not been settled by the agreement to dismiss the judicial review action. The issue of the conservation authority's jurisdiction was distinct from potential environmental damage represented by the development, and not covered by the settlement agreement.

With respect to the public interest argument, the motions judge focused on the harm caused by the continuation of litigation. Mr. Justice Doherty agreed that finality in litigation is an important consideration but ruled that 170 Ontario's expectations were dependent on the wording of the agreement. If the testimony of the defendant at the OMB fell outside that agreement, there was no actual harm. Even if that were not the case, however, the Court ruled that the plaintiff had not shown it had suffered any damage as a result of the alleged breach of the agreement, since it was the plaintiff themselves who had initiated the appeal to the OMB. The defendant's testimony before the OMB, and the granting of standing to the defendants to participate in the hearings, were not additional damages to the plaintiff. Indeed, the plaintiff had objected to the OMB granting standing to Pointes, an argument that was rejected. The Court concluded the threat to the defendant's right to express themselves, by accessing the regulatory institutions of the state, outweighed whatever harm the plaintiff might have suffered.

Able Translations v Express International Translations

In this case, Able Translations (Able) sued Philippe Vitu and his company, Express International Translations (Express), for defamation. The defendants moved for an order dismissing the lawsuit under section 137.1 and were successful. Able appealed. Able is a large translation company operating in Canada. Vitu and his wife operated a much smaller company providing French and English translations and interpreter services. Able sued the defendants for defamation based on two internet posts made by Vitu in August 2015. The posts were made on an internet bulletin board used by people in the translation industry. Many posts on the board were critical of Able's business practices and related to the company's reputation for mistreating freelance reporters. Vitu's posts, however, were directed against a former vice-president of the company, Peter Fonesca, who was a candidate in the 2015 federal election. The posts were critical of Fonesca, alleging that he was aware of his former employer's business practices and that he should not be elected to Parliament. He suggested organizing a press conference to denounce Fonesca's candidacy.

The Court of Appeal considered the posts as relating to a matter of public interest. Mr. Justice Doherty concluded the posts were about the suitability of Fonesca as a candidate for Parliament. Arguably, if the posts had been about Able's corporate employment practices, they might not have been considered a matter public interest. Such allegations, if untrue, might very well give rise to a defamation claim. But in this instance, the posts, while assuming some knowledge of Able's reputation, were clearly about the upcoming election.

The Court rejected Able's arguments that its case had sufficient merit to be allowed to continue. The Court emphasized the fact that the posts did not actually reference the plaintiff and that any such reference was implicit at best. Moreover, the Court further concluded, given the nature of the matter being debated, that the defendant likely had a valid defence to the allegation of defamation. In particular, both the motions judge and the Court concluded that Vitu's comments would likely be protected as "fair comment," given that they took place during an election campaign and were related to that campaign.

Finally, the Court concluded that on a balancing of the competing interests, the litigation should not be allowed to continue. The Court concluded that the harm suffered by Able was slight, at best, but that the contents of the comments – namely, the suitability of a candidate for election to Parliament – was a topic of significant importance. Free and open debate, and the ability to subject candidates to public scrutiny, are essential elements of our system of democracy. Given this, the Court easily determined that the litigation should be dismissed as a SLAPP. The lawsuit, the Court argued, was designed to prevent members of the public from criticizing a candidate for office.

Armstrong v Corus Entertainment

William Armstrong, a London, Ontario, city councillor, was running for re-election in 2014. He sued his opponent, Nancy McSloy, for defamation, along with three individuals in her campaign and Corus Entertainment, the owner of a local radio station. The case focused on comments made by McSloy during the campaign. She claimed Armstrong had been convicted of sexual assault "many years ago" and that his conviction was part of a pattern of bullying and intimidation. She also asserted she was concerned for her safety and the safety of community members.[12] These statements were repeated on a local radio talk show. It was true that twenty-five years earlier Armstrong had been convicted of sexual assault. The defamation claim focused on McSloy's allegations of a pattern of bullying and intimidation, suggesting that Armstrong was unethical and prone to criminality. He argued that the statements were clearly defamatory and that they were made with malice. The defendants moved to have the case dismissed.

The question of whether or not the statements related to a matter of public interest was not in dispute; all parties agreed that statements regarding the fitness of a candidate for office, made during an election campaign, met that requirement. As a result, the onus was on Armstrong to demonstrate that his case passed the merit and public interest tests. The motions judge found that Armstrong had succeeded in demonstrating that his lawsuit had substantial merit, and also that the defendant had no valid defences to his claim. Additionally, he was satisfied that the harm suffered by Armstrong was sufficiently serious that the public interest justified permitting the lawsuit to continue. As a result, the defendant's motion was initially dismissed.

On appeal, Mr. Justice Doherty took a different view. The motions judge had treated the defendants as largely one entity. Mr. Justice Doherty, however, assessed the grounds for a SLAPP determination under section 137 for each specific defendant. This seems appropriate, particularly where one of the defendants is a media outlet. The defences to a claim of defamation are different for media than for individuals, and it is important that they be considered carefully. In this case, Corus made the argument that their broadcast of McSloy's comments, as well as any subsequent publication, were covered by the defence of responsible communication. Mr. Justice Doherty found that Corus had more than established a basis for putting this defence on the record. He then considered whether or not the material filed by Armstrong was sufficient to conclude there was no reasonable basis for the defence to succeed. He found Armstrong's material failed to do this. Of particular importance was the fact that during an election campaign it is appropriate that a broadcaster publish the comments and views of candidates, that the comments made by McSloy were clearly her "opinion," and no listener would interpret the broadcast as reflecting Corus endorsing that view. The broadcast, Mr. Justice Doherty found, was careful and balanced in its coverage, and had sought comment from Armstrong and his campaign team, which they had refused. As a result, the Court found sufficient grounds to view Corus has having a valid defence to the claim.

With respect to the primary individual defendants, the Court found that Armstrong had, in general, established the merits of his claim. He was able to demonstrate that the comments had clearly been made about him and that they were damaging to his reputation. He was further able to establish that there wasn't a valid defence against the defamation claim. However, the Court was not persuaded that the public interest warranted allowing the litigation to proceed. In this regard the Court found that the injury suffered by Armstrong was relatively minor. Significantly, the Court put great stock in the fact that Armstrong won re-election by a fairly wide margin. This suggested that the public had been unconvinced by the allegations and that his reputation had not been affected. The Court emphasized the importance of granting a fairly wide scope for free expression during election campaigns. Mr. Justice Doherty stated that

> Against what I would characterize as modest evidence of harm or potential harm to Mr. Armstrong stands the very strong public interest in promoting freedom of expression by candidates during the electoral process. The public expects and benefits from vigorous debate among candidates. The rhetoric can become personal and overly zealous. No doubt, candidates have in the past, and will in the future, step over the line between strongly stated opinions and defamatory comments. However, the message to be taken from the enactment of s.1371.1 is that not every foot over the defamatory foul line warrants dragging the offender through the litigation process. By enacting s.137.1, the Legislature acknowledged that, in some circumstances, permitting the wronged party to seek vindication through litigation comes at too high a cost to freedom of expression.[13]

The fact that Armstrong won re-election made it relatively simple for the Court to come to the determination that the public interest warranted not permitting the litigation to proceed. It will be interesting to see what the Court might do in future cases where the candidate pursuing litigation loses. The logic of the analysis followed by the Court suggests that the same outcome should be arrived at regardless of whether a candidate wins or loses. One of the difficulties is that what "causes" an electoral victory or an electoral defeat is not easily determined. It is rarely possible to pinpoint the extent to which a comment made during the campaign has influenced voter choices. For this reason, the determination of "harm" in these cases will often be difficult to assess, while the value in promoting free expression in the electoral context will generally be clear.

Analysis

The decision to dismiss a case risks undermining the rule of law and preventing a potentially injured plaintiff from seeking redress. By contrast, allowing SLAPP lawsuits to proceed permits plaintiffs to curtail other parties' right to freedom of expression and encourages the abuse of the judicial process. One way to approach this question might be to ask what is it about freedom of expression that the courts should be concerned about? Is it all expression, or is it only certain types of expression?

The legislation gives us a partial answer to this question, by stipulating that its provisions apply to expression on public issues. The public interest in these cases should be understood in a democratic context. This, I would argue, is what Mr. Justice Doherty was expressing when he stated that commentary on government or the courts would always be a matter of public interest. Curtailing criticism of, or comment about, the functioning of our institutions of government is fundamentally an erosion of democratic accountability. If we look at the specific outcomes in the cases it is clear that the democratic implications of the cases were significant considerations for the Court.

Overall, of the six cases that were considered by the Ontario Court of Appeal, two were permitted to go ahead, and four were dismissed. The cases that were allowed, *Veneruzzo v Storey* and *Platnick v Bent*, both involved what seem to be fairly classic private law disputes. The parties are all individuals and they are suing over allegedly defamatory statements. In each case, the issues also raise potentially serious and real damage to the plaintiff's reputation. In *Platnick*, for example, the ability of the plaintiff to earn his livelihood as a medical practitioner was clearly in jeopardy. In these cases, where individuals are suing individuals, it is often more difficult to determine what might be the public issue at stake. In *Veneruzzo*, the Court could find no public issue at stake, but determined that the defendant was trying to create a different narrative about a motor vehicle accident by impugning the character of the victim and her family. In general, those cases that involve individuals suing each other over largely private matters should rarely be found to be a SLAPP.

These cases are quite different from those that were deemed to be SLAPPs and dismissed. In these cases, the Court had relatively little difficulty in determining that there was an issue of public interest. In *Able Translations*, while there had been a lengthy conflict between the parties, the actual comments made were not about the plaintiff, but rather about the suitability of an electoral candidate. In *Pointes* the case involved testimony about a development project before the OMB. The litigation could clearly be seen as an attempt to prevent the defendants from fully participating in public regulatory processes. Finally, in *Armstrong v Corus*, the case involved one candidate for office suing another candidate and her campaign workers for defamation. As in *Able Translations*, the Court emphasized the importance of understanding the case within the context of an ongoing election. If candidates begin suing each other over every critical comment or remark, then the ability of our electoral system to function properly would be seriously undermined.

Conclusion

In general, the Ontario Court of Appeal has applied section 137.1 in a way that is sensitive, not only to the values of freedom of expression, but also to the democratic values that underpin freedom of expression. Cases involving what are private disputes, or individual versus individual litigation, were allowed to continue (*Vereruzzo v Storey*; *Platnick v Bent*). Cases involving more collective democratic risks, individuals or corporations suing individuals and/or community groups, as well as cases involving participation in regulatory or democratic processes, were not permitted to continue (*Able Translations v Express*; *1704604 Ontario v Pointes Protection Association*; *Armstrong v Corus*). Appropriately, cases that involve politicians suing other politicians were not found to pass the public interest test and were not permitted to proceed.

Access to the courts, and the ability for people to seek redress for injuries suffered, is a cornerstone of the rule of law and our judicial process. At the same time, the use of the courts, and the assertion of injury, for the purpose of silencing critics or to limit the democratic and political expression/activities of others, undermines the rule of law and should be considered an abuse of the courts. The difficulty is in determining which cases are meritorious and therefore should be allowed to proceed, and which cases should be curtailed. The Ontario legislative framework strikes an appropriate balance and reverses many of the features of SLAPP lawsuits that make them effective political strategies. The legislation, along with the approach taken by the Ontario Court of Appeal, indicates that the Court is very much aware of the democratic implications of SLAPP lawsuits.

There are, of course, issues that are still to be resolved. In particular, the assessment of the extent to which the plaintiff has suffered damages is a difficult question to determine with any precision. This is particularly so when we are dealing with questions of reputation. The decision of the Court in *Armstrong* is particularly troubling in this regard. Tying the seriousness of the "injury" to the electoral outcome raises potentially serious issues in future cases and may lead to a downgrading of the significance of the electoral context. In virtually all cases where candidates are suing each other over things said during an election campaign, the courts should be very hesitant to permit litigation to continue. When individuals decide to put their name forward as candidates, they subject themselves to a degree of scrutiny, and an expectation of critical comment on their behaviour and their past, from which they would otherwise be insulated and protected. Indeed, there is a long history of defamation case law in which the courts have resisted the temptation to entertain litigation emanating from electoral contests.[14] The electoral context means that these cases cannot be treated in the same way as any other case.

Several of these cases have now been appealed to the Supreme Court of Canada. The Supreme Court granted leave to hear appeals in *Platnick v Bent* and *170 Ontario v Pointes*, cases representing very different ends of the SLAPP continuum. *Platnick* is a classic private dispute, while *Pointes* is the case that most closely reflects the characteristics of a traditional SLAPP lawsuit. These cases provide an important test for the approach developed by the Ontario Court of Appeal and the extent to which the courts are willing to seriously restrict access to the courts in favour of public expression and engagement.

Both judgments of the Ontario Court of Appeal were upheld by the Supreme Court, and the Court appears to have broadly affirmed the overall direction charted by the Ontario Court of Appeal.[15] Interestingly, the decision of the Supreme Court in *Pointes* was a unanimous decision that the litigation should not be allowed to proceed, while in *Platnick* the Court divided 5–4 in supporting the continuation of the lawsuit. It appears that the Court felt much more comfortable stopping a case that fit the parameters of a public interest lawsuit and that clearly operated to adversely affect public engagement. In *Platnick*, on the other hand, the Court was divided on how to articulate the public interest dimensions of the legislation when more traditional issues of defamation were at play. The majority was more prepared to favour the interests of access to the courts, while the dissenting judgment was more inclined to maximize comment and public expression. The dissenting judgment was written by Justice Abella, who has now retired from the bench, so the balance on the Court will have shifted for future cases. In light of the split decision in *Platnick*, we should expect more direction from the Court in future cases.

Overall, though, it is clear that, for the moment, section 137.1 has provided the courts with a robust and effective tool for dealing with SLAPP litigation. Moreover, it does not simply privilege expression over the rule of law. It preserves the ability of parties to seek recourse to the Court and provides an effective vehicle for interrogating the public interest element of free speech, along with the democratic implications of the litigation. The Court has effectively reinforced the strength of the legislation through its consideration of this first group of cases.

NOTES

1 In 2008 Quebec introduced a much more limited series of legislative regulations restricting lawsuits that are considered to have been introduced for an "improper purpose." For a discussion of the Quebec legislation, see Normand Landry, "From the Streets to the Courtroom: The Legacies of Quebec's Anti-SLAPP Movement," *Review of European and Community International Environmental Law* 10, no. 1 (2010): 58–69. In British Columbia, the NDP government passed legislative

regulations governing SLAPPs in 2000, but the legislation was repealed in 2001 when the government was defeated and replaced by Gordon Campbell's Liberal Party. In several other jurisdictions, most notably New Brunswick and Nova Scotia, private members bills have been introduced to try and restrict SLAPP lawsuits, but none have been successfully enacted. More recently, in 2019 British Columbia enacted new Anti-SLAPP legislation that is largely based on the Ontario model.

2 See Jennifer Brown, "Anti-Slapp Legislation Re-introduced in Ontario," *Canadian Lawyer*, 8 December 2014, for an overview of the controversy.

3 The term "SLAPP" developed principally within the context of American public interest law in the 1970s and '80s. In Canada, the phenomena of SLAPPs became more apparent in the 1990s, and the courts, in several important cases, expressed their unease with this sort of lawsuit (*Fraser v Saanitch* 1997; *MacMillan Bloedel v Galiano Island Trust* 1995; *Daishowa v Friends of the Lubicon* 1998). See also Chris Tollefson, "Strategic Litigation against Public Participation: Developing a Canadian Response," *Canadian Bar Review* 73, no. 2 (1994): 200–33; Chris Tollefson, "Strategic Lawsuits and Environmental Politics: Daishowa Inc. v. Friends of the Lubicon," *Journal of Canadian Studies* 31, no. 1 (1996): 119–32.

4 George Pring, "SLAPPS: Strategic Lawsuits against Public Participation," *PACE Environmental Law Review* 7, no. 1 (1989): 3–21; George Pring and Penelope Canan, "Strategic Lawsuits against Public Participation," *Social Problems* 35, no. 5 (1998): 506–19; George Pring and Penelope Canan, *SLAPPS: Getting Sued for Speaking Out* (Philadelphia: Temple University Press, 1996); Byron Sheldrick, *Blocking Public Participation: The Use of Strategic Ligitation to Silence Political Participation.* (Waterloo, ON: Wilfrid Laurier University Press, 2014).

5 Pring and Canan, *Getting Sued*; Sheldrick, *Blocking Public Participation*.

6 *Veneruzzo v Storey*, 2018 ONCA 688 (CanLII), para 27; *1704604 Ontario Ltd. v Pointes Protection Association*, 2018 ONCA 685 (CanLII), para 61.

7 *1704604 Ontario*, paras 77–8.

8 Sheldrick, *Blocking Public Participation*, 19.

9 *Patnick v Bent*, 2018 ONCA 687 (CanLII), para 38; *1704604 Ontario v Pointes*, para 55.

10 *Platnick v Bent*, para 101.

11 *1704604 Ontario v Pointes*, para 21.

12 *Armstrong v Corus Entertainment Ltd.*, 2018 ONCA 689 (CanLII), para 7.

13 Ibid., para 90.

14 Ian Loveland, *Political Libels: A Comparative Study* (Oxford: Hart Publishing, 2000).

15 *Bent v Platnick*, 2020 SCC 23 (CanLII); *1704604 Ontario v Pointes*, 2020 SCC 22 (CanLII).

10 Denial, Deplatforming, and Democracy: Thinking about Climate Change in the Age of Social Media

CHRISTOPHER BENNETT

In July 2019, Instagram crossed the billion-user threshold.[1] It was not the first social networking site to do so. WeChat (1.1 billion), WhatsApp (1.6 billion), and YouTube (2 billion) were already there. Eclipsing them all is Facebook, with 1.3 billion users on Facebook Messenger and 2.375 billion on Facebook itself. The dramatic growth in the use of social networking platforms is a clear sign that approaches to communication and expression are changing. How people articulate their ideas, interact with others, and form their beliefs is increasingly dominated by our relationships on social networking sites.

Growing reliance on social networking raises an important question about freedom of expression: How will the value, justification, and limits of free expression evolve along with the means of our expression? With respect to social media companies, we can distinguish between two broad categories of issues relating to freedom of expression. One has to do with privacy: for many, the worry is that social media companies (as well as various online platforms that serve other purposes, such as Amazon) not only know a vast number of details about users' lives but in fact rely on and profit from that data.[2] The other has to do with information. As they are eager to repeat, social media companies connect individuals, empowering each of us to express ourselves and, more importantly, find the audience that we want for our expression. The worry here is about the debasement of discourse, including both its tone and its content.

It is that second category – worries about the content of online communication – that motivates this chapter. At its simplest, the puzzle can be described as follows: on the one hand, thanks to social media, individuals can observe and participate in a vastly greater number of conversations; on the other, the content of those conversations and the information that circulates within them is, to put it mildly, often not very good, both in the sense of its provenance and its truth value. This has led many to advocate all manner of techniques to restrict, manage, or limit online speech to improve its content; the universe of online thought pieces, itself an important contributor of information that circulates via social media, abounds with nervous hand-wringing, sometimes with calls to tackle misinformation.[3]

Here, I focus on climate change denial. (Anti-vaccination, and the mawkishly labelled "vaccine hesitancy," serve as an illustrative analogy.) I ask: Does the prevalence of climate change denial on social media companies warrant deplatforming some users? In what follows, I try to avoid reproducing a misleading bifurcation of camps on this question. For some, climate change denial and its constant renewal via social media justifies the limitation of free expression or, bluntly, censorship. Climate change denial constitutes harmful falsehoods that, perhaps regrettably, warrant interfering in the liberty of some to express themselves. For others, climate change denial is precisely the sort of speech that requires protection. No matter how false and manufactured,[4] individuals must be allowed to speak their minds and freely form their opinions, perhaps because of principled commitments to autonomy and democracy and perhaps because of practical worries about speech-limiting policies.

Instead of endorsing one of those two positions, I outline an autonomy-based justification for reconsidering the design of social media platforms. Proper appreciation of the significance of democracy to individual autonomy reveals the importance of fostering healthier conversations online. I develop a three-part line of reasoning. First, I consider whether climate change denial is valuable. Perhaps unsurprisingly, I find that it is not. Second, I consider the deplatforming impulse, where one might interpret the lack of value found in climate change denial as implying that advocates of the view should be deprived of online platforms. I caution against giving in to this impulse, noting several pitfalls to this form of content moderation as a response to climate change denial (for further pitfalls to be found when attempting to regulate social media, see Mathen, this volume). Third, I argue that the problem posed by climate change denial (and by anti-vaxxers) requires deeper thinking about the place of social media companies in democratic societies. Those committed to free expression, especially those committed to it as a necessary condition of a functioning democracy, must abandon the view that online conversations are the new terrain where freedom of expression must be protected and consider instead the properties that online platforms must have to nourish individuals' expressive capacities. I argue that greater attention to user consent and control over the design of social media platforms is required.

One final preliminary comment is in order. In this chapter, I am primarily concerned with moral arguments. The insight underlying the line of reasoning presented above is that considering whether climate change deniers should be deplatformed should lead us to think harder about the role that social media companies should play in contemporary society, given prevailing democratic ideals. I do conclude by sketching a few suggestions that illustrate what the right kind of democratic control within social media platforms might look like. Of course, the full development and institutionalization of the solutions requires a great deal of empirical work. For example, determining whether a particular policy is *Charter* compliant, as well as whether that policy can successfully achieve its aims, given that social media companies operate across so many jurisdictions (a concern discussed in Mathen, this volume), requires answering further questions. That said, it is the underlying rationale for such a project that I seek to contribute to in this chapter.

The Value of Climate Change Denial

What Is Climate Change Denial?

There are two related ways of conceiving of climate change denial, one narrow and one broad. On the narrow view, climate change denial is "the deliberate and deceptive misrepresentation of the scientific realities of climate change, such as the fact that climate change is happening, its anthropogenic causes, and its damaging impacts."[5] This narrow view supports a range of significant claims about climate change denial: organized, intentional climate change denial by well-funded institutions is on the rise;[6] intentional climate change denial continues to shape public opinion, especially (but not only) in the United States;[7] these deliberate efforts to deny, misconstrue, and obfuscate influence politics and policy.[8]

On the broad view, climate change denial is a complex set of phenomena, all of which sit on a spectrum that runs from genuine, good-faith rejection of some claim about the climate, on one end, to dishonest, insincere rejection, on the other. Between these two poles lies a range of psychologically complex denial, whereby people "are presented with information that is too disturbing, threatening or anomalous to be fully absorbed or openly acknowledged."[9] This conception of denial, which fits with other examples of denial that are unrelated to climate, underpins a range of work on climate change denial.[10] The key difference between the narrow and the broad views is that the former is always deliberate. Adopting the broader view sensitizes our view to the wider range of attitudes that exist in political communities, where most individuals, while not active, intentional, self-conscious deniers, still hold a set of views about climate change that amount to a failure to acknowledge its reality, as well as its personal, social, and political implications. In this chapter, I take the broader view. The disconnect widely felt between individuals' knowledge about climate change and their apathetic or hostile view of personal and collective responsibility constitutes an ongoing impediment to meaningful action on climate change, an impediment to which many individuals do not intentionally contribute.[11] Only some contributors to online conversations deliberately aim to mislead; a significant proportion of denial on social media is far more psychologically complex.

What Is Deplatforming?

Deplatforming refers to a subset of actions that restrict some individual or individuals from expressing their views by removing a medium or venue that they would otherwise employ to express themselves (see also D'Orazio, this volume).[12] Straight away, notice that delineating deplatforming from other (non-deplatforming) restrictions on free expression is difficult. If I steal the bullhorn through with which you amplify your views, most would not agree that I have deplatformed you, even though I am restricting your freedom of expression by removing your preferred medium. The concept more often applies to larger-scale acts or events, where a speaker is disinvited from a university campus or a social media company closes a particular account.

An example might help. Take Twitter's suspension of an account. Some such events will count as deplatforming, but only some. On the one hand, suspending an account because it coordinates a clear-cut case of conspiracy to commit a crime fits the general definition given above, but not the common usage of the term "deplatforming." On the other, suspending an account because it espouses anti-transgender views fits the concept more clearly.[13] One can immediately see the possibility of a grey area.

For example, hate speech laws in Canada prohibit the advocacy of genocide (*Criminal Code* section 318). Some Twitter users will make claims about the historical relation between Indigenous peoples and the Canadian state; others will interpret the tweets as criminalized under section 318, while the original tweeter defends the tweet as espousing a legitimate intellectual position. While we may want to draw a strong line between deplatforming and barring criminal behaviour, it will not always be easy. That said, I proceed on the assumption that there is a core set of deplatforming cases where a Twitter account is banned or could be banned for the non-criminal empirical views that it defends.

Is Climate Change Denial Valuable?

In this section, I argue that climate change is not valuable. Following J.S. Mill's discussion of free expression, I divide this argument into three analytical categories: truth seeking, autonomy, and harm. In this section, I argue that climate change does not contribute to any truth-seeking exercise, that it has little autonomy-enhancing deliberative value, and that it is harmful.

DOES CLIMATE CHANGE DENIAL CONTRIBUTE TO INDIVIDUALS' PURSUIT OF THE TRUTH?

First, a word on the "truth-tracking defence of expressive liberties."[14] This defence starts with a simple thought: any opinion can be truth and every act that suppresses an opinion risks suppressing an insight into the truth.[15] Proscribing free expression is therefore definitely bad in one way: it can deprive individuals of some truth that may help them to reason about and to execute their life plans properly.[16] Insofar as proper reasoning and plan execution are significant conditions of an autonomous life, and insofar as that requires grasping a range of truths, the exchange of ideas supported by individuals' free expression appears to be valuable. Knowing the truth is good for what it helps people do, help that restrictions on speech risk threatening.

Even falsehoods have their place in the truth-seeking exercise.[17] A false opinion partly developed with reference to truth can help to spread those truths. For example, someone might agree that CO_2 is a greenhouse gas but reject that it contributes to a changing global climate. That opinion is partly true. Others exposed to such an opinion may learn the truth (CO_2 is a greenhouse gas) but reject the falsehood (it does not contribute to climate change).

In general terms, the thought is that there should be a presumption in favour of individuals freely expressing their opinions because everyone's autonomy depends on knowing and articulating truths, with which all opinions help. This line of reasoning produces a weak reason in favour of free expression. After all, wherever it turns out that, because of some particular circumstances, suppressing an opinion will lead to a greater regard for the truth, then that defence of free expression no longer holds. Moreover, appealing to this defence raises worries of circularity. For some advocates of deplatforming deniers, the thought is that the continued permission for individuals to rehearse debunked claims about the climate online impedes everyone's ability to form true beliefs. For opponents to assert that this permission is a useful part of a truth-seeking system begs, rather than answers, the question of whether free expression is necessary to all truth-seeking exercises.

Here it is useful to distinguish between free expression as a rule that promotes the good (a consequentialist approach) and as a right that constrains how an individual can be treated (a deontic approach). If free expression is an individual permission whose value depends on the promotion of human well-being, then the truth-tracking justification proceeds as explained above. If, however, one conceives of free expression as an individual's right, then the significance of an opinion's truth to the justification of its holder's right to articulate that opinion is less obvious. After all, if the point is that people have a weighty interest in speaking their mind, an interest weighty enough to support a right,[18] then the truth of their opinion, as well as its value or lack thereof to listeners, is irrelevant. Against this attempt to drive a wedge between the truth-tracking defence and the deontic interpretation of free expression there is the claim that individuals have a weighty interest in free expression because there is an intrinsic connection between knowing and speaking. In Mill's words, "assuming that the true opinion abides in the mind, but abides as a prejudice, a belief independent of, and proof against, argument – this is not the way in which truth ought to be held by a rational being. This is not knowing the truth. Truth, thus held, is but one superstition the more, accidentally clinging to the words which enunciate a truth."[19]

Even if the freedom to articulate and discuss one's ideas is part of what it is to know something (a plausible claim), it does not follow that deniers must be permitted to use a given platform. It is not obvious that the intellectual interest that everyone has in speaking their mind would be set back were a social media company to take steps to limit the reach of certain voices. After all, deniers can freely talk among themselves, enjoy debates housed by willing institutions, and discuss their views with non-deniers who make themselves available in other ways.

Moreover, the potential audience that deniers might reach via social media platforms do not have a truth-relevant interest in hearing further climate change denial.[20] With respect to the truth, deniers present information that has been thoroughly debunked, recycle argumentative strategies, and often argue in the alternative (using incompatible lines of reasoning).[21] Further exposure to these is not helpful to listeners' formation of true beliefs. For one, rather than re-debunking the same ideas, that end would be better served through exposure to information on the functioning of the climate and the role of humans within it. Furthermore, deniers often mislead through their argumentative strategies.[22] Arguing in the alternative has the effect of bombarding listeners with lines of reasoning that create illusory breadth in deniers' evidence. Those who wish to learn about climate change would be better served learning without having to dig through those tactics.

THE "DELIBERATIVE VALUE OF FREE DISCUSSION"[23]: DOES CLIMATE CHANGE DENIAL HELP PROTECT OR PROMOTE INDIVIDUALS' AUTONOMY?

Insofar as a vanishingly small subset of individuals form life plans around the intention to argue against the consensus position that the climate is changing (i.e., the "warmist conspiracy"),[24] then the ability to articulate one's view, especially via amplifying platforms, is part of one's exercise of autonomy. More generally, however, climate change denial does not help enrich the intellectual environment in which we exercise our deliberative capacities – enrichment that would, if real, help us develop our deliberative capacities.

In principle, the defence of free expression on the grounds of its value to individuals' deliberative capacities is strong. The thought is that individuals' deliberation is a crucial ingredient in their happiness and well-being. It is this uniquely human capacity that makes us responsible agents. The goal is to avoid "ape-like imitation" and instead "use observation to see, reasoning and judgement to foresee, activity to gather materials for decision, discrimination to decide, and ... firmness and self-control to hold to his deliberate action."[25] For individuals to engage in that practice, they require a range of conditions, both positive and negative.[26] The former include good intellectual habits and skills, as well as education on a range of topics. The latter include freedoms of thoughts and action, which include freedom of expression. Freedom of expression distributed among members of a shared society allows everyone to represent their views clearly and comprehensively, thereby expanding everyone's menu of options for how to live: "experiments in living not only express the autonomy of the agent at the time of action, but they provide materials for the agent and others in future deliberations."[27] This is material that we can accept or reject; the point is that it is more for us to process.

Further exposure to climate change denial is *one* way of exercising our deliberative capacities. Thankfully, there are others. It follows therefore that climate change deniers cannot claim access to particular platforms, especially educational ones, on the grounds that it improves the deliberative capacities of members of those institutions. In my view, debates about how to reduce the remaining areas of uncertainty in climate projects,[28] which jurisdictions and industries are better suited to a cap-and-trade system and which are better suited to a carbon price/tax, how to balance investment in proven renewable energy technologies with experimental technologies that have huge upsides, how to include all those affected by such decisions in the decision-making process itself, how to represent the interests of future generations in such processes, how to compensate those victims of unavoidable loss and damage of climate change, how to set the limits of adaptation … All of these questions represent fascinating, evidence-driven subjects whose study will reward the student by improving their deliberative capacities, in addition to helping improve existing knowledge about climate change and the menu of policies that might help respond to it. No one's deliberative capacities require for their development further exposure to climate change denial.

In addition to the autonomy-relevant interest that we all have in exercising our deliberative capacities, we also have autonomy-relevant interests in controlling what reasons we consider with those capacities.[29] The thought runs as follows: when agent A restricts the freedom of expression of agent B to interfere in the reasoning of agent C, A infringes on C's autonomy: "to regard himself as autonomous in the sense I have in mind a person must see himself as sovereign in deciding what to believe and in weighing competing reasons for action."[30] Autonomy is both the control over the reason for which we act *and* the reasons for which we formulate our reasons. Any effort to improve the quality of a debate by, say, limiting the number of voices espousing climate change denial cannot but restrict all of its participants' autonomy.[31]

The case for climate change denial is not so simple, as it raises the related problem "that false or misleading information can undermine autonomous agency and responsibility."[32] Evidence shows that individuals' opinions on climate change often follow from elite cues.[33] In short, not all reasons are made equal.

Some cues – especially ones tailored for individuals by, say, a targeted marketing firm – have greater purchase on our minds than others. As such, the view that I undermine my own autonomy in arguing for deplatforming climate change deniers is too simple. The information that I see in my daily life, especially as it is presented to me online, reflects a constant battle among actors who wish to influence my behaviour through that information. Exposure to a wider range of information (including climate change denial) is not always autonomy enhancing.[34] Indeed, the quality of options matters enormously.[35] I may therefore choose to permit others to restrict the information in ways that enhance my autonomy.

 For me, that includes climate change denial. To generalize this line of reasoning, we can ask if properly motivated individuals would agree to such restrictions on the grounds that doing so enhances everyone's autonomy. That is, we can defend hypothetical consent to such restrictions. Put briefly: if we take autonomy to be "the actual ability to exercise independent rational judgment, as a good to be promoted,"[36] then it is clear that individuals will accept restrictions on speech where they help promote individual autonomy so defined. Deplatforming denial exposes people to an intellectual position that neither helps develop their deliberative capacities nor helps their pursuit of the truth.

Is Climate Change Denial Harmful?

Directly, no; indirectly, yes.[37] Perhaps the clearest way to object to a set of acts, including speech acts, is to argue that they together harm individuals. For many, to show that a set of speech acts is harmful is not sufficient to show that it should be in some way restricted.[38] I do not quarrel with that position directly.[39] Here I explain the connection between climate change denial and the harms of climate change. As becomes clear below, harm is a flexible notion, making its application to this discussion difficult. Before getting to that complication, I begin with the relationship of harm to individual liberty.

The position that harm provides the moral warrant for interference in individuals' liberty is most commonly associated with Mill. In his words,

> the sole end for which mankind are warranted, individually or collectively, in interfering with the liberty of action of any of their number, is self-protection … [The] only purpose for which power can be rightfully exercised over any member of a civilized community, against his will, is to prevent harm to others. His own good, either physical or moral, is not sufficient warrant.[40]

In case one is tempted to impute to Mill the view that speech acts cannot harm, note that he writes elsewhere in *On Liberty* that opinions are correctly subject to restriction if the circumstances warrant it.[41] To use Mill's own example: the opinion that corn dealers starve the poor is acceptably expressed in the press, for example, but not to an angry mob outside of a corn dealer's house. Furthermore, omitted acts are equally important. Where an agent fails to discharge a duty, thereby leading to others' harm, that agent can be held responsible.[42] In the right circumstances, failure to prevent some harmful speech act might constitute precisely such an omission. His view thus runs something like this: individuals can justly protect themselves from harm. Individuals, via social and political institutions, must protect one another from harm, even where that depends on restricting individuals' liberty. This applies to some opinions and omissions, as it does to obvious cases of harmful acts.

It is tempting to argue that climate change denial is harmful because it prevents meaningful action on climate change, action that would prevent harm.[43] Here, the analogy between climate change denial and anti-vaccination advocacy is helpful.[44] Their points of commonality are as follows: both consist of empirical claims that the relevant scientific experts reject; advocates of both have found receptive audiences via social media; both employ similar rhetorical strategies (e.g., framing their efforts as merely informing others', rather than advocating particular actions). The difference is that the harm of anti-vaccination advocacy is clear and direct, as the resurgence of previously rare (if not eradicated) diseases following from a decrease in vaccination rates would not have happened but for the spread of anti-vaccination messages.[45] It is not equally clear that a rapid and widespread transition away from fossil fuels would have happened in the absence of climate change denial.

For those who believe that counterfactual to be correct and who believe that climate change denial continues to impede that transition, then the identification of harm is easy and the analogy to the anti-vaccination movement complete. It follows, then, that the significance of the interest in good health of those who will suffer as a result of reduced vaccination rates caused by the anti-vaccination movement outweighs the interest that anti-vaccination advocates, as well as their listeners, have in a free exchange of ideas.[46] In short, anti-vaccination advocates harm those who suffer from diseases that can be prevented by vaccination. By analogy, so do climate deniers, as they promote inaction about climate change.

There are, however, reasons to think that the harm of climate change denial is not as readily identified as that of the anti-vaccination movement. I will consider two. First, the causal link between climate change denial and inert climate policies, for example, contains many steps and involves many mediating agents. In short, deniers might point out that their words do not emit carbon; that is the result of individuals' choices. While this drives a wedge between denial and harm, it invites the response that climate change denial is indirectly harmful in the sense that its harm requires the complicity of some agent who acts in ways motivated by denial. Perhaps, then, the correct response is, both perspectives considered, to express moral condemnation of both.

There is a further wrinkle in the harm-based justification for deplatforming. A particular climate denier might object that one instance (or one social media account) is, on its own, not harmful – in fact, it will make virtually no difference to the harms that take place, since there are thousands of instances that together motivate harmful inaction. If harm occurs where one agent sets back the interests of another agent, then no instance of denial meets that standard of harm, and so is not harmful. No instance of denial can be deplatformed, then, for the harm that it does.

The response to this line of argument is that, when considering the moral quality of acts whose effects are vanishingly small, if not imperceptible, but where those acts together produce a harmful state of affairs, the moral quality of those acts depends on what they together do.[47] The implication, then, is that deplatforming should be rule-driven. After all, since the harm-based objection to climate change denial depends on its collective effects, then responses to it should aim to shape those collective effects via systematic, rather than ad hoc, policies.

Does Deplatforming Follow?

The Deplatforming Impulse: Reasons and Worries

For many, the natural impulse in response to the above analysis is to advocate for deniers' deplatforming. The line of reasoning proceeds as follows: since climate change denial helps sustain neither true beliefs nor individuals' deliberative capacities, and since it is harmful, then deniers' free expression can be justly limited. The key normative claim is that climate change denial is harmful. Whether one takes the presence of harm to be sufficient to license restrictions on speech, or whether one weighs the speakers' rights against the rights that belong to the victims of climate change, the argument is that deplatforming is justified. That particular feature of the case for deplatforming – that it depends on the success enjoyed by deplatforming – opens it up to a range of significant, and familiar, objections. I present two that I take to be instructive, before turning to some suggestions in the next section.

SLIPPERY FISH

The first objection runs as follows: Deplatforming deniers on the most popular social media sites will only push them to find new venues for their views, likely pulling at least some of their audience with them, which will in turn exacerbate the "echo chamber" problem, the problem where social media users cluster ideologically within platforms such that they only ever encounter information that they already accept. Any move that leads to platforms being dominated by individual echo chambers will exacerbate that problem by removing the possibility that platform design can introduce heterogeneity into users' experience.

The evidence that echo chambers do in fact form is compelling. One representative paper demonstrates that Facebook users inclined to interact with scientific information and users inclined to interact with conspiracy theories behave remarkably similar.[48] Their "likes" – indication of support for a piece of content – are remarkably uniform in the information liked: 78 per cent of users interacting with scientific pages only "like" that type of page; the same is true for 92 per cent of users interacting with pages posting conspiratorial information.[49] Users build networks of friends who share these same convictions and same uniform behaviour. It follows, then, that information shared via this platform spreads within thought communities, with only preferred content (i.e., posts confirming accepted information) being shared. A growing number of papers confirm these sorts of trends across platforms.[50]

If users of a particular ideological persuasion or with certain beliefs feel that they are systematically disadvantaged by a given platform, then it is reasonable to assume that they will avoid that platform.[51] With that in mind, while we may wish to deplatform climate change deniers, this may have the result of driving users to platforms that do not have such a policy, increasing ideological homogeneity within social media platforms.

WHO DECIDES?

Who decides what information is considered sufficiently harmful to warrant deplatforming? And what if the shoe were on the other foot? That is, how would those who wish to deplatform deniers feel if, instead, Twitter reduced the visibility of tweets advocating for action on climate change or Facebook suspended accounts arguing for the same?

This worry has bite because of the incentives under which social media companies operate.[52] Quite apart from substantive political questions, social media companies rely on advertising and, more generally, on particular forms of user engagement. There is no reason to think that that interest will converge with some interest that we all have in, for example, securing access to high-quality information. Indeed, there is reason to think that those two sets of interests come apart.[53] It seems, then, that we should be predisposed not to trust social media companies' interference in the content of the online discussion that they house. The obvious alternative is to suggest that governments draft regulations that guide that interference. I do not investigate that alternative in any depth because I do not find it to be plausible. Even on the implausibly optimistic assumption that democratic governments might come up with guidelines that could in fact temper social media companies' worst tendencies (perhaps by diversifying the values for which they seek to optimize their platforms), not all governments are democratic. Subsuming the content of online conversations to parochial state regulations would, given the lack of political freedoms in many jurisdictions, reproduce that lack of freedom online.

Democratic Alternatives

I have now done two things. First, I outlined the case against taking climate change denial to be valuable. Second, I presented two serious worries about inferring from that first point that deniers should be deplatformed. Despite those worries, though, the problem of climate change denial on social media platforms persists. What is to be done?

To begin, recall a point made at the beginning of this chapter, that I wish to avoid reproducing an unhelpful division between two camps, one that favours restricting free expression where justified and one that favours unlimited free expression. Recall also a subsequent point, where, in discussing the deliberative value of free expression, I introduced the notion that individuals have autonomy-relevant interests in forming their own beliefs, as well as controlling the reasons for which they form their beliefs. For example, I have autonomy-relevant interests in making up my own mind about climate change; I also have autonomy-relevant interests in forming my climate beliefs using evidence that I myself deem to be significant.

It seems to me that these two points together direct our attention to the following idea: when we consider the case for deplatforming denial, we should really be considering questions about what options of institutional design are available to us that can include those who are sceptical that the climate is changing without allowing them to dominate online conversations. I stress the significance of this topic. Insofar as social media represents a massively important information source for many, including citizens who vote in democratic elections, then supporting individuals' exercise of their deliberative capacities on social media platforms in a way that nourishes those capacities is quite important.

We can arrive at the same point another way. Free expression is intimately linked with democracy; freedom of expression within a political community is necessary for that community to be democratic.[54] The basic thought is that in a democracy, individuals must have unfettered access to political deliberation. There are several, compatible justifications for this claim.[55] The first two are already familiar. Some take free expression to help establish the truth of some matter, which of course helps when deliberating over policies in a democratic context. Furthermore, free expression protects space where citizens can exercise, and thereby improve, their deliberative capacities. Finally, insofar as democracy makes individuals into both the authors and the subjects of laws, speech regulations can produce inequalities in political ineffectiveness, thereby granting some citizens less authorial power than others, which is unjustly undemocratic. On this view, free expression generates democratic value of three sorts: better-quality decisions, flourishing people, and respectful government. In sum: "a majority decision is not fair unless everyone has had a fair opportunity to express his or her attitudes or opinions or fears or tastes or presuppositions or prejudices or ideals ... to confirm his or her standing as a responsible agent in, rather than a passive victim of, collective action."[56]

It is in no way clear to me that individuals who rely on an online echo chamber for information, and consequently whose views fall into place with those received from that same community, have had a fair opportunity to express their attitudes or opinions. The evidence cited above shows clearly that as users engage with those communities, their opinions tend to shift in a polarized direction. Those with contrary opinions at best keep them to themselves, and more often are excluded from the community. The suggestion in those papers is that this is at least in part a function of platform design. With that in mind, at least some possible improvements in that design should be taken as enhancements, rather than restrictions, on freedom of expression, enhancements that protect the notion of "fair opportunity" mentioned above. In this way, such enhancements are similar to public education. One of the many reasons to favour state-funded education in a democracy is that it helps to secure citizens' fair opportunity to participate in the democratic process. Revisions to the design of social media companies can appeal to an analogous justification.

Democratic Control

In this final section, I will focus on one suggestion. My previous move was to suggest that instead of thinking of social media platforms as the terrain for the next battle between free and restricted speech, we should think about what properties they should have, given their growing significance to democracy. Rather than ask how to integrate social media into democracy, my approach here is to ask how democracy can be brought to social media.

The autonomy-relevant interest in controlling the reasons for which we form our beliefs implies a negative interest against others' interference in the reasons that we encounter. Should a social media platform remove climate change denial from our feeds, for example, then it appears that that negative interest has been set back. How can control be returned to users in such a situation? By seeking their consent. Now, this is a practice with some precedent in the form of a given platform's terms and conditions of use. As I am sure is a universal experience, nobody reads these terms and conditions.[57] While that experience is cautionary, the lesson is that this consent-seeking exercise should not take the form of lengthy documents rendered in impenetrable legalese.

My suggestion, then, is that social media companies, perhaps in conjunction with other stakeholders, should devise principles that, for example, curb the tendency towards polarization and echo chambers on their platforms, then seek users' consent, not in a consultation with a small sample, but on an individual basis. Ask users to agree to certain principles of content diversity, for example. The general point is as follows: if social media companies are to house the conversations so vital to the functioning of a healthy democracy, then they should themselves be democratized. While evidence shows that disconfirming evidence does not always have the effect of shifting beliefs,[58] that is not necessarily the point. Rather, there is still value in preventing echo chambers from spiralling towards opposite poles.

Questions might include: Do you agree to have x per cent of the posts that you see contain information (or come from sources) with which you disagree? Do you want to see information that confirms what you already believe? Wording these questions precisely and compellingly is beyond my area of expertise, and of course different terms (e.g., "fact-checking") will engender unnecessary controversy. I find it hard to believe, though, that questions posed in the abstract will evoke a desire in individuals to avoid educational content, close off their minds, and commit to ideological homogeneity. Imagine that upon opening a given platform, users were each asked simple and direct questions about the principles that should guide their experience on that platform. In addition to the principled virtue of granting them more control over the reasons for which they form their beliefs, this would have the practical effect of licensing the policies necessary to counter harmful polarization around issues like climate change denial on social media platforms, without necessarily deplatforming deniers.

Conclusion

This chapter opens with a question about how the changing means of expression are influencing the justification for freedom of expression, a question that matters in part because of a worry about the ways in which the design of social media platforms leads to conversations that, via their tone and content, mislead people. With that in mind, considering deplatforming and the case of climate change denial helps to show that it is not enough to have confidence that those predisposed to think for themselves can in fact do so. We all need help, especially when it comes to the segment of our lives that is expressed on our social media. Reflecting on the case of climate change denial directs us to think about how to support each of our efforts to think for ourselves in a world dominated by social media.

NOTES

1 This and following data from Statista (https://www.statista.com/). For social media data, see "Most Popular Social Networks Worldwide as of January 2021, Ranked by Number of Active Users," Statista, January 2021, https://www.statista.com /statistics/272014/global-social-networks-ranked-by-number-of-users/.

2   For work on that problem, see Ari E. Waldman, *Privacy and Trust* (Cambridge: Cambridge University Press, 2018), and Jennifer Rothman, *The Right of Publicity: Privacy Reimagined for a Public World* (Cambridge, MA: Harvard University Press, 2018)

3   Many distinguish misinformation from disinformation, with the former referring to incorrect information and the latter to incorrect information designed and spread with the intention of deceit. Nothing in this chapter hinges on such a distinction. What I care about here is that some speech is false; I do not much care about the intention behind its falsity. For examples of nervous hand-wringing, see Julia Carrie Wong, "How Facebook and YouTube Help Spread Anti-vaxxer Propaganda," *Guardian*, 1 February 2019, https://www.theguardian.com/media/2019/feb/01/facebook-youtube-anti-vaccination-misinformation-social-media; Olga Khazan, "Wealthy L.A. Schools' Vaccination Rates Are as Low as South Sudan's," *Atlantic*, 16 September 2014, https://www.theatlantic.com/health/archive/2014/09/wealthy-la-schools-vaccination-rates-are-as-low-as-south-sudans/380252/ (an article based on a surprisingly difficult to verify statistic); and Jennifer Monte de Oca, "Anti-vaxxers: Public Health Enemy Number One?," *Medium*, May 13, 2019, https://medium.com/@writtenbyjenny/anti-vaxxers-public-health-enemy-number-one-9d74f28b21a0. The list goes on.

4   Riley E. Dunlap, "Climate Change Skepticism and Denial: An Introduction," *American Behavioral Scientist* 57 (2013): 691–8; Riley E. Dunlap and Aaron M. McCright, "Organized Climate Change Denial," in *The Oxford Handbook of Climate Change and Society*, ed. John S. Dryzek, Richard B. Norgaard, and David Scholsberg (Oxford: Oxford University Press, 2011), 144–60; S. Vanderheiden, *Atmospheric Justice: A Political Theory of Climate Change* (Oxford: Oxford University Press, 2008), 38–40.

5   Catriona McKinnon, "Should We Tolerate Climate Change Denial?," *Midwest Studies in Philosophy* 40, no. 1 (2016): 205; see also Dunlap, "Climate Change Skepticism and Denial."

6   Constantine Boussalis and Travis G. Coan, "Text Mining the Signals of Climate Change Doubt," *Global Environmental Change* 36 (2016): 89–100.

7   For a snapshot of American public opinion on climate change, see Anthony Leiserowitz et al., *Climate Change in the American Mind* (New Haven, CT: Yale Program on Climate Change Communication, 2019).

8   Naomi Oreskes and Erik M. Conway, *Merchants of Doubt: How a Handful of Scientists Obscured the Truth on Issues from Tobacco Smoke to Global Warming* (London: Bloomsbury, 2012) esp. ch. 6; Justin Farrell, "Corporate Funding and Ideological Polarisation About Climate Change," *Proceedings of the National Academy of Sciences of the United States of America* 113, no. 1 (2016): 92–7.

9   Stanley Cohen, *States of Denial: Knowing about Atrocities and Suffering* (Cambridge: Polity, 2001), 1.

10 See, for example, Kari Marie Norgaard, "Climate Denial: Emotions, Psychology, Culture, and Political Economy," in *The Oxford Handbook of Climate Change and*

Society, ed. John S. Dryzek, Richard B. Norgaard, and David Schlosberg (Oxford: Oxford University Press, 2011), 399–413.

11 Ibid., 400.

12 Also known as "no platforming." The National Union of Students in the United Kingdom has had a no platform policy since 1973, which indicates that these issues have been around for a while. For their most recent policy (at time of writing), see "NUS' No Platform Policy: Key Information, Background and FAQs," National Union of Students, 13 February 2017, https://www.nusconnect.org.uk/resources /nus-no-platform-policy-f22f.

13 Suspensions for this reason have occurred. Those claiming to have been deplatformed for this reason are listed in a Twitter thread by Sam Barber (@SamBarber1910) from 15 November 2018, https://twitter.com/SamBarber1910 /status/1063250389791883264?s=19. See also Holly Lawford-Smith, "An Open Letter to Twitter's Board of Directors," 3 June 2019, https://hollylawford-smith.org /an-open-letter-to-twitters-board-of-directors/.

14 David O. Brink, Mill's Progressive Principles (Oxford: Oxford University Press, 2013), 152.

15 J.S. Mill, Utilitarianism and On Liberty (Oxford: Blackwell, 2003), 100.

16 Brink, Mill's Progressive Principles, 152–3.

17 Mill, Utilitarianism and On Liberty, 128.

18 Joseph Raz, The Morality of Freedom (Oxford: Oxford University Press, 1986), 165.

19 Mill, Utilitarianism and On Liberty, 114.

20 I specify truth relevance because, below, I discuss the possibility that there are deliberative-capacity-relevant interests in hearing climate change denial.

21 Shaun W. Elsasser and Riley E. Dunlap, "Leading Voices in the Denier Choir: Conservative Columnists' Dismissal of Global Warming and Denigration of Climate Science," American Behavioral Scientist 57, no. 6 (2013): 754–76.

22 N. Koteyko, R. Jaspal, and B. Nerlich, "Climate Change and 'Climategate' in Online Reader Comments: A Mixed Methods Study," Geographical Journal 179, no. 1 (2013): 74–86.

23 Brink, Mill's Progressive Principles, 152.

24 In the early days of public awareness about climate change, "warmists" and "coldists" (and indeed "staticists," as a middle-ground position) occupied intellectual positions generally represented as equally legitimate. See H. Rheingold, "On Language: Succinctly Spoken," New York Times, 27 August 1989.

25 Mill, Utilitarianism and On Liberty, 134.

26 Brink, Mill's Progressive Principles, 157.

27 Mill, Utilitarianism and On Liberty, 132.

28 For example, the precise extent of climate sensitivity.

29 Though I do not want to use this language any further, we might say that we have a first-order interest in deliberating and a second-order interest in controlling what we deliberate about.

30   T. M. Scanlon, "A Theory of Freedom of Expression," *Philosophy and Public Affairs* 1, no. 2 (1972): 215; see also Thomas Nagel, "Personal Rights and Public Space," *Philosophy and Public Affairs* 24, no. 2 (1995): 83–107.

31   Scanlon, the original proponent of that first conception of autonomy, later recognized that it is far too expansive, ruling out even regulations against false advertising. See T.M. Scanlon, "Freedom of Expression and Categories of Expression," *University of Pittsburgh Law Review* 40 (1978): 532.

32   Susan J. Brison, "The Autonomy Defense of Free Speech," *Ethics* 108, no. 2 (1998): 329.

33   R.J. Brulle, J. Carmichael, and J.C. Jenkins, "Shifting Public Opinion on Climate Change: An Empirical Assessment of Factors Influencing Concern over Climate Change in the U.S., 2002–2010," *Climatic Change* 114, no. 2 (2012): 169–88; J. Carmichael and R.J. Brulle, "Elite Cues, Media Coverage, and Public Concern: An Integrated Path Analysis of Public Opinion on Climate Change, 2001–2013," *Environmental Politics* 26, no. 2 (2017): 232–52.

34   G. Dworkin, *The Theory and Practice of Autonomy* (Cambridge: Cambridge University Press, 1988), 62–81.

35   Raz, *The Morality of Freedom*, 205, 373–80.

36   Scanlon, "Freedom of Expression and Categories of Expression."

37   I proceed with a relatively simple conception of harm in which agent A harms agent B, thereby setting back B's interests. See J. Feinberg, *The Moral Limits of the Criminal Law*, vol. 1, *Harm to Others* (Oxford: Oxford University Press, 1984), 33–4. There are, of course, many ways of conceptualizing harm. For an outline of the main competitors, see Victor Tadros, "What Might Have Been," in *The Law of Torts*, ed. John Oberdiek (Oxford: Oxford University Press, 2014), 181–6.

38   See, for example, Scanlon, "A Theory of Freedom of Expression," 204.

39   For some who do, see Susan J. Brison, "Speech, Harm, and the Mind-Body Problem in First Amendment Jurisprudence," *Legal Theory* 4, no. 1 (1998): 39–61; Frederick Schauer, "The Phenomenology of Speech and Harm," *Ethics* 103 (1993): 635–53; K. Greenawalt, *Speech, Crime, and the Uses of Language* (Oxford: Oxford University Press, 1989).

40   Mill, *Utilitarianism and On Liberty*, 94.

41   Ibid., 64.

42   Ibid., 17–18.

43   An argument defended by T. Lavik, "Climate Change Denial, Freedom of Speech and Global Justice," *Nordic Journal of Applied Ethics* 10, no. 2 (2015): 75–90.

44   Lavik defends this claim in part by developing an analogy between climate change denial and a thought experiment in which pharmaceutical companies seek to undermine scientific inquiry that shows their drug to be harmful: ibid., 75–6.

45   T.C. Smith, "Vaccine Rejection and Hesitancy: A Review and Call to Action," *Open Forum Infectious Diseases* 4, no. 3 (2017); J.K. Olive et al., "The State of the Anti-vaccine Movement in the United States: A Focused Examination of Nonmedical Exemptions in States and Counties," *PLoS Medicine* 15, no. 6 (2018): https://doi.org/10.1371/journal.pmed.1002578; Azhar Hussain et al., "The

Anti-vaccination Movement: A Regression in Modern Medicine," *POLS1Medicine* 10, no. 7 (2018), doi:10.7759/cureus.2919; Ayelet Evrony and Arthur Caplan, "The Overlooked Dangers of Anti-vaccination Groups' Social Media Presence," *Human Vaccines & Immunotherapeutics* 13, no. 6 (2017): 1475–6.

46 Lavik, "Climate Change Denial, Freedom of Speech and Global Justice," 10–11; developing Scanlon, "Freedom of Expression and Categories of Expression."

47 Derek Parfit, *Reasons and Persons* (Oxford: Oxford University Press, 1984), 67–86, esp. 83–6.

48 Walter Quattrociocchi, Antonio Scala, and Cass R. Sunstein, "Echo Chambers on Facebook," SSRN, 13 June 2016, https://ssrn.com/abstract=2795110.

49 Ibid., 4.

50 F. Zollo et al., "Debunking in the World of Tribes," *PloS One* 12, no. 7 (2017), https://doi.org/10.1371/journal.pone.0181821; D. Mocanu et al., "Collective Attention in the Age of (Mis)Information," *Computers in Human Behavior* 51 (2015): 1198–204; A. Bessi et al., "Science vs. Conspiracy: Collective Narratives in the Age of (Mis)Information," *PLoS ONE* 10, no. 2 (2015), https://doi.org/10.1371/journal.pone.0118093.

51 A problem that is especially pronounced on the platform Discord, which provides a greater degree of anonymity than some social media platforms. See their report acknowledging the issue: "Discord Transparency Report: Jan–June 2020," *Discord Blog*, 27 August 2020, https://blog.discord.com/discord-transparency-report-jan-june-2020-2ef4a3ee346d.

52 A. Manolica, T. Roman, and A.I. Roman, "Lie It or Not: Facebook Advertising Triggers," *Ovidius University Annals, Series Economic Sciences* 19, no. 1 (2019): 450–6; J. Claussen, T. Kretschmer, and P. Mayrhofer, "The Effects of Rewarding User Engagement: The Case of Facebook Apps," *Information Systems Research* 24, no. 1 (2013): 186–200; I. Pletiokosa Cvijkj and F. Michahelles, "Online Engagement Factors on Facebook Brand Pages," *Social Network Analysis and Mining* 3, no. 4 (2013): 843–61.

53 E. Bakshy, S. Messing, and L.A. Adamic, "Exposure to Ideologically Diverse News and Opinion on Facebook," *Science* 348, no. 6239 (2015): 1130–2.

54 For a recent example of a view with significant pedigree, see R. Dworkin, "Foreword," in *Extreme Speech and Democracy*, ed. I. Hare and J. Weinstein (Oxford: Oxford University Press, 2009), v–ix; J. Weinstein, "Hate Speech Bans, Democracy and Political Legitimacy," *Constitutional Commentary* 32 (2017): 715–82.

55 R. Langton, "Whose Right? Ronald Dworkin, Women, and Pornographers," *Philosophy and Public Affairs* 19, no. 4 (1993): 311–59.

56 Dworkin, "Foreword."

57 J.A. Obar and A. Oeldorf-Hirsch, "The Biggest Lie on the Internet: Ignoring the Privacy Policies and Terms of Service Policies of Social Networking Services," *Information, Communication and Society*, 2 April 2018, 1–20.

58 Cass R. Sunstein, *Going to Extremes: How Like Minds Unite and Divide* (Oxford: Oxford University Press, 2009), ch. 1.

11 The Tension between Freedom of Expression and Language Rights in Canada: The *Ford* and *Devine* Legacy after Thirty Years

STÉPHANIE CHOUINARD AND EMMANUELLE RICHEZ

Freedom of expression is an intrinsically social phenomenon that often involves the use of socially created languages.[1] When expression is in a written or oral form, whether it is in a private or a public setting, a choice must be made: What language(s) will be used when expressing oneself? As most people only understand and speak, or at least only master fully, one language – their mother tongue – forbidding them from using this language amounts to forbidding them from expressing themselves clearly and authentically.[2]

Language is an ad hoc jurisdiction in Canada; both orders of government can legislate on the issue of language in their respective spheres of competence. At Confederation, the right to use either French or English in federal and Quebec legislative assemblies and courts of law was established in section 133 of the *British North America Act*.[3] Canadian governments have subsequently enacted language legislation, either by granting equal standing to both French and English (Canada and New Brunswick) or granting special status to English (Manitoba) or French (Quebec). The federal and New Brunswick provisions were later entrenched in the *Canadian Charter of Rights and Freedoms*[4] and interpreted by the Supreme Court of Canada (SCC) as a "precise scheme" representing a constitutional minimum emanating from the "historical compromise arrived at by the founding people who agreed upon the terms of the federal union."[5] Courts may not expand or modify the language provisions contained within it; changes to the scheme must only be achieved through formal amendments to the Constitution.[6] According to the "precise scheme" theory, other *Charter* rights and freedoms, such as freedom of expression, may not be used to limit or modify language rights provisions contained within it. Furthermore, since freedom of expression is conceived as a negative right, unlike language rights, it cannot be used to require the services of the state.[7]

However, the tension between freedom of expression and other, non-constitutional linguistic legislation remained after the entrenchment of freedom of expression in section 2(b) of the *Charter*. The SCC rendered two controversial decisions in 1988 (*Ford v Quebec*,[8] *Devine v Quebec*[9]) striking down provisions forbidding the use of language other than French in commercial signage and advertising in Quebec and extending freedom of expression to commercial expression. However, the Court has also recognized that the goal of protecting the French language and Quebec's *visage linguistique* was a "pressing and substantial concern" pursuant to section 1 of the *Charter*, mitigating the *Charter*'s protections of freedom of expression as well as crafting a compromise between these *Charter* rights at a moment when they held particular political salience.

Since this watershed moment, very little attention has been paid in academia to the impact of language legislation on freedom of expression, while questions of language in commercial signage and advertising have expanded beyond Quebec, and new issues have arisen in a wide range of areas such as language of work, municipal powers, and language choice in judicial proceedings. This chapter will seek to shed light on the evolution of this tension between freedom of expression and language legislation since *Ford* and *Devine* in these different domains. It will analyse instances where freedom of expression can peacefully coexist with language rights, ones where one type of right will take precedence over the other, or ones where a compromise must be struck between the two. The chapter will demonstrate that although courts have upheld citizens' freedom of language choice in the private sphere, they have maintained the concern to protect the French language in the public sphere as a valid and tangible constraint to freedom of expression in the last thirty years, building on their original compromise, with consequences reaching outside the province of Quebec, into Yukon and Ontario.

Ford and *Devine*: Laying the Groundwork

The 1988 *Ford* and *Devine* cases were not only the first SCC cases where freedom of commercial expression was being tested, but also the first ones where freedom of expression and language rights intersected in Canada. These are twin cases where the right of Quebec business owners to use public signs (both indoors and outdoors) and commercial advertising, as well as to name their businesses, in the language of their choice was being tested, as several sections of the *Charter of the French Language*[10] (hereinafter *CFL*) limited commercial expression to the sole use of French.[11] These business owners argued that freedom of expression, protected under section 2(b) of the *Charter* and section 3 of the Quebec *Charter of Human Rights and Freedoms*,[12] should entitle them to the use of the language of their choice. The Court was presented with two separate questions – namely, whether commercial expression was protected by freedom of expression, and whether the freedom to use the language of one's choosing was protected by the same.

The first question was not fully answered. According to the Court, it is not necessary ... to delineate the boundaries of the broad range of expression deserving of protection ... Although the expression in this case has a commercial element, it should be noted that the focus here is on choice of language and on a law which prohibits the use of a language.[13]

Commercial speech is important insofar as it "serves individual and societal values in a free and democratic society."[14] Since the Court had already adopted a "large and liberal interpretation" of the relevant provisions of the *Charter*, it concluded that "there [was] no sound basis on which commercial expression [could] be excluded of the protection of s. 2(b)."[15] The Court then turned to discussing whether commercial expression *in the language of one's choice* fell within the boundaries of the protection of freedom of expression. Its response to this second question was much clearer. Language was indeed understood as falling within the purview of the freedom of expression, as explained below:

> Language is so intimately related to the form and content of expression that *there cannot be true freedom of expression by means of language if one is prohibited from using the language of one's choice*. Language is not merely a means or medium of expression; it colours the content and meaning of expression. It is, as the preamble of the [CFL] itself indicates, a means by which a people may express its cultural identity. It is also the means by which the individual expresses his or her personal identity and sense of individuality.[16]

From this interpretation, the Court then considered that sections of the *CFL* restricting language choice were an infringement on both the *Charter* and the Quebec *Charter*.[17] The final question regarded whether this infringement was justifiable under section 1 of the *Charter* and section 9.1 of the Quebec *Charter*. The Court recognized that Quebec's language policy had a "serious and legitimate" aim: the survival of the French language and "assuring that the reality of Quebec society is communicated through the '*visage linguistique*.'"[18] However, it did not accept the Quebec government's position that the exclusive use of French in commercial signage was a necessary, proportional, and/or justified impingement on section 2(b) of the *Charter* to attain the policy's aim. Rather, it offered a suggestion to amend the policy: the French language would have to be markedly predominant, while allowing any other language to be used in commercial signage, in order to meet the aim of protecting Québec's *visage linguistique* while infringing as little as possible on freedom of expression.[19]

In sum, *Ford* and *Devine* have drawn three lessons for subsequent cases pertaining to language choice and freedom of expression. First, the language used in one's expression will from now on be "inextricably connected to the exercise of the freedom"[20] of expression. Second, commercial expression is important enough in a democratic society to be granted protection under freedom of expression.

However, and this is the final lesson, French, as the language of the minority in Canada, is deemed worthy of particular protections in the public realm (what the Court called the *visage linguistique*) – even in the province of Quebec, where it is the most widely spoken language – with the potential to circumscribe private entities' linguistic freedom of expression. These lessons will have long-lasting impacts in a number of different domains where freedom of expression and language intersect.

We will now present this jurisprudence and its outcomes for freedom of expression, in turn, in the domains of commercial signage and advertisement, language of work, municipal powers, and judicial proceedings.

Commercial Signage and Advertising

As discussed above, the *Ford* and *Devine* decisions set the path for language choice to be taken seriously in cases of freedom of commercial expression. The Government of Quebec, however, was not willing to apply the SCC's proposed compromise, which was to allow languages other than French to be used in commercial signage in the province, provided they were used in smaller fonts and either underneath or to the right of the French wording. Less than a week after the *Ford* and *Devine* decisions were rendered, the National Assembly of Quebec enacted the controversial Bill 178, *An Act to Amend the Charter of the French Language*,[21] which stated that public signage outdoors, as well as inside shopping centres and on public transportation, shall be solely in French. Quebec invoked section 33 of the *Charter*, also known as the "notwithstanding clause," to override the SCC decisions, to much furore in the rest of the country.

A group of anglophone Quebeckers resorted to international law, and on 11 April 1991 submitted a complaint to the United Nations Human Rights Committee (UNHRC) claiming that the Governments of Quebec and Canada violated freedom of expression as protected under article 19 of the *Optional Protocol to the International Covenant on Civil and Political Rights*. They also alleged that section 33 of the *Charter* was a violation of the provision of effective remedies as per article 2 of the *Covenant*. The UNHCR indeed found the use of the notwithstanding clause problematic, but also noted the impossibility for complainants to seek further remedies once a case had been heard by the SCC.[22] While this decision had no legal impact on the *CFL*, it effectively shamed Quebec, and, by association, Canada, on the international stage.[23]

Once the five-year override period expired, Quebec further amended the *CFL* in 1993 with Bill 86,[24] which enacted the compromise suggested by the SCC in 1988: to ensure the marked predominance of French while allowing for the use of any other language (underneath or to the right of the French characters and in smaller font)[25] on any commercial signage, advertisement, or business name. The validity of this legislation was challenged less than a decade later in *Entreprises W.F.H. Ltée c Québec* by a business that had been found guilty of violating section 58 of the *CFL*. Its commercial sign displayed French and English words of the same size and omitted the translation of certain words from English to French.[26] The owners claimed that the *CFL*'s provisions were overly infringing on their freedom of expression as French was no longer in a vulnerable position in Quebec. In 2001, the Court of Appeal of Quebec dismissed the case, as section 58 of the *CFL* embodied the compromise found in the *Ford* decision and the plaintiffs did not demonstrate that French was less vulnerable than it was in 1988.[27]

A similar case was brought before the provincial Court of Québec in 2015 by a group of businesses arguing for less restrictions on commercial signage.[28] In *Quebec v Boulangerie Maxie's*, the *Ford* and *Devine* decisions were once again upheld as formulating a reasonable limitation on freedom of expression, seeing as the defendants did not present persuasive proof that the situation of French had sufficiently evolved in the province to merit a change in the equilibrium struck in 1988 between protection of French and freedom of expression.[29]

Finally, Ontario is the only other province where challenges to bilingual signage by-laws have been brought before the courts. According to provincial legislation, an Ontario municipality located in an area designated in the schedule of the *French Language Services Act* (*FLSA*) "may pass a by-law providing that the administration of the municipality shall be conducted in both English and French and that all or specified municipal services to the public shall be made available in both languages,"[30] but does not specifically mandate these municipalities to enforce bilingualism on commercial signs. Accordingly, Russell Township opted to enforce bilingualism on any new commercial signage. Howard Galganov, an English-language rights activist from Quebec, and Jean-Serge Brisson, a French Canadian libertarian business owner from Russell, challenged the constitutional validity of the township's by-law. They argued, first, that it was outside the township's jurisdiction; second, that it violated section 2(b) of the *Charter*; and third, that it violated sections 19 (freedom of expression) and 27 (protection of minority cultural rights) of the *International Covenant on Civil and Political Rights*.[31]

In *Galganov v Russell* (2010), the Ontario Superior Court of Justice refused to grant standing to Galganov as he did not reside in the township but agreed to hear Brisson. The Court first declared the by-law *intra vires* according to Ontario's *Municipal Act*.[32] Next, it examined whether the by-law infringed on freedom of expression. The Court recalled the *Devine* decision, which stated that "while there is a right to express oneself in a language of one's choice, there is no corresponding right to express oneself *exclusively* in one's own language."[33] It then used the two-step freedom of expression test laid out in *Irwin Toy Ltd. v Québec* (1989)[34] and determined that the applicant had not clearly proved to the Court that his freedom of expression had been restricted. The Court added that if that had been the case, the *Oakes* test would have shown that its restriction was reasonable and justified under section 1 of the *Charter*.[35] Finally, it rejected the allegation that the by-law violated international law since Canada, and not Ontario, was the *Covenant*'s signatory, and that the *Covenant* had not been incorporated into Canadian law.[36] Brisson's application was therefore dismissed.

Brisson and Galganov appealed this decision. In 2012, the Court of Appeal for Ontario confirmed the 2010 decision in part. Weiler, Sharpe, and Blair Js. agreed that only Brisson had standing and that the by-law was *intra vires*.[37] They distanced themselves from the trial court's view by ruling that the by-law was indeed a violation of Brisson's freedom of expression, as it compelled the use of both French and English on commercial signs. However, this violation would pass the *Oakes* test and be justified by section 1 of the *Charter*. In the justices' view, the by-law's objective, "the preservation and enhancement of the equality of status of the French language in the Township,"[38] was reasonable for a bilingual township, proportional to the township's goal, and framed in such a way as to limit as little as possible one's freedom of expression.[39] According to the Court, the benefits of protecting and promoting the equal status of French and English outweighed the minimal infringement on freedom of expression. Brisson had not mobilized international law arguments in this appeal, so the Court of Appeal did not take them into account. The appeal was dismissed. Galganov and Brisson submitted an application to appeal this decision before the SCC in 2012, but were denied a hearing.[40]

In sum, the jurisprudence on bilingual commercial signage and advertising is clear, thirty years after the groundwork laid by *Ford* and *Devine*: these precedents still hold a lot of weight. Provisions found in section 1 of the *Charter* continue to trump freedom of expression, at least when it comes to the protection and promotion of French, Canada's more vulnerable official language, in the public sphere. Whether it could also be used to protect English, Canada's majority language, in areas where ethnocultural groups massively advertise in a different language, such as in the case of British Columbia,[41] remains a hypothetical question for the time being, as it has not yet been tested in court. One could foresee that multiculturalism rights, rather than language rights, would be the ones to intersect with freedom of expression in such a proceeding, leading into unchartered territory.

Commercial signs are not the only aspect of business proceedings where the issue of language has intersected with freedom of expression; the language in which employers and employees conduct their business has also been in the legislative crosshairs. We now turn to this issue.

The Language of Work

The *CFL* stipulates that "workers have the right to carry on their activities in French" in Quebec.[42] More specifically, the law mandates that all companies of fifty employees or more must put in place a francization program "intended to generalize the use of French at all levels of the enterprise through [notably] the use of French in information technologies."[43] In the case of *Chiasson c Québec,* both anglophones and francophones working in pharmaceutical companies in Montreal challenged the Office québécois de la langue française's (OQLF) interpretation of the law, according to which the exclusive use of French software is mandated in the workplace when a French version of the software is available.[44] The plaintiffs took the view that using French as opposed to English software reduced their work efficiency and infringed on their freedom of expression.[45] The Quebec Superior Court decided in this case that employees had the right to use French software in the workplace when available, but that nothing should prevent their employers from offering access to software in an English version or in any other language.[46]

Since the Court reached this decision through a textualist analysis of the *CFL,* it decided that it was unnecessary to determine whether the law violated freedom of expression.[47] Invoking *Ford,* however, the Court declared *obiter dicta* that though the *CFL* mandates that companies' management and personnel have knowledge of French, the OQLF cannot negatively evaluate a company that allows its employees to speak their language of choice, since doing so would infringe upon freedom of expression.[48] Similarly, companies cannot be evaluated negatively for using multilingual working documents or for communicating in multiple languages with clients, as this would also amount to an infringement of freedom of expression.[49]

Freedom of expression was used less successfully to circumscribe measures put in place to promote French as a minority language within the Ottawa municipal government. In 2001, the City of Ottawa adopted a by-law and a policy that established rules for the delivery of bilingual services on its territory and the use of bilingualism within its municipal administration.[50] In *Canadians for Language Fairness v Ottawa* (2006), a group of anglophone citizens challenged the constitutionality of the City of Ottawa's bilingualism scheme, notably on the grounds of freedom of expression.[51] From their point of view, the designation of various employment positions within the municipal government as bilingual was infringing upon the rights of the anglophone majority.[52] By encouraging anglophone employees to speak French in order to further their career development, the City was responsible for "a blatant abrogation of the right to express oneself in one's language of choice without fear of penalty or repercussion."[53]

The Ontario Superior Court of Justice referred to the two-step test developed in *Irwin Toy* to determine whether there was an infringement of freedom of expression.[54] The first step consisted of determining whether the activity at stake conveyed or attempted to convey meaning. Here, the Court asserted that the "activity of being required to learn a second language in order to obtain a certain employment is not one that has a meaning or any content."[55] Since the first part of the test had not been met, it was unnecessary to move to the second step, which would have had to decide whether the impugned action has the purpose or the effect of restricting freedom of expression.[56] Nevertheless, the Court argued that the purpose and effect of the City of Ottawa's bilingualism scheme were constitutional. On the one hand, the scheme aimed to guarantee citizens access to services in the official language of their choice.[57] On the other, it wanted municipal employees to work in their language of choice, which would in turn facilitate the delivery of bilingual services.[58] The Court concluded that in promoting the right to express oneself in English or French, the City of Ottawa did not attempt to curb the expression of any thoughts or opinions.[59]

The jurisprudence on freedom of expression and the language of work appears to favour the claims of the linguistic minority. In the *Chiasson* case, workers who for the most part were anglophone Quebeckers, were given the right to use software in their language in private businesses. In the *Canadians for Language Fairness* case, the francophone minority in Ottawa got to keep bilingual municipal job postings, which gave them greater employment opportunities and increased their likelihood of receiving municipal services in their native tongue. Though the courts seem to have favoured equally French and English here as minority languages, it is important to note that *Chiasson* dealt with employment conditions in the private sector, while *Canadians for Language Fairness* dealt with those in the public sector. The following section on municipal powers emphasizes the role played by the public/private dichotomy on the jurisprudence on freedom of expression and language.

Municipal Powers

Some municipalities in Quebec unsuccessfully made freedom of expression arguments when they opposed *An Act to reform the municipal territorial organization of the metropolitan regions of Montréal, Québec and the Outaouais*, better known as Bill 170.[60] The Quebec National Assembly passed the bill in 2000, thereby mandating the merger of several small municipalities into three large cities so as to improve the management and delivery of public services.[61] For many municipalities with majority anglophone populations, the merger constituted a threat to the vitality of the Anglo-Quebecker minority's institutions. Under the new law, boroughs in the new City of Montreal emanating from former municipalities could maintain their bilingual status as per the *CFL*.[62] As such, a third of newly created boroughs (nine out of twenty-seven) enjoyed a bilingual status after the passing of the law.[63] Nevertheless, Bill 170 declared Montreal to be a "French-speaking city."[64] This declaration was judged inadequate by the plaintiffs, considering the linguistic makeup of Montreal.[65] Furthermore, the Anglo-Quebecker community saw it as a deliberate assimilation plan that breached its constitutional rights.[66]

In *Baie d'Urfé c Québec* (2001), Bill 170 was first challenged at the Quebec Superior Court on many counts of unconstitutionality. Of interest to this chapter is how freedom of expression was invoked to counter the municipal mergers. Here, the Municipality of Baie d'Urfé and that of L'Ancienne-Lorette refused to collaborate with the merger transition committee on the premise that the government had refused to submit Bill 170 to a referendum despite several polls, petitions, and local referendums in which citizens expressed their disapproval of it.[67] The Court declared that freedom of expression, as protected by the Canadian *Charter* and the Quebec *Charter*,[68] did not entail a right to a particular tribune provided by the state.[69] Although a referendum can provide a valuable forum in which to promote expression, there is no constitutional obligation for the state to consult citizens before adopting a law.[70] The Court was of the opinion that the refusal to organize a referendum on municipal mergers had nothing to do with the fundamental freedom of expression, as no restriction or suppression of expression was present in the case.[71] Even though the plaintiffs were not given the opportunity to participate in a public consultation, they still maintained the possibility of expressing their opinion publicly on the question of the merger.[72] The Court stressed that expressing an opinion is one thing, but imposing one's opinion outside an election is another.[73]

The merged municipalities ultimately appealed the decision in *Baie d'Urfé* before the Court of Appeal of Quebec.[74] Appellants developed another argument based on freedom of expression to discredit Bill 170, albeit again unsuccessfully.[75] They argued that by forcing municipal employees and council members to collaborate with the transition committee, the law forbade these individuals from resorting to dissidence or non-collaboration, which constitute protected forms of expression.[76] The law, according to the appellants, would also infringe on their freedom by compelling them to participate in a project that goes against their political conviction.[77] In response, the Court indicated that no provision in the law prevented anyone from expressing themselves and formulating opinions on whatever matter.[78]

At both the trial and appeal levels, the plaintiffs unsuccessfully invoked the unwritten constitutional principle of the protection of minorities to maintain existing anglophone municipal structures.[79] In *Baie d'Urfé*, the Court was of the opinion that unwritten principles cannot be used to contradict existing constitutional provisions or to expand the existing constitutional language rights regime.[80] Provinces maintain unlimited constitutional power over municipal government, and the right to municipal government for anglophones in Quebec is not explicitly recognized in the written constitution.[81] As the justices explained in *Westmount*, this constitutional silence is not a vacuum to be filled thanks to the unwritten principle of the protection of minorities; the fathers of Confederation could have explicitly protected anglophone municipalities if they wanted to.[82] This restrictive approach to the principle of the protection of minorities was not the one used in *Lalonde v Ontario,* however, to save l'Hôpital Montfort, the only French university hospital in Ontario.[83] The freedom of expression jurisprudence thus does not seem to favour the rights of the anglophone minority in the public sphere.

Judicial Proceedings

As discussed in the introduction to this chapter, both the *Constitution Act, 1867* and the *Charter* protect the right to be heard in one's official language of choice before a federal court, or before a Quebec or New Brunswick provincial court. The *Criminal Code,*[84] at sections 530 and 530.1, further strengthens these guarantees. However, these provisions only cover these governments' obligation to provide documentation in the accused's official language and the right for them to express themselves in court in the official language of their choice. Moreover, the right to express oneself in the official language of one's choice does not only belong to the accused, but also to the opposing party and counsel. Language rights, therefore, do not cover the entirety of judicial proceedings, such as the submission or reception of evidence and the choice of the language used by adversaries.

The issue of the language of submitted evidence was brought before the Yukon courts in 1994 in *R. v Rodrigue.*[85] The accused, Mr. Rodrigue, requested that the evidence submitted by the Crown in his case, which was heard in French, also be made available in French. Said evidence contained

> statements and notes made by members of the Royal Canadian Mounted Police, transcripts of testimony provided by an informant at the preliminary inquiry, the criminal record of that informant and notes taken while interviewing the informer, in the course of an investigation into a criminal charge against the informer.[86]

The accused relied both on language rights (section 133 of the *Constitution Act, 1867*; section 5 of the *Yukon Languages Act*; section 530 of the *Criminal Code*; section 20(1) of the *Charter*; and sections 21 and 24 of the *Official Languages Act* [*OLA*]) and on freedom of expression (section 2(b) of the *Charter*) to support his request. The judge interpreted these language rights to cover the accused's written arguments and pleadings, but not evidence.

Following SCC jurisprudence set out in the so-called 1986 trilogy (*Macdonald v City of Montreal,*[87] *Bilodeau v A.G.,*[88] and *Société des Acadiens v Association of Parents*[89]), which framed the limits on language rights in the judiciary for over a decade,[90] Garson, LaFlamme, and McDonald Js. from the Supreme Court of Yukon refused to interpret the above provisions so as to include access to evidence in one's language of choice. They argued that "[if] the legislator had wanted to impose a positive obligation on the Crown regarding its own written pleadings, arguments or the disclosure of evidence, this would have been explicitly stated."[91] Furthermore, the judges interpreted freedom of expression as being limited to protecting the freedom of the accused and their counsel to use the official language of their choice. Recalling the SCC's decision in *Ford*, which reiterated part of the *Macdonald* decision, the justices highlighted the difference between freedom of expression and "special guarantees of language rights" found in the Constitution, which are a "precise scheme" and should be limited to an individual's interaction with government.[92] It appears the Court in this instance chose to interpret evidence submitted for the purpose of a proceeding as belonging to the private, rather than the public, sphere, and therefore not subject to constitutional language protection.[93]

The question of language of proceedings reappeared before the courts, this time through the issue of the language used by the opposing counsel during trial, in 2000, in *Lavigne v Quebec (AG)*.[94] Mr. Lavigne, who requested to be tried in English in a Quebec court, also wished for the representative of the Attorney General's Office to plead in that language. He was therefore not only claiming rights for himself to speak the official language of his choice, as protected by the Constitution, but, as the Court notes, also as a "listener" of the proceedings.[95]

Lavigne based his argument on language rights (section 133 of the *Constitution Act, 1867*; section 530.1 of the *Criminal Code*; section 18 of the *OLA*; and section 15 of the *CFL*), on freedom from discrimination (section 15 of the *Charter* and section 10 of the Quebec *Charter*), and on freedom of expression (section 2(b) of the *Charter*). The Superior Court of Quebec determined, first, that section 133 of the *Constitution Act, 1867* covers the language rights of both the accused and the state representatives. It contains no right for the accused to oblige another person to address them in their own language.[96] Section 530.1 of the *Criminal Code*, for its part, only covers the right of the accused to have a justice of the peace, judge, or jury who speaks their language, and does not mention the Crown's representatives.[97] Moreover, the *OLA* only applies in federal courts, while section 15 of the *CFL* does not apply to court proceedings. Section 7 of the *CFL*, for its part, echoes section 133 of the *Constitution Act, 1867*, and protects the language rights of all parties in a Quebec court. The Court also rejected Mr. Lavigne's argument that his right to life, liberty, and security of the person (section 7 of the *Charter*) or that his right to natural justice were compromised, since he was provided with an interpreter, as well as his argument that he would be discriminated against according to section 15 of the *Charter* and section 10 of the Quebec *Charter*. Finally, the Court was clear that as long as Mr. Lavigne could express himself in his own language and was provided with an interpreter to understand the proceedings happening in another language, his freedom of expression was not violated.[98]

Finally, in *Morand c Québec*,[99] the Quebec Court of Appeal refused to recognize the appellant's right to receive an official, authenticated English translation of a decision emanating from a Quebec court. The appellant argued that several *Charter* rights, among them section 2(b), would grant him the right to an official ruling in the official language of his choice.[100] The Court decided that the historical compromise struck in section 133 of the *Constitution Act, 1867* should be interpreted in such a way as to grant both the public representatives (in this occurrence the judge) and the individuals being heard the right to use the official language of their choice. This compromise was respected since the Government of Quebec could provide the parties with a translated, but not authenticated, copy of the decision upon request. Moreover, the Court underlined once again, citing *Ford,* that *Charter* rights, such as freedom of expression, could not be mobilized to modify or enlarge that compromise.[101]

In sum, constitutional language guarantees for judicial proceedings have imposed strong boundaries on freedom of expression. The state of the jurisprudence relies heavily on the SCC's interpretation of language rights in judicial proceedings found in the 1986 trilogy, which supported a restrictive interpretation of these rights and warned against any attempt by the courts to "read into" constitutional provisions so as to extend them beyond the letter of the law. This controversial interpretation[102] has granted freedom of language choice for both parties involved in any case. It does not grant the accused any special rights beyond ensuring the availability of a judge or jury who can understand them in their official language of choice in a federal, Quebec, or New Brunswick court, and ensuring simultaneous interpretation when necessary. It thus appears that in the domain of judicial proceedings, freedom of expression in one's language of choice is accorded to all individuals and not only the accused, whether this expression is deemed to belong to the private (in the case of the evidence submitted to the Court) or the public (in the case of the counsel or the judge's expression) realm. No language is deemed worthy of supplementary protection in this field.

Conclusion

This jurisprudential analysis reveals that while freedom of expression is considered fundamental in Canada, the question of the language(s) chosen (or imposed) for one's expression is a complex issue that must take into account important elements of the Canadian language rights regime. The "precise scheme" of language rights set out in the 1867 and 1982 Constitutions has significantly framed language choice in a court of law, pitting linguistic minorities against linguistic majorities. Case law in which the Court framed freedom of expression as belonging to the private sphere saw mixed results. However, when anglophones – either in a majority or minority setting – claimed more language rights in the public sphere on the basis of freedom of expression, the courts always found in favour of the French community. Due to the constitutional parallelism approach, whereby linguistic groups are treated equally regardless of their official language,[103] the same fate should apply to francophones hoping to make language rights gains in the public sphere. Nevertheless, this case law does not exist and the fact remains that the jurisprudence has overwhelmingly maintained the concern for protecting the French language in freedom of expression cases in the public sphere over the last thirty years. In other words, the compromise between language rights and freedom of expression first struck by the SCC in 1988 has since been upheld, to francophones' benefit.

Moreover, what the SCC has identified as an unwritten constitutional principle in its 1998 *Secession Reference*[104] – namely, the principle of the protection of minorities (to the benefit of official-language minorities)[105] – has acted as a constraint on freedom of expression in the public realm when it benefited the French-language minority. This was the case in *Canadians for Language Fairness*, where the Court followed the example set out in *Lalonde*[106] and used the principle of minority protection to understand the purpose of Ontario's *French Language Services Act* as "to promote the use of French and English and to advance the equalization of status or use of English and French while offering services in French and thus protecting the rights of the minority francophone population in Ontario."[107]

However, the mobilization of this same principle by Anglo-Quebeckers in cases pertaining to commercial signage and municipal amalgamation in Montreal has proven unproductive. In *Entreprises W.F.H. Ltée*, the Court explained bluntly that the principle did not apply to Anglo-Quebeckers since "French-language Canadians are the majority in Québec, but largely the minority in Canada and in America [and therefore, protection of French in commercial signage] is a legitimate objective in the actual circumstances."[108] In *Baie d'Urfé*, the Court reminded the appellants of the limited power of unwritten principles, which "cannot neutralize the [provincial] legislator's unlimited power on municipal institutions nor serve as constitutional base for the creation of a third order of government for the protection of language rights."[109] This precedence of the "written constitution"[110] over unwritten principles is reiterated in *Westmount*, once again to protect Quebec's powers in the domain of municipalities.

In other words, protection of the French language, the more vulnerable of the country's two official languages, in the public realm has been interpreted by the courts as a justifiable infringement on freedom of expression and a reasonable goal set out by legislators. This is evident in cases involving Quebec municipalities, as well as cases pertaining to the *visage linguistique* of both Quebec and regions of other provinces where francophone communities comprise a sizable portion of the demographic. The use of the unwritten principle of the protection of minorities, successfully by Franco-Ontarians but unsuccessfully by Anglo-Quebeckers, also points to the courts' preference for the protection of the French language in the public sphere. It must be noted that freedom of expression jurisprudence is not the only context in which the courts have found against members of the majority challenging on the basis of *Charter* rights governmental policy meant to support a minority. In *R v Kapp*, the SCC notably declared that an affirmative action program for Indigenous peoples did not infringe the equality rights of non-Indigenous Canadians.[111]

As we have seen above, the issue of freedom of expression also intersects with provincial language regimes. As language is an ad hoc jurisdiction, freedom of expression in one's language of choice may be extended or limited based on the legislation adopted by each province. In Quebec specifically, the provincial government has added a layer of complexity to the original federal bargain struck in 1867 with the adoption of Bill 101, a bill specifically aimed at protecting the French language. Its provisions have repeatedly been on a collision course with freedom of expression in several domains of provincial jurisdiction – resulting in the striking of several compromises between freedom of expression and language protection that could not likely be achieved in other parts of the country, unless other provinces also significantly altered their own language regime. In other words, the Canadian federal system makes it possible for freedom of expression, when intersecting with language, to be interpreted differently across the country, an unexpected feature of the Canadian federal system. It confirms earlier findings according to which the SCC has attempted to reconcile the *Charter* with federalism, allowing for "policy variation among provincial governments,"[112] akin to what Jeremy Clarke has dubbed the "federalist dialogue" between the provinces and the courts.[113] However, the prevalence of the protection of the French language adds a layer of complexity to what Jeremy Clarke previously observed in his analysis of the SCC's *Charter* cases.[114]

Some questions remain from the above overview of the jurisprudence. For example, does freedom of expression protect expression *solely* in languages other than French or English – for example, in the case of a business advertising only in Chinese languages?[115] If such a case is brought before a court in the future, the issue of the intersection of freedom of expression with section 27 of the *Charter* pertaining to the protection of Canada's multicultural heritage, rather than language provisions, could then make the jurisprudence more intricate. Finally, with the adoption of Bill C-91, *An Act respecting Indigenous languages*[116] in February 2019, one could foresee that freedom of expression in Indigenous languages, both on- and off-reserve, would be a new domain for the courts to explore in the near future.

NOTES

1 Richard Moon, *The Constitutional Protection of Freedom of Expression* (Toronto: University of Toronto Press, 2000), 3.
2 José Woehrling, "La réglementation linguistique de l'affichage public et la liberté d'expression: *P.G. Québec c. Chaussure Brown's Inc.,*" *McGill Law Journal* 32, no. 4 (1987): 880–1.
3 *British North America Act*, 1867 (UK), 30–31 Vict., c 3.
4 *Canadian Charter of Rights and Freedoms*, Part 1 of the *Constitution Act, 1982*, Schedule B of the *Canada Act 1982* (UK), 1982, c 11.
5 *MacDonald v City of Montreal*, [1986] 1 SCR 460 at para 104. This "historical compromise" was first interpreted in such a way as to restrict the scope of language rights. This interpretation was later overturned (see *R. v Beaulac*, [1999] 1 SCR 768).
6 *MacDonald v City of Montreal* at para 104.
7 Woehrling, "Réglementation linguistique," 883–4.
8 *Ford v Quebec (Attorney General)*, [1988] 2 SCR 712.
9 *Devine v Quebec (Attorney General)*, [1988] 2 SCR 790.
10 *Charter of the French Language*, LRQ, c C-11, ss 57–61.
11 In *Ford*, sectionss 58 and 69 of the *CFL* were under scrutiny; in *Devine*, sections, 59, 60, and 61 were also called into question.
12 *Charter of Human Rights and Freedoms*, c C-12.
13 *Ford v Quebec* at paras 59–60. Many doctrinal sources underline the difficulty for the SCC to circumscribe the aspects of commercial expression that were constitutionally protected. See Yves de Montigny, "Les rapports difficiles entre la liberté d'expression et ses limites raisonnables," *Revue générale de droit* 22, no. 1 (1991): 129–50; Keith Dubick, "Commercial Expression: A 'Second-Class' Freedom?," *Saskatchewan Law Review* 60 (1996): 91–130.
14 *Ford v Quebec* at para 54.
15 Ibid., para 59. We also note that a few years later, in *RJR-MacDonald Inc. v Canada (AG)*, [1995] 3 SCR 199, the SCC also ruled that commercial speech was not of lesser value than other kinds of speech because of profit motivation.
16 Ibid., para 40. Emphasis added.
17 Ibid., para 60.
18 Ibid., para 73. Emphasis in original.
19 Ibid. This is the compromise the Government of Quebec would subsequently adopt in 1993. We will return to this later.
20 Dubick, "Commercial Expression," 100.
21 *Bill 178: An Act to Amend the Charter of the French Language*, ch. 54, SQ 1988.
22 United Nations Human Rights Committee, 47th session, *Ballantyne, Davidson, McIntyre v Canada*, Communications Nos. 359/1989 and 385/1989, UN Docs. CCPR/C/47/D/359/1989 and 385/1989/Rev.1 (1993), s 7.3, http://hrlibrary.umn.edu/undocs/html/v359385.htm.

23 Sophia Müller, *Talking Back: An Examination of Legislative Sequels Produced by the National Assembly of Quebec in Response to Judicial Invalidation of the* Charter of the French Language (PhD diss., University of Ottawa, 2017), 167.

24 *Bill 86: An Act to amend the Charter of the French language*, SQ 1993, c 40.

25 *Ford v Québec* at para 73.

26 *Entreprises W.F.H. Ltée c Québec (Procureure Générale du)*, 2001 CanLII 17598 (QC CA), para 4.

27 Ibid., para 73.

28 *Quebec (Attorney General) v 156158 Canada Inc. (Boulangerie Maxie's)*, 2015 QCCQ 354 (CanLII).

29 *Boulangerie Maxie's*, paras 289–94.

30 *French Language Services Act*, RSO 1990, c F.32, s 14.

31 *Galganov v Russell (Township)*, 2010 ONSC 4566 (CanLII) at para 9.

32 *Municipal Act*, 2001, SO 2001, c 25.

33 *Galganov v Russell (Township)* 2010 at para 169. Emphasis in original.

34 *Irwin Toy Ltd. v Quebec (Attorney General)*, [1989] 1 SCR 927.

35 *Galganov v Russell (Township)* 2010 at paras 172–88.

36 Ibid., para 201.

37 *Galganov v Russell (Township)*, 2012 ONCA 409 (CanLII) at para 49.

38 Ibid., para 67.

39 Ibid., para 85.

40 La Presse Canadienne, "Galganov et Brisson déboutés en Cour suprême," *Le Droit*, 6 December 2012, https://www.ledroit.com/archives/galganov -et-brisson-deboutes-en-cour-supreme-150dd5047f1828291e189a7869494 4ca.

41 Tristin Hopper, "Richmond, B.C., Considers Banning Chinese-Only Signs Amid Uproar over City's 'Un-Canadian' Advertisements," *National Post*, 19 October 2014, https://nationalpost.com/news/politics/richmond-b-c-considers-banning -chinese-only-signs-amid-uproar-over-citys-un-canadian-advertisements.

42 *Charter of the French Language*, s 4.

43 Ibid., ss 138–41.

44 *Chiasson c Québec (Procureur Général)*, [2000] RJQ 1836, EYB 2000–18911 at para 13.

45 Ibid., paras 1–7.

46 Ibid., para 60.

47 Ibid., para 63.

48 Ibid., para 55.

49 Ibid., para 56.

50 City of Ottawa, *By-Law No. 2001-170*, 9 May 2001; City of Ottawa, *Bilingualism Policy*, 9 May 2001.

51 *Canadians for Language Fairness v Ottawa (City)*, 146 CRR (2d) 268, 26 MPLR (4th) 163 at para 13.

52 Ibid., para 29.
53 Ibid.
54 *Canadian for Language Fairness*, para 19; *Irwin Toy Ltd. v Quebec (Attorney General)*, [1989] 1 SCR 927.
55 *Canadian for Language Fairness*, para 121.
56 Ibid., para 122.
57 Ibid., para 123.
58 Ibid.
59 Ibid.
60 *Bill 170: An Act to reform the municipal territorial organization of the metropolitan regions of Montréal, Québec and the Outaouais*, SQ 2000, c 56.
61 *Baie d'Urfé (Ville) c Québec (Procureur général)*, [2001] RJQ 1589, EYB 2001–24836 at para 16.
62 *An Act to reform the municipal territorial organization of the metropolitan regions of Montréal, Québec and the Outaouais*, Schedule I, s 11.
63 *Baie d'Urfé*, para 69.
64 *An Act to reform the municipal territorial organization of the metropolitan regions of Montréal, Québec and the Outaouais*, Schedule I, s 1.
65 *Baie d'Urfé*, para 70.
66 Ibid., para 70.
67 Ibid., paras 224–5.
68 *Canadian Charter of Rights and Freedoms*, Part 1 of the *Constitution Act, 1982*, Schedule B to the *Canada Act 1982* (UK), 1982, c 11, s 2(b); *Charter of Human Rights and Freedoms*, CQLR c C-12, s 3.
69 *Baie d'Urfé*, para 227.
70 Ibid.
71 Ibid., para 228.
72 Ibid., para 229.
73 Ibid., para 232.
74 *Westmount (Ville de) c Québec (Procureur Général du)*, [2001] RJQ 2520, AZ-50101773; *Beaconsfield (Ville) c Québec (Procureur général)*, 2001 CanLII 39759 (QC CA), EYB 2001–26336; *Beaconsfield (Ville de) c Québec (Procureur Général du)*, 2001 CanLII 11448 (QC CA); *Dollard-des-Ormeaux (Ville de) c Québec (Procureur Général du)*, 2001 CanLII 20374 (QC CA), EYB 2001–26332; *Hampstead (Ville de) c Québec (Procureur Général du)*, 2001 CanLII 16454 (QC CA), EYB 2001–26335; *Saint-Laurent (Ville de) c Québec (Procureur Général du)*, 2001 CanLII 15469 (QC CA), EYB 2001–26334; *Côte Saint-Luc (Cité de) c Québec (Procureur Général du)*, 2001 CanLII 14969 (QC CA), EYB 2001–26331; *Baie d'Urfé*.
75 *Westmount*, para 188.
76 Ibid., para 189.
77 Ibid.
78 Ibid., para 190.

79 *Baie d'Urfé*, paras 183–91; *Westmount*, paras 95–111.

80 *Baie d'Urfé*, para 186.

81 Ibid., para 187.

82 *Westmount*, para 106.

83 *Lalonde v Ontario (Commission de restructuration des services de santé)*, 2001 CanLII 21164 (ON CA).

84 *Criminal Code*, RSC 1985, c C-46.

85 *R. v Rodrigue*, 1994 CanLII 5249 (YK SC).

86 Ibid., 2.

87 *MacDonald v City of Montreal.*

88 *Bilodeau v A.G. (Man.)*, [1986] 1 SCR 449.

89 *Société des Acadiens v Association of Parents*, [1986] 1 SCR 549.

90 The 1986 trilogy was overturned in 1999 in *R. v Beaulac*, [1999] 1 SCR 768.

91 *R. v Rodrigue*, 9.

92 Ibid., 11–12.

93 A similar case was heard by the SCC in 2013. In *Conseil scolaire francophone de la Colombie-Britannique v British Columbia*, [2013] 2 SCR 774, 2013 SCC 42 (CanLII), the Court refused to grant the appellants the right to submit documentation in French to a court of British Columbia, as the right to a bilingual trial does not exist in this province. Freedom of expression, however, was not mobilized as an argument by either the appellants or the bench in its decision.

94 *Lavigne v Quebec (Attorney General)*, 2000 CanLII 30033 (QC CS).

95 Ibid., para 10.

96 Ibid., paras 13–14.

97 Ibid., para 15.

98 Ibid., paras 25–7.

99 *Morand c Québec (Procureur général)*, 2000 CanLII 2218 (QC CA).

100 Ibid., para 6.

101 Ibid.

102 Leslie Green and Denise Réaume. "Second Class Rights? Principle and Compromise in the Charter," *Dalhousie Law Journal* 13 (1990): 564–93.

103 Emmanuelle Richez, "Losing Relevance: Quebec and the Constitutional Politics of Language," *Osgoode Hall Law Journal* 52, no. 1 (2014): 218–20.

104 *Reference re Secession of Quebec*, [1998] 2 SCR 217.

105 Stéphanie Chouinard, "L'impact du Renvoi relatif à la sécession du Québec sur le droit linguistique canadien, ou de la force normative mitigée du principe constitutionnel de protection des minorités," in *Réimaginer le Canada. Vers un État multinational?*, ed. Félix Mathieu and Dave Guénette (Quebec: Presses de l'Université Laval, 2019), 313–40.

106 *Lalonde v Ontario (Health Services Restructuring Commission)*, 2001 CanLII 21164 (ON CA).

107 *Canadians for Language Fairness*, para 92.

108 *Entreprises W.F.H. Ltée c Québec (Procureure Générale du)*, para 116. Unless otherwise noted, all translations come from the authors.

109 *Baie d'Urfé (Ville) c Québec (Procureur général)*, para 187.

110 *Westmount (Ville de) c Québec (Procureur Général du)*, para. 104.

111 *R. v Kapp*, [2008] 2 SCR 483, 2008 SCC 41.

112 James Kelly, "Reconciling Rights and Freedoms during Review of the Charter of Rights and Freedoms: The Supreme Court of Canada and the Centralization Thesis, 1982–1999," *Canadian Journal of Political Science* 34, no. 2 (2001): 339.

113 Jeremy Clarke, "Beyond the Democratic Dialogue, and Towards a Federalist One: Provincial Arguments and Supreme Court Responses in Charter Litigation," *Canadian Journal of Political Science* 39, no. 2 (2006): 293–314; Jeremy Clarke, "In the Case of *Federalism v. Charter*: The Processes and Outcomes of a Federalist Dialogue," *International Journal of Canadian Studies* 36 (2007): 41–71.

114 See Clarke, "Beyond the Democratic Dialogue" and "In the Case of *Federalism v. Charter.*"

115 Hopper, "Richmond, B.C., Considers Banning Chinese-Only Signs."

116 Bill C-91: *An Act respecting Indigenous languages*, 1st Sess, 42nd Parl, 2019.

12 Teiakwanahstahsontéhrha' – We Extend the Rafters

DAVID NEWHOUSE*

Before all words are spoken, we send greetings to the universe and to all living things.
We give thanks for the rising of the sun and the light and life that it brings.
We give thanks for another day of life.

I start in this fashion, with words of thanksgiving. The Thanksgiving Address, which reminds us of the nature of the universe, its structure and functioning, the roles and responsibilities of all its aspects, creates an attitude of humility and gratitude. Traditional Haudenosaunee protocol also requires an acknowledgment of the other; a ceremony "at woods' edge," as it is called. It signals to those whose village we are about to enter that we have arrived, asks for permission to enter, and gives time to refresh ourselves from the journey. It allows time to collect our thoughts, to pay our respects, to thank the universe and our protectors for their watchfulness and allows our prospective hosts to ready themselves. The ceremony "at woods' edge" is an important aspect of Haudenosaunee diplomacy.

I grew up in the Six Nations of the Grand River community near Brantford, Ontario. Since 1784, we have lived on land that was provided to us in return for service by the British during the war that created the United States of America. The war had profound effects upon our communities, effects that we are still dealing with 235 years later. One of the effects of the war was to push us to the margins of the new societies that were emerging in North America at the time. Our marginalization continues. It's from this position on the margins that I speak. We remain outsiders to the structures and institutions of Canada.

In Haudenosaunee communities, families lived in large communal structures called longhouses. When the family grew too large or a new family emerged, the structure was enlarged through a process called "extending the rafters." The longhouse remained intact and the new family integrated into the lives of the families living within it. Can the rafters of the university be extended to include Indigenous peoples and their knowledges? Answering this question requires us to think of Indigenous peoples not just as people with culture or people with problems but as people with knowledge and knowledge-producing institutions, structures, and processes. Can the university accommodate these?

The university has played a large role in colonization, furnishing and transmitting the ideas that are used to advance this political project in Canada. It is good to see that there is now a desire to change, to see the university as a force for good, but we have to be careful that we don't continue the work of Indian residential schools. These schools were intended to replace Indigenous thought and knowledge with European thought and knowledge: to kill the Indian in the child.

In the six years since the release of the Truth and Reconciliation Commission's *Final Report* in 2015, Canadian universities have engaged in a process called "Indigenization." This process is intended to create a university environment that is amicable to us and that pays attention to our self-determined goals and objectives. It is intended to correct the mistakes of the past. Extending the rafters, so to speak, is a complex ethical process that requires considerable thought and discussion.

Starting in a traditional way by giving thanks helps us to reflect upon the task before us and to approach it with good minds. How might we extend our traditional practices to our scholarly endeavours? Can we create norms of scholarship that are appropriate to our understandings of the work of the university? Ought our scholarly endeavours be consistent with our cultural practices? Can we bring our knowledge to the university? Can we shape this eight-hundred-year-old institution so that it fits us as well?

I see the university as a speech community with structures of power and rules about what can be said, how things can be said, and where they can be said. Freedom of expression as expressed in the idea of academic freedom is not just about the individual capacity to speak freely with the protection of the system. Academic freedom is about the capacity of the system to welcome and create speech spaces for Indigenous speech and knowledge that has been excluded. Can the rafters indeed be extended?

Indigenous peoples have been part of the university experience in North America since the institution's establishment in the seventeenth century. We have been mascots, students, administrators, professors, and objects of research. There is, after a hundred years of research, much written about Indigenous peoples: some of it is even true and useful. It would be fair to say that Indigenous peoples did not go to universities to find themselves or to study themselves, to learn about their cultures, or how their societies functioned. Indigenous peoples were enticed to enter universities as preparation for high-level participation in the labour market or to meet the goals established for them by groups outside of Indigenous communities. The university served as another instrument of assimilation. I am hopeful that we can find ways so that this project is not completed. While I'm hopeful, I also recognize that doing so will require enormous effort on the part of all of us.

I've been teaching at Trent University for more than twenty-five years, in both the Indigenous Studies Department and the School of Business. About twenty years ago, a colleague and I were leading a fourth-year business administration seminar on organizational change. We decided that we would conduct the seminar as a talking circle. We explained the rationale for the circle, how it worked and began.

At the start of every class, each student was expected to speak about the readings for the day. At the end of the third week, we received a note from the program director explaining that he had received a complaint from some students in the course that they were being subjected, against their will, to Indigenous teaching. They argued that they had come to a business class not an Indigenous studies class. The reaction to the use of an Indigenous pedagogical approach was strong and rooted in prejudice. We did not, however, abandon the practice. Today, twenty-five years later, Indigenous pedagogies and research methodologies are an accepted part of the university landscape.

When I speak in my first-year Indigenous studies class of the church's role in colonization, some students report in their course evaluations that I am bashing the church. When I speak of England's, France's, and Spain's roles in colonization, the same students complain that I am bashing Europeans. When I present Indigenous views of politics or Canada, I am accused of white-bashing. Students are upset because I am not supporting the standard orthodoxies. The reactions have become muted over the last five years as students learn of the impact of Indian residential schools and the partnership between church and state that fuelled them.

A few years ago, I was invited to give a talk in a School of Business speakers series. I chose to speak about capitalism as an ethical system, as having a structured set of values that were used to determine the worth of a particular object or action. Those that were related to increasing economic worth were more highly regarded than those that did not. I asserted that Indigenous peoples also had ethical systems and a set of values and were using them to determine the worth of any particular action.

The two sets of values were different and as a result there was an emerging conflict. I also argued that capitalism was an extraordinarily resilient and adaptive system and that resisting it was difficult. I titled the talk "Aboriginal Encounters with Capitalism: Resistance Is Futile." The reaction to the talk was instructive: My non-Indigenous colleagues were incensed, saying that I had said that Indigenous society was going to disappear. How could I, as chair of Indigenous Studies, say such things? My Indigenous colleagues said: Hmm. This is something we should talk about and explore further. Starting an academic conversation about issues that are important to us is challenging, as my non-Indigenous colleagues want to determine what we can investigate and say.

We are in a time of reconciliation. When I think of reconciliation, I think of the Haudenosaunee ceremony of "polishing the silver covenant chain."[1] Polishing removes the grime and tarnish that coats the chain's silver and restores its shiny lustre. We do this work with enthusiasm, for we hope that things will be different, and also wariness, for we've been here before many times over the last half century. There is more than a century of accumulated grime and much polish to bring out. We will need bright polish and strong hands to make it shiny again.

My intent is to look forward, to talk about what I see as emerging. The Elders within our communities at Trent are urging us to look forward and not backward while also understanding the past so we can work to ensure that it is not replicated. All of us know the history, so I'm not going to repeat it here.

However, having said that, I want to start on 2 June 1537 with the *Sublimis Deus* issued by Pope Paul III. After considerable debate, he declared that the Indians of the New World were truly men, that they were rational beings with souls. What this means is that in the eyes of the Europeans, we were capable of thought and possessed the ability to reason. Europeans spent the next four centuries denying the quality of our thought and ignoring it. Our ideas about the nature of the world, proper ethical relationships between ourselves and the elements of the universe, truth, social relationships, governance, these were all ignored or treated as exotic curiosities. Our answers to the question "What does it mean to be human?" were ignored. The only people who were capable of answering this question were Europeans, and they desired that all would become rational like them. European thought was considered to be the pinnacle of human thought. The attempt to replace our thought with European thought is one of the aspects of the colonial enterprise that drove the Indian residential school policy. Our thought until recently has been systematically excluded from the institution that we call the university. The institution recruited our bodies but was not interested in our knowledge.

About fifteen years ago, my department nominated Professor Shirley Williams for the university's annual research award. Shirley, an Anishinaabe Elder appointed to the university on the basis of the depth of her Indigenous Knowledge, had produced the first Odawa-English lexicon for use in helping those interested in learning Nishnaabemowin. It took her about five years of hard work, interviewing Elders and speakers, thinking through the categories of words, and deciding upon a format for presentation, in addition to translating words accurately. The Awards Committee chair wrote to me to ask if the work was real research. The committee didn't know how to deal with it, believing that it was mere cataloguing or documenting words in a language.

I wrote back saying that a student at UBC had just received her doctorate for doing just what Shirley did. I also described the work that she did in putting together the lexicon as research conducted in the same fashion as other research in linguistics or anthropology. This did not convince the committee, and the file was considered to be ineligible as it wasn't considered research. Two decades later, the Social Sciences and Humanities Research Council has an official research category for Indigenous research, developed in collaboration with an Indigenous advisory panel.

In 2009, our university underwent a visioning exercise in which it asked for submissions about a new vision. We held focus groups, conducted surveys, and did all the usual things. Nothing that was emerging from the discussions resonated with me or spoke to the mission of the university as it pertains to our knowledge. At a meeting, I proposed the following statement: "Indigenous Knowledges are a valid means by which to understand the world." If you look online, you will see the statement displayed on the university president's website. They are twelve small words but a good rebuttal to the denial of the last few centuries. It's a small action, but I think that our future will be built upon thousands of small actions.

The predominant way in which we are seen by the academy is as people with culture. We add the cultural colour and flavour to the institution. We help the university to chalk up diversity and equity points. And as Indigenous peoples, we do our best to ensure that our culture is present in all sorts of ways. This cultural-representation project is important: we need to be seen. The real work of the academy, however, is about knowledge; its production and transmission from one generation to another.

We have to work to have the academy see us as people with knowledge in addition to people with culture. And we have to help the academy to realign its work so that it serves us in ways that are important to us. This realignment is what I want to speak to next.

As a scholar, I came to the academy without the usual academic credentials and background. In one sense it was freeing in that I had to learn the disciplinary rules and could ask questions that others weren't asking. I wasn't trapped by any disciplinary framework or tradition. I could invent as I went.

I decided after the large effort of the Royal Commission on Aboriginal Peoples (RCAP) never to write about the so-called Indian Problem. As many of you may know, the Indian Problem rests at the heart of Canadian public policy and drives much of the research enterprise surrounding Indigenous peoples. I thought that the RCAP, after spending $56 million, had explored the Indian Problem in sufficient depth to provide a solid direction and foundation for future public policy and set out the parameters of a way forward.

I wrote a paper for the RCAP entitled "From the Tribal to The Modern"; it was a reflective piece that argued that there was a new Aboriginal society emerging after the 1969–71 White Paper discussion. This event I've characterized as the official end of what I'm calling "the Long Assault";[2] a century and a half of formal state attempts at transformation and absorption. We live and work in the shadow of this long assault and its effects are still felt. It will take a few generations to fully recover from its horrible actions.

Instead of writing about the Indian Problem, I was going to write about two things: the development of our own society and something that I later have come to call "the Canada Problem."[3]

I conceptualized a modern Aboriginal society as being built out of ideas from both our traditions and those we encountered in non-Indigenous education institutions. We are a pragmatic people with a strong desire to foreground our own ideas using what we used to call cultural knowledge and which we now call Traditional Knowledge or Traditional Indigenous Knowledge. We wanted to use our own ideas to build better lives, better families, clans and houses, leaders, communities, nations.

The modern university is the institution that the West has developed as the site for the exploration of its own ideas, the building of its own knowledge about itself, its problems and solutions. The university is not part of our intellectual and institutional heritage. That doesn't mean, however, that as latecomers we cannot influence it or be part of it. Indeed, we are attempting that through the project of Indigenization.

Indigenization is the process whereby institutions begin to adjust to our presence, not just our bodies but our knowledge, our knowledge systems and structures, and our truth tests. Indigenization, in my mind, is about creating a site within the university for the exploration of our own ideas, first for ourselves and then for all of humanity. It is a site of enormous complexity and potential. It can also be a site of considerable tension and promise.

I want to try to give you a sense of this complexity, tension, and promise.

I have been confused by what we have come to call Indigenization. It seemed to mean different things in different places and was often presented as a linear process with different sequential phases. By contrast, I see Indigenization as not occurring in linear phases; rather, in a modern and complex institution like a university, one can be in all phases simultaneously depending upon one's location within it. ·

The first phase involves bringing our bodies into universities; our absence has been noted and is framed as a social or educational inequity. The goal is to increase the enrolments of Indigenous peoples in the academic programs of the university. New academic programs of interest to Indigenous peoples should be created as well.

The second phase involves bringing our cultural practices into the university. The institution creates new spaces where we may have feasts, powwows, Elders, and traditional peoples. The space may be decorated with local Indigenous motifs and materials and may be a showplace and meeting place. The spaces may be built using Indigenous notions of space articulated by Indigenous architects. Visible Indigenous spaces are thereby created.

The third phase involves bringing our knowledge and creating a place for it. This place has been confined to Indigenous studies programs or programs related to Indigenous peoples. This phase has an early or entry phase in which Indigenous Knowledge is introduced to students through the academic literature and limited engagement with Indigenous Knowledge holders. There is a second part to this phase whereby Indigenous Knowledge holders are engaged as academic instructors.

The fourth phase involves the spread of Indigenous Knowledge beyond its foundational area in Indigenous studies. Indigenous Knowledge and Indigenous Knowledge holders appear in other disciplines within the university: philosophy, business, education, environmental studies, literatures, politics, etc.

Adam Gaudry at the University of Alberta sees Indigenization as a spectrum ranging from activities focusing on equity to activities focusing on epistemology and pedagogy. He, and others, question whether one can Indigenize the modern university or whether separate Indigenous institutions should be established.

As you can see, Indigenization is a fairly complex phenomenon. While it has developed in response to the Truth and Reconciliation Commission's 2015 Calls to Action, it is also grounded in a growing movement within Indigenous societies to assert control over the structures and the processes of everyday life. Since 1972, we have seen the emergence of an Indigenous modernity that forms the context and foundation of modern Indigenous societies. This modernity is imbued with an ethos that is confident, aggressive, assertive, insistent, desirous of creating a new world out of Indigenous and Western ideas, and self-consciously and deliberately acting out of Indigenous thought. This desire and the Indigenous-led political, cultural, and social actions of the last four decades have shaped a modern Indigenous society.

Yet, in my view, this does not tell the whole story. The last three decades have also seen the creation of a new Indigenous person, one who lives in this new world with what I have come to call "postcolonial consciousness."

Modern Indigenous society is defined by postcolonial consciousness. It's a society that is aware that it has been colonized in many ways. It's a society that is aware of the implications of its colonization and that is choosing deliberately, consciously, and systematically to deal with that colonization. It's a society that is coming to terms with what has happened to it. It's a society that is determined to overcome its colonial legacy. It's a society that is starting to possess the ways and means to achieve its own goals.

Postcolonial consciousness will be the defining force of Indigenous society over the coming generations. Postcolonial Indians are angry and want to dismantle the master's house – or at least renovate it so that it suits their desires more easily. Postcolonial Indigenous peoples understand the nature of power and the way in which it flows to create realities. Postcolonial Indigenous peoples study Canada and are unwilling to accept the place they have been assigned within it. Postcolonial Indigenous peoples want more than a simple passing reference in history texts or to be the passive policy objects of government or corporations. They are actively influencing and shaping institutions to ensure that they meet their needs and desires. They are actively creating a new future.

Postcolonial consciousness creates tensions: it creates a desire to go back and start over again while remaining fully conscious that as a colonized people we can't go back and start over again. The world lost as a result of colonization cannot be regained. We can only go forward. Postcolonial consciousness is imbued with a strong sense of history and tradition and a desire to see these forces affect the present and the future.

Postcolonial consciousness also creates a tension with the current descendants of the colonizers. "Post," in some people's view, implies a departure, but the creation of North American postcolonial reality is different from African or Asian postcolonial realities. In our case, the colonizers are not leaving and will continue to be a huge political, social, cultural, and intellectual presence. The Supreme Court of Canada says we're all here to stay. We have to develop our own society in the shadow of the state whose actions have led to our colonization and almost destruction. We exist in a state of constant awareness that we live on the edge of absorption and that maintaining our identities requires constant vigilance and assertions of visibility.

What are the implications of this idea of postcolonial consciousness? It results, I believe, in a broader definition of governance. It means that postcolonial Indians will not be content merely with political self-government. Postcolonial Indigenous peoples see all aspects of Indigenous life as ground for Aboriginal influence. The restoration of Aboriginal governance then becomes a central theme of modern Aboriginal societies. Broadly speaking, Indigenous governance seeks stewardship and direction over the structures and processes of everyday life.

Behind this notion is a strongly held desire to use ideas, theories, notions, traditions, customs, and ceremony emanating from traditional thought either as the basis for or as key informing aspects of contemporary Indigenous institutions, organizations, structures, processes, and actions. This does not mean a rejection of ideas emanating from what we have come to call the West. What is desired is to see that Indigenous ideas are moved to a position of primary importance in those aspects of public policy that affect the core elements of Aboriginal life.

How do these ideas affect us in universities, particularly around the idea of academic freedom?

I see Indigenous scholarship rooted in Indigenous Knowledge as a fundamental part of this governance landscape. The ability and capacity to decide for oneself what is a problem, the parameters of the problem, the nature of enquiry into the problem, and the enquiry itself, including the definition of method, the data to be gathered, the analyses to be done, the interpretation of data, the construction of options and solutions, the dissemination of results, the translation of these results into action, and the eventual re-examination and reappraisal of the scholarship and its ideas – these are central to governing.

Indigenous scholarship comes to the table with its central notion of "complex understanding." Complex understanding occurs when we begin to see a phenomenon from various perspectives and to discern the relationships among these perspectives. Complex understanding doesn't seek to replace one view with another, but rather to find a way of ensuring that all views are given due consideration. It doesn't work in an either/or fashion. A phenomenon is not one thing or another but all things at one time. Complex understanding allows for our understanding to change depending upon where we stand to see or upon the time that we look or who is doing the looking. Complex understanding is grounded in a view of a constantly changing reality that is capable of transformation at any time.

Complex understanding is based on dialogue rather than dialectic. In this sense, it is deeply rooted in traditional Aboriginal notions of how one comes to understand. The notion can create a broader and deeper understanding of a phenomenon. It fosters a conversation among different disciplines, perspectives, knowledge systems, methods of enquiry. It fosters understanding without necessarily inviting competition. Challenge is present through the attempt to understand and explain the sometimes differing, sometimes similar views.

Indigenous scholarship doesn't just engage the intellect. It engages the mind, spirit, and body, and it considers all in its exploration.

Indigenous scholarship also brings with it a willingness to engage other disciplines and other ways of knowing. Indigenous scholarship does not reject the knowledge that has been gained by the West in its exploration of physical, social, or spiritual reality. Indigenous scholarship brings these ideas to the table and considers them alongside Aboriginal ideas, accepting or rejecting them on the basis of their usefulness.

Indigenous scholarship also brings with it a sense of mind and intellect grounded in Indigenous experience, thought-world, and view of reality. All these factors are important to creating legitimacy in the eyes of Indigenous peoples. It gives a sense of concreteness to Indigenous thought. It restores a sense of intellectual Indigeneity, bringing to visibility a part of the four elements of human beings usually seen when discussing Indigenous peoples.

Indigenous scholarship also brings with it a sense of agency, an ability to shape the world through one's thought, action, and feelings.

The promise of Indigenous scholarship is that ideas from Indigenous thought can build healthy individuals and communities. Abraham Maslow thought so, and I hope that we do as well.

As many of you may be aware, one of the central ideas in psychology is the idea of need. This idea has affected much of our work in areas such as social work, organizational behaviour, and psychological counselling, to name a few. Few of you may be aware of the origins of Abraham Maslow's work on the hierarchy of needs, which figures so prominently in this area.

Abraham Maslow was a graduate student at Columbia University in the 1930s with an interest in cross-cultural psychological issues. In 1938, Maslow agreed to spend some time among the Blackfoot in Alberta. His ideas about the emotional life of Blackfoot members were turned upside down. He found that Blackfoot members, despite their economic poverty, were more emotionally secure than most members of American society. He found, to his amazement, "that about eighty to ninety percent of the population must be rated as high in ego-security as the most secure individuals in our own society, who comprise perhaps five to ten percent at most."[4]

As a result, he began to investigate why this might be so since it appeared so much at odds with what he was expecting and the common understanding of Indigenous society at the time. His explorations led him to explore the notion of well-being among the Blackfoot, which in turn led him directly to their ideas about the whole human being and balance among different aspects. He translated his understanding into what we commonly call Maslow's Hierarchy of Needs (but which we ought to call Maslow's Hierarchy of Blackfoot Needs). His whole approach to psychology was changed as a result of his experience with the Blackfoot. He oriented it to the study of human well-being rather than human illness and dysfunction, and focused it on the following questions: What is a healthy human being? And, how can we assist human beings in being healthy? The Blackfoot roots of Maslow's ideas were finally recognized at the end of the twentieth century.

The academy is a powerful institution, but it is not immutable. Its rafters have been extended many times over the centuries. Bringing Indigenous Knowledge into it will not destroy it, nor will it shake its foundations. The primacy of reason is important, even to those who hold to the idea of the good mind. Bringing Indigenous Knowledge into it is a project that involves dialogue, discussion, and debate. It requires the creation of an atmosphere that supports a broad definition of enquiry, that accepts the interrelatedness of reason and passion, that accepts the notion of multiple truths rather than a single truth, and that above all accepts that Indigenous people have something to offer beyond opportunities for research into social problems.

We do not have a tradition of separating the spiritual from the secular. For traditional people, the spiritual and secular are intertwined to form a seamless reality. Bringing Indigenous Knowledge into the modern secular university means bringing our spirituality. For many, the spiritual aspects of Indigenous Knowledge are problematic. They are seen as inappropriate for inclusion within an Enlightenment institution and are often seen as incompatible the work of the academy. For us, the spiritual facilitates our work. It forces us to think of relationships and connections, of impact and effect, and it awakens our consciousness to new truths.

The spiritual also reminds us of the ethics of our work, to approach it, as the Anishinaabe say, in a good way, and as the Haudenosaunee say, with a good mind. The spiritual also reminds us of our responsibilities as academics: to tell the truth, to be conscious of our method, to be aware of our emotions and their effects. The spiritual envelopes us in an ethic of responsibility and respect and relationship. It does not allow us to live outside the world but requires that we live fully within it.

It is possible to do all of these things without a spiritual foundation, as our Enlightenment colleagues will tell us. This is indeed true. Yet for us, it would not be consistent with the idea of the good mind and would be asking us to forget who we are. It would not be in keeping with the dialogue postulated by the Guswentah. It would be asking us to continue the old assimilationist activities of the university.

Using Haudenosaunee social theory, I conceptualize the Indigenization project as one of "extending the rafters." The addition of a new family to our longhouses required the addition of extra rooms. The rafters were extended to add these new rooms. The addition to the house improves life for all.

We are now part of the academy. Indigenous Knowledge is part of the academy. The challenge to us as academics, as scholars, is to ensure that this knowledge does not remain only in the one room we have created.

Indigenous Knowledge is starting to move beyond its original academic home in Indigenous studies. Disciplines such as environmental studies, sustainability studies, women's studies, anthropology, geography, social work, and health studies now incorporate Indigenous Knowledge into their teaching and research.

The national granting councils – the Social Science Humanities Research Council (SSHRC) and the Canadian Institutes of Health Research (CIHR) – acknowledge that Indigenous Knowledge is real and important. Both SSHRC and CIHR have been grappling with how to accommodate this extension of their rafters. I find it remarkable that within a short time Indigenous Knowledge has become an integral part of the university research environment. It bodes well, I think, for our future as it shows that we have begun to be able to refute the legacy of the last four hundred years and give full expression to the sentiment of the 1537 papal bull.

We are now fully engaged in extending the rafters. I can point to the growing number of Indigenous strategic plans that are emerging across academia. They are evidence of this engagement. We've done some of the easy things: developed academic programs, recruited students, improved supports for Indigenous students, and built new academic spaces reflective of Indigenous notions of space and place. The hard part – bringing our knowledge into the university in significant and substantive ways – is also underway.

Extending the rafters also brings a discussion about ethics. As I stated before, I see the university is a speech community with an ever-evolving set of rules regulating what can be said and who can speak with what authority. As an Indigenous scholar, I belong to at least two distinct speech communities: the university speech community, which tells me that I have academic freedom; the Indigenous speech community, which tells me that I have academic responsibilities.

My academic responsibilities involve making a contribution to the decolonization, resurgence, revitalization, and development of Indigenous communities. It is telling that there is no word for freedom within Indigenous languages. Yet as a tenured academic, I have an enormous amount of freedom and am expected to exercise it within the frame of ethical responsibility that comes with my traditional Indigenous background.

I've been guided over the years by a conversation that I had with Eber Hampton, the former president of the First Nations University of Canada (FNUNIV). The FNUNIV board was resisting the move to tenure and the idea of academic freedom. Eber created an Elders Advisory Committee and asked its members for advice. After a few days of discussion, the Elders advised that Indigenous academic staff at the FNUNIV had a responsibility to speak the truth and to make clear the grounds for their truth claims, and that the board had to respect this responsibility even when they didn't like the truths that were being spoken.

So, I see academic freedom through this Cree lens: it's the responsibility to speak the truth. Speaking the truth also means making the grounds that I use for my truth claim visible so that it can be evaluated by others. The exercise of my responsibility also means that I have to make room for other truth claims. I don't have to agree with others' truths, but I have to respect them. However, engaging in a dialogue may result in the emergence of additional truths as we bring our minds together.

I recall a talk by a young Indigenous scholar who was studying community dynamics. Educated in sociology and anthropology, she characterized what she saw as factionalism. I asked how, based upon her own intellectual traditions as a Haudenosaunee person, she would describe what she saw.

She responded that she saw the search for one mind (which is the Haudenosaunee way of describing the process of deliberation and debate). We chatted for a bit and, after a while, one of my colleagues said that it doesn't matter what it's called, it's still factionalism.

Sociology, I remarked at the time, was a little more than a hundred years old. The search for one mind was about a thousand years old. Over the past three decades, we have come to understand that both can exist simultaneously.

Perhaps the way forward is through the concept of Etuaptmumk, or "two-eyed seeking."

The concept creates an ethical speech community that provides space for both Indigenous Knowledge and other forms of knowledge in respectful conversation.

It affirms that both sets of knowledge have something to contribute to the understanding of the human condition and ought to be included in our teaching, research, and service as academics. It has proven to be foundational in creating a new research community.

Perhaps our conversations about inclusion of new voices and academic freedom might also be informed by the ethics of two-eyed seeing.

I am reminded of Hiawatha and the Peacemaker's work to convince Atatarho of the message of peace. They came to him and told him the message. He was unable to hear, saying, "No, not yet." They continued their work, bringing others to the message. Each time they came back they were greeted with the response "No. Not yet." Finally, they stood, in huge numbers, before Atatarho. He saw and was convinced. Hiawatha combed the snakes from his hair and his mind became the good mind. His body was straightened and he accepted the message. Our numbers are gathering.

At the end of a meeting, a speaker would also perform a small ritual similar to the opening: And now that the words have been spoken and our business is concluded, we cover the fire and return to our homes and families. May you find them in good health and joyful at your return. May they greet you with happiness and affection. May you journey well.

NOTES

* This paper is based on a talk given at the Harry Crowe Foundation Conference: Free Speech on Campus, held on 22 February 2019. Indigenous argument is often presented in narrative form. This contribution reflects that tradition.

1 Treaties and agreements between the Haudenosaunee and their new European neighbours were depicted using the metaphor of a silver chain. Silver required polish from time to time. Polishing the silver covenant chain came to be seen as the metaphor for the review and renewal of treaties and agreements.

2 For my first-year classes, I discuss Indigenous history since the arrival of Europeans through two conceptual lenses: the Long Assault and the Great Healing. The Long Assault is the period in which new European settler states, specifically Canada and the United States, actively attempted to dispossess Indigenous peoples of their lands,

territories, cultures, languages, and spirituality, and the Great Healing is the period starting from the withdrawal of the White Paper in 1971 in which Indigenous peoples begin to actively and in large numbers speak back to the state and advance their own ideas about the relationship with it and how to heal from the effects of the Long Assault.

3   The Canada Problem is the idea behind Indigenous politics of the last century. It has two aspects: how to live with this new entity called Canada and how to live well within it as Indigenous peoples.

4   Edward Hoffman, *The Right to Be Human: A Biography of Abraham Maslow* (New York: Jeremy P. Tarcher, 1988), 123.

13 Faculty Free Speech in Canada: Trends, Risks, and Possible Futures

JEFFREY ADAM SACHS

Campus free speech is always and everywhere in crisis, and never before has it been more always in crisis than now, nor more everywhere in crisis than here.

With some exaggeration, this may serve as a fitting summary of the public debate surrounding academic freedom and campus free speech. In Canada (though certainly not only in Canada), members of the media are warning darkly that "the radicals have taken over."[1] Powerful student mobs, afire with a zeal for "social justice," are intimidating into silence anyone who stands in their way. "Political correctness has become the new orthodoxy," announces one commentator.[2] "Welcome to the new Cultural Revolution," declares another.[3] And dissident professors, we are told, are often the first casualties. "Students are at least free to speak their minds once they leave the universities," notes columnist Barbara Kay. "But pity the rare faculty member at odds with the leftist echo chamber he is condemned to inhabit for decades. Faculty and administration can be very tough on their own."[4]

While hyperbolic, these claims deserve to be taken seriously. Freedom of expression (which is distinct from, but closely related to, academic freedom) is an important part of the university mission. Without the ability to freely share their opinions, engage in classroom instruction, and participate in disciplinary and public debates, faculty members cannot perform their twin responsibilities of acquiring and disseminating knowledge. Therefore, it is vital that we determine whether faculty in Canada are no longer able to freely express themselves or are less free now than they were in the past. Unfortunately, the issue remains poorly understood. The available literature on academic freedom in Canada describes many important developments and trends germane to faculty free speech, including the rise of contingent labour,[5] the dependence of faculty on government and corporate support,[6] threats to institutional autonomy,[7] and issues of shared governance.[8] However, much of what we know on the topic remains impressionistic and anecdote-driven.

This chapter attempts to introduce some rigour to the question of faculty free speech. Specifically, it investigates the causes and nature of formal faculty punishment in Canada for protected speech, focusing on terminations and lesser disciplinary action (e.g., suspensions). This focus has its limitations. Many types of faculty punishment are informal, such as departmental mobbing or chastisement. These types of punishment are rarely disclosed to the public and are difficult to identify, and as a result are not discussed below. It is also possible that faculty engage in self-censorship for reasons besides avoiding punishment, such as career advancement or social acceptance. However, it is precisely because formal terminations and disciplinary action are public that they warrant extra attention. When a professor is fired for criticizing university leadership, this sends a powerful message to other faculty that more private forms of punishment simply cannot match. Therefore it poses a special threat to faculty free speech and academic freedom.

This chapter is divided into two principle sections. In the first, I survey recent episodes (from 2010 to 2020) of faculty being punished for their speech. Generally, the speech at issue in these episodes falls into one of two categories: university-related speech and speech offensive to a particular social group. I argue that punishment for either types of speech is rare in Canada, though it may be more common in some contexts than in others. In the second section, I consider three possible explanations for the relative scarcity of faculty punishment, focusing on the *supply* of controversial speech, the *demand* for faculty punishment, and the administrative *response* to those demands. Though necessarily speculative, the chapter concludes by arguing that certain features of post-secondary education in Canada – in particular, the grounding of academic free speech in collective agreements and the relative absence of political polarization around higher education – have helped to protect faculty free speech.

Punishing Faculty for Their Speech: Recent Episodes and Contexts

Canadian faculty are very rarely punished for protected speech. An extensive search of press reports, databases, and other sources found only fifteen clear cases between 2010 and 2020 in which a faculty member was fired or forced by their college or university to resign from a position due at least in part to protected speech.[9] A further thirteen were professionally disciplined, typically in the form of a paid or unpaid suspension. In several cases, these disciplinary acts were followed by the resignation of the faculty member involved, though these were uncommon. In at least three cases, fired faculty were eventually permitted to return to work at the same university, and many lesser punishments were later reversed.

These are rough numbers, and they almost certainly undercount the phenomenon. Minor forms of punishment are less likely to be reported in the media or other databases, and news of more serious ones may be blocked by employee confidentiality rules. Still, these numbers give us a basic sense of the frequency with which punishment to faculty is meted out and, crucially, the forms and contexts in which they occur.

University-Related Speech

The most common form of protected faculty speech to result in punishment is speech critical of university leadership, co-workers, or corporate or government partners. As several scholars have argued, Canadian higher education has grown increasingly corporatized in recent years,[10] a development characterized both by the increased dependence of universities on commercial partnerships and by the internal adoption by universities of "corporate values, policies and modes of governance."[11] As Howard Woodhouse argues, the result of this development has been a two-fold assault on academic freedom in Canada. First, the institutional autonomy of universities has been steadily ceded to business and government. And second, individual faculty members face increasing constraints on what they can research, publish, and say.[12]

The role of corporate and governmental partnerships is visible in several faculty terminations. For instance, in 2011, the University of Calgary removed Joe Arvai as head of its Enbridge Centre after he expressed opposition to Enbridge's proposed Northern Gateway Pipeline. An investigation by the Canadian Association of University Teachers (CAUT) later revealed that the university had grown alarmed by the prospect of Enbridge withdrawing its financial support in response. Similar motivations were responsible for the termination of Ramesh Thakur by the University of Waterloo and Wilfrid Laurier University in 2011. In both of these cases, the faculty members were terminated due to criticism of these universities' corporate partnerships.

These cases also reflect the special challenges experienced by faculty who serve as directors of research institutes or centres. By holding an administrative position and an academic one simultaneously, there can be considerable confusion about whether and to what extent their activities are protected under academic freedom.[13] This confusion is compounded when they are expected to act as the "public face" of their unit and to maintain good relations with various stakeholders. Such was evidently the case with Andrew Potter, who was appointed director of McGill University's Institute for the Study of Canada in 2016. In March of the following year, Potter authored a newspaper column about what he called the "essential malaise" of Quebec society. In the ensuing backlash, McGill administrators informed Potter that his actions had damaged the university's relations with the province and its political leaders so badly that his only option was to resign or be fired. Indeed, when criticized by Gerald Butts, then a senior advisor to Prime Minister Justin Trudeau, McGill's president explained that she did not "believe that academic freedom protects us in our roles as administrator where we cannot be viewed as expressing our own opinion but rather the opinion of our organization and/or institution."[14]

The University of Toronto made a similar argument during the so-called Azarova Affair. In September 2020, Dean Edward Iacobucci abruptly withdrew an initial offer of employment to Dr. Valentina Azarova, who was then in talks to accept the directorship of the Faculty of Law's International Human Rights Program. This decision caused enormous controversy, as it came immediately after a wealthy alumnus had expressed his concerns to the dean over Azarova's scholarship on the Israeli-Palestinian conflict. In its defence, the university took great pains to emphasize that the position for which Azarova was being considered was "non-academic" and therefore not protected by academic freedom.[15]

In other cases, however, the speech at issue was directed inward, typically in the form of criticism towards a university program or its personnel. In 2014, Robert Buckingham was removed as head of the University of Saskatchewan's School of Public Health and fired from his faculty position after he criticized a proposed university restructuring. Rod Cumberland, an instructor at the Maritime College of Forest Technology, was fired in 2019 for criticizing the forest industry's use of the herbicide glyphosate. When Gerald Redmond, a fellow instructor at the college and its former executive director, was quoted in the media as saying that Cumberland's termination was likely due to the college's close ties to the industry, he was immediately fired as well. And university criticism seems to have been at least partially responsible for the firing of Rick Mehta by Acadia University in 2018. In its letter notifying Mehta of his termination, the university accused him of "damaging the reputation of the institution by attacking the University and colleagues on social media." It went on to say that he had given the public the impression that Acadia was "an intolerant environment" where "vulnerable students may be attacked."[16]

Criticism of the university or its leadership is also a major cause of faculty suspensions and course removals. Many of these cases involve the accusation by university administrators that a faculty member failed to maintain workplace "collegiality," thereby undermining the "effective functioning" of their departments (see, for example, the suspensions of Chris Bart, Devashish Pujari, Sourav Ray, George Steiner, and Wayne Taylor by McMaster University in 2013). Yet we find evidence here again that administrators often view these episodes more in terms of public relations than internal collegiality. Thus, administrators only chose to suspend Morteza Shirkhanzadeh (Queen's University in 2014) and Derek Pyne (Thompson Rivers University in 2018) after the professors made their criticism of their colleagues public.

Offensive Speech

While speech critical of the university or that might damage its corporate or governmental partnerships is responsible for the bulk of faculty punishment, a smaller number involve speech deemed offensive to social groups. Andrew Potter's perceived anti-Quebec speech is one such example, but most cases feature disparagement of women or specific religions, ethnicities, or sexualities. For instance, Ryerson University fired Ayman Alkasrawy from his position as a teaching assistant in 2017 after comments came to light that were perceived as antisemitic. Accusations of antisemitic speech were also levelled against University of Lethbridge professor Anthony Hall in 2016, resulting in a one-year suspension without pay. Meanwhile, David Mullan of Cape Breton University and Jean Laberge of CEGEP du Vieux Montreal were both disciplined (though not terminated) by their institutions for alleged homophobic speech. And in 2020, Professor Kathleen Lowrey was removed from an administrative position at the University of Alberta over comments that critics deemed transphobic.

Based on these and similar cases, we can reach three tentative conclusions. First, there appears to be an increase in the number and severity of faculty punishments for offensive speech in recent years, though a lack of comprehensive data makes it impossible to know for certain. Second, criticism of faculty that resulted in formal punishment was more likely to come from the political Left than Right. In other words, offensive speech typically associated with conservativism (e.g., opposition to homosexuality or feminism) was more likely to be responsible for faculty punishment than offensive speech associated with liberalism, though here again we are limited by incomplete data. And third, pressure from students and the larger public was much more likely to play a role in these cases than in those involving speech critical of the university or its corporate partnerships.

However, all of these conclusions should be qualified by an important caveat. In many cases where faculty members engage in controversial speech, they are also engaging in controversial behaviour. Indeed, the two often seem to go hand in hand, making it difficult to determine to what extent their speech contributed to the administrative punishment, or indeed whether their speech was a pretext for punishing them on other grounds. The example of Rick Mehta is again instructive. While initial accounts of his termination focused on his "politically incorrect" speech, it was later revealed that he had publicly outed one of his students as a rape survivor. Absent this outrageous behaviour, would Mehta have still been fired on account of his speech? It is impossible to say, but it does illustrate the way that speech and conduct can both be contributing factors.

Evaluating and Explaining the Status of Faculty Free Speech in Canada

To be fired or professionally disciplined for protected speech is an extremely uncommon event in the Canadian academy. To be fired or disciplined for offensive or so-called politically incorrect speech is even less common, despite the often alarmist language many commentators have used to describe the state of academic free speech. To understand why, it is helpful to consider three potential explanations. First, Canadian faculty may be unwilling to express controversial opinions or uninterested in doing so. Second, potential audiences for controversial faculty speech, such as students, administrators, or the general public, may be disinclined to seek a faculty member's punishment. And third, faculty may possess strong free speech rights that prevent their termination or punishment. We can formulate these as, respectively, supply-based, demand-based, and rights-based explanations.

Canadian Faculty and the Supply of Controversial Speech

The idea that Canadian faculty are unlikely to engage in controversial speech is not an unreasonable one. Michiel Horn, in his history of academic freedom in Canada, notes the importance of the German concept of *Lehrfreiheit* – the freedom to teach and publish – during the Canadian academy's formative years.[17] Unlike in the more activist British or American traditions of academic freedom, German professors were regarded as civil servants, with all the attendant expectations about circumspection and institutional loyalty such a status carries. Outside of the performance of their professional duties, they operated under "an implicit obligation to maintain political neutrality," an obligation that Horn suggests was present early on in Canada as well.[18]

This German influence in Canadian higher education began to wane in the 1930s, but according to many scholars, faculty apoliticism continued to linger. Writing in the mid-1960s, John Porter contends in *The Vertical Mosaic* (1965) that most professors maintain a facade of studious political neutrality.[19] Over a decade later, Janet Scarfe and Edward Sheffield would argue that while professors had grown more political in recent years, their engagement was typically limited to advising government and participating in the civil service.[20] Similarly, Michael Horn and Douglas Owram both claim that due to their financial dependence on government and industry largesse, Canadian academics are typically hesitant to engage in controversial or "politically incorrect" speech.[21]

More recently, some have claimed that many faculty engage in political self-censorship, especially those who are conservative. Virtually by definition, self-censorship is extremely difficult to identify, and no empirical research has been conducted to date in Canada. However, a small number of studies among American faculty suggest that it does happen, albeit with uncertain scope and consequence. For example, Yoel Inbar and Joris Lammers show that many conservative social psychologists report experiencing a hostile professional climate on account of their political beliefs.[22] A survey of philosophers found similar results, as well as a stated reluctance by conservative philosophers to defend arguments with "right-leaning conclusions."[23] In their study of conservative faculty, Jon Shields and Joshua Dunn liken the experience of being a conservative in the academy to being "in the closet." Many of their interview subjects describe being forced to conceal their political opinions from their colleagues in order to achieve professional success.[24] All of this suggests that faculty self-censorship does occur, especially among members of the political Right.

These same dynamics may exist in Canada as well. Though recent data is unavailable, a survey from 2000 found that Canadian faculty come overwhelmingly from the political Left.[25] Given recent trends in the United States and Europe, it is likely that the academy's political imbalance has become even greater in the intervening decades.[26] If this is the case, conservative and centrist faculty may self-censor for fear of drawing attention to themselves or angering their peers. Liberal faculty, meanwhile, may self-censor for a different reason. While the majority on campus, their views may make them ideological minorities off campus. Depending on the audience, they may choose to avoid discussing certain issues or expressing controversial opinions, especially if they are contingent faculty who lack tenure.

Yet there is reason to believe that the prevalence of both apoliticism and self-censorship is exaggerated. First, whereas Porter could confidently assert in the 1960s that Canadian faculty were apolitical, the intervening decades have undermined this claim considerably. During the 1970s and '80s, faculty were deeply active in anti-war movements and the Quebec sovereignty debate. Since then, they have been prominent in social justice issues as well.[27] Recent decades have also seen rapid unionization, first in Quebec and then elsewhere in the country. By the mid-2000s, more than 80 per cent of Canadian faculty were unionized. This process, along with the attendant labour actions and contract negotiations, have injected faculty into the centre of academic governance and generated new opportunities for conflict with administrators. And while there are few signs of labour militancy in Canada, Jonah Butovsky, Larry Savage, and Michelle Webber speculate that the combination of financial austerity and threats to university autonomy may be triggering increased political activism.[28] Second, historical accounts suggest that the prevalence of academic self-censorship has fluctuated wildly depending on the political and institutional context.[29] Faculty composition, including the liberal-to-conservative ratio, also differs dramatically depending on the academic discipline, university, and department. And in Canada, where tenure and collective agreements offer broad protections for controversial speech, faculty should be expected to have less reason to self-censor.

As a result, it seems unlikely that faculty are disinclined to engage in controversial or offensive speech. However, there is still much we do not know about these dynamics and further research is sorely needed.

Canadian Faculty and the Demand for Faculty Punishment

By contrast, there is good reason to conclude that students and the broader public in Canada are generally uninterested in demanding that faculty be fired or disciplined for their speech, especially compared to the United States.

First, student activism in Canada is focused primarily on issues of university governance and affordability. This is due to the public nature of higher education funding, which invites student scrutiny and mobilization in a way it does not in contexts where tuition is the responsibility of students themselves.[30] Moreover, while many students in Canada care deeply about "social justice" issues, significant differences exist when compared with American students. Canadian undergraduates are only half as likely as their American counterparts to say that society is racist. They are also significantly less likely to believe that racism is a serious problem on their campuses or that students should be required to take courses on the experiences of minorities or women.[31] All of this suggests that Canadian students may be less willing or able to target faculty members for speech perceived as offensive towards certain groups.

Attitudes towards higher education are also much more positive than they are in the United States, where a growing number of Americans, especially Republicans and conservatives, view the professoriate with deep suspicion. According to a recent Pew survey, only half of all Americans and just 33 per cent of Republicans believe that colleges and universities have a positive impact on the country. Republicans were also much less likely than Democrats (48 per cent vs. 84 per cent) to have confidence that professors will act in the public's best interest.[32] By contrast, 78 per cent of Canadians say universities have a positive impact on the direction of the country.[33] While a partisan breakdown is unavailable, other polls show lower levels of partisan polarization on many campus free speech issues. A 2018 Environics/CAUT survey found that Liberal, Conservative, and NDP supporters all share broadly similar attitudes towards the acceptability of various kinds of speech (e.g., anti-abortion, anti-Israel, racist) on university and college campuses.[34] And while important gaps do exist (for example, 75 per cent of Liberal supporters rate free speech on campus as secure, while only 51 per cent of Conservatives and 61 per cent of New Democrats say the same), they are generally much smaller than those in the United States.

One reason may be the comparative weakness of Canadian right-wing media. We have seen in the United States the importance of conservative media and higher education watchdog organizations (e.g., Campus Reform, Turning Point USA, the College Fix) in identifying and publicizing controversial academic speech. Many public campaigns to fire an offending professor have their origin in these organizations, which excel in generating outrage among their audience.[35] Canada has few organizations that play a comparable role. For example, Turning Point USA, which maintains the controversial "Professor Watchlist" of supposedly liberal faculty, has struggled to establish a presence in Canada and has been virtually dormant since its introduction in 2017.[36] Other watchdog groups like the Society for Academic Freedom and Scholarship and the Campus Freedom Index (a publication of the Justice Centre for Constitutional Freedoms) operate largely outside the public eye.

In the absence of strong political polarization over views of the academy and campus free speech, it may be the case that students and other members of the public are less willing or able to target a professor for punishment. However, this may currently be changing. Recently unveiled policies on campus free speech in Ontario and Alberta mark a new, more nakedly partisan phase in the debate.[37] Similar policies were proposed by the federal Conservative Party in 2017.[38] A growing number of faculty have found themselves targeted on social media.[39] And established right-wing outlets like Rebel Media, plus new entrants like the *Post Millennial*, may have a larger impact in the future.

Canadian Faculty and Employment Rights

Finally, one major reason for the scarcity of faculty punishment for speech is the robust employment protections most of them enjoy.

The free speech rights of Canadian faculty are derived principally from the academic freedom sections of collective agreements between faculty unions and administrators. While varying in their particulars, these agreements typically guarantee faculty the right to criticize their institution, to teach and conduct research free from official censorship, and to comment publicly on matters germane to their academic expertise. In the event that the university or college fails to uphold these provisions, the faculty association can engage in internal mediation with administrators or, if necessary, pursue legal action.

This approach has its advantages. By locating academic freedom within administrative law, Canadian faculty generally enjoy greater free speech protections than non-unionized faculty elsewhere, particularly in the United States, where First Amendment rights are limited to those working in public institutions. Many of the faculty punishments described in this chapter were overturned or reduced due to arbitration between administrators and their faculty unions. However, by relying so heavily on arbitral decisions, whose interpretations of academic freedom are often narrowly drawn or contradictory (or, in the words of one administrative law scholar, "soft and shifting – bog-like"), faculty are often left unsure of the limits of permissible speech. The resulting uncertainty can have a chilling effect that more explicit guidelines would avoid.[40]

For that reason, litigants in numerous court cases have sought to ground academic freedom and faculty free speech in section 2(b) of the *Charter of Rights and Freedoms*. At issue is whether colleges and universities are government actors. In *Lavigne v Ontario Public Service Employees Union* (1991), the Supreme Court determined that colleges are "an emanation of government," and are therefore subject to the *Charter*.[41] Universities, however, enjoy a much more ambiguous status. In *McKinney v University of Guelph* (1990), the Court found that while universities are established by an act of government and serve a clear public function, they are autonomous institutions. This insulates them from governmental interference, but it also means that administrators are not obligated to respect section 2(b) freedoms.

Yet, more recently, lower courts have begun reaching the opposite conclusion. For example, in *Pridgen v University of Calgary* (2010), the Alberta Court of Queen's Bench ruled that the University of Calgary had violated two students' section 2(b) rights when it disciplined them over controversial Facebook comments.[42] In *R. v Whatcott* (2014), the Saskatchewan Court of Appeal reached a similar verdict after a group of activists was arrested for distributing pro-life literature on the University of Regina campus without permission.[43] These decisions suggest that there may be a growing willingness by the courts to extend *Charter* rights onto campus. However, much depends on the provincial legislation establishing the university and the extent to which it demonstrates that it is controlled by the government or serving a government function.[44] Moreover, all of these recent cases focus on the free speech of students or members of the public engaging in expressive acts while on university property.[45] Faculty free speech rights, as well as academic freedom more generally, have yet to be addressed by the courts.[46]

A notable exception is a comment made by LaForest J. in *McKinney v University of Guelph*, for which he wrote the majority decision. "Academic freedom and excellence," he affirms, are "necessary to our continuance as a lively democracy."[47] He further states, "the preservation of academic freedom is also an objective of pressing and substantial importance."[48] But LaForest goes on to explain that he understands academic freedom purely in terms of an *institutional* right of the university to determine its own affairs free from government censorship, not as an *individual* right possessed by faculty. "Any attempt by government to influence university decisions," he writes, "especially decisions regarding appointment, tenure and dismissal of academic staff, would be strenuously resisted by the universities on the basis that this could lead to breaches of academic freedom."[49] Thus, while the Supreme Court does affirm in *McKinney* the importance of academic freedom, it does not do so in a way that bolsters faculty free speech. Rather, it actually serves to further insulate the university's personnel decisions from *Charter* review.[50]

Lastly, we should note that CAUT offers a robust definition of faculty free speech, one considerably more expansive than the one offered by the American Association of University Professors (AAUP). The AAUP limits a faculty member's free speech to areas germane to his or her academic expertise. In addition, the AAUP warns faculty that "their special position in the community imposes special obligations," and therefore that when engaging in extramural speech, they should "at all times be accurate," "exercise appropriate restraint," and "show respect for the opinions of others."[51] CAUT, by comparison, makes no such mention of academic expertise. Moreover, it explicitly affirms that academic staff "must not be hindered or impeded in exercising their civil rights as individuals, including the right to contribute to social change through free expression of opinion on matters of public interest." It also insists that they "must not suffer any institutional penalties because of the exercise of such rights."[52] Together, this represents an emphatic affirmation of faculty free speech, one potentially better suited to an age of social media and outrage mobs.

The problem is enforcement. CAUT (like the AAUP) may censure universities for violating faculty free speech, but nothing more severe. As a result, it typically relies on members of the public and other academics to pressure the offending university or college. Alternatively, it may launch an investigation or attempt to work with the university on the faculty member's behalf. These interventions have been successful in the past, resulting, for instance, in new policies at Queen's University on faculty whistle-blowers.[53] However, many of CAUT's recommendations have been ignored, showing that there are limits to its powers of persuasion.

Some (Very Tentative) Conclusions

Contrary to the dire warnings heard in the media, faculty free speech in Canada has not disappeared. Terminating a professor for protected speech, whether via forced resignation or outright firing, remains an extremely rare event, as does lesser punishment. Moreover, when such incidents do occur, they are more likely to be due to criticism of university leadership or its governmental or corporate partners than because of some "politically incorrect" statement about race, gender, or a particular social group. This suggests that the corporatization of higher education, a process underway in Canada since the 1990s, presents a greater threat to faculty free speech than public outrage over controversial remarks. However, terminations and lesser disciplinary action for offensive and politically incorrect speech do occur and warrant close attention. The cause is unclear, but speech offensive to the Left seems to be a more common cause of punishment than speech offensive to the Right.

As for *why* faculty punishment is such a rare event – and how much longer it will *remain* rare – there is still much we do not know. Based on the available evidence, it seems unlikely that Canadian faculty are unusually apolitical or apt to self-censor, though there is a need for more research. More probable is that they are rarely targeted for punishment because of the relative absence of partisan polarization around higher education and the professoriate. Students also may be less mobilized around "social justice" issues. Finally, Canadian faculty tend to enjoy strong free speech and employment protections. So long as these features remain intact, the free speech of faculty should remain on relatively firm footing.

However, there are several concrete steps that administrators and faculty associations should consider taking to further entrench academic free speech. First, in the past, administrators have exploited the concept of "collegiality" to censor or punish faculty for their speech. Faculty should be aware of this problem and carefully define collegiality in their collective agreements. Second, they should also seek to explicitly affirm in their collective agreements the right of faculty members to express themselves outside of the academy (i.e., in their personal capacity) without fear of punishment. The language supplied by CAUT can serve as a model in this regard. And lastly, both administrators and faculty should develop strategies for dealing with public pressure campaigns, whether originating on campus or off. These are likely to be a permanent feature of the higher education landscape, so it will be important to have a firm policy already in place.[54]

NOTES

1 Margaret Wente, "The Radicals Have Taken Over: Academic Extremism Comes to Canada," *Globe and Mail*, 3 December 2016.
2 Tom Flanagan, "We Can't Ignore the Warning Signs on U.S. Campuses," *Globe and Mail*, 21 December 2015.
3 Margaret Wente, "The Cultural Revolution (Read: The Triumph of Hysteria) Comes to Campus," *Globe and Mail*, 13 November 2015.
4 Barbara Kay, "Universities Are Bastions of Censorship," *National Post*, 28 March 2014.
5 Karen Foster and Louise Birdsell Bauer, *Out of the Shadows: Experiences of Contract Academic Staff* (Ottawa: Canadian Association of University Teachers, 2018), https://www.caut.ca/sites/default/files/cas_report.pdf.
6 Claire Polster, "The Nature and Implications of the Growing Importance of Research Grants to Canadian Universities and Academics," *Higher Education* 53, no. 5 (2007): 599–622.
7 Len Findlay, "Institutional Autonomy and Academic Freedom in the Managed University," in *Academic Freedom in Conflict: The Struggle over Free Speech Rights in the University*, ed. James L. Turk (Toronto: James Lorimer and Company, 2014), 49–61.
8 Peter MacKinnon, *University Commons Divided: Exploring Debate and Dissent on Campus* (Toronto: University of Toronto Press, 2018), 7–20.
9 Sources included press reports, the Canadian Association of University Teachers (CAUT), the CanLII database, the Society for Academic Freedom and Scholarship, and the Justice Centre for Constitutional Freedoms. To merit inclusion, a case must involve a faculty member, dean, or program director of a public Canadian university or college who was professionally disciplined, suspended, denied an expected promotion, fired, or forced to resign for protected speech. Protected speech is defined here as legal speech (e.g., non-defamatory) that does not violate a university or college's policy on harassment, discrimination, academic integrity,

insubordination, or respectful work environment. Accounting for these last two categories of speech was especially challenging, as their definitions vary greatly across institutions and can be easily abused by would-be censors. Wherever possible, I have been guided by arbitration decisions, CAUT investigations, and the language of collective agreements. More broadly, I have defined protected speech as speech that falls under the umbrella of academic freedom, as defined by CAUT.

10 James Turk, ed., *The Corporate Campus: Commercialization and the Dangers to Canada's Colleges and Universities* (Toronto: James Lorimer and Company, 2000); Adrienne S. Chan and Donald Fischer, eds., *The Exchange University: Corporatization of Academic Culture* (Vancouver: UBC Press, 2008).

11 Jamie Brownlee, *Academia, Inc.: How Corporatization Is Transforming Canadian Universities* (Halifax: Fernwood, 2015), 4.

12 Howard Woodhouse, *Selling Out: Academic Freedom and the Corporate Market* (Montreal: McGill-Queen's University Press, 2009).

13 Arbitrators have struggled to determine the boundaries of academic freedom in such cases, with much depending on the language of the collective agreement and the administrator's job description. In *Board of Governors of Ryerson University v Ryerson Faculty Association* (2012), which involved a tenured faculty member who was disciplined for speech and conduct that occurred while serving as associate dean, the arbitrator noted that "the traditional perception of the 'shop floor' with its rigid separation of management and labour" (para 40) becomes blurred in the university setting. As a result, he determined that the faculty member never fully exited the academic bargaining unit and the protections it provides.

14 Dylan C. Robertson, "Inside McGill University's Andrew Potter Meltdown," *Canadaland*, 4 May 2017, https://www.canadaland.com/inside-mcgill-university-andrew-potter-meltdown/.

15 Canadian Association of University Teachers, *CAUT Report on Academic Freedom at the Faculty of Law, University of Toronto,* October 2020, https://www.caut.ca/sites/default/files/caut-report-on-academic-freedom-at-the-faculty-of-law-university-of-toronto_2020-10_0.pdf.

16 Mairin Prentiss, "Controversial Prof Fired for Privacy Breach, Harassment, Acadia Letter Reveals," *CBC News*, 12 September 2018, https://www.cbc.ca/news/canada/nova-scotia/rick-mehta-acadia-university-1.4819220.

17 Michiel Horn, *Academic Freedom in Canada: A History* (Toronto: University of Toronto Press, 1998).

18 Ibid., 8.

19 John Porter, *The Vertical Mosaic: An Analysis of Social Class and Power in Canada* (Toronto: University of Toronto Press, 1965).

20 Janet Scarfe and Edward Sheffield, "Notes on the Canadian Professoriate," *Higher Education* 6, no. 3 (1977): 354–5.

21 Michiel Horn, "Running for Office: Canadian Professors, Electoral Politics and Institutional Reactions, 1887–1968," in *Historical Identities: The Professoriate in*

Canada, ed. P. Stortz and L. Panayaotidis (Toronto: University of Toronto Press, 2006); Douglas Owram, *The Government Generation: Canadian Intellectuals and the State, 1900–1945* (Toronto: University of Toronto Press, 1986).

22 Yoel Inbar and Joris Lammers, "Political Diversity in Social and Personality Psychology," *Perspectives on Psychological Science* 7, no. 5 (2012): 496–503.

23 Uwe Peters, Nathan Honeycutt, Andreas De Block, and Lee Jussim, "Ideological Diversity, Hostility, and Discrimination in Philosophy," *Philosophical Psychology* 33, no. 4 (2020): 511–48.

24 Jon A. Shields and Joshua M. Dunn Sr., *Passing on the Right: Conservative Professors in the Progressive University* (Oxford: Oxford University Press, 2016), 83–107.

25 M.R. Nakhaie and Barry D. Adam, "Political Affiliation of Canadian University Professors," *Canadian Journal of Sociology* 33, no. 4 (2008): 873–98.

26 On political ideology among US academics, see Neil Gross and Solon Simmons, eds., *Professors and Their Politics* (Baltimore: Johns Hopkins Press, 2014). For Europeans, see Herman G. van de Werfhorst, "Are Universities Left-Wing Bastions? The Political Orientation of Professors, Professionals, and Managers in Europe," *British Journal of Sociology*, no. 71 (2020): 47–73.

27 Sandra Smeltzer and Sara Cantillon, "Guest Editors' Introduction: Scholar-Activist Terrain in Canada and Ireland," *Studies in Social Justice* 9, no. 1 (2015): 7–17.

28 Jonah Butovsky, Larry Savage, and Michelle Webber, "Assessing Faculty Attitudes toward Faculty Unions: A Survey of Four Primarily Undergraduate Universities," *Working USA: A Journal of Labor and Society*, no. 18 (2015): 247–65.

29 Michiel Horn, "The Mildew of Discretion: Academic Freedom and Self-Censorship," *Dalhousie Review* 72, no. 4 (1993): 439–66.

30 Olivier Bégin-Caouette and Glen A. Jones, "Student Organizations in Canada and Quebec's 'Maple Spring,'" *Studies in Higher Education* 39, no. 3 (2014): 413–14.

31 Ivan Katchanovski, Neil Nevitte, and Stanley Rothman, "Race, Gender, and Affirmative Action Attitudes in American and Canadian Universities," *Canadian Journal of Higher Education* 45, no. 4 (2015): 18–41.

32 Kim Parker, "The Growing Partisan Divide in Views of Higher Education," Pew Research Center, 30 January 2019, https://www.pewresearch.org/social-trends /2019/08/19/the-growing-partisan-divide-in-views-of-higher-education-2/.

33 "Post-secondary Education, the Future of Canada, and Federal Policy," Abacus Data, accessed 21 June 2021, https://www.dropbox.com/sh/tjnu5f77d4zx75p /AADJema4nTtmS8KWbi2eCWzxa?dl=0.

34 Environics, "Canadian Attitudes Toward Free Speech," 2018 (unpublished report commissioned by CAUT; in possession of the author).

35 See Colleen Flaherty, "Being Watched," *Inside Higher Ed*, 22 November 2016, https://www.insidehighered.com/news/2016/11/22/new-website-seeks-register -professors-accused-liberal-bias-and-anti-american-values; Peter Schmidt, "Professors' Growing Risk: Harassment for Things They Never Really Said," *Chronicle of Higher Education*, 22 June 2017, https://www.chronicle.com/article

/professors-growing-risk-harassment-for-things-they-never-really-said/; Anthony Fucci and Theresa Catalano, "Missing the (Turning) Point: The Erosion of Democracy at an American University," *Journal of Language and Politics* 18, no. 3 (2019): 346–70; Robby Soave, *Panic Attack: Young Radicals in the Age of Trump* (New York: All Points Books, 2019), 239–44.

36 Raffy Boudjikanian, "Canadian Offshoot of U.S. Libertarian Campus Group Says It Provides Needed Counterpoint to Liberal Bias," *CBC News*, 22 May 2018, https://www.cbc.ca/news/politics/turning-point-canada-scheer-1.4658239.

37 Paolo Loriggio, "Ontario Post-Secondary Schools Expected to Now Have Free-Speech Policies in Place," *Canadian Press*, 7 January 2019, https://globalnews.ca/news/4823953/ontario-post-secondary-schools-free-speech-policies/; "UCP Prepares to Roll out Ford-Flavoured Post-secondary Changes in Alberta," *Edmonton Journal*, 6 May 2019.

38 Marie-Danielle Smith, "Take Away Federal Funding if Universities Don't Protect Free Speech on Campus, Andrew Scheer Says," *National Post*, 19 April 2017.

39 Christina Frangou, "The Growing Problem of Online Harassment in Academe," *University Affairs*, 23 October 2019, https://www.universityaffairs.ca/features/feature-article/the-growing-problem-of-online-harassment-in-academe/; Wanda Cassidy, Chantal Faucher, and Margaret Jackson, "Adversity in University: Cyber-bullying and Its Impacts on Students, Faculty and Administrators," *International Journal of Environmental Research and Public Health* 14, no. 8 (2017): 888–906.

40 Charles T. Gillin, "The Bog-Like Ground on Which We Tread: Arbitrating Academic Freedom in Canada," *Canadian Review of Sociology* 39, no. 3 (2002): 319.

41 *Lavigne v Ontario Public Service Employees Union*, [1991] 2 SCR 211. See also *Douglas/Kwantlen Faculty Association v Douglas College*, [1990] 3 SCR 570.

42 *Pridgen v University of Calgary*, 2012 ABCA 139.

43 *R. v Whatcott*, 2012 ABQB 231.

44 See *Lobo v Carleton University*, 2012 ONSC 254; and *BC Civil Liberties Association v University of Victoria*, 2016 BCCA 162.

45 On this trend, see Dwight Newman, "Application of the *Charter* to Universities' Limitation of Expression," *Revue de droit de l'Universite de Sherbrooke/Sherbrooke Law Review*, no. 45 (2015): 133–55.

46 For an overview of recent jurisprudence on universities and the *Charter*, see Franco Silletta, "Revisiting *Charter* Application to Universities," *Appeal*, no. 20 (2015): 79–98.

47 *McKinney v University of Guelph*, [1990] 3 SCR 234.

48 Ibid., 281.

49 Ibid., 233.

50 In a separate, concurring opinion in the *McKinney* case, L'Heureux-Dubé J. writes that "while universities may perform certain public functions that could attract *Charter* review, I am able to accept that the hiring and firing of their employees are not properly included within this category."

51 "1940 Statement of Principles on Academic Freedom and Tenure," American Association of University Teachers, accessed 21 June 2021, https://www.aaup.org/report/1940-statement-principles-academic-freedom-and-tenure.

52 "Academic Freedom: CAUT Policy Statement," Canadian Association of University Teachers, accessed 21 June 2021, https://www.caut.ca/about-us/caut-policy/lists/caut-policy-statements/policy-statement-on-academic-freedom.

53 Jenna Zucker, "Queen's Dispute Highlights Issues of Academic Freedom, Harassment," *Globe and Mail*, 13 November 2015.

54 For a good example of this, see the Resource Library in PEN America's *Campus Free Speech Guide*, available at https://campusfreespeechguide.pen.org/.

14 On Silence: Student Refrainment from Speech

SHANNON DEA*

In the thrust and parry of free speech debates, it can sometimes seem as though all speech is desirable and all refrainment from speech is cause for concern. Of course, no serious scholar or jurist working in the field really holds this exaggerated view. Political philosopher John Horton puts it well:

> The right to freedom of expression is not an obligation or requirement always and in all circumstances to give overt expression to what one thinks or feels. A person also has the right to remain silent, unless there is a specific reason in a particular case for why this would be wrong. We might, for example, quite properly feel ashamed of what we feel or think, and therefore prefer to keep it to ourselves.[1]

Nonetheless, in recent years, a number of surveys and media reports have raised the alarm that post-secondary students are engaging in self-censorship, with the implication that the putative self-censorship is both a bad thing and reflective of a dangerous trend on university campuses.

In this chapter I provide resources for assessing the charge that post-secondary students are self-censoring. The argument is advanced in three broad steps. First, I argue that both a duality at the heart of the concept of self-censorship and the term's negative lay connotation should incline us to limit the charge of self-censorship to a specific subset of its typical extension. I argue that in general we ought to use the neutral term "refrainment from speech," reserving the more normatively charged "self-censorship" for cases of bad refrainment. In the second step of the argument, I seek to narrow down what counts as bad refrainment by mapping broad categories of possible reasons for and consequences of refrainment from speech. I argue that in general refrainment from speech is only bad if it is for bad (or what I will later term *vicious*) reasons or has pernicious consequences. When considering pernicious consequences, I argue that we should be concerned in particular about systems that perpetuate the coercive silencing of marginalized voices. I draw on Kristie Dotson's work to describe two means by which marginalized voices are systemically silenced: testimonial quieting and testimonial smothering. After considering these types of silencing, I circle back to the post-secondary context to assess whether there is cause for concern if, as some reports suggests, US college students are refraining from speech within the educational context.

I here focus on US students because the surveys in question do. I am not aware of surveys tracking university student refrainment from speech in Canada. That said, US news stories and policies often produce downstream consequences in Canada, and therefore warrant attention by Canadians. At bottom, the worry about student refrainment from speech is a salvo in the culture wars – and in particular in a popular narrative that we are in the grip of a campus free speech crisis. While that narrative has its origins in the United States, it has been a common theme in Canada since 2016; so, it is worth getting clear on how to assess it. This chapter is one part of that project.

Self-Censorship versus Refrainment

"Self-censorship" tends to be used broadly to mean any occasion on which, without direct coercion by a third party, a person who has something to say nonetheless remains silent. I argue that this is a mistake for both popular and scholarly reasons.

First, in lay and media usage, the connotation of "self-censorship" is always bad. "Censorship" has a negative valence. That is, we generally agree that censorship is a regrettable thing and that those who practise it are blameworthy for doing so. The prominence of the word "censorship" in the phrase "self-censorship" means that the same shadow darkens self-censorship. Even though there are important differences between typical third-party censorship and self-censorship, the terminology negatively disposes us towards the latter phenomenon because of the associations it suggests with the former. To characterize all refrainment from speech as self-censorship begs the question by assuming from the outset that all such refrainment is bad. By recasting what is often termed "self-censorship" as "refrainment from speech," we put ourselves in position to see that refrainment from speech takes many forms, some of which are cause for concern and some of which are not. People refrain from speech for a variety of reasons and with a range of different consequences. As we shall see in the next section, both reasons for and consequences of refrainment from speech are relevant to our assessment of that refrainment.

My reasons for preferring "refrainment from speech" to "self-censorship" extend beyond these terms' popular connotations. In the small but useful literature providing conceptual analysis of so-called self-censorship, theorists have identified a duality at the heart of self-censorship that makes it importantly distinct from garden-variety censorship.[2] However, the popular conversation has not taken up that insight, I think largely because of its complexity. Increasingly, "self-censorship" as the public uses it and "self-censorship" as scholars use it assume the status of homophones – two words that are pronounced the same, but which bear very distinct meanings. Thus, any gains that are made on the scholarly side in providing a more nuanced, less negatively charged characterization of self-censorship creates the risk of the public and the scholarly specialists talking past each other without realizing that they are doing so.

John Horton follows Gerald MacCallum[3] in regarding censorship as in general[4] triadic in form. On this account, censorship occurs when some agent x prevents speaker y from uttering z. Horton adds that not only the content of an utterance, but its manner, time, or place of expression may be thus suppressed (that is, censored).[5] However, Horton denies that all cases in which x prevents y from uttering z count as censorship. For instance, it is not censorship when the chair of a meeting stops participants in the meeting from all talking at once, or when a judge stops a witness from uttering hearsay during a trial.

A puzzle at the heart of the notion of self-censorship resides in the fact that in cases of self-censorship the same person seems to occupy two opposing roles: x (preventing the utterance) and y (being the utterer so prevented). Censorship is usually understood as a kind of coercion, but it is not clear what it means to coerce oneself.[6] To think through this implied internal tension, Horton compares self-censorship with self-deception, self-control, and self-restraint – all phenomena that involve a similarly divided self – but ultimately finds self-censorship quite different from these other concepts. On most accounts, we do not consciously or intentionally self-deceive. Rather, self-deception happens as it were behind our own backs. By contrast, self-censorship is typically understood as something we do consciously and intentionally (if not always willingly). Horton offers a quite different reason for differentiating self-censorship from self-control and self-restraint. Even though self-censorship is arguably a form of self-control or self-restraint, it is distinct from those broader categories because they are often regarded as virtuous and praiseworthy, whereas the usual attitude to self-censorship is "uncertainty or ambivalence," as if self-censorship were "generally under some sort of moral cloud."[7]

For Horton, self-censorship involves a bifurcation between two commitments on the part of the speaker. This produces a further bifurcation within self-censorship as a concept because of the inherent tension between the *self* part of the concept and the *censorship* part. The "self" prefix seems to assign agency to the speaker, and thereby to weaken worries about coercion. However, the coercion implied by the word "censorship" seems to implicate a third party, making the speaker an instrument rather than the author of censorship. If the self is the author of the censorship, then it seems not to be censorship at all. And if the self is merely the instrument of censorship, then "self-censorship is little more than a particular form of ordinary censorship, because responsibility remains with those whose will is dominant."[8] Horton continues, "in the most interesting and distinctive instances of self-censorship, we understand ourselves neither to be merely exercising self-control nor to be simply subject to ordinary censorship."[9] While Horton thus spells out the two sides of self-censorship, he rejects the suggestion that there are two kinds of self-censorship. Instead, he regards self-censorship as operating on a continuum, with some cases "closer to simple self-restraint while others are closer to straightforward censorship."[10]

Philip Cook and Conrad Heilmann agree with Horton that the concept of self-censorship is characterized by a duality between self and other, autonomy and heteronomy. However, unlike Horton, they resolve the duality by arguing that there are two kinds of self-censorship – public and private. In public self-censorship, "individuals internalise some aspects of the public censor and then censor themselves."[11] By contrast, *"private self-censorship* is the suppression by an agent of his or her own attitudes where a public censor is either absent or irrelevant. Private self-censorship is a process of regulation between what an individual regards as permissible to express publicly, and that which he or she wishes to express publicly."[12] Cook and Heilmann argue that principle of free speech does not apply directly to private self-censorship since the absence of an external censor makes it non-coercive.

Whether we adopt Horton's continuum model or Cook and Heilmann's binary model, the self-censorship scholarship makes clear that refrainment from speech is not typically coercive in the way that ordinary third-party censorship is, nor does it necessarily constitute a freedom of expression violation. By contrast, the implicature of most recent popular discussions of self-censorship is that self-censorship is both indirectly coercive and a freedom of expression violation. By adopting the more neutral term "refrainment from speech," we avoid equivocating between two very different usages, and free ourselves from the bias that attaches to the popular usage.

This is not to say that the term "self-censorship" should have no lay usage. Popular (that is, non-scholarly) discussions of self-censorship tend to assume that self-censorship is a regrettable phenomenon for which someone deserves blame. It is thus apt to use the term "self-censorship" for bad refrainment from speech, just so long as the more neutral term is used for the broader category. But what makes some kinds of refrainment bad? In the next section, I argue that some reasons for refrainment and some consequences of refrainment make some refrainment bad.

Refrainment from Speech: Reasons and Consequences

Both freedom of expression and (self-)censorship are typically considered under the remit of law and political theory; by contrast, Horton emphasizes the moral aspects of self-censorship, and finds moral intuitions a useful guide to the character of self-censorship. He observes that acts of self-censorship, depending on the circumstances, may be instances of moral virtue or of moral weakness. Further, our tendency to direct praise or blame at either the refraining would-be speaker or a third party can clarify whether we regard the speaker as author or instrument of the self-censorship.

While I here depart from Horton by considering refrainment from speech in general and not self-censorship per se, I follow him in shifting the focus from politics to ethics. A political approach to expression can be too totalizing in its emphasis on broad rights and freedoms. By contrast, the moral domain permits assessment of each case on its own merit. Such an approach is thus not only normatively useful, but descriptively revealing. I am here primarily interested in the descriptive side of the project; so, I will not plump for a particular normative approach. Instead, I agnostically borrow notions from two distinct normative systems – deontology and consequentialism – in order to highlight how varied the types of refrainment from speech are, and in particular to make clear that many forms of refrainment are not in the least (to repeat Horton's phrase) "under some sort of moral cloud." Deontologists regard the rules guiding an agent's actions as the proper locus of moral praise and blame. By contrast, consequentialists regard the good or bad results of one's actions as the morally relevant feature. I propose that the varieties of refrainment from speech can be usefully mapped by considering both the reasons for the refrainment and the consequences.

People's reasons to refrain from speech may be governed by vice, virtue, or neither.[13] Let's call a reason that is neither vicious (that is, pertaining to vice) nor virtuous "neutral." When I was a small child, someone in my class left the classroom hamster cage open and the hamster escaped. When the teacher asked who had left the cage open, the culprit remained silent for fear of punishment, and so the entire class was punished. The guilty child's silence is an example of vicious refrainment. They refrained from speech in order to avoid blame and punishment.[14] By contrast, when your mother told you, "If you can't say something nice about a person, don't say anything at all," she was counselling virtuous refrainment. Frequently, in conversation, an interlocutor's remark prompts us to think of a possible reply, but the conversation moves on in a different direction before we can interject, and we never make the reply. Our silence in that situation is neither virtuous nor vicious, but neutral.

So much for the reasons for refrainment from speech. What about the consequences of such refrainment? Irrespective of whether one refrains from speech for virtuous, vicious, or neutral reasons, that refrainment can have beneficial, pernicious, or benign effects in the world. Consider a situation in which someone refrains from speech because their point has already been made and they want to make sure that there is time for other speakers to provide different perspectives. The audience profits from this speaker's generous refrainment. This is beneficial refrainment. By contrast, if someone with a novel and germane perspective is prevented from participating in a conversation, the audience is worse off as a result. Their refrainment is therefore pernicious. If one's refrainment from speech makes no one either better or worse off, then that refrainment is benign.

The intersection of two triadic categories produces nine different types of refrainment: virtuous refrainment may produce beneficial, pernicious, or benign consequences, as may vicious and neutral refrainment.

		Reasons for refraining		
		Virtuous	Neutral	Vicious
Consequences of refraining	Beneficial	GOOD	GOOD	BAD
	Benign	GOOD	NEITHER GOOD NOR BAD	BAD
	Pernicious	?	?	BAD

When we map it in this way, it quickly becomes apparent that refrainment is not inherently bad. In particular, virtuous refrainment that produces beneficial or benign results seems to be good. Vicious refrainment, whatever its consequences, is bad.[15] Neutral refrainment with benign results would seem to be neither good nor bad. It is not clear in the abstract how to assess refrainment that mixes virtuous reasons with harmful results or neutral reasons with beneficial or pernicious results. Such cases may simply require individual assessment. For now, it is enough to notice that from a moral perspective, refrainment is complex and particular. It is simplistic to treat all refrainment as if it were a bad thing.

Sometimes, the harm that is done when someone refrains from speech concerns not merely the content of the speech that the audience was unable to hear, but the cause of the refrainment. Coerced refrainment from speech is often (although not always[16]) harmful in itself, irrespective of the content of the speech that did not occur. Further, pernicious coerced refrainment is even more pernicious if it is part of a pattern of coercion, and more pernicious still if that pattern reinforces unjust and oppressive systems of power. It is to that matter that we now turn.

Can the Subaltern Speak?

In 1988, Gayatri Chakravorty Spivak provocatively asked, "Can the subaltern speak?"[17] While Spivak was particularly interested in colonial populations outside the system of imperial power, feminist philosophers have extended the question to consider the range of ways that marginalized people in general (not only the colonial *subaltern*) are silenced in virtue of their marginalization. In an influential 2011 paper within this tradition, Kristie Dotson offers a characterization of two types of silencing – testimonial quieting and testimonial smothering.[18]

In testimonial quieting, a marginalized speaker performs a speech act, but their utterance receives no uptake because their audience does not recognize them as a knower. By way of example, Dotson cites Patricia Hill Collins's argument that common stereotypes about Black women in the United States compromise people's ability to take US Black women seriously as knowers. Another example of the same phenomenon that has recently begun to receive scholarly and media attention is the differential pain-management techniques medical clinicians have long used for Black and white patients because clinicians are led by bad science about how Black people experience pain to downplay Black patients' own testimony about their pain levels.[19]

Testimonial smothering, on the other hand, is Dotson's name for the phenomenon of marginalized speakers refraining from speech because they perceive their audience as unwilling or unable to receive their testimony in good faith. Dotson lists three conditions that are present in cases of testimonial smothering:

1. the content of the speech is risky;
2. the audience demonstrates incompetence to take up the testimony; and
3. that incompetence arises out of pernicious ignorance.

She offers a range of examples of Black women refraining from speech on various topics related to race. For instance, she describes Black women who refrain from discussing domestic violence in Black communities because of the risk that white listeners will hear that testimony in ways that are biased by false but pervasive stereotypes about Black masculinity. The audience will thus wrongly regard the discussion of domestic violence as lending confirmation to those stereotypes. To be unable to discuss domestic violence leaves Black women vulnerable – not because Black women are disproportionately subject to domestic violence but because all women are. Their refrainment from speech on the topic due to testimonial smothering is thus pernicious.

One striking fact about Dotson's account of testimonial quieting and testimonial smothering is that both phenomena emerge from the relationship between the speaker and audience. Dotson follows Jennifer Hornsby in understanding speech acts not as isolated acts performed by speakers alone but as acts that occur within a relationship of dependence between speaker and audience. For Hornsby, the success of speech acts requires what she terms *reciprocity* between the speaker and the audience. A speech act is successful, that is, when the audience not only understands the speaker's words but also takes those words as the speaker meant them to be taken.

To understand what it means to take words as the speaker means them to be taken, consider the following example. You are walking with a colleague to a meeting. The colleague is struggling to carry a pile of books, a laptop, a coffee, and a box of pastries for the meeting. You are carrying just a water bottle. The colleague, looking for help, sarcastically asks, "Can I take that for you?" If you accede and hand the colleague your water bottle, it is a sign that you have understood the semantic content of their question, but not their intended pragmatic effect. By failing to "catch" your colleague's sarcasm, you have failed to understand their words as they meant them to be taken. Your colleague's speech act has failed because the two of you were not in the right reciprocal relationship for the exchange.

One way that audience members can do a better job of ensuring communicative reciprocity is by being aware of their own epistemic limitations. Dotson describes listening to someone explain something about physics. Throughout the exchange, Dotson remains aware of her own limited background in physics. This intellectual humility helps her avoid communicative misfires with her interlocutor. She is attuned to the possibility that she might not understand what is said, and so she is quick to ask questions or to slow the conversation down if her understanding starts to flag. If Dotson is ignorant about physics, it is not pernicious ignorance because of her awareness of her own limitations.

By contrast, Dotson argues, many white listeners are as ignorant of Black reality as Dotson is of physics. However, they are unaware of their own ignorance and thus don't take the same care as listeners when listening to Black speakers as Dotson does when listening to a physicist. She relays a story about a white woman too quickly dismissing a Black woman's account of what it's like to raise Black sons in the United States. Dotson writes, "It was very likely the woman never had to scale the epistemic distance between raising white sons and raising black sons in the United States and was entirely unaware of the epistemic difference that distance highlighted."[20]

Thus, it is not only the different social locations of speaker and audience that lead to testimonial quieting and smothering, but the incapacity of more privileged speakers to recognize their social location *as* a social location, and moreover one that might affect their capacity for communicative reciprocity. We will come back to this point soon in the context of post-secondary education.

FIRE's 2017 Survey

As I suggested at the outset, I am focusing here on the reasons and consequences of refrainment from speech because of surveys, media reports, and commentary in recent years about US college students who report refraining from speech in class or on campus.[21] As our earlier discussion made clear, the mere fact that college students refrain from speech should not in itself be cause for concern since we refrain from speech all the time – often for virtuous or neutral reasons, and often with beneficial or benign effects. Further, refrainment from speech is not necessarily coerced, and not all coercion is bad or systemic. Nonetheless, the news that students refrain from speech in class has been greeted both by free expression groups and the media with widespread concern and disapproval.

In this section, I look at the survey conducted in 2017 by the Foundation for Individual Rights in Education (FIRE) on what students at US colleges think about free expression. While there have been similar reports in recent years from the Heterodox Academy, the Cato Institute, and the Knight Foundation, I focus on FIRE's survey in particular because it made the biggest commotion about so-called self-censorship, and that commotion received wide uptake.

In October of 2017, FIRE issued a press release about the survey. The headline read, "NEW SURVEY: Majority of college students self-censor, support disinvitations, don't know hate speech is protected by First Amendment."[22] The lede sentence reprised the headline: "A new report from the Foundation for Individual Rights in Education finds a majority of students on college campuses self-censor in class, support disinviting some guest speakers with whom they disagree, and don't know that hate speech is protected by the First Amendment." Further down the page, the release listed highlights from the survey results. The final highlight read, "In class, 30 percent of students have self-censored because they thought their words would be offensive to others. A majority of students (54 percent) report self-censoring in the classroom at some point since the beginning of college."

These results quickly became canon. In an opinion piece about colleges' putative suppression of viewpoint diversity, John Villasenor and Ilana Redstone Akresh note that the FIRE survey "found that 54 percent of student respondents have curtailed their own expression in class."[23] Elsewhere, Susan Carini reports that the "survey showed that a majority of students self-censor in class."[24] Similarly, Frank Furedi notes that FIRE's survey "found that the majority of students on American university campuses self-censor in classrooms."[25] Debra Soh erroneously cites the FIRE survey as finding that "54 per cent of students self-censor to avoid offending someone."[26] (In fact, the survey finds that 30 per cent *of the 54 per cent of students who refrain from speech* – that is, just over 16 per cent – claimed to have stopped themselves saying something because they thought they might offend someone.)

With respect to FIRE's own publicity about the survey results and the ways in which those results are taken up by others, the tone is typically disapproving. In FIRE's publicity, student self-censorship is presented as a problem – a phenomenon about which readers should be concerned. FIRE treats it as of a piece with such worrisome matters as speaker disinvitations and student ignorance about the First Amendment. Similarly, when authors and publications outside of FIRE cite the survey's student self-censorship results, they typically do so in order to reinforce familiar narratives about a campus free speech crisis.

However, this pattern misrepresents the actual (as opposed to glossed) survey data, and indeed the survey questions themselves. While both FIRE and other authors discussing the survey repeatedly characterize student respondents to the survey as reporting that they have self-censored, none of the survey's sixty-four questions explicitly asks about self-censorship. The conclusions about student self-censorship in the classroom that were, and continue to be, widely circulated are characterizations of student replies to the following five questions from the survey:

Q7: In my college classes, I feel comfortable sharing my ideas and opinions.
Q8: In my college classes, there are times when I share my ideas and opinions even when I am uncomfortable doing so. [Asked only of respondents who answered "disagree" or "strongly disagree" to Q7.]
Q9: Which of the following were reasons that you shared your ideas or opinions when you felt uncomfortable in class? [Asked only of respondents who answered "agree" or "strongly agree" to Q8.]
Q10: In my college classes, I have stopped myself from sharing my ideas or opinions.
Q11: Which of the following were reasons that you stopped yourself from sharing your ideas or opinions in class? [check all that apply] [Asked only of respondents who answered "strongly Agree" or "agree" to Q10.][27]

The way that the survey was reported by FIRE and others distorts the data, both because a survey that never explicitly asked about self-censorship was broadly reported as if it had, and because the supposed bad news that students are self-censoring was emphasized over the overwhelmingly good news that emerged in the replies to this same suite of questions.

While FIRE's own press release emphasizes self-censorship, student replies to question 7 revealed that 87 per cent of students feel comfortable sharing ideas and opinions in their college classrooms.[28] Among the 13 per cent of students who at times feel uncomfortable sharing ideas and opinions in class, 56 per cent speak up despite their discomfort.[29] This puts the combined percentage of students who feel comfortable speaking up or who speak up even when it's uncomfortable to do so at 94 per cent. It is difficult to see these results as anything but good news for campus expression.

It is against this backdrop that we must understand the finding that 54 per cent of respondents have at some point stopped themselves from sharing their ideas or opinions in class. By that point in the survey, 94 per cent of respondents had already replied that they feel comfortable speaking up or that they speak up even when it feels uncomfortable to do so. Therefore, we ought not to read the finding that 54 per cent of students have stopped themselves from speaking up as evidence of a chilling effect. There are lots of reasons for people not to say their piece. Indeed, FIRE's survey shows exactly this. On average, respondents chose two reasons for not speaking up with a little more than one-quarter of students (27 per cent) selecting three or more reasons. FIRE reports as follows:

> Among the listed reasons for not expressing themselves in the classroom, students most often selected that they thought they might be incorrect or mistaken (53%). Almost half of students (48%) self-censored because they thought another student might judge them, and just under one-third of students (30%) did not speak up because they thought their peers might consider their words offensive.[30]

Again, only the 54 per cent of students who said they sometimes don't speak up had the chance to answer this question. Thus, among all students surveyed, 29 per cent don't speak up because they think they might be wrong, 26 per cent don't speak up because they are afraid another student might judge them, and 16 per cent don't speak up because they are afraid of causing offence.

It is noteworthy that the most common reason for students not to speak up in class is that they think they might be wrong. This result fits nicely with the earlier result that the overwhelming majority of students feel comfortable contributing to class discussions. It is perfectly possible to feel comfortable in a learning environment and to wish not to make errors there. I recall my own undergraduate years, in which I was a happy, confident student who loved to participate but who would nonetheless shrink a bit and try to avoid the German professor's gaze if I wasn't sure about the verb conjugation he was drilling us on. My silence in those moments was garden-variety embarrassment, not self-censorship. Of course, as teachers sometimes know better than learners, mistakes can be pedagogically useful, but that doesn't stop them being scary for students, even in the most supportive learning environment.

Students' refrainment from speech when they think they are mistaken has an interesting, unreported flip side in students' answers to question 9 of the FIRE survey: "Which of the following were reasons that you shared your ideas or opinions when you felt uncomfortable in class?" None of FIRE's discussions of the 2017 survey and none of the media discussions of it take up the answer to question 9. To see what students said, we need to look at the data tables.[31] The tables reveal that, as with the "why not speak up?" question, respondents each had multiple reasons to speak up despite their discomfort; on average, respondents selected 2.8 (so, typically 2 or 3 each) of the listed reasons. By far, the most common reason students indicated for speaking up even when it is uncomfortable is "I needed to participate in class because it affects my grade," which was selected by 69.3 per cent of respondents to the question. This answer is unsurprising, and reinforces the common perception among post-secondary instructors that participation grades boost class participation.

The second most popular response was "I thought my idea or opinion was correct." Notice that this reason for speaking up mirrors the main reason students don't speak up – namely, that they thought they were incorrect. However, the two answers do not perfectly mirror each other.

Students' choice to remain silent when they think they are wrong is the most common answer across all genders, races, and family income levels. Admittedly, there is a discernible gender divide, with women more prone than men to select this reason, and yet it is also the top answer for men. Across other demographic categories, the distribution is more or less even.

Matters are very different among respondents who speak up even when uncomfortable. Among this group, there are very clear gender, race, and income lines. Whereas 53.4 per cent of men report that they speak up in class even when it is uncomfortable because they think are right, only 25.4 per cent of women selected this answer. Across racial categories, there is wide variation, with zero Black respondents, 38.7 per cent of white respondents, 42.5 per cent of "other" respondents, and 56.1 per cent of Hispanic respondents selecting "I thought my idea or opinion was correct." The most striking variation occurs across family income levels, where the "I thought my idea or opinion was correct" reply was strongly correlated to family income. Only 23.8 per cent of respondents with family incomes under $40,000 per year selected this option, compared to 43 per cent in the $40,000 to $80,000 range, 60.8 per cent in the $80,000 to $120,000 range, and 91.2 per cent in the $120,000 or higher range.

Now, caution is warranted here. Since just over 7 per cent of subjects were presented with this question (because only that proportion both feels uncomfortable speaking up and does so anyway), we only have data from 93 students. The sample size is especially small for non-white students (total n = 27 for the three non-white racial categories combined) and students from the highest family income level (n = 3). Nonetheless, the results offer some *prima facie* cause for concern that a self-confidence gap may lead more women and lower-income students to refrain from participating in class when they feel uncomfortable.

In sum, then, FIRE's charge that a majority of students self-censor is wildly overblown. What the survey does show is that most students either feel comfortable speaking up in class or don't let their discomfort prevent them speaking up; that most students refrain from speech from time to time, usually for innocuous reasons; that professors are in general doing a good job of using participation grades to get students to speak up in class; and that women and lower-income students may lack the self-confidence to speak up as much as their classmates do.

Communicative Reciprocity and Student Refrainment from Speech

We earlier considered communicative reciprocity, and in particular Dotson's account of two different kinds of failures of communicative reciprocity: testimonial quieting and testimonial smothering. The first occurs when a listener fails to take up what the speaker has to say; the second occurs when the speaker has good reason to expect that there will be no uptake by the listener. I want to conclude by drawing some connections between Dotson and Jeffrey Sachs, who has provided some of the most balanced analysis of the FIRE results.

In a piece in the *Washington Post*, Sachs offers two main reasons for thinking that (to express it in the terminology I have been using) much student refrainment is for neutral or virtuous reasons, and has beneficial or benign results, and thus that commentators' concerns are overblown. First, Sachs argues that some student refrainment from speech is healthy. Sachs writes, "While we should want students to be free to speak their minds, we also want them to develop the skills necessary to navigate complex and diverse environments. This, in part, is what those skills look like."[32] Second, Sachs notes that students who identify as "very conservative" are much more likely than their peers to report that they refrained from speech because they thought their professor might give them a lower grade. However, Sachs argues that this fear does not derive from actual grading practices. He adduces various evidence that grading is more or less unaffected by the relative political stripes of the student and professor, except for some evidence that suggests conservative professors may grade conservative student work more highly than liberal or centrist work.

Let us consider the first of these two points in light of Dotson's account. Recall the pernicious ignorance of the white listener in Dotson's story who did not even realize that there was any epistemic distance between herself and the Black speaker. Recall, too, Dotson's awareness of her own ignorance when listening to a physicist, and the effort she takes to ensure reciprocity within that exchange. When young people pursue higher education, we hope that they will stretch beyond their narrow horizons to learn new perspectives. A key part of learning new perspectives – whether in physics or critical race studies – is recognizing the gaps in one's own knowledge and perspectives and being willing to hear others. While that of course requires speech on the part of those from whom students learn, it also requires silence and intellectual humility from the students themselves. While some commentators seem shocked that students would ever refrain from speech, such refrainment, at least some of the time, is crucial to the core purpose of education. Further, it supports communicative reciprocity – and helps to prevent testimonial quieting – by training students to provide uptake to unfamiliar perspectives.

What about Sachs's second point regarding students' fear of receiving a lower grade? Does that fear suggest that some college students are engaged in testimonial smothering of the type Dotson describes? Recall the three conditions of testimonial smothering:

1. the content of the speech is risky;
2. the audience demonstrates incompetence to take up the testimony; and
3. that incompetence arises out of pernicious ignorance.

Are students smothering their risky testimony because they perceive their professors to be perniciously ignorant and hence incompetent to receive that testimony in good faith? Again, the evidence Sachs cites shows that if students are afraid of political biases affecting their professors' grades for them, that fear does not stem from the professors' actual grading practices. That is, while the students may perceive the content of the speech to be risky, their professors have not in their grading practices demonstrated incompetence to take up the testimony.

That means that either the fears are caused by something other than the professors' grading or they are unfounded. There are a number of possible causes for students' unwarranted fear of receiving lower grades. One possibility that goes unexplored in the discussions of student refrainment from speech is that this fear may be nothing new. Students have always been intimidated by their teachers, and have always rightly or wrongly inclined to the view that the best way to get a good grade is to pretend to agree with the teacher. It is possible that conservative students are particularly prone to this view because it is part of the nature of conservatism to be risk averse. If this is right, then the survey results indicating that students are afraid of losing grades should not be read as any indication of a new trend in post-secondary education. Alternatively, the student fears might be the result of increasing pressure on students to get higher grades in order to gain admittance to post-graduate programs, etc. In that case, the change is a reflection not of the "intolerant Left" (as is often intimated) but of increasing extrinsic pressures on students. In either of these cases – i.e., nothing has changed, or extrinsic pressures have changed – the solution to student fears lies not in stoking free speech panic but in better pedagogy and program design.

A further possible cause for students' mistaken fear about losing grades is the narrative about a campus free speech crisis and biased liberal professors that has been whipped up in recent years, in large part thanks to groups like FIRE and Heterodox Academy, generous sponsorship by the Koch Foundation,[33] and the viral power of social media. In that case, it is the purveyors of that mythology who, ironically, bear most of the blame for the students' consequent refrainment from speech. If, however, students are largely unaffected by this campaign of misinformation, then their fear of their professors is simply unfounded. By refraining from speech because of a fear founded on no good evidence, they are acting out of cowardice, and are hence guilty of vicious refrainment. Indeed, their refrainment is not only vicious but pernicious because of the way in which it is being co-opted in support of the mythology of a campus free speech crisis. And, just as with the student in my long-ago classroom who liberated the hamster, if they aren't brave enough to tell the truth, the whole class will be punished.

NOTES

* I acknowledge that I live and work on Treaty 4 territory – the territories of the nêhiyawak, Anihšinápěk, Dakota, Lakota, and Nakoda, and the homeland of the Métis/Michif Nation. My thanks to Emmett Macfarlane and to fellow panelists and audience members at the Freedom of Expression in Canada workshop held in October 2019 at the Balsillie School of International Affairs in Waterloo, Ontario, for stimulating discussion that helped strengthen this chapter. Thanks also to Tim Kenyon for generative conversations about silencing, to *University Affairs* for publishing my earliest thoughts on the topic, and to the anonymous referees who provided helpful feedback on the chapter. This research was supported by a Social Sciences and Humanities Research Council of Canada Insight Development Grant.

1 John Horton, "Self-Censorship," *Res Publica* 17, no. 1 (2011): 101.
2 There is a fairly extensive literature on self-censorship, but most of it does not seek to analyse the concept. Much of the self-censorship literature considers particular domains in which self-censorship occur – for instance, the media and the military – but do not ask what self-censorship is.
3 Gerald MacCallum, "Negative and Positive Freedom," in *The Liberty Reader*, ed. David Miller (Edinburgh: Edinburgh University Press, 2006), 100–23.
4 But not necessarily. Horton allows that there may be exceptions.
5 Horton, "Self-Censorship," 95.
6 This puzzle is also taken up by several other theorists. See, for instance, Philip Cook and Conrad Heilmann, "Two Types of Self-Censorship: Public and Private," *Political Studies* 61, no. 1 (March 2013): 178–9; Randal Marlin, "The Muted Bugle: Self-Censorship and the Press," in *Interpreting Censorship in Canada*, ed. Klaus Petersen and Allan Hutchinson. (Toronto: University of Toronto Press, 1999), 291; and Mark Cohen, *Censorship in Canadian Literature* (London: McGill-Queen's University Press, 2001), 9.
7 Horton, "Self-Censorship," 97.
8 Ibid., 99.
9 Ibid.
10 Ibid., 105.
11 Cook and Heilmann, "Two Types of Self-Censorship," 139.
12 Ibid.

13 Any moral philosophers reading this will notice here my unusual deployment of virtue ethical terminology in a deontological application. I adopt this gambit to avoid getting sidetracked explaining unfamiliar deontological terminology to a multidisciplinary audience. For the purposes of the present characterization, not much hangs on whether we assess the speaker's refrainment using the lens of deontology or virtue ethics.

14 It is worth saying that not all refrainment from speech to avoid punishment is vicious. There is a difference between staying quiet in order to avoid legitimate punishment and staying quiet to avoid unwarranted or excessive punishment. Thank you to an anonymous referee for making this point.

15 A consequentialist might argue that vicious refrainment that produces beneficial results is good. If indeed some vicious refrainment turns out to be good, that only lends further support to my larger points that not all refrainment from speech is bad, and that assessing the goodness or badness of refrainment from speech is complex and particular.

16 Consider non-disclosure agreements in research and development departments.

17 Gayatri Spivak, "Can the Subaltern Speak?," in *Marxism and the Interpretation of Culture*, ed. Cary Nelson and Lawrence Grossberg (Urbana: University of Illinois Press, 1998), 271–313. In deploying Spivak in the context of discussing testimonial silencing, I follow Kristie Dotson, "Tracking Epistemic Violence, Tracking Practices of Silencing," *Hypatia* 26, no. 2 (Spring 2011): 236–57.

18 Dotson, "Tracking Epistemic Violence."

19 Kelly Hoffman et al., "Racial Bias in Pain Assessment and Treatment Recommendations, and False Beliefs about Biological Differences between Blacks and Whites," *Proceedings of the National Academy of Sciences of the United States of America* 113, no. 16 (2016): 4296–301.

20 Dotson, "Tracking Epistemic Violence," 249.

21 See Kelsey Ann Naughton, *Speaking Freely: What Students Think about Expression at American Colleges*, Foundation for Individual Rights in Education (FIRE), 11 October 2017, https://d28htnjz2elwuj.cloudfront.net/wp-content/uploads/2017/10/11091747/survey-2017-speaking-freely.pdf; Sean Stevens, "The Campus Expression Survey: Summary of New Data," *Heterodox Academy*, 20 December 2017, https://heterodoxacademy.org/blog/the-campus-expression-survey-summary-of-new-data/; Emily Ekins, "The State of Free Speech and Tolerance in America," Cato Institute, 31 October 2017, https://www.cato.org/survey-reports/state-free-speech-tolerance-america; and *Free Expression on Campus: What College Students Think about First Amendment Issues*, Gallup/Knight Foundation, 2018, https://kf-site-production.s3.amazonaws.com/publications/pdfs/000/000/248/original/Knight_Foundation_Free_Expression_on_Campus_2017.pdf. See also Emily Chamlee-Wright, "Coaching Students through the Self-Censorship Dilemma," *Forbes*, 4 October 2019, https://www.forbes.com/sites/emilychamleewright/2019/10/04/coaching-students-through-the-self-censorship-dilemma/#79af39557a12; *Chasm*

in the Classroom: Campus Free Speech in a Divided America, PEN America, 2 April 2019, https://pen.org/wp-content/uploads/2019/04/2019-PEN-Chasm-in-the -Classroom-04.25.pdf; and Debra Mashek, "When College Students Self-Censor, Society Loses," *The Hill*, 3 October 2018, https://thehill.com/opinion /education/409549-when-college-students-self-censor-society-loses.

22 FIRE, "NEW SURVEY: Majority of College Students Self-Censor, Support Disin-vitations, Don't Know Hate Speech Is Protected by First Amendment," FIRE press release, 11 October 2017, https://www.thefire.org/new-survey-majority-of-college -students-self-censor-support-disinvitations-dont-know-hate-speech-is-protected -by-first-amendment/.

23 John Villasenor and Ilana Redstone Akresh, "3 Ways That Colleges Suppress a Diversity of Viewpoints," *Chronicle of Higher Education*, 28 September 2018, https://www.chronicle.com/article/3-Ways-That-Colleges-Suppress/244673.

24 Susan Carini, "Emory Conference Explores Academic Freedom, Free Speech on Campus," *Emory Report*, 9 April 2019, https://news.emory.edu/stories/2019/04 /er_conference_free_speech/campus.html.

25 Frank Furedi, "Why Opinion Polls Keep Getting It Wrong," *Spiked*, 21 May 2019, https://www.spiked-online.com/2019/05/21/why-opinion-polls-keep-getting -it-wrong/.

26 Debra Soh, "How to Win the War on Free Speech," *Globe and Mail*, 13 November 2017; updated 14 November 2017, https://www.theglobeandmail.com/opinion /how-to-win-the-war-on-free-speech/article36943894/.

27 Naughton, *Speaking Freely*, 22. The bracketed sentences are reproduced from the original.

28 Ibid., 9.

29 Ibid.

30 Ibid.

31 YouGov, FIRE0001 data tables, May/September 2017, https://d28htnjz2elwuj .cloudfront.net/wp-content/uploads/2017/09/27154057/fs-survey-01-tabs.pdf, 32–6.

32 Jeffrey Sachs "Do Universities Have a Self-Censorship Problem?," *Washington Post*, 16 April 2019, https://www.washingtonpost.com/politics/2019/04/16/do -universities-have-self-censorship-problem/.

33 See Aaron Freedman, "Why Should We Care about Faux Free-Speech Warriors? Because the Koch Brothers Are Paying Their Bills," *American Prospect*, 20 June 2019, https://prospect.org/justice/care-faux-free-speech-warriors -koch-brothers-paying-bills./.

15 Deplatforming in Theory and Practice: The Ann Coulter Debacle

DAX D'ORAZIO

Over the last few decades, the perception that North American university campuses are increasingly intolerant has gained impressive traction.[1] While much of this discourse echoes some familiar critiques of higher education from the culture wars, a moral panic that was once largely confined to the op-ed pages is now official government policy.[2] Solidifying the perception that freedom of speech is under attack is a particular type of campus controversy, one that tends to attract a disproportionate amount of media coverage and public scrutiny: when an invited speaker is cancelled, interrupted, or otherwise unable to address an audience. This protest tactic is colloquially known as "no platforming" or "deplatforming" (in this chapter I use the latter term). Because there is a reflexive assumption that university campuses are the most appropriate venue for entertaining potentially controversial and uncomfortable ideas,[3] it is not entirely surprising that deplatforming generates such controversy. In this sense, campus is emblematic of a deeply entrenched liberal ideal, as a literal "marketplace of ideas."[4] Thus, deplatforming has become a central pillar of contemporary critiques of higher education, often referenced as evidence that campus is an inhospitable environment for conservative ideas and individuals.

Although contemporary media coverage might give the impression that these controversies are novel, deplatforming on university campuses has a much longer history. As Evan Smith notes, the practice has been animating concerns for freedom of speech since the 1960s in Europe and North America.[5] Although social protest has been a consistent theme of campus life in the postwar era, many trace the popularization of deplatforming as a legitimate tactic to the British National Union of Students, who adopted an explicit institutional "no platform" policy in 1974 (one that remains today in altered form).[6] Smith refers to this policy as "a bureaucratic measure that formalised the ad hoc protests that had occurred over the last half decade."[7] Essentially, students were concerned about an influx and normalization of far-right discourses on campus and they were actively engaged in protest tactics that would diminish such forms of expression.

Nonetheless, more recent and sensational incidences of deplatforming have sharpened scrutiny and criticism. In March of 2017, student protestors deplatformed Charles Murray at Middlebury College. Allison Stanger, a Middlebury faculty member and Murray's interlocutor for the event, suffered a concussion while both of them were accosted.[8] In response, the college disciplined sixty-seven students who were involved.[9] In February of 2017, a peaceful-protest-turned-riot forced the cancellation of a planned Milo Yiannopolous's planned visit to the Berkeley campus of the University of California. The riot resulted in more than $100,000 in damage and managed to raise the ire of President Trump, who warned that colleges might risk public funding if they did not guarantee freedom of speech.[10] In October of 2017, the University of Florida paid more than half a million dollars in associated security fees for an event featuring Richard Spencer that resulted in Governor Rick Scott declaring a state of emergency.[11] Although the talk was cut short rather than cancelled, this case illustrates some of the incredible challenges universities face when potentially harmful individuals seek a platform on campus.[12] In Canada, too, instances of deplatforming have made headlines and catalyzed debates about freedom of speech on campus. In March of 2018, a fire alarm effectively cancelled an appearance by Faith Goldy at Wilfrid Laurier University, although she later addressed supporters outside and vowed to return to campus.[13] In March of 2017, a talk by Ezra Levant was disrupted by protestors on the Ryerson campus,[14] after the event was relocated due to security concerns.[15] A few months later, Ryerson cancelled a panel titled "The Stifling of Free Speech on University Campuses" amid an inundation of complaints and an inability to provide adequate security.[16] The proposed panel originally included Goldy and Jordan Peterson, among others, although the panel was later moved to a different venue and excluded Goldy.

In response to the controversy generated by deplatforming, this chapter asks a simple question: Does deplatforming *work*? Admittedly, this question is both broad and ambitious. Providing a sufficient answer would require both precise measurements for defining success and a long-range comparative data set. Instead, I pose the question as a way to delve into some relevant political theory and philosophy to map the various justifications one might marshal in assessing the legitimacy of the tactic. Further, I am curious to know if there is a potential disjuncture between deplatforming *in theory* and deplatforming *in practice*, and what this might say about its potential effectiveness.

To do this, I analyse a seminal case study from approximately a decade ago that foreshadows the contemporary moral panic about freedom of speech on campus: Ann Coulter's aborted visit to the University of Ottawa in 2010. Because of Coulter's high profile, as well as some well-organized opposition, the planned event garnered an impressive amount of national (and even some international) media coverage. Coulter's is a compelling case for two reasons. First, she is not just a popular and bestselling author, but also someone whose ideas have influenced official policy in the United States. Therefore, the consequences of her deplatforming (i.e., potentially reduced credibility) might have wide-ranging effects. Second, as will be outlined below, Coulter inhabits a liminal space between offensive speech and potentially illegal speech (at least in Canada). Therefore, the potential effectiveness of deplatforming might inform and enhance strategies for responding to speech that is potentially harmful but not *prima facie* illegal. Although university affairs are typically seen as mundane, cases such as these are instructive because they test the boundaries of acceptable debate, something that necessarily involves public discourse at the margins of society.[17]

Overall, my research suggests that deplatforming is prone to generating unintended consequences and, for this reason, ought to be considered carefully and deployed only in extreme circumstances. I use a qualitative mixed-methods approach that includes reviews of relevant scholarly literature (primarily political theory and philosophy), reviews of relevant news and opinion (primarily newspaper articles and op-eds), access to information (ATI) records solicited from the University of Ottawa (administrative correspondence, security reporting, external complaints, and donor records), and semi-structured personal interviews with individuals proximate to the Coulter protest (four students, three protest organizers, and one former executive of the Student Federation of the University of Ottawa).

The chapter proceeds in three parts. The first section provides context for Coulter's abortive appearance, including a brief background on Coulter herself and a chronology of the protest and the talk's eventual cancellation. The second section considers deplatforming in theory by outlining some relevant political theory and philosophy with a particular focus on potential justifications. Importantly, not all the literature discussed here explicitly endorses deplatforming; rather, it provides some justifications that could be marshalled in support of deplatforming on campus. This section is organized along three interconnected levels that include merit, harm reduction, and discursive strategy. The third section considers deplatforming in practice by outlining some of the political and/or strategic considerations at play when it is deployed. I shed light on why incidences of deplatforming catalyze a disproportionate amount of media attention and public scrutiny and then outline two possible unintended consequences of the practice: greater exposure and unearned moral and intellectual legitimacy.

The Ann Coulter Debacle

Conservative firebrand and pundit Ann Coulter was slated to speak on the University of Ottawa campus on 23 March 2010. She was on a three-day tour through Canada (London–Ottawa–Calgary) organized by the International Free Press Society and the Clare Boothe Luce Policy Institute.[18] Known for her abrasive and often offensive polemics, Coulter has slowly become an American institution in the realm of punditry, despite her long history of objectionable (typically racist) comments. More recently, her ideas have been credited as a blueprint for President Trump's populist electoral success, and she herself has been open about her influence on the former president,[19] although Trump now disputes this.[20] Interestingly, her ultimately unsuccessful event at the University of Ottawa was the first time that she had ever been prevented from speaking on a campus.[21] This novelty and symbolism – a Canadian campus shutting down an American speaker – easily led to headlines across North America.[22]

The event cancellation itself was the result of a confluence of factors. First, student protestors mounted a well-organized campaign in opposition to Coulter, hoping that the university administration would explicitly bar her from campus. Their campaign included back-channel communications with senior administration,[23] gathering signatures (as well as organizational endorsements), distributing literature on campus and online, soliciting supporters to contact the senior administration, and inviting students (and others) to protest at the event. An organizer described the process as a "grassroots" effort that included ample "word of mouth" mobilization.[24] The campaign boasted the explicit support of the Student Federation of the University of Ottawa (SFUO),[25] which went as far as banning posters advertising the event in the University Centre.[26] Despite student protestors finding a sympathetic ear in the SFUO, the senior administration did not cancel the event outright. Instead, the provost and vice-president academic, Francois Houle, sent an ill-fated message to the organizers on 19 March,[27] essentially warning Coulter that Canadian hate speech laws might proscribe some of her standard fare.[28]

Obviously, the email would cause a freedom of speech controversy and be widely condemned (it was originally leaked by the National Post in Canada).[29] Although criticism within Canadian media was not surprising, it was not confined to the op-ed pages.[30] The Canadian Association of University Teachers, for example, expressed concern directly to Houle, noting that his missive "raises serious questions about the University of Ottawa's respect for freedom of expression and academic freedom."[31] Coulter added more controversy during an exchange with a young Muslim woman the previous evening (in London, Ontario). During the Q&A, the woman asked how she ought to travel, since Coulter had previously remarked that Muslims should not be able to fly (but rather should take "flying carpets"). Coulter eventually told the woman to "take a camel."[32] This confrontation was widely reported, so it was no surprise that the evening in Ottawa was met with raucous protest.[33]

On 19 March, University of Ottawa Protection Services noted that there would likely be more than a hundred students at the event to protest. Days later, they noticed that student organizing had intensified, as campus was blanketed with promotional material. Security consisted of five Protection Services members, two members of the Ottawa Police (one constable and one sergeant), and Coulter's personal bodyguard (Floyd Resnick). Although estimates of the crowd varied from a few hundred to as many as two thousand, reliable sources suggest the former is accurate.[34] The event itself had approximately 460 registered attendees and it was not an open event (online registration only). Access to the auditorium was restricted to one entrance where organizers were verifying registration, but the situation became "unmanageable" shortly after admittance began, according to Protection Services. At one point, a fire alarm was triggered, although it was quickly remedied because there was no evacuation order. In its internal report, Protection Services described the quickly spiralling situation as follows:

> As the crowd started arriving, it was quickly realized that there was not sufficient security and extra resources were requested … There were several people in the crowd that were not registered and when they found out that their name was not on the list, they refused to leave the registration table area, which caused severe issues with the access to the room. The registration volunteers were being overpowered by the people wanting access and the crowd was trying to force their way past them.[35]

A small handful of protestors registered for the event, gained admission, and disrupted it from the inside.[36] According to the former SFUO executive, this was no small feat, as the organizers of the event had rejected the registrations of those who they thought were left-wing activists.[37] Eventually, in a conversation between Protection Services, Resnick, and Ottawa Police, a decision was made that it would be unsafe for Coulter to appear. However, the ultimate source of this decision has been disputed, largely due to the media narrative shaped by Coulter's own statements. According to internal Protection Services reports,

> All parties involved agreed that the event could not be continued. Public Safety was the overall deciding factor for the cancellation … All parties agree that in the best interest of everyone, the decision to cancel the event was the appropriate action to take given the circumstances we were faced with.[38]

However, additional data suggests otherwise. According to an Ottawa Police media relations officer, it was Coulter's security (presumably Resnick) who ultimately decided to nix the event, even after being offered alternative courses of action.[39] The former SFUO executive confirmed this, explaining that they had approached the head of Protection Services explicitly, due to a worry that a contrived cancellation on the part of Coulter would generate undue criticism of the

SFUO.[40] After the debacle, a prepared statement from the University of Ottawa read, in part, "the organizers themselves decided at 7:50 p.m. to cancel the event and so informed the University's Protection Services staff on site." Nonetheless, the precise details of the conversation that led to this decision are still unclear, and many questions therefore remain. For example, what alternative courses of action might have been pitched?[41] For those who were there, one thing *was* clear: the cancellation could also be reasonably attributed to "a combination of overcapacity and utter disorganization," as reporter Daniele Hamamdjian described it.[42]

A related question is whether or not deplatforming was the explicit strategy of the protestors. Although the data suggests that it was,[43] there is *some* divergence, particularly in the approach of the SFUO.[44] Regardless, one can reasonably say that the noticeable lack of an explicit plan made deplatforming more likely. Inside the lecture hall and addressing the irate crowd, Levant alleged that Houle's earlier advisory emboldened student protestors by "telegraph[ing] to the community that the University of Ottawa is not a place for free debate."[45] He alleged that the SFUO followed the lead of the senior administration,[46] when in fact it was the SFUO that had been pressuring the administration behind the scenes.[47] Interestingly, one of the organizers explained the administrative receptivity to concerns from the SFUO and broader University of Ottawa community historically and contextually. According to them, the previous university president (Gilles Patry) had a much more antagonistic relationship with student activists. Part of then President Allan Rock's appeal was that his political experience (as a former Liberal cabinet minister) would allow him to repair a broken relationship.[48]

Predictably, Coulter used the controversy as an opportunity for more media coverage and "indulged in a media orgy of invective," criticizing both the University of Ottawa (as "bush league") and the student protestors (who allegedly victimized *her*).[49] Several months later, it was revealed that Rock had actually seriously considered re-inviting Coulter in an attempt to satiate critics and rehabilitate the university's reputation. In the end he yielded to advice suggesting that such an opportunity would be manipulated by Coulter to further amplify her profile.[50]

Deplatforming in Theory

In general, there are three interconnected levels of justification for deplatforming. These justifications were key in the present case, but they also strongly correlate with the secondary literature (academic and non-academic work) and some other recent incidences of deplatforming (based on news media). First, deplatforming is justified by appealing to the concept of merit. Importantly, contemporary discussions about freedom of speech on campus sometimes make a significant analytical error by conflating this principle with academic freedom. Freedom of speech is typically conceptualized as a general non-interference principle because individuals in liberal democracies are understood to have some inviolable boundaries as citizens. Conversely, academic freedom is *not* a general right, but instead one tailored to particular professional duties. Thus, academic freedom "is a *special* right of academics – a right to freedom from prescribed orthodoxy in their teaching, research, and lives as academics."[51]

Put more concretely, it "is actually a complex set of beliefs, traditions, procedures, and legal rulings that govern many of the relationships between faculties and their employing institutions, the government, students, and the broader public."[52] Despite a noticeable gap between professional rules and norms and actual law,[53] there is wide recognition that academic freedom is at once a functional *right* necessary to perform professional duties and a professional *obligation* (with reasonable limits likewise tailored to the university's mission). Thus, while the principle of freedom of speech emphasizes content neutrality (on the part of the state, institution, etc.), the university is typically *not* neutral regarding the content of speech.[54] In fact, scholarship is normally premised upon concepts such as merit, rigour, and excellence. Because it is reasonably assumed that relevant experts vet ideas presented in an academic context, they are likely to benefit from some form of distinction.[55] This epistemic gatekeeping, while potentially exclusionary, is absolutely crucial for the university, because it ensures that information emanating from inside its walls has satisfied some scholarly threshold. The implications of this are clear: not all opinions are equal and not everyone is automatically entitled to a platform on campus.

The obvious response to those who invoke merit is that none of these potentially restrictive conventions ought to apply to speakers who come from *outside* the university (who might merely express an interest in an attractive venue). One might also contend that the umbrella of academic freedom (and perhaps free speech more broadly) extends to include the presentation of ideas, concepts, and arguments *at all stages* of their development. Thus, there is a legitimate worry that the relatively strict meritocratic standards of peer review, for example, could be invoked to restrict expression in other venues on campus. To further complicate matters, one might also make distinctions regarding the form of gatekeeping (i.e., a controversial pundit renting university space vs. being invited and/or hosted by an academic).

However, there is an argument to be made that the university campus is not analogous to the town square. Here, we see that universities are hybrid in practice, concurrently public *and* private institutions. If one accepts the premise that universities have a particular autonomy non-analogous to purely *public* expression, legitimate reasons to restrict platforms might include a well-founded anticipation of disruption to the normal operations of the university (especially if violence is likely), discourse that is likely to contravene applicable laws (i.e., hate speech), and/or (most controversially) sufficient pressure applied to the university by those who argue that a platform could cause harm. In all of these circumstances, the university would be regulating the content of speech, whether or not one agrees with each of these rationales. Ultimately, the point would be that universities should have wide discretion in regulating speech on campus in accordance with their own unique mission and norms. Further, considering that there is a plethora of other publicly available platforms, universities are not suppressing speech simply by reserving the right to restrict space to those who align with its particular institutional mission (and one could make the case that this would necessarily preclude pundits like Coulter).

In another version of the appeal to merit, some have emphasized that freedom of speech should not be equated with freedom from consequences.[56] Essentially, while someone might have the right to expression in a way others might fight objectionable (and potentially harmful), they do not have a right to be immune from social criticism in response to their expression. The question, then, is what consequences would be appropriate for objectionable speech. At least one of them might be restricted platforms, particularly in spaces that are not strictly public or that have an institutional commitment to some other principle or goal (much like universities).[57]

Second, deplatforming is justified by appealing to harm reduction. Since at least the early 1990s, there have been some significant changes in the way scholars conceptualize harm in relation to speech,[58] particularly in stretching the concept to include newly theorized harms[59] and highlighting the links between knowledge production and harm.[60] Traditionally understood as something that accrues primarily though clear cause and effect, harm can also be understood to result from a poisoned environment. While cumulative pollution might render the assignment of responsibility difficult,[61] the potentially permissive environment that is created by speech might lead to more serious harm. Accordingly, harm can be both indirect and temporal (see Bennett, in this volume). Although the topic of pornography infamously failed to engender consensus among feminist theorists,[62] the issue itself remains an apt illustration of this theory and approach. Essentially, while pornography itself cannot "leap off the shelf and assault women,"[63] it leaves in its wake a psychosocial effect that cannot be easily separated from the inferior status of women and the gendered violence visited upon them.[64] The internalization of disparaging views of women (which is reasonably imbibed from pornography) may eventually form the raw materials for a variety of physical (and emotional) abuses.[65]

More relevant to the present case is scholarship on hate speech, however; this is the key discursive pillar of the objections to Coulter analysed below. Jeremy Waldron argues that hate speech vitiates a "public good" of inclusion that is an integral part of liberal democracies, and that hate speech further attacks the dignity of its targets and their membership in the larger community.[66] He uses the concept of "group libel" to capture the essence of the latter, whereby the law ought to prevent efforts to impugn groups with negative associations such that it would logically flow that equal standing within a political community could be questioned.[67] Legal restrictions preventing the most extreme of these targeted manifestations of hatred are legitimate because they provide a crucial prerequisite – a public *assurance* – for a system based upon egalitarian membership: "Hate speech and group defamation are actions performed in public, with a public orientation, aimed at undermining public goods."[68]

At the individual level, Richard Delgado and Jean Stefancic catalogue a number of troubling potential reactions among the recipients of hate speech, ranging from mild physical responses to deeper psychological and emotional harm, contributing to self-destructive behavioural patterns.[69] Repeated exposure to harmful speech can lead to a general "cultural mistrust,"[70] whereby targets of hate speech might close themselves off from the broader society, internalize the stereotypes to which they have been exposed, devalue their own self-worth, and/or react with anger and frustration.[71]

Although hate speech constitutes a "psychic tax" for those it targets,[72] it might also produce cognitive effects within a larger audience. While someone passively receiving these hate messages may tend towards discounting them, when they experience other situations involving those targeted, previously received ideas may catalyze unconscious associations.[73] Further, the toleration of hateful speech sends a potent signal to the entire polity that egalitarian principles can in practice *coexist* with tacit identity-based exceptions.[74] In this sense, there might also be a direct connection between discriminatory speech and concrete political movements,[75] because the former may create a permissive environment in which the latter can thrive.

Harm reduction was the most consistent justification reflected in the primary data. According to some of the organizers of the opposition to Coulter's talk, the main protest message was kept simple for strategic purposes: "no hate speech on our campus."[76] The possibility of Coulter speaking was "scary" for one, a racialized woman who described her general experience at the University of Ottawa as "alienating."[77] Stunned that fellow students would even want to invite someone like Coulter to campus, she viewed the prospect as "a really big threat."[78] Although she did not in fact attend the protest out of fear – and was relieved that white organizers were at the forefront – she was motivated to participate in its organization because "nobody should feel unsafe or attacked or unwanted" on campus.[79] Another organizer argued that it would be a "waste of time" to debate the minutia of whether or not Coulter's speech constitutes hate speech. Instead, protestors could legitimately "shut it down" because "[her] ideas have concrete impact on people's lives."[80]

As mentioned, in advance of the scheduled event, organizers used a variety of outreach strategies that included both printed and online materials. In a section of the printed literature titled "What You Can Do," a number of suggestions are offered, including sending President Allan Rock an email asking him to cancel the event. An attached draft letter frames the event as potentially causing harm to marginalized communities. The scheduled event, according to the organizers,

> presents a worrying situation for many students on campus against whom and against whose communities Ms. Coulter has promoted hatred ... As a campus which promotes a right to respect, diversity, and multiculturalism, a figure of such offense, hatred, and oppression has no place in our community.

The accompanying petition asks President Rock and the administration to bar Coulter from campus "in order to promote a safe space for community members and students through limiting possible discrimination and hate speech on campus." Its preamble likewise cites the reasonably anticipated harm that could be done to marginalized communities based upon Coulter's previous public commentary:

> Ann Coulter in numerous public interviews, speeches, books, and columns has been cited making discriminatory, hateful, and violent comments against: women, Muslims, LGBTQ persons, persons of colour, migrants, Jewish persons, persons with disabilities and other marginalized communities.

Importantly, all of the promotional materials suggested that Coulter's standard fare might be classified as hate speech under Canadian law. The aforementioned literature (email appeal) begins with "BAN HATE SPEECH," the email argues that freedom of speech is balanced with freedom from discrimination on prohibited grounds, the petition explicitly references section 319 of the *Criminal Code*, and some of the posters include the phrase "BAN HATE SPEECH" alongside some objectionable quotes from Coulter. During the protest itself, crowds boisterously chanted, "No more hate speech on our campus!"[81] The point here is not to definitively conclude that any of Coulter's speech might run afoul of applicable Canadian law. Rather, this suggests that these appeals to relevant laws were ultimately efforts to justify speech restrictions based upon a specific conceptualization of harm. Not only would Coulter allegedly harm individuals as a direct result of her commentary, but she would also contribute to a potentially poisoned environment that would be at odds with the declared mission of the university.

Third, deplatforming is justified by appealing to a broader discursive strategy that attempts to halt the normalization of potentially harmful speech over time. Aside from the material and/or psychological harm that speech might inflict, extreme speech can tangibly shift discursive territory. The Overton window is an oft-cited conceptual framework for understanding how policy options exist in a narrow but constantly shifting spectrum of legitimacy and possibility.

Contemporary events have seen it "firmly embedded in the vernacular of seemingly every political news outlet" due to its analytical relevance.[82] Essentially, in any particular discursive environment there are what might be called boundaries of acceptable debate that are conditioned by what seems intuitively possible at the moment. Importantly, these boundaries are neither static nor easily defined. They are constantly shifting due to a synthesis of factors that might range from explicit legal prohibitions to implicit (unwritten) rules, norms, and conventions. While exposure to extreme speech might not necessarily catalyze support for a specific idea or position, it might render less extreme (but equally problematic) speech more palatable. Thus, the window of acceptable debate can perceptibly shift over time towards more extreme positions if and when extremity is gradually normalized.

One of the most exemplary cases of this discursive strategy involved the phenomenon of Holocaust denial in the 1990s. The UK trial between Penguin Books (as publisher of historian Deborah Lipstadt) and disgraced historian David Irving is now infamous.[83] The case illustrated that an idea or argument could be so nefarious that merely entertaining it publicly might bestow upon it some unearned legitimacy, and this in turn could result in the infliction of *harm*. Further, Holocaust denial could be seen in the public eye as just one of a number of different (and perhaps equally legitimate) competing viewpoints. Accordingly, Lipstadt argues that "free speech does not guarantee them [Holocaust deniers] the right to be treated as the 'other side' of a legitimate debate."[84] In other words, since racism is "irrational," it is impossible to combat the wider effects of Holocaust denial with reasoned discussion.[85]

This basic non-normalization argument has become commonplace in contemporary anti-racist and anti-fascist politics and activism, on campus and elsewhere.[86] Its most noteworthy pillar is an explicit scepticism of the "marketplace of ideas" analogy that is reflected in liberal democratic theory and jurisprudence.[87] It therefore questions the assumption that an unrestricted marketplace will naturally tend towards the dominance of normatively "good" ideas.[88] This may be the case for at least two reasons. First, some ideas may be relatively more popular not because of their intrinsic merit but because of their disproportionate *power*. It may, then, be a mistake to assume that all ideas have enjoyed a full hearing, or that commonly accepted ideas have naturally been subjected to rigorous scrutiny. This epistemological position is a common tradition under the broad aegis of critical political theory and philosophy, popularized more recently by Michel Foucault,[89] but typically finding its roots in the writing of Friedrich Nietzsche.[90] Second, ideas do not always appeal to one's rational or logical sensibilities; indeed, it is difficult to ignore the overestimated liberal investment in individual rational calculation. The archetypical liberal subject as a rational information gatherer is at minimum misleading and at most a woefully inadequate paradigm for understanding the circulation of ideas.[91] Therefore, at the very least, the market analogy relies upon an over-optimistic presupposition, according to Jason Stanley:

> The argument for the "marketplace of ideas" presupposes that words are used only in their "descriptive, logical, or semantic sense." But in politics, and most vividly in fascist politics, language is not used simply, or even chiefly, to convey information but to elicit emotion. The argument from the "marketplace of ideas" model for free speech works only if the underlying disposition of the society is to accept the force of reason over the power of irrational resentments and prejudice.[92]

Accordingly, the problem with Coulter is not just that her ideas are harmful *prima facie*, but that they have a caustic effect on the discursive environment *as a whole* by normalizing a specific tenor of speech and eroding possibilities for respectful public debate.[93] In essence, there is a potential *double* movement in political discourse. The first is a shift to the (far) right and a redefinition of a "new normal."[94] The second is a shift downward in the quality of public debate by normalizing speech that is ad hominem, sensationalistic, and hateful.[95] Protest organizers recognized these discursive dynamics and pointed out other ways that power imbalances might shape the contours of debate about freedom of speech more broadly. One remarked that when there are alleged violations of freedom of speech (such as in the Coulter case), "it's always the freedom of speech of the most privileged and the people who have the most power to be able to do harm."[96] Another similarly referred to a predictable "pattern" in debates about freedom of speech: those who "believe vehemently in the principle of freedom of speech under any circumstances" might not have been exposed to or affected by speech that "led to harm or violence."[97] In other words, categorical approaches to freedom of speech might also be a reflection of privilege.

Promotional materials for the protest also reflected some of this non-normalization justification in broad terms. Posters and email appeals included an encouragement to "support positive space on campus," ostensibly by helping to keep Coulter off campus. The petition explicitly invoked relevant hate speech prohibitions as a reasonable limit for freedom of speech on campus and conveyed the desire to "promote a safe space for community members and students through limiting possible discrimination and hate speech on campus." Similarly, the letter for President Rock asked that he and the university "assist in the preservation of the culture of our campus and right of our students to enjoy that culture free of discrimination and oppression."

Deplatforming in Practice

Against these various justifications for deplatforming we can contrast a more familiar (perhaps reflexive) justification for a large margin of appreciation for freedom of speech in liberal democracies (and especially on campus). Stretching all the way back to Socrates, Western political theory and philosophy has exalted an abstract individual free from illegitimate external constraint.[98] More recently, most people associate the liberal paradigm of contemporary democracies with the truth-based defence of John Stuart Mill.[99] According to him, since humans are fallible in their intellect, only by constant collision with error can truth be attained.[100] As such, every instance of censorship is an assumption of infallibility.[101] Further, one ought to eschew orthodoxy because even normatively good ideas need to be sustained through occasional epistemic competition.[102]

However, despite some persuasive arguments for (and against) deplatforming,[103] a separate and more interesting question is the strategic environment in which the tactic is employed. At the outset, this raises an interesting paradox: it is entirely possible to have a moral and intellectual case for a specific course of action (such as deplatforming) but not a strategic one (as the present case vividly illustrates). It also begs a further question: despite a litany of other (and likely more serious) threats to freedom of speech on campus (declining funding, contingent faculty, etc.), why do incidences of deplatforming tend to attract a disproportionate amount of media attention and public criticism? I think there are at least two reasons for this.

First, as outlined earlier, deplatforming highlights (often in a sensational way) the theoretical or philosophical tensions between a reflexive liberal paradigm of freedom of speech and a host of nuanced challenges to this paradigm.[104] Because freedom of speech is considered a hallowed right in liberal democracies (not without inconsistency, of course), even the most thoughtful and careful critiques of it can precipitate moral panic.[105] Two protest organizers conveyed these tensions in their justifications for deplatforming. For them, the law is not an accurate barometer for morality.[106] According to one, deplatforming as a form of "direct action" fills in the gaps because Canadian "laws are quite limited in what they can accomplish in terms of keeping people safe from harm in a preventative way."[107] Existing laws grant too great a margin of appreciation for speech if and when speech (like Coulter's) can "lead to individual racist attacks."[108] Further, deplatforming also highlights (and even compounds) some of the existential tensions at play in the contemporary university. Although campus life is often imagined in idyllic terms – as relatively democratic, autonomous, and representative of society's diversity (although not perfectly) – in practice it is marked by incredibly divergent views regarding the ends to which the institution should strive. In the context of deplatforming, one of these existential tensions is unambiguous: freedom of speech as a non-interference principle and precondition for scholarly communities and a desire to minimize potential harm done to those who may be vulnerable.

Second, some of the most well-known incidences of deplatforming – including the present case and some of those previously mentioned – typically feature individuals who inhabit a discursive liminal space. This space is between the merely offensive, on the one hand, and what is actually proscribed by law, on the other. In the middle is a simultaneously vast and opaque discursive territory where it is difficult to draw definitive boundaries of acceptable debate. Situating the university campus in this discursive territory only compounds the difficulty. Since the university is a publicly funded institution, it ought to be subject to existing freedom of expression laws, but it is also in some sense a private institution with its own *particular* mission.[109] On this latter point, it legitimately restricts some forms of expression in accordance with this mission (e.g., through student codes of conduct). This is because there are some compelling prerequisites for an equal and open scholarly environment – namely, something approximating "dignitary safety."[110] Likewise, the concept of merit as expressed in academia provides a rationale for restricting the scope of expression tied to the particular mission of generating truth and knowledge. Again, there is a disjuncture here between freedom of speech understood as a principle of non-interference and the particularities of the university as an institution that might reasonably limit freedom of speech.

This gap – between the existing external legal framework and the particular institutional rules and norms of the university – is precisely what has been exploited in order to generate controversy.[111] Essentially, in a concurrently strategic and ironic fashion, conservative provocateurs have constructed an immanent critique of the university campus by demonstrating that it violates its own values and principles in practice. Therefore, it is no accident that Yiannopoulos (and later Coulter, who also had a scheduled appearance at the University of California cancelled)[112] sought a platform at Berkeley specifically. Wanting to capitalize on the symbolic meaning and significance of that campus – the birthplace of the Free Speech Movement of the 1960s[113] – Yiannopoluos was reported to have created a "Mario Savio Freedom of Speech Award" with which he planned to honour Ann Coulter as its inaugural winner.[114] Savio's son would later call this plan "some kind of sick joke."[115] Although Yiannopolous has now fallen into disrepute and has largely faded from the public eye,[116] his meteoric rise was propelled at least in part by his methodical weaponizing of a perception that has gained impressive traction in the wake of the culture wars: that the university campus is where freedom of speech goes to die.[117] Likewise, Coulter has consistently portrayed campuses as breeding grounds for extremism and the origins of sociocultural tumult, especially at Berkeley, where the " 'Free Speech' movement kicked off the campus riots in 1964."[118] For example, in her book released the year after the University of Ottawa debacle, she writes, "The closest this country has been to the violent mobs of the French Revolution was the upheaval of the anti-war protests and race riots of the late sixties – all led by liberals."[119]

Regarding the efficacy of deplatforming, the present case points to two primary potential pitfalls. First, it might counter-intuitively increase the exposure of harmful ideas. If one believes that mere exposure to Coulter's speech is enough to potentially cause harm – irrespective of context – the publicity generated as a result of the cancellation inordinately multiplied Coulter's reach in Canada. Therefore, one approach to harm reduction might be an effort to limit the total number of individuals exposed to Coulter, and particularly those who might be immediately harmed (based on their identity) or those who are the "unconverted," so to speak. The outcry precipitated by these events might also suggest that Canadians have a reflexive sympathy for those who have had their speech suppressed, irrespective of the content of their speech. Coulter and Levant are undoubtedly media savvy and were only too willing to take advantage of this sympathy in order to generate some incredible media coverage. Of course, this is why attempting to speak on campus is such a potent political strategy for "controversy entrepreneurs" like them. If successful, gaining a platform within a university might provide some symbolic legitimacy because of the associated esteem of the institution. Even if a speaker is not strictly an academic, speaking on campus still connotes legitimacy because it is assumed that access is not extended to just anyone who tries to book a lecture hall. If unsuccessful, denial of a platform can be a vehicle for media exposure and public sympathy, as well as a chance to portray political opponents in an unsavoury light. Given this dynamic, it is possible that minimizing potential controversy and any associated publicity is a potent counter-response, particularly if and when a speaker's explicit strategy is to elicit them. This minimization might preclude explicit protest but it need not be a tacit acceptance of potentially harmful speakers. There are potential alternatives that can simultaneously cultivate an environment of support for those who are likely to be negatively affected *and* grapple with the nuances of a non-ideal strategic environment.[120]

Based on my interviews, protest organizers were not unaware of this dynamic, but were instead hoping that rebuking Coulter would have a performative or declaratory effect. According to the former SFUO executive, the biggest discussion that took place among organizers was whether or not Coulter would "win" if the event were shut down.[121] However, there was a notable divergence among organizers and protestors (as mentioned), and a lack of an explicit protest strategy arguably resulted in a more uncompromising approach in practice. Although one organizer was at the time happy that the protest might have led directly to the decision to cancel the event, they now question whether or not the cancellation may have been a contrived opportunity to generate controversy.[122] In the moment, though, organizers experienced a "general sense of victory," despite not being able to properly convey that it was Coulter who ultimately cancelled the event.[123] However, it is hard to reconcile this optimism with an overwhelmingly (and perhaps predictable) negative media portrayal.[124]

Second, and more significantly, deplatforming risks providing unearned moral and intellectual legitimacy. This strategic dynamic was particularly evident in the Coulter case because of her already existing profile and reach, but also because there are long-standing critiques of contemporary university campuses that further amplified her claims.[125] In this latter sense, then, she was hypothesis testing by potentially appearing on campus. Essentially, there is a popular perception that universities are an inhospitable place for conservatives, and her inability to speak merely confirmed this perception. This particular strategy on the part of Coulter is not surprising. More compelling, however, is the degree to which Coulter and others have done two simultaneous but largely irreconcilable things: systematically devaluing the virtue of victimhood while portraying *themselves* as a virtuous victim. In the inevitable stream of post-cancellation media engagements and subsequent news and opinion pieces, Coulter was given ample space to portray herself as a victim and contemporary university campuses as intolerant. For example, in response to the letter from Houle, Coulter claimed that "he is guilty of promoting hatred against an identifiable group: conservatives."[126] This accords with some of her previous writing and public statements. Tellingly, her book from 2008 begins with this line: "Liberals always have to be the victims, particularly when they are oppressing others."[127]

But how does someone who is clearly *not* a marginal individual by any means claim to be a victim and garner an impressive amount of coverage and sympathy? At least part of this puzzle is the degree to which liberal democratic societies generate a reflexive sympathy for those who might have their speech suppressed, irrespective of its content. Additionally, the media has an innate stake in freedom of speech as a principle and might therefore have a predilection for portraying the issue in more categorical terms. But the response to Coulter's deplatforming might also be read more symptomatically to highlight the ways in which her claims can be understood as a deliberate obfuscation of victimhood in order to garner political capital. Alyson M. Cole refers to this phenomenon as an "inversion" that "nurtur[es] a general hostility to all claims of victimization, while at the same time elevating an impossibly pure archetype of True Victimhood."[128] While this might seem rational or strategic from Coulter's perspective as a pundit consistently on the front lines of the culture wars, it is still striking in its irony:

> As the Left desperately struggles to disengage from "victim politics," the Right jockeys to carve out a space within it. While conservative critics deem victimism to be a pervasive threat and call to restrain victims, they nevertheless become in effect practitioners of victim politics by devising and promoting new groups of victims.[129]

Despite Cole diagnosing this dynamic in contemporary American politics more broadly, she notes, curiously, that the university campus looms large in the discourses that invert victimhood.[130] Thus, one might add conservatives on campus to this list of new victims.

In a similar tone, Rebecca Stringer argues that contemporary politics has been marked by a collective eschewal of the identity category of "victim," a move intimately tied to notions of self-sufficiency that form the core of neoliberal discourse and politics.[131] For her, this represents not the disappearance of the category of victim but its *reversal*, by altering "the perception of who can and cannot be seen as a real and legitimate victim."[132] This is a fitting description of Coulter's claims, as she so clearly "mirrored" the discourse of her detractors, hoping to shore up her own legitimacy as a potential victim while portraying them as serious threats to the vitality of campus (and even society).[133] The point, then, is that deplatforming might have a counter-intuitive effect for reasons completely detached from the moral concern one has for those most negatively affected by speech. It risks the potential of solidifying already existing perceptions on two fronts: that well-intentioned and legitimate invocations of victimhood on campus are merely cynical power plays, and that supposed violations of freedom of speech are a more fundamental threat to a liberal democratic society (rather than harmful speech itself).

This places protestors in an unsavoury double bind. Not confronting harmful speech might broadcast to the community the message that members of marginalized groups can be impugned with impunity. It might also demonstrate that the institution prioritizes a commitment to abstract principles like freedom of speech even if disproportionate material harm is a potential result. Confronting harmful speech with protest, though, might reinforce stereotypes about campus communities and amplify speech that ought to be mitigated. Although it is beyond the scope of this chapter to offer specific prescriptions, the present data and analysis suggests that there is a noticeable disjuncture between the theory of deplatforming and the practice of deplatforming. Whereas the former may be informed by sound theoretical and philosophical justifications, the latter is prone to unintended consequences. Therefore, deplatforming may not be as effective as is typically assumed. This is particularly the case when its targets are within the liminal space discussed earlier – between merely offensive speech and potentially illegal speech – but it is likely that the tactic becomes more effective the closer a speaker is to the latter end of that spectrum. In any case, considering these unintended consequences, deplatforming is a tactic that should not be expected to tend towards its intended effect in the absence of extremity (i.e., *prima facie* violations of law).

Although deplatforming has been a relatively frequent occurrence on university campuses since at least the 1960s, the practice and its associated justifications have become the focus of much contemporary debate.[134] Rather than assessing its legitimacy primarily based upon theoretical and philosophical justifications, I think practical considerations ought to be equally considered and weighed. Perhaps a more fruitful measure of deplatforming's effectiveness, then, is the degree to which it isolates and/or reduces support for *ideas*, rather than the degree to which it isolates and/or reduces support for *individuals*.[135] Importantly, while harmful individuals may be denied a platform in a particular instance, their harmful ideas are still free to circulate. This strategic calculation necessarily includes thinking through any potential unintended consequences and making difficult strategic decisions in a non-ideal environment. Ultimately, decision making that includes these practical and strategic considerations would be beneficial on multiple fronts: reducing exposure to harmful ideas and hopefully mitigating harm itself, conserving the time and resources of university administrations that are often ill-equipped to weather such controversies, and attenuating the popular misconception that universities are somehow destroying freedom of speech.

NOTES

1 Ellen Schrecker, *The Lost Soul of Higher Education: Corporatization, the Assault on Academic Freedom, and the End of the American University* (New York: New Press, 2010), 122. See also "Free Speech under Attack," *CBC News: The National*, 17 April 2017, YouTube video, 15:22, https://www.youtube.com/watch?v=k5g9AlCQFaM.

2 Joe Friesen, "Ontario Colleges Adopt Single Free-Speech Policy as Universities Rush to Meet Deadline," *Globe and Mail*, 16 December 2018, https://www.theglobeandmail.com/canada/article-ontario-universities-scramble-to-release-common-free-speech-policy/; Emma Graney, "UCP Prepares to Roll Out Ford-Flavoured Post-Secondary Changes in Alberta," *Edmonton Journal*, 6 May 2019, https://edmontonjournal.com/news/politics/ucp-prepares-to-roll-out-ford-flavoured-post-secondary-changes-in-alberta.

3 The university "is the ultimate mental gymnasium, full of advanced equipment, skilled trainers, and therapists standing by, just in case." Jonathan Haidt and Greg Lukianoff, *The Coddling the American Mind: How Good and Bad Ideas Are Setting Up a Generation for Failure* (New York: Penguin, 2018), 9.

4 As Schrecker notes, "campuses are among the last few places where it is still possible to deal with complicated ideas or entertain unorthodox opinions." Schrecker, *The Lost Soul of Higher Education*, 4.

5 Evan Smith, "50 Years of Snowflakes," *Research Professional*, 4 November 2018, https://www.researchresearch.com/news/article/?articleId=1378065.

6 For a brief FAQ and additional context, see National Union of Students, "Implementing 'No Platform' policies," 24 March 2015, https://www.nusconnect.org.uk/resources/implementing-no-platform-policies; National Union of Students, "NUS' No Platform Policy," 13 February 2017, https://www.nusconnect.org.uk/resources/nus-no-platform-policy-f22f.

7 Evan Smith, "45 Years On: The History and Continuing Importance of 'No Platform,'" *New Socialist*, 18 April 2019, https://newsocialist.org.uk/45-years-history-and-continuing-importance-no-platform/.

8 Taylor Gee, "How the Middlebury Riot Really Went Down," *Politico*, 28 May 2017, https://www.politico.com/magazine/story/2017/05/28/how-donald-trump-caused-the-middlebury-melee-215195.

9 Stephanie Saul, "Dozens of Middlebury Students Are Disciplined for Charles Murray Protest," *New York Times*, 24 May 2017, https://www.nytimes.com/2017/05/24/us/middlebury-college-charles-murray-bell-curve.html.

10 Thomas Fuller and Christopher Mele, "Berkeley Cancels Milo Yiannopoulos Speech, and Donald Trump Tweets Outrage," *New York Times*, 1 February 2017, https://www.nytimes.com/2017/02/01/us/uc-berkeley-milo-yiannopoulos-protest.html.

11 Monique O. Madan, "UF Paid Richard Spencer's $300K Security Fees – By Mistake. Now They Want the Money Back," *Miami Herald*, 29 January 2018, https://www.miamiherald.com/news/state/florida/article197316814.html.

12 Anemona Hartocollis, "University of Florida Braces for Richard Spencer," *New York Times*, 17 October 2017, https://www.nytimes.com/2017/10/17/us/florida-richard-spencer.html.

13 Laura Booth, "Faith Goldy Talk at Wilfrid Laurier University Shut Down by Fire Alarm after Protest," *Toronto Star*, 20 March 2018, https://www.thestar.com/news/canada/2018/03/20/faith-goldy-talk-at-wilfrid-laurier-university-shut-down-by-fire-alarm-after-protest.html.

14 Lauren Malyk, "Protesters Disrupt Ezra Levant Talk at Ryerson," *Ryersonian*, 23 March 2017, https://ryersonian.ca/protesters-disrupt-ezra-levant-talk-at-ryerson/.

15 Christopher Blanchette, "Ezra Levant Event Relocated Due to Security Concerns," *Ryersonian*, 22 March 2017, https://ryersonian.ca/ezra-levant-event-relocated-due-to-security-concerns/.

16 Jack Hauen, "Facing Pushback, Ryerson University Cancels Panel Discussion on Campus Free Speech," *National Post*, 16 August 2017, https://nationalpost.com/news/canada/facing-pushback-ryerson-cancels-panel-discussion-on-campus-free-speech.

17 In this sense, "academia's squeaky wheels are the canaries in the coal mine, perched at the edge of a slippery slope." Likewise, controversial speakers from outside the university community are increasingly testing these boundaries. Schrecker, *The Lost Soul of Higher Education*, 39.

18 Matthew Pearson, "Host U of O Draws Ire of U.S. Firebrand," *Ottawa Citizen*, 23 March 2010, http://www.ottawacitizen.com/story_print.html?id=2714542.

19 "Ann Coulter Interview," *Skavlan*, 8 October 2018, YouTube video, 13:57, https://www.youtube.com/watch?v=hxTtjGamJtI; "Zero Tolerance: Ann Coulter Interview," *Frontline PBS*, 22 October 2019, YouTube video, 50:19, https://www

.youtube.com/watch?v=VXOFHr6tGMQ. Coulter begins speaking about Trump at 8:15 in the second video.

20 Quint Forgey, "Trump Fires Back at 'Wacky Nut Job' Ann Coulter," *Politico*, 9 March 2019, https://www.politico.com/story/2019/03/09/trump-ann-coulter-1214720.

21 Zev Singer and Kristy Nease, " 'Free Speech in Canada Leaves Much to Be Desired': Ann Coulter after Event Cancellation," *National Post*, 23 March 2010, https://nationalpost.com/news/free-speech-in-canada-leaves-much-to-be-desired-ann-coulter-after-event-cancellation. She has, however, catalyzed much protest. See, for example, Jennifer Amsler, "Coulter Avoids Pie in the Face," *Arizona Daily Wildcat*, 22 October 2004, https://wc.arizona.edu/papers/98/44/01_1.html.

22 Ian Austen, "Free Speech Debated after Ann Coulter Cancels Appearance," *New York Times*, 24 March 2010, https://www.nytimes.com/2010/03/25/world/americas/25coulter.html; Andrew Cohen, "Even Canadians Can't Tolerate Ann Coulter," *Vanity Fair*, 24 March 2010, https://www.vanityfair.com/news/2010/03/ann-coulter-unwelcomed-guest.

23 One interviewee was privy to these communications between the SFUO and administration. (Please note: the names of interviewees have been withheld in this chapter in order to respect their desire for anonymity and to mitigate any potential risks associated with identification.)

24 Personal interview with protest organizer, 11 December 2018.

25 Then president of the SFUO, Seamus Wolfe, was quoted as saying, "Anyone that consistently promotes hatred of violence towards any individual or group of people should not be permitted to use a public institution, like a university, as a soapbox for that hatred and promotion of violence." Jennifer Pagliaro, "Ann Coulter Went Home," *Maclean's*, 23 March 2010, https://www.macleans.ca/education/uniandcollege/coulters-u-of-o-event-canceled/.

26 Pearson, "Host U of O Draws Ire of U.S. Firebrand."

27 The operative passage of the email reads, in part: "I therefore encourage you to educate yourself, if need be, as to what is acceptable in Canada and to do so before your planned visit here ... I therefore ask you, while you are a guest on our campus, to weigh your words with respect and civility in mind. There is a strong tradition in Canada, including at this University, of restraint, respect and consideration in expressing even provocative and controversial opinions and urge you to respect that Canadian tradition while on our campus."

28 In a letter dated 16 March 2010, Wolfe directly wrote to President Rock on behalf of the SFUO executive to thank him. It read, in part: "While we may disagree in our method of response to such a situation, it is heartening to know that our values of a positive community are shared. I trust that Ms. Coulter's event will proceed with its usual passion and vitriol, and I do not doubt that it will be received with antagonism by many students who oppose her paradigm of intolerance. As ever, we appreciate your collaboration and support."

29   Bruce Cheadle, "Watch Your Mouth, Ann Coulter Warned for Canadian Tour,"
     Toronto Star, 22 March 2010, https://www.thestar.com/news/canada/2010/03/22
     /watch_your_mouth_ann_coulter_warned_for_canadian_tour.htm. Internal
     correspondence gleaned from ATI requests made matters worse by highlighting
     President Rock's unfiltered opinion of Coulter. See "Editorial: Allan Rock's
     Faulty Concepts of Free Speech," *National Post*, 2 July 2010, https://nationalpost
     .com/full-comment/editorial-allan-rocks-faulty-concept-of-free-speech. On 18
     March, he wrote directly to Houle to suggest that while the university should not
     obstruct the event in any way, security costs ought to be the responsibility of the
     organizers and Houle (as provost) ought to convey applicable freedom of expres-
     sion laws in Canada. He prefaced his advice with the following: "Ann Coulter is
     a mean-spirited, small-minded, foul-mouthed poltroon. She is 'the loud mouth
     that bespeaks the vacant mind.' She is an ill-informed and deeply offensive shill
     for a profoundly shallow and ignorant view of the world. She is a malignancy
     on the body politic. She is a disgrace to the broadcasting industry and a leading
     example of the dramatic decline in the quality of public discourse in recent times.
     D'accord."
30   ATI data reveals that the University of Ottawa kept an inventory of dozens of
     print and TV media coverage, which was almost exclusively and overwhelmingly
     negative. ATI data also reveals that the University of Ottawa's Advancement
     Services kept records related to negative responses from alumni. Many of these
     responses mention that they will no longer consider donating because of the
     scandal.
31   Canadian Association of University Teachers, letter to Vice-President Academic
     and Provost Francoise Houle, 22 March 2010, https://www.caut.ca/docs/default
     -document-library/ottawau_coulter.pdf?sfvrsn=0.
32   Randy Richmond, "Firebrand Singes Muslim," *London Free Press*, 23 March 2010,
     https://web.archive.org/web/20100328222923/http://www.lfpress.com/news
     /london/2010/03/22/13322401.html.
33   She was also protested in Calgary, but it was mostly peaceful. See "Coulter in Cal-
     gary," *Calgary Herald*, 29 March 2010, YouTube video, 2:11, https://www.youtube
     .com/watch?v=bplbcqZZcEk.
34   John Baglow, "A Different View on the Coulter File," *National Post*, 25 March
     2010, https://nationalpost.com/full-comment/john-baglow-a-different-view
     -on-the-coulter-file.
35   University of Ottawa, Protection Services, Incident Reports, 23 March 2010.
36   Once the letter was sent, they wanted to "get as many of our people in the room
     as possible" because they could ask challenging questions, according to the for-
     mer SFUO executive. Personal interviews with protest organizers, 25 October
     2018 and 11 December 2018. See also "Protest Cancels Ann Coulter Speech in
     Ottawa," Associated Press, 24 March 2010, YouTube video, 1:55, https://www
     .youtube.com/watch?v=mOP_kbU7XxA.

37 They described it as needing to "sneak" people through the online registration process. Personal interview with former SFUO executive, 25 October 2018.

38 University of Ottawa, Protection Services, Incident Reports, 23 March 2010.

39 Kady O'Malley, "Ann Coulter's Adventures in Ottawa: So, What Happened Last Night?" *CBC News*, 24 March 2010, https://web.archive.org/web /20100327123602/http://www.cbc.ca/politics/insidepolitics/2010/03/ann -coulters-adventures-in-ottawa-so-what-really-happened-last-night.html.

40 They explained that "campus security never told her that [it was unsafe]" and that the SFUO enjoyed "a very good relationship with [Protection Services]." Personal interview with former SFUO executive, 25 October 2018.

41 Internal reports also noted that Resnick was alone on site only to assess the situation. He had told Protection Services personnel that if he had arrived *with* Coulter he would have immediately turned around after seeing the protest numbers.

42 "Coulter Protesters Attack Free Speech: Levant," *CTV News Calgary*, 24 March 2010, https://web.archive.org/web/20120201033459/http://calgary.ctv.ca/servlet /an/local/CTVNews/20100324/coulter_cancellation_100324/20100324 /?hub=CalgaryHome.

43 All three of them said that deplatforming Coulter was the explicit goal, although one noted that at the protest itself "some people clearly wanted to shut it down and others just wanted to protest." Personal interviews with protest organizers, 17 December 2018, 22 November 2018, and 11 December 2018.

44 Theirs was essentially disruption but not cancellation, due to strategic concerns. Personal interview with former SFUO executive, 25 October 2018

45 Singer and Nease, "'Free Speech in Canada Leaves Much to Be Desired.'"

46 Pagliaro, "Ann Coulter Went Home."

47 The former SFUO executive described the Houle email as "100% ... directly from the SFUO" and a "compromise" that they "weren't unhappy with." Personal interview, 25 October 2018.

48 In their words, "He brought with him an approach to conflict resolution that was quite diplomatic," and thus the Houle letter could be reasonably interpreted as "an attempt by the administration to demonstrate to students that they were listening." Personal interview with protest organizer, 11 December 2018. The former SFUO executive also noted the close nature of their relationship, emphasizing that they understood each other, in essence, because of Rock's political pragmatism. Personal interview, 25 October 2018.

49 Michael Rowe, "Sorry Ann Coulter, Canada's Just Not That into You," *Huffington Post*, 25 May 2010, https://www.huffpost.com/entry/sorry-ann-coulter -canadas_b_513865.

50 Dean Beeby, "Plan to Invite Coulter Back Thwarted by University of Ottawa Advisers," *Globe and Mail*, 30 June 2010, https://beta.theglobeandmail.com/news /national/plan-to-invite-coulter-back-thwarted-by-university-of-ottawa-advisers /article4323285/.

51 James L. Turk, "Introduction," in *Academic Freedom in Conflict: The Struggle over Free Speech Rights in the University*, ed. James L. Turk (Toronto: Lorimer, 2014), 11.

52 Schrecker, *The Lost Soul of Higher Education*, 10.

53 Stanley Fish, *Versions of Academic Freedom: From Professionalism to Revolution* (Chicago: University of Chicago Press, 2014), xi.

54 Joan W. Scott's recent writing is particularly instructive on this point: "The principle of academic freedom was not, as critics sometimes describe it, an endorsement of the idea that in the university anything goes. The call for faculty autonomy rested on the guarantee of quality provided by disciplinary bodies whose role is to establish and implement norms and standards and so to certify their members' professional competence." Joan W. Scott, *Knowledge, Power, and Academic Freedom* (New York: Columbia University Press, 2019), 48.

55 Haidt and Lukianoff refer to this process of meritocratic peer review as "institutionalized disconfirmation." See *The Coddling of the American Mind*, 109.

56 As one of the protest organizers put it, "Freedom of speech doesn't mean freedom from repercussions from that speech." Personal interview, 22 November 2018.

57 Bryan W. Van Norden, "The Ignorant Do Not Have a Right to an Audience," *New York Times*, 25 June 2018, https://www.nytimes.com/2018/06/25/opinion/free-speech-just-access.html.

58 For a brief summary of some of these works, see Catherine A. MacKinnon, "Foreword," in *Speech & Harm: Controversies over Free Speech*, edited by Ishani Maitra and Mary Kate McGowan (Oxford: Oxford University Press, 2012), vi–xviii.

59 Mary Kate McGowan, *Just Words: On Speech and Hidden Harm* (New York: Oxford University Press, 2019).

60 The concept of epistemic injustice is an apt example. See Ian James Kidd, José Medina, and Gaile Pohlhaus Jr., *The Routledge Handbook of Epistemic Injustice* (London: Routledge, 2017).

61 Another way to think about this is that some problems may be *structural* in nature, making assignments of *individual* responsibilities difficult, if not counterproductive. See Iris Marion Young, "Responsibility and Global Justice: A Social Connection Model," *Social Philosophy and Policy* 23, no. 1 (2006): 102–30; Eduardo Bonilla-Silva, *Racism without Racists: Color-Blind Racism and the Persistence of Racial Inequality in the United States* (Lanham, MD: Rowman and Littlefield, 2006).

62 Brenda Cossman and Shannon Bell, "Introduction," in *Bad Attitudes on Trial: Pornography, Feminism, and the Butler Decision*, ed. Brenda Cossman, Shannon Bell, Lise Gotell, and Becki L. Ross, 3–47 (Toronto: University of Toronto Press, 1997), 7. For perhaps the best volume capturing the various feminist approaches to the topic, see Drucilla Cornell, *Feminism and Pornography* (New York: Oxford University Press, 2000).

63 Catharine A. MacKinnon, *Only Words* (Cambridge, MA: Harvard University Press, 1993), 15.

64 MacKinnon believes that (heterosexual male) consumers of pornography face the inevitability of deeply imbibing and then recreating the sexual fantasies depicted: "Sooner or later, in one way or another, the consumers want to live out the pornography further in three dimensions. Sooner or later, in one way or another, they do" (19).

65 Andrea Dworkin, for example, argues that "male power is the raison d'etre of pornography; the degradation of the female is the means of achieving this power." Andrea Dworkin, *Pornography: Men Possessing Women* (New York: Perigee Books, 1981), 25. See also Michelle J. Anderson, "Silencing Women's Speech," in *The Price We Pay: The Case against Racist Speech, Hate Propaganda, and Pornography*, ed. Laura J. Lederer and Richard Delgado (New York: Hill and Wang, 1995), 123. For more recent scholarship that casts a critical eye on the potentially harmful effects of pornography, see McGowan, *Just Words*. For a summary and analysis of some of the most prominent arguments against pornography, see Amanda Cawston, "The Feminist Case against Pornography: A Review and Re-evaluation," *Inquiry: An Interdisciplinary Journal of Philosophy* 62, no. 6 (2019): 624–58.

66 Jeremy Waldron, *The Harm in Hate Speech* (Cambridge, MA: Harvard University Press, 2012), 4–5.

67 Ibid., 47.

68 Ibid., 100.

69 Richard Delgado and Jean Stefancic, *Understanding Words That Wound* (Boulder, CO: Westview Press, 2012), 13–14.

70 Mari J. Matsuda covers the range of consequences that would leave one deeply distrustful: "Victims are restricted in their personal freedom. To avoid receiving hate messages, victims have to quit jobs, forgo education, leave their homes, avoid certain public places, curtail their own exercise of speech rights, and otherwise modify their behavior and demeanor." Mari J. Matsuda, "Public Response to Hate Speech: Considering the Victim's Story," in *Words That Wound: Critical Race Theory, Assaultive Speech, and the First Amendment*, ed. Mari J. Matsuda, Charles R. Lawrence III, Richard Delgado, and Kimberlé Williams Crenshaw (Boulder, CO: Westview Press, 1993), 24.

71 Richard Delgado, "Words That Wound: A Tort Action for Racial Insults, Epithets, and Name Calling," in *Words That Wound: Critical Race Theory, Assaultive Speech, and the First Amendment*, ed. Mari J. Matsuda, Charles R. Lawrence III, Richard Delgado, and Kimberlé Williams Crenshaw (Boulder, CO: Westview Press, 1993), 91.

72 Mari J. Matsuda, "Public Response to Hate Speech: Considering the Victim's Story," *Michigan Law Review* 87, no. 8 (1989): 2323.

73 These (un)conscious associations can have substantial impacts upon discourse, especially if they catalyze prejudicial credibility deficits. See, for example,

Miranda Fricker, *Epistemic Injustice: Power and the Ethics of Knowing* (New York: Oxford University Press, 2007).

74 Delgado, "Words That Wound," 93; Richard Delgado and Jean Stefancic, *Must We Defend Nazis? Hate Speech, Pornography, and the New First Amendment* (New York: New York University Press, 1997), 8–9.

75 Alexander Tsesis, *Destructive Messages: How Hate Speech Paves the Way for Harmful Social Movements* (New York: New York University Press, 2002).

76 Personal interview with protest organizer, 11 December 2018.

77 Personal interview with protest organizer, 17 December 2018.

78 Ibid.

79 Ibid. As she recounted, "I do remember feeling like, 'Thank God that I don't have to go at the forefront and try to shut this thing down.' I don't think it would have worked so well had there not been so many white people involved."

80 Personal interview with protest organizer, 22 November 2018.

81 Associated Press, "Protest Cancels Ann Coulter Speech in Ottawa.".

82 Joseph G. Lehman, "The Overton Window and Free Speech," *Impact: The Magazine of the Mackinac Center for Public Policy*, 2 October 2018, https://www.mackinac.org/25904.

83 Deborah E. Lipstadt, *History on Trial: My Day in Court with David Irving* (New York: HarperCollins, 2005), 18.

84 Ibid., 17.

85 She writes: "[Holocaust deniers] are using [freedom of speech] not as a shield, as it was intended by the Constitution, but as a sword. There is a qualitative difference between barring someone's right to speech and providing him or her with a platform from which to deliver a message." Deborah E. Lipstadt, *Denying the Holocaust: The Growing Assault on Truth and Memory* (New York: Free Press, 1993), 26.

86 Nesrine Malik, "The Myth of the Free Speech Crisis," *The Guardian*, 3 September 2019, https://www.theguardian.com/world/2019/sep/03/the-myth-of-the-free-speech-crisis; Jasmine Zine, "The Alt-Right and the Weaponization of Free Speech on Campus," *Academic Matters*, 21 November 2018, https://academicmatters.ca/the-alt-right-and-the-weaponization-of-free-speech-on-campus/; Kate Manne and Jason Stanley, "When Free Speech Becomes a Political Weapon," *Chronicle of Higher Education*, 13 November 2015, https://www.chronicle.com/article/When-Free-Speech-Becomes-a/234207.

87 For example, Mark Bray explicitly rejects the "marketplace of ideas" analogy: "Historically, fascist and fascistic ideas have thrived in open debate. Sometimes public discourse has been sufficient to squash fascism. But sometimes it hasn't been – which is why anti-fascists refuse to pin their hopes for the freedom and security of humanity on processes of public discourse that have already shown themselves to be fallible." Mark Bray, *Antifa: The Anti-fascist Handbook* (New York: Melville House, 2017), 147–8.

88 This optimism forms a consistent thread in normative liberal theory, often expressed as a broader optimism invested in pluralism and tolerance. For an example of this ("the liberal wager"), see Stephen L. Newman, "Finding the Harm in Hate Speech: An Argument against Censorship," *Canadian Journal of Political Science* 50, no. 3 (2017): 695.

89 For Foucault, there is no objective truth in the sense that it represents a shared core or foundation that can be vindicated by an appeal to universal standards. What constitutes truth, then, is at least a partial function of politics. What becomes "true" may have a traceable logic or justification but nonetheless necessitates an examination of why one discourse became intelligible as opposed to another; in other words, the requisite conditions for intelligibility, acceptability, and propagation, or what Foucault calls "a nexus of knowledge-power." Michel Foucault, *The Politics of Truth*, ed. Sylvère Lotringer (Los Angeles: Semiotext(e), 2007), 61.

90 For an unsympathetic view of this lineage, see Ronald Beiner, *Dangerous Minds: Nietzsche, Heidegger, and the Return of the Far Right* (Philadelphia: University of Pennsylvania Press, 2018), 7. Other theoretical or philosophical traditions that feature amalgams of these ideas include critical race theory, critical discourse analysis, and diverse engagements with Antonio Gramsci.

91 For Bray (in contradistinction to Mill), progressive advances in society are not a result of "a rational process of analysis," but come about "through the ongoing struggle of competing interests, which are perpetually shaped by shifting economic and social factors." Likewise, on university campuses, progressive advances are the accumulation of material agitation. In this sense, the university is not a neutral institution and knowledge production is inherently political. Bray, *Antifa*, 160, 163–5.

92 Jason Stanley, *How Fascism Works* (New York: Random House, 2018), 68–9.

93 This was precisely what Rock had argued in the email to Houle referenced earlier.

94 Susan Estrich, *Soulless: Ann Coulter and the Right-Wing Church of Hate* (New York: Regan, 2006), 40.

95 "What she succeeds in doing is dividing us against each other, polarizing us whether we want to be polarized or not (and often we do not), playing to the lowest common denominator, and not only moving the ideological line to the right, but moving it downward in the process." Ibid., 6.

96 Personal interview with protest organizer, 18 December 2018.

97 Personal interview with protest organizer, 11 December 2018.

98 For an excellent overview of the history of the concept in Western political theory and philosophy, see Jacob Mchangama, "Clear and Present Danger: A History of Free Speech," *Blog of the American Philosophical Association*, 30 January 2019, https://blog.apaonline.org/2019/01/30/clear-and-present-danger-podcast-philosophy-outside-academia/.

99 Richard Moon, *The Constitutional Protection of Freedom of Expression* (Toronto: University of Toronto Press, 2000), 9–12.

100 John Stuart Mill, *On Liberty, Utilitarianism and Other Essays*, ed. Mark Philp and
     Frederick Rosen (Oxford: Oxford University Press, 2015).

101 Ibid., 19.

102 Ibid., 36–7.

103 For a review and analysis of some relevant arguments, see Eric Heinze,
     "No-Platforming and Safe Spaces: Should Universities Censor More (or Less)
     Speech than the Law Requires?," *Croatian Political Science Review* 55, no. 4
     (2018): 79–108.

104 There are, however, nuanced challenges that take a "Millian" approach more on
     its own terms, rather than presenting an alternative theoretical approach. See, for
     example, Bennett (in this volume).

105 This was evident in the responses from major Canadian newspapers, although
     one should note that the fourth estate is particularly sensitive to issues related to
     freedom of expression. For a brief summary of some of the most important re-
     sponses, see Carson Jerema, "Ann Coulter: Canadian Free Speech Hero,"
     Maclean's, 25 March 2010, https://www.macleans.ca/education/uniandcollege
     /ann-coulter-canadian-free-speech-hero/.

106 In one protest organizer's words, "I don't think we can tie our activism to what is
     and isn't legal." Personal interview, 22 November 2018.

107 Personal interview with protest organizer, 11 December 2018.

108 Ibid.

109 The potential application of the *Charter* on campus is still indeterminate. For a
     classic case that found that universities are not legally considered part of the gov-
     ernment, see *McKinney v University of Guelph*, [1990] 3 SCR 229.

110 Sigal Ben-Porath, *Free Speech on Campus* (Philadelphia: University of Pennsylva-
     nia Press, 2017), 62.

111 Pearl Eliadis has previously used the term "controversy entrepreneur" to refer
     to pundits who perform this edgework. I think this is an apt description. Pearl
     Eliadis, "The Controversy Entrepreneurs," *Maisonneuve*, 20 August 2009, https://
     maisonneuve.org/article/2009/08/20/controversy-entrepreneurs/. See also Rich-
     ard Moon, "The Attack on Human Rights Commissions and the Corruption of
     Public Discourse," *Saskatchewan Law Review*, no. 73 (2011): 93–129.

112 Merrit Kennedy, "After Ann Coulter Speech Cancellation, Protesters Rally at
     Berkeley," *Two-Way*, National Public Radio, 27 April 2017, https://www.npr
     .org/sections/thetwo-way/2017/04/27/525898344/after-ann-coulter-speech
     -cancellation-protesters-rally-at-berkeley.

113 Robert Cohen, "What Might Mario Savio Have Said about the Milo Protest at
     Berkeley?" *The Nation*, 7 February 2017, https://www.thenation.com/article
     /what-might-mario-savio-have-said-about-the-milo-protest-at-berkeley/.

114 Savio was "the Berkeley rebellion's most famous voice and most prominent
     leader." Robert Cohen, *Freedom's Orator: Mario Savio and the Radical Legacy of
     the 1960s* (New York: Oxford University Press, 2009), 82.

115   William Wan, "Milo's Appearance at Berkeley Led to Riots. He Vows to Return This Fall for a Week-Long Free-Speech Event," *Washington Post*, 26 April 2017, https://www.washingtonpost.com/news/grade-point/wp/2017/04/26/milos-appearance-at-berkeley-led-to-riots-he-vows-to-return-this-fall-for-a-week-long-free-speech-event/?utm_term=.4bd9e03d497c.

116   Charlie May, "The Fall of Milo: Breitbart's Former Star Is Now Hawking Supplements on Infowars," *Salon*, 21 February 2018, https://www.salon.com/2018/02/21/the-fall-of-milo-breitbarts-former-star-is-now-hawking-supplements-on-infowars/.

117   Ryan Holiday, "I Helped Create the Milo Trolling Playbook. You Should Stop Playing Right Into It," *The Observer*, 7 February 2017, https://observer.com/2017/02/i-helped-create-the-milo-trolling-playbook-you-should-stop-playing-right-into-it/.

118   Ann Coulter, *Demonic: How the Liberal Mob Is Endangering America* (New York: Crown Forum, 2011), 158.

119   Ibid., 157.

120   For a more contemporary and thoughtful discussion of this strategic environment, see Shannon Dea, "Free Speech and the Battle for the University," *Academic Matters*, 21 November 2018, https://academicmatters.ca/free-speech-and-the-battle-for-the-university/.

121   The strategy that was settled on, at least at the SFUO level, was to be "a bit obnoxious" at the event itself, to make the opposition "clear," but not to obstruct to a level that would allow Coulter to become a martyr in the public eye. Personal interview with former SFUO executive, 25 October 2018.

122   In their words, "If they could come up with a somewhat sensationalized explanation as to why it was cancelled, and if they have a monopoly over mainstream media airspace in order to shape the narrative of why it was cancelled and demonize protestors in the process, then it may also have been cancelled for opportunistic purposes." Personal interview with protest organizer, 11 December 2018.

123   Personal interview with former SFUO executive, 25 October 2018.

124   Jerema, "Ann Coulter: Canadian Free Speech Hero."

125   See, for example, Joe Friesen, "Conservatives' On-Campus Flyers Maligning 'Left-Wing' Professors Anger Academics, Faculty Representatives," *Globe and Mail*, 12 September 2019, https://www.theglobeandmail.com/canada/article-conservatives-on-campus-flyers-maligning-left-wing-professors-anger/.

126   Pearson, "Host U of O Draws Ire of U.S. Firebrand."

127   Ann Coulter, *Guilty: Liberal "Victims" and Their Assault on America* (New York: Crown Forum, 2008), 1.

128   Alyson M. Cole, *The Cult of True Victimhood: From the War on Welfare to the War on Terror* (Stanford, CA: Stanford University Press, 2007), 22.

129   Ibid., 4.

130   Ibid., 24.

131 Rebecca Stringer, *Knowing Victims: Feminism, Agency and Victim Politics in Neo-liberal Times* (New York: Routledge, 2014), 8.

132 Ibid., 11.

133 Ibid., 38.

134 Interestingly, the former SFUO executive claimed that "we [the organizers] didn't have that word, 'deplatform,' " at the time of the protest. At the very least, it hadn't yet fully entered the lexicon of contemporary political contestation. Personal interview with former SFUO executive, 25 October 2018.

135 Sometimes there is an overestimation of the effectiveness of deplatforming associated with this conflation. See, for example, Zack Beauchamp, "Milo Yiannopoulos's Collapse Shows That No-Platforming Can Work," *Vox*, 5 December 2018, https://www.vox.com/policy-and-politics/2018/12/5/18125507/milo-yiannopoulos-debt-no-platform; Taylor Link, "Milo Yiannopoulos Attacks His Fans for Failing to Support Him Emotionally and Financially," *Salon*, 26 August 2018, https://www.salon.com/2018/08/26/milo-yiannopoulos-attacks-his-fans-for-failing-to-support-him-emotionally-and-financially/; Shree Paradkar, "Giving Maxime Bernier a Platform Legitimizes His Dangerous Ideas," *Toronto Star*, 25 September 2019, https://www.thestar.com/opinion/star-columnists/2019/09/25/giving-maxime-bernier-a-platform-legitimizes-his-dangerous-ideas.html.

Selected Bibliography

Alexander, Basil S. "Exploring a More Independent Freedom of Peaceful Assembly in Canada." *Western Journal of Legal Studies* 8, no. 1 (2018): 1–18.

Alexander, Larry. "Compelled Speech." *Constitutional Commentary* 23, no. 1 (2006): 147–61.

Anderson, Michelle J. "Silencing Women's Speech." In *The Price We Pay: The Case against Racist Speech, Hate Propaganda, and Pornography*, edited by Laura J. Lederer and Richard Delgado. New York: Hill and Wang, 1995.

Appiah, Kwame Anthony. "What's Wrong with Defamation of Religion?" In *The Content and Context of Hate Speech: Rethinking Regulation and Responses*, edited by Michael Herz and Peter Molnar. Cambridge: Cambridge University Press, 2012.

Bagdikian, Ben. *The Media Monopoly*. Boston: Beacon Press, 1992.

Bakshy, E., S. Messing, and L.A. Adamic. "Exposure to Ideologically Diverse News and Opinion on Facebook." *Science* 348, no. 6239 (2015): 1130–3.

Bambauer, Derek E. "Against Jawboning." *Minnesota Law Review* 100 (2015): 51–128.

Barry, Ann Marie. *Visual Intelligence: Perception, Image, and Manipulation in Visual Communication*. Albany: State University of New York Press, 1997.

Beiner, Ronald. *Dangerous Minds: Nietzsche, Heidegger, and the Return of the Far Right*. Philadelphia: University of Pennsylvania Press, 2018.

Benkler, Yochai, Robert Faris, and Hal Roberts. *Network Propaganda: Manipulation, Disinformation, and Radicalization in American Politics*. Oxford: Oxford University Press, 2018.

Ben-Porath, Sigal. *Free Speech on Campus*. Philadelphia: University of Pennsylvania Press, 2017.

Bercuson, David, Robert Bothwell, and J.L. Granatstein. *Petrified Campus: The Crisis in Canada's Universities*. Toronto: Random House, 1997.

Berger, John. *Ways of Seeing*. London: British Broadcasting Corporation; New York: Penguin, 1977.

Berlin, Isaiah. "Two Concepts of Liberty." In *Liberty: Incorporating Four Essays on Liberty*, edited by Henry Hardy. Oxford: Oxford University Press, 2013.

Berman, Paul, ed. *Debating P.C.: The Controversy over Political Correctness on College Campuses*. New York: Dell, 1992.

Besco, Randy, and Erin Tolley. "Does Everyone Cheer? The Politics of Immigration and Multiculturalism in Canada." In *Federalism and the Welfare State in a Multicultural World*, edited by Elizabeth Goodyear-Grant, Richard Johnston, Will Kymlicka, and John Myles. Montreal: McGill-Queen's University Press, 2018.

Bird, Brian. "The Call in *Carter* to Interpret Freedom of Conscience." *Supreme Court Law Review (2d)* 85, no. 2 (2018): 107–41.

Bleich, Erik. *The Freedom to Be Racist? How the United States and Europe Struggle to Preserve Freedom and Combat Racism*. Oxford: Oxford University Press, 2011.

Bloom, Allan. *The Closing of the American Mind: How Higher Education Has Failed Democracy and Impoverished the Souls of Today's Students*. New York: Simon and Schuster, 2012.

Boussalis, Constantine, and Travis G. Coan. "Text Mining the Signals of Climate Change Doubt." *Global Environmental Change* 36 (2016): 89–100.

Brink, David O. *Mill's Progressive Principles*. Oxford: Oxford University Press, 2013.

Brison, Susan J. "The Autonomy Defense of Free Speech." *Ethics* 108, no. 2 (1998): 312–39.

– "Speech, Harm, and the Mind-Body Problem in First Amendment Jurisprudence." *Legal Theory* 4, no. 1 (1998): 39–61.

Brown, Marvin. "Academic Freedom: The Troubling Present and Questionable Future." In *Pursuing Academic Freedom: "Free and Fearless"?*, edited by Len Findlay and Paul M. Bidwell. Saskatoon: Purich Publishing, 2001.

Brownlee, Jamie. *Academia, Inc.: How Corporatization Is Transforming Canadian Universities*. Halifax: Fernwood Publishing, 2015.

Brulle, R.J., J. Carmichael, and J.C. Jenkins. "Shifting Public Opinion on Climate Change: An Empirical Assessment of Factors Influencing Concern over Climate Change in the U.S., 2002–2010." *Climatic Change* 114, no. 2 (2012): 169–88.

Buckley, William F., Jr. *God and Man at Yale: The Superstitions of "Academic Freedom."* Chicago: Regnery, 1951.

Calvert, Clay. "Hate Speech and Its Harms: A Communication Theory Perspective." *Journal of Communication* 47, no. 1 (1997): 4–19.

Cameron, Jamie. "The Past, Present, and Future of Expressive Freedom under the Charter." *Osgoode Hall Law Journal* 35, no. 1 (1997): 1–74.

Cameron, Jamie, and Bailey Fox. "Toronto's 2018 Municipal Election, Rights of Democratic Participation, and Section 2(b) of the Charter." *Constitutional Forum* 30, no. 1 (2021): 1–18.

Chan, Adrienne S., and Donald Fischer, eds. *The Exchange University: Corporatization of Academic Culture*. Vancouver: UBC Press, 2008.

Chouinard, Stéphanie. "L'impact du Renvoi relatif à la sécession du Québec sur le droit linguistique canadien, ou de la force normative mitigée du principe constitutionnel de protection des minorité." In *Réimaginer le Canada. Vers un État multinational?*, edited by Félix Mathieu and Dave Guénette. Quebec: Presses de l'Université Laval, 2019.

Clarke, Jeremy. "Beyond the Democratic Dialogue, and Towards a Federalist One: Provincial Arguments and Supreme Court Responses in Charter Litigation." *Canadian Journal of Political Science* 39, no. 2 (2006): 293–314.

– "In the Case of *Federalism v. Charter*: The Processes and Outcomes of a Federalist Dialogue." *International Journal of Canadian Studies* 36 (2007): 41–71.

Cohen, Mark. *Censorship in Canadian Literature*. Montreal: McGill-Queen's University Press, 2001.

Cohen, Stanley. *States of Denial: Knowing about Atrocities and Suffering*. Cambridge: Polity, 2001.

Cook, Philip, and Conrad Heilmann. "Two Types of Self-Censorship: Public and Private." *Political Studies* 61, no. 1 (March 2013): 178–96.

Crandall, Erin, and Andrea Lawlor. "Third Party Policy and Electoral Participation after *Harper v. Canada*: A Triumph of Egalitarianism?" In *Policy Change, Courts, and the Canadian Constitution*, edited by Emmett Macfarlane. Toronto: University of Toronto Press, 2018.

Delgado, Richard, and Jean Stefancic. *Understanding Words That Wound*. Boulder, CO: Westview Press. 2012.

Desai, Anuj C. "The Transformation of Statutes into Constitutional Law: How Early Post Office Police Shaped Modern First Amendment Doctrine." *Hastings Law Journal* 58 (2007): 671–727.

Dotson, Kristie. "Tracking Epistemic Violence, Tracking Practices of Silencing." *Hypatia* 26, no. 2 (Spring 2011): 236–57.

D'Souza, Tanya, Laura Griffin, Nicole Shackleton, and Danielle Walt. "Harming Women with Words: The Failure of Australian Law to Prohibit Gendered Hate Speech." *UNSW Law Journal* 41, no. 3 (2018): 939–76.

Dubick, Keith. "Commercial Expression: A 'Second-Class' Freedom?" *Saskatchewan Law Review* 60 (1996): 91–130.

Dunlap, Riley E. "Climate Change Skepticism and Denial: An Introduction." *American Behavioral Scientist* 57 (2013): 691–9.

Dworkin, Gerald. *The Theory and Practice of Autonomy*. Cambridge: Cambridge University Press, 1988.

Dworkin, Ronald. "Foreword." In *Extreme Speech and Democracy*, edited by I. Hare and J. Weinstein. Oxford: Oxford University Press, 2009.

– "Reply to Jeremy Waldron." In *The Content and Context of Hate Speech: Rethinking Regulation and Responses*, edited by Michael Herz and Peter Molnar. Cambridge: Cambridge University Press, 2012.

Elsasser, Shaun W., and Riley E. Dunlap. "Leading Voices in the Denier Choir: Conservative Columnists' Dismissal of Global Warming and Denigration of Climate Science." *American Behavioral Scientist* 57, no. 6 (2013): 754–76.

Emerson, Thomas I. "The Doctrine of Prior Restraint." *Law and Contemporary Problems* 20 (1955): 648–71.

Esmonde, Jackie. "The Policing of Dissent – The Use of Breach of the Peace Arrests at Political Demonstrations." *Journal of Law and Equality* 1 (2002): 246–78.

Feasby, Colin. "*Libman v. Quebec (Attorney General)* and the Administration of the Process of Democracy under the Charter: The Emerging Egalitarian Model." *McGill Law Journal* 44, no. 1 (1998): 5–38.

Findlay, Len. "Institutional Autonomy and Academic Freedom in the Managed University." In *Academic Freedom in Conflict: The Struggle over Free Speech Rights in the University*, edited by James L. Turk. Toronto: James Lorimer and Company, 2014.

Fish, Stanley. *Versions of Academic Freedom: From Professionalism to Revolution.* Chicago: University of Chicago Press, 2014.

Galanter, Marc. "Why the Haves Come Out Ahead: Speculations on the Limits of Legal Change." *Law and Society Review* 9, no. 1 (1974): 95–160.

Geertz, Clifford. *The Interpretation of Cultures.* New York: Basic Books, 1973.

Gelber, Katharine, and Luke McNamara. "The Effects of Civil Hate Speech Laws: Lessons from Australia." *Law and Society Review* 49, no. 3 (2015): 631–64.

– "Evidencing the Harms of Hate Speech." *Journal for the Study of Race, Nation and Culture* 22, no. 3 (2016): 324–41.

Grazia, Edward de. "Obscenity and the Mail: A Study of Administrative Restraint." *Law and Contemporary Problems* 20 (1955): 608–20.

Green, Leslie, and Denise Réaume. "Second Class Rights? Principle and Compromise in the Charter." *Dalhousie Law Journal* 13 (1990): 564–93.

Greenawalt, Kent. *Speech, Crime, and the Uses of Language.* Oxford: Oxford University Press, 1989.

Gross, Neil, and Solon Simmons, eds. *Professors and Their Politics.* Baltimore: Johns Hopkins University Press, 2014.

Hindman, Matthew. *The Internet Trap: How the Digital Economy Builds Monopolies and Undermines Democracy.* Princeton, NJ: Princeton University Press, 2018.

Horn, Michiel. *Academic Freedom in Canada: A History.* Toronto: University of Toronto Press, 1998.

– "Running for Office: Canadian Professors, Electoral Politics and Institutional Reactions, 1887–1968." In *Historical Identities: The Professoriate in Canada*, edited by P. Stortz and L. Panayaotidis. Toronto: University of Toronto Press, 2006.

Horton, John. "Self-Censorship." *Res Publica* 17, no. 1 (2011): 91–106.

Ilg, Michael. "Economy of Pain: When to Regulate Offensive Expression." *International Journal of Constitutional Law* 16, no. 3 (2018): 806–35.

Inbar, Yoel, and Joris Lammers. "Political Diversity in Social and Personality Psychology." *Perspectives on Psychological Science* 7, no. 5 (2012): 496–503.

Jay, Timothy. "Do Offensive Words Harm People?" *Psychology, Public Policy, and Law* 15, no. 2 (2009): 81–101.

Kalvin, Harry. *The Negro and the First Amendment.* Chicago: University of Chicago Press, 1966.

Karanicolas, Michael. "Subverting Democracy to Save Democracy: Canada's Extra-Constitutional Approaches to Battling 'Fake News.'" *Canadian Journal of Law and Technology* 17, no. 2 (2019): 201–26.

Katchanovski, Ivan, Neil Nevitte, and Stanley Rothman. "Race, Gender, and Affirmative Action Attitudes in American and Canadian Universities." *Canadian Journal of Higher Education* 45, no. 4 (2015): 18–41.

Kelly, James B. "Reconciling Rights and Freedoms during Review of the Charter of Rights and Freedoms: The Supreme Court of Canada and the Centralization Thesis, 1982–1999." *Canadian Journal of Political Science* 34, no. 2 (2001): 321–55.

Koteyko, N., R. Jaspal, and B. Nerlich. "Climate Change and 'Climategate' in Online Reader Comments: A Mixed Methods Study." *Geographical Journal* 179, no. 1 (2013): 74–86.

Kreimer, Seth F. "Censorship by Proxy: The First Amendment, Intermediaries, and the Problem of the Weakest Link." *University of Pennsylvania Law Review* 155 (2006): 11–101.

Landry, Normand. "From the Streets to the Courtroom: The Legacies of Quebec's Anti-SLAPP Movement." *Review of European and Community International Environmental Law* 19, no. 1 (2010): 58–69.

Langille, Brian, and Benjamin Oliphant. "The Legal Structure of Freedom of Association." *Queen's Law Journal* 40 (2014): 249–99.

Langton, Rae. "Whose Right? Ronald Dworkin, Women, and Pornographers." *Philosophy and Public Affairs* 19, no. 4 (1993): 311–59.

Lavik, Trygve. "Climate Change Denial, Freedom of Speech and Global Justice." *Nordic Journal of Applied Ethics* 10, no. 2 (2015): 75–90.

Lawlor, Andrea, and Erin Crandall. "Understanding Third Party Advertising: An Analysis of the 2004, 2006 and 2008 Canadian Elections." *Canadian Public Administration* 54, no. 4 (2011): 509–29.

Lazer, David M.J., Matthew A. Baum, Yochai Benkler, Adam J. Berinsky, Kelly M. Greenhill, Filippo Menczer, Miriam J. Metzger, et al. "The Science of Fake News." *Science* 359, no. 6380 (2018): 1094–6.

Leets, Laura. "Experiencing Hate Speech: Perceptions and Responses to Anti-Semitism and Antigay Speech." *Journal of Social Issues* 58, no. 2 (2002): 341–61.

Lee-Won, Roselyn J., Tiffany N. White, Hyunjin Song, Ji Young Lee, and Mikhail R. Smith. "Source Magnification of Cyberhate: Affective and Cognitive Effects of Multiple-Source Hate Messages on Target Group Members." *Media Psychology* 23, no. 5 (2019): 1–22.

Levin, Abigail. *The Cost of Free Speech: Pornography, Hate Speech, and their Challenge to Liberalism*. Houndmills, UK: Palgrave Macmillan, 2010.

Loveland, Ian. *Political Libels: A Comparative Study*. Oxford: Hart Publishing, 2000.

MacCallum, Gerald. "Negative and Positive Freedom." In *The Liberty Reader*, edited by David Miller. Edinburgh: Edinburgh University Press, 2006.

Macfarlane, Emmett. *Governing from the Bench: The Supreme Court of Canada and the Judicial Role*. Vancouver: UBC Press, 2013.

MacKinnon, Catharine. *Only Words*. Cambridge, MA: Harvard University Press, 1993.

MacKinnon, Peter. *University Commons Divided: Exploring Debate and Dissent on Campus*. Toronto: University of Toronto Press, 2018.

Marlin, Randal. "The Muted Bugle: Self-Censorship and the Press." In *Interpreting Censorship in Canada*, edited by Klaus Petersen and Allan Hutchinson. Toronto: University of Toronto Press, 1999.

Matsuda, Mari J. "Public Response to Racist Speech: Considering the Victim's Story." In *Words That Wound: Critical Race Theory, Assaultive Speech, and the First Amendment*, edited by Mari J. Matsuda, Charles R. Lawrence III, Richard Delgado, and Kimberle Williams Crenshaw. Boulder, CO: Westview Press, 1993.

Matsuda, Mari J., Charles R. Lawrence III, Richard Delgado, and Kimberle Williams Crenshaw, eds. *Words That Wound: Critical Race Theory, Assaultive Speech, and the First Amendment*. Boulder, CO: Westview Press, 1993.

McElroy, Wendy. *Sexual Correctness: The Gender-Feminist Attack on Women*. Jefferson, NC: McFarland Publishing, 1996.

McGowan, Mary Kate. *Just Words: On Speech and Hidden Harm*. New York: Oxford University Press, 2019.

– "On 'Whites Only' Signs and Racist Hate Speech: Verbal Acts of Discrimination." *Speech and Harm: Controversies over Free Speech*, edited by Ishani Maitra and Mary Kate McGowan. Oxford: Oxford University Press, 2012.

McKinnon, Catriona. "Should We Tolerate Climate Change Denial?" *Midwest Studies in Philosophy* 40, no. 1 (2016): 205–16.

Meyerson, Michael I. "Rewriting *Near v. Minnesota*: Creating a Complete Definition of Prior Restraint." *Mercer Law Review* 52 (2001): 1087–145.

Mill, John Stuart. *On Liberty*. London: Penguin, 1982; first published 1859.

Modood, Tariq. "Hate Speech: The Feelings and Beliefs of the Hated." *Contemporary Political Theory* 13, no. 1 (2014): 104–9.

Montigny, Yves de. "Les rapports difficiles entre la liberté d'expression et ses limites raisonnables." *Revue générale de droit* 22, no 1 (1991): 129–50.

Moon, Richard. "The Attack on Human Rights Commissions and the Corruption of Public Discourse." *Saskatchewan Law Review* 73 (2010): 93–129.

– *The Constitutional Protection of Freedom of Expression*. Toronto: University of Toronto Press, 2000.

– *Putting Faith in Hate: When Religion is the Source or Target of Hate Speech*. Cambridge University Press, 2018.

Müller, Sophia. *Talking Back: An Examination of Legislative Sequels Produced by the National Assembly of Quebec in Response to Judicial Invalidation of the Charter of the French Language*. PhD diss., University of Ottawa, 2017.

Nagel, Thomas. "Personal Rights and Public Space." *Philosophy and Public Affairs* 24, no. 2 (1995): 83–107.

Nakhaie, M.R., and Barry D. Adam, "Political Affiliation of Canadian University Professors." *Canadian Journal of Sociology* 33, no. 4 (2008): 873–98.

Newman, Dwight. "Interpreting Freedom of Thought in the Canadian Charter of Rights and Freedoms." *Supreme Court Law Review (2d)* 91 (2019): 107–22.

Newman, Stephen L. "Finding the Harm in Hate Speech: An Argument against Censorship." *Canadian Journal of Political Science* 50, no. 3 (2017): 679–97.

Nunziato, Dawn C. "The Beginning of the End of Internet Freedom." *Georgetown Journal of International Law* 45 (2014): 383–410.

– "How (Not) to Censor: Procedural First Amendment Values and Internet Censorship Worldwide." *Georgetown Journal of International Law* 42 (2011): 1123–60.

Oliphant, Benjamin. "The Nature of the Fundamental Freedoms and the *Sui Generis* Right to Collective Bargaining: The Case of Vulnerable and Precarious Workers." *Canadian Labour and Employment Law Journal* 21 (2019): 319–60.

Oreskes, Naomi, and Erik M. Conway. *Merchants of Doubt: How a Handful of Scientists Obscured the Truth on Issues from Tobacco Smoke to Global Warming.* London: Bloomsbury, 2012.

Owram, Douglas. *The Government Generation: Canadian Intellectuals and the State, 1900–1945.* Toronto: University of Toronto Press, 1986.

Peters, Uwe, Nathan Honeycutt, Andreas De Block, and Lee Jussim. "Ideological Diversity, Hostility, and Discrimination in Philosophy." *Philosophical Psychology* 33, no. 4 (2020): 511–48.

Polster, Claire. "The Nature and Implications of the Growing Importance of Research Grants to Canadian Universities and Academics." *Higher Education* 53, no. 5 (2007): 599–622.

Porter, John. *The Vertical Mosaic.* Toronto: University of Toronto Press, 1965.

Pring, George. "SLAPPS: Strategic Lawsuits against Public Participation." *Pace Environmental Law Review* 7, no. 1 (1989): 3–21.

Pring, George, and Penelope Canan. *SLAPPS: Getting Sued for Speaking Out.* Philadelphia: Temple University Press, 1996.

– "Strategic Lawsuits against Public Participation." *Social Problems* 35, no. 5 (1998): 506–19.

Raz, Joseph. *The Morality of Freedom.* Oxford: Oxford University Press, 1986.

Redish, Martin H. "Compelled Commercial Speech and the First Amendment." *Notre Dame Law Review* 94, no. 4 (2019): 1749–74.

Richez, Emmanuelle. "Losing Relevance: Quebec and the Constitutional Politics of Language." *Osgoode Hall Law Journal* 52, no. 1 (2014): 191–233.

Ryder, Bruce. "The *Little Sisters* Case, Administrative Censorship, and Obscenity Law." *Osgoode Hall Law Journal* 39, no. 1 (2001): 207–27.

Scanlon, T.M. "Freedom of Expression and Categories of Expression." *University of Pittsburgh Law Review* 40 (1978): 519–50.

– "A Theory of Freedom of Expression." *Philosophy and Public Affairs* 1, no. 2 (1972): 204–26.

Scarfe, Janet, and Edward Sheffield. "Notes on the Canadian Professoriate." *Higher Education* 6, no. 3 (1977): 337–58.

Schauer, Frederick. *Free Speech: A Philosophical Inquiry*. Cambridge: Cambridge University Press, 1982.
- "The Phenomenology of Speech and Harm." *Ethics* 103 (1993): 635–53.
- "Too Hard: Unconstitutional Conditions and the Chimera of Constitutional Consistency." *Denver University Law Review* 72, no. 4 (1994): 989–1005.
Schrecker, Ellen. *The Lost Soul of Higher Education: Corporatization, the Assault on Academic Freedom, and the End of the American University*. New York: New Press, 2010.
Scott, Joan W. *Knowledge, Power, and Academic Freedom*. New York: Columbia University Press, 2019.
Sheldrick, Byron. *Blocking Public Participation: The Use of Strategic Litigation to Silence Political Expression*. Waterloo, ON: Wilfrid Laurier University Press, 2014.
Shields, Jon A., and Joshua M. Dunn Sr. *Passing on the Right: Conservative Professors in the Progressive University*. Oxford: Oxford University Press, 2016.
Simpson, Robert Mark. "'Won't Somebody Please Think of the Children?' Hate Speech, Harm, and Childhood." *Law and Philosophy* 38 (2019): 79–108.
Sirota, Léonid. "True Allegiance: The Citizenship Oath and the *Charter*." *National Journal of Constitutional Law* 33, no. 2 (2014): 137–68.
Small, Tamara A. "Digital Third Parties: Understanding the Technological Challenge to Canada's Third Party Advertising Regime." *Canadian Public Administration* 61, no. 2 (2018): 266–83.
Soral, Wiktor, Michat Bilewicz, and Mikotaj Winiewski. "Exposure to Hate Speech Increases Prejudice through Desensitization." *Aggressive Behavior* 44 (2017): 136–46.
Spivak, Gayatri. "Can the Subaltern Speak?" In *Marxism and the Interpretation of Culture*, edited by Cary Nelson and Lawrence Grossberg. Urbana: University of Illinois Press, 1998.
Stanley, Jason. *How Fascism Works*. New York: Random House, 2018.
Strossen, Nadine. *Defending Pornography: Free Speech, Sex, and the Fight for Women's Rights*. New York: New York University Press, 2000.
- *Hate: Why We Should Resist It with Free Speech, Not Censorship*. Oxford: Oxford University Press, 2018.
Sumner, L.W. *The Hateful and the Obscene: Studies in the Limits of Free Expression*. Toronto: University of Toronto Press, 2004.
Sunstein, Cass. *#Republic: Divided Democracy in the Age of Social Media*. Princeton, NJ: Princeton University Press, 2017.
- *Going to Extremes: How Like Minds Unite and Divide*. Oxford: Oxford University Press, 2009.
- "Why the Unconstitutional Conditions Doctrine is an Anachronism (with Particular Reference to Religion, Speech, and Abortion)." *Boston University Law Review* 70 (1990): 593–621.
Taylor, Charles. *Human Agency and Language*. Cambridge: Cambridge University Press, 1985.

Thompson, John B. *The Media and Modernity: A Social Theory of the Media*. Stanford, CA: Stanford University Press, 1995.

Thoreau, Henry David. "Civil Disobedience." In *Anti-Slavery and Reform Papers*, edited by H.S. Salt. London: Swan Sonnenschein, 1890.

Tollefson, Chris. "Strategic Lawsuits and Environmental Politics: Daishowa Inc. v. Friends of the Lubicon." *Journal of Canadian Studies* 31, no. 1 (1996): 119–32.

– "Strategic Litigation against Public Participation: Developing a Canadian Response." *Canadian Bar Review* 73, no. 2 (1994): 200–33.

Tufekci, Zeynep. *Twitter and Tear Gas: The Power and Fragility of Networked Protest*. New Haven, CT: Yale University Press, 2017.

Turk, James. ed. *The Corporate Campus: Commercialization and the Dangers to Canada's Colleges and Universities*. Toronto: James Lorimer and Company, 2000.

Vaidhyanathan, Siva. *Antisocial Media: How Facebook Disconnects Us and Undermines Democracy*. Oxford: Oxford University Press, 2018.

Vance, Carole S. *Pleasure and Danger: Exploring Female Sexuality*. London: Pandora Press, 1992.

Vanderheiden, Steve. *Atmospheric Justice: A Political Theory of Climate Change*. Oxford: Oxford University Press, 2008.

Vidal-Naquet, Pierre. *Assassins of Memory: Essays on the Denial of the Holocaust*. New York: Columbia University Press, 1992.

Volokh, Eugene. "The Law of Compelled Speech." *Texas Law Review* 97, no. 2 (2018): 355–95.

Waldron, Jeremy. *The Harm in Hate Speech*. Cambridge, MA: Harvard University Press, 2012.

Weinstein, James. "Hate Speech Bans, Democracy and Political Legitimacy." *Constitutional Commentary* 32 (2017): 715–82.

West, Caroline. "Words That Silence? Freedom of Expression and Racist Hate Speech." In *Speech and Harm: Controversies over Free Speech*, edited by Ishani Maitra and Mary Kate McGowan. Oxford: Oxford University Press, 2012.

White, Aidan. "Dissent and Collective Action in Oppressive Times." In *Disciplining Dissent: The Curbing of Free Expression in Academia and the Media*, edited by William Bruneau and James L. Turk. Toronto: James Lorimer and Company, 2004.

Williams, Matthew L., Peter Burnap, Amir Javed, Han Liu, Sefa Ozalp. "Hate in the Machine: Anti-Black and Anti-Muslim Social Media Posts as Predictors of Offline Racially and Religiously Aggravated Crime." *British Journal of Criminology* 60, no. 1 (2019): 93–117.

Woehrling, José. "La réglementation linguistique de l'affichage public et la liberté d'expression: P.G. Québec c. Chaussure Brown's Inc." *McGill Law Journal* 32, no. 4 (1987): 878–904.

Woodhouse, Howard. *Selling Out: Academic Freedom and the Corporate Market*. Montreal: McGill-Queen's University Press, 2009.

Zivi, Karen. "Doing Things with Hate Speech." *Contemporary Political Theory* 13, no. 1 (2014): 94–100.

Contributors

Christopher Bennett, Assistant Professor, Department of Political Science, University of Waterloo

Jamie Cameron, Professor Emeritus, Osgoode Hall Law School, York University

Stéphanie Chouinard, Associate Professor, Department of Political Science, Royal Military College (Kingston) and Queen's University

Erin Crandall, Associate Professor, Department of Politics, Acadia University

Shannon Dea, Dean of Arts and Professor of Philosophy, University of Regina

Dax D'Orazio, Department of Political Science, University of Alberta

Andrea Lawlor, Associate Professor, Department of Political Science, King's University College, Western University

Emmett Macfarlane, Associate Professor, Department of Political Science, University of Waterloo

Carissima Mathen, Professor of Law, University of Ottawa

Richard Moon, Distinguished University Professor and Professor of Law, University of Windsor

David Newhouse, Director and Professor, Chaney Wenjack School for Indigenous Studies, Trent University

Benjamin J. Oliphant, Gall Legge Grant Zwack LLP, Vancouver, BC

Emmanuelle Richez, Associate Professor, Department of Political Science, University of Windsor

Jeffrey Adam Sachs, Department of Politics, Acadia University

Byron M. Sheldrick, Department of Political Science, University of Guelph

Léonid Sirota, Senior Lecturer, Auckland University of Technology Law School

Cara Faith Zwibel, Director, Fundamental Freedoms Program, Canadian Civil Liberties Association

Index